PENGUIN CLASSICS

AGAINST SLAVERY

Mason Lowance is professor of English at the University of Massachusetts, Amherst. His books include *Increase Mather* (1974), *Massachusetts Broadsides of the American Revolution* (1976), *The Language of Canaan* (1980), *The Typological Writings of Jonathan Edwards* (1993), and *The Stowe Debate: Rhetorical Strategies in "Uncle Tom's Cabin"* (1994). He has held a Guggenheim Fellowship and a National Endowment for the Humanities Fellowship, and has been a fellow of the National Humanities Institute at Yale University and a life member of the American Antiquarian Society.

Dean Grodzins and William Pannapacker are lecturers in history and literature at Harvard University specializing in nineteenth-century American literature.

AGAINST SLAVERY
AN ABOLITIONIST READER

EDITED AND WITH AN INTRODUCTION
BY MASON LOWANCE

PENGUIN BOOKS

PENGUIN BOOKS

Published by the Penguin Group
Penguin Putnam Inc., 375 Hudson Street,
New York, New York 10014, U.S.A.
Penguin Books Ltd, 27 Wrights Lane,
London W8 5TZ, England
Penguin Books Australia Ltd, Ringwood,
Victoria, Australia
Penguin Books Canada Ltd, 10 Alcorn Avenue,
Toronto, Ontario, Canada M4V 3B2
Penguin Books (N.Z.) Ltd, 182–190 Wairau Road,
Auckland 10, New Zealand

Penguin Books Ltd, Registered Offices:
Harmondsworth, Middlesex, England

First published in Penguin Books 2000

1   3   5   7   9   10   8   6   4   2

LIBRARY OF CONGRESS CATALOGING-IN-PUBLICATION DATA
Against slavery : an abolitionist reader / edited and with an
introduction by Mason Lowance.
p.   cm. — (Penguin classics)
Includes bibliographical references.
ISBN 0 14 04.3758 4
1. Antislavery movements—United States—History Sources.
2. Slavery—Moral and ethical aspects—United States—History
Sources.   3. Abolitionists—United States—History—19th century
Sources.   4. Abolitionists—United States—History—18th century
Sources.   I. Lowance, Mason I., 1938–   .   II. Series.
E449.A29   2000
326'.8'0973—dc21   99–16211

Printed in the United States of America
Set in Stempel Garamond
Designed by Ellen Cipriano

Dedicated to

PROFESSOR EMERITUS ARTHUR BANKS, JR.,

MOREHOUSE COLLEGE

and to the memory of

MRS. LOUISE JACKSON

CONTENTS

AGAINST SLAVERY

GENERAL INTRODUCTION

Freedom is and has always been America's root concern,
a concern that found dramatic expression in the abolitionist
movement. The most important and revolutionary reform in
our country's past, it forced the American people to
come to grips with an anomaly that would not down—
the existence of slavery in the land of the free.

—BENJAMIN QUARLES,
THE BLACK ABOLITIONISTS, 1969

Thus begins one of this century's best studies of the abolitionist movement of the nineteenth century, written by an African American scholar who, with John Hope Franklin, explored the role of slavery in American society and the contributions of abolitionists to emancipation, before either topic reached the mainstream of American historical studies. Franklin and Quarles were writing in the 1940s and 1950s, when African American scholars were denied access to some college and university libraries in the United States, but their pioneering studies, both researched at the Library of Congress when other resources were closed to them, are monumental works of scholarship on antebellum America, and Franklin's *From Slavery to Freedom: A History of Negro Americans*, first published in the 1940s, is still in print.

The purpose of this anthology of abolitionist writings is to make available to the scholar and student primary documents representing the antislavery and abolitionist movements of the eighteenth and nineteenth centuries. Each selection is introduced and annotated, and the section introductions provide an examination of the historical and cultural contexts out of which the texts were developed. Following this general introduction, the anthology includes background documents showing the rise of antislavery sentiment in America when it was still a colony of Great Britain, excerpting the writings of Samuel Sewall, Cotton Mather, John Woolman, Phillis

Wheatley, Thomas Jefferson, and Frederick Douglass, whose "What to the Slave Is the Fourth of July?" (1852), a piece written well after the colonial period, is a hostile response to a nation which celebrates annually the fundamental Enlightenment principle of natural rights by reaffirming that "all men are created equal" while tolerating the right of slaveholders to own human beings.

Americans began debating the slavery issue in the late seventeenth century, when the Quakers, who had opposed slavery in Great Britain, developed arguments against the expansion of chattel slavery in North America, but their voices were muted compared to the overwhelming economic development of the plantation system in the Southern colonies. Early opponents of slavery were primarily religious figures, like the founder of Methodism, John Wesley, who wrote a treatise attacking the institution in the mid-eighteenth century. The Quaker meetings collectively opposed slavery, and one among them, John Woolman, eloquently told of the anguish of conscience he suffered when required by his employer, a New Jersey lawyer, to write an indenture of sale for the purchase of a slave. Moreover, slavery was challenged by natural rights theorists of the Enlightenment, and it is one of the ironies of American history that the most eloquent articulation of those principles composed by an American, the Declaration of Independence, should have been authored by Thomas Jefferson, master of a Virginia plantation and the owner of slaves.

Because the charter document of the United States, the Constitution, failed to adequately treat or even to confront the question of slavery, the legacy of the early importation of Africans to North America to serve as laborers on Southern plantations and as domestic servants and laborers in some Northern colonies was transmitted to the nineteenth century, just as the new nation "conceived in liberty and dedicated to the proposition that all men are created equal," as Abraham Lincoln would eloquently rephrase it in his Gettysburg Address, was attempting to define its objectives and establish its identity. Remarkably, the flexibility of the Constitution as an ever-changing charter document, whose amendment system permitted alteration of the original plan, gave opponents of slavery the opportunity not only to argue the moral degradation of humanity brought about by the "peculiar institution," but to set forth an objective of immediate and unconditional emancipation of the slaves through an amendment to the Constitution itself.

These changes did not come easily. As Section II shows, the Bible was used by proslavery and antislavery advocates alike either to argue for the retention and extension of slavery, or to demand its termination. Theodore Dwight Weld, James Freeman Clarke, Alexander McLeod, and Robert Dale Owen were but four of many who were opposed to slavery and used their Bibles to frame theological arguments designed to persuade readers, and listeners, that slavery was morally wrong and that owning slaves was fundamentally a sin in the biblical sense of the term. These theological arguments gained some momentum in the early nineteenth century, but they were delivered by less powerful voices that those of the leading opponents of slavery who wrote and debated between 1830 and 1865, the period of the militant and aggressive "abolitionist crusade." Section III is the main section of this anthology, and it includes the writings of some of the leading abolitionists of these crucial decades, including William Lloyd Garrison, Wendell Phillips, Lydia Maria Child, David Walker, and Harriet Beecher Stowe.

Thus it is critical to distinguish between the broad phrase "antislavery movement" and the specific intellectual and political crusade of the abolitionists between 1830 and 1865, when the institution of slavery was officially ended in the United States through the Thirteenth Amendment to the Constitution. "Antislavery" is a sweeping phrase that refers to those individuals and groups who opposed the enslavement of human beings as chattel property, especially during the period 1776–1865, while the United States government officially sanctioned slavery despite the protestations of its charter documents. The Constitution of 1787 did not openly discuss slavery as an issue, but allowed it as a practice by disregarding the application of constitutional principles to chattel slaves of African American descent. The status of the mother usually determined the status of the child, so that the natural reproduction of slaves in the United States greatly expanded the enslaved population even after Congress outlawed the *importation* of slaves in 1808. The "antislavery movement" grew up during this period to oppose all aspects of slavery and the slave trade, but its moral arguments and

influence were not sufficient to overcome the "Slave Power" of the
Southern states and the economic demand for slave labor induced
by Eli Whitney's invention of the cotton gin in the 1790s and the
worldwide demand for cotton goods. Like Virginia tobacco, which
was exported to England and Europe even during the years of the
American Revolution, American cotton exports were extensive in
the first half of the nineteenth century and gave enormous power to
the slaveholding states, who were able not only to retain the institution in their plantation societies, but also to persuade Congress to
grant slaveholding privileges to some of the new territories being
secured by the federal government, such as the Louisiana Purchase
and the Annexation of Texas. Meanwhile, the slave population continued to grow. According to the first official census, 1790, there
were approximately 55,000 free blacks living mostly in the North,
and this figure had risen to 250,000 by 1820. By contrast, the same
census showed that in 1790 there were some 700,000 African slaves
in the United States. By 1820, there were over 1 million slaves concentrated in the Southern states, and by 1860, on the eve of the Civil
War, there were over 4 million African Americans in the United
States who were owned by an American citizen. Although most of
the Northern states had abolished slavery in the late eighteenth and
early nineteenth centuries, and although in 1808 Congress had prohibited by law the importation of slaves, thus abolishing the slave
trade for Americans, slavery continued to flourish in the Southern
states because the slave population expanded rapidly and because
the laws were frequently disobeyed and Africans continued to be
smuggled into the United States.

The "antislavery" philosophy must be distinguished from the
"abolitionist movement" or "abolitionist crusade," which was a
specific, historical group action that is associated with the publication of David Walker's *Appeal* in 1829 and William Lloyd Garrison's *The Liberator* in 1831. Walker, an African American, was an
early proponent of racial equality, with special emphasis on political and social equality, and he was joined by the Garrisonians, who
not only argued for equality and for an end to racial prejudice, but
who emphatically called for "immediate, unconditional emancipation," without compensation to the slaveowners. These abolitionists were characterized by a militant and demanding tone and by
exceptional organizational skills, so that their message of reform

was naturally evangelical; and the movement adopted many of the tactics of the American Tract Society, whose expansion and missionary zeal had reached all corners of the new nation through national, regional, and local state organizations.

William Lloyd Garrison (1805–1879) is generally considered to be the dean of the abolitionist movement in the United States. Influenced early in his life by the Quaker rejection of chattel slavery and its inhuman practices, Garrison became one of the earliest and most outspoken advocates of the complete and total emancipation of the slaves, which he first articulated in Benjamin Lundy's paper, *The Genius of Universal Emancipation.* With the publication of the first issue of *The Liberator* on January 1, 1831, Garrison identified his voice with the searing admonition "I am in earnest—I will not equivocate—I will not excuse—I will not retreat a single inch,—and I will be heard." He was a brilliant organizer, and founded two antislavery societies to carry on his work. He made a modest living by directing their programs and spreading the gospel of antislavery through the regional and local chapters of the national organizations. In 1833, when the Garrisonians formed the American Antislavery Society, they immediately developed local chapters to represent the objectives of the national organization, and the principal players in the national movement traveled frequently to meetings of the local groups. Thus abolitionism and Christian reform paralleled each other in method and scope if not in objectives and message, and the American culture of the early nineteenth century was well used to oratory by reformers whose causes were well known.

At the same time, during the 1820s and 1830s, American women were beginning to perceive the association between their own oppressed condition and that of the African slaves, so that the aggressive abolitionist movement led by Garrison and his followers gave them an opportunity to develop arguments for female emancipation that paralleled the arguments for the abolition of slavery. As Ellen Dubois put it,

> By contrast with the moral reform movement, Garrisonian abolitionism provided women with a political framework that assisted the development of a feminist movement. As Garrisonians, women learned a way to view the world and a theory and practice of social

change that they found most useful in elaborating their protofeminist insights. In addition, the antislavery movement provided them with a constituency and a political alliance on which they were able to rely until the Civil War. Thus, American feminism developed within the context of abolitionism less because abolitionists taught women that they were oppressed than because abolitionists taught women what to do with that perception, how to develop it into a social movement. Two aspects of the way that Garrisonians approached social reality were particularly important to the development of nineteenth-century American feminism: the ability to perceive and analyze entire institutions, and the assumption of absolute human equality as a first principle of morality and politics. Both habits of mind, though seemingly abstract, were derived from the concrete task facing abolitionists, to make slavery a burning issue for northern Whites. The women who built the women's rights movement borrowed these approaches and found them eminently useful in overcoming obstacles that had stopped other protofeminists. The habit of institutional analysis permitted Garrisonian women to escape the control of the clergy and move beyond pietistic activism. The principle of absolute human equality freed them from the necessity of justifying all their duties in terms of woman's sphere. (Ellen Dubois, "Women's Rights and Abolition: The Nature of the Connection," in *Feminism and Suffrage: The Emergence of an Independent Women's Movement in America, 1848–1869* [Ithaca, N.Y.: Cornell University Press, 1978])

The role of women abolitionists is exceptionally well represented in this collection by Lydia Maria Child's *An Appeal in Favor of That Class of Americans Called Africans* (1833), which was an early and militant call for unconditional emancipation without compensation to slaveowners and an argument for full political and social equality of blacks and whites. Like William Lloyd Garrison, Lydia Child had blatantly defied the cultural customs, political system, and social conventions of both the North and the South, and like Garrison, she suffered disapproval not only from her fellow Bostonians, but also from her father and sibling members of her own family. The "women's sphere" had been violated in two specific ways in Lydia Child's treatise. First, as a woman she had entered the sanctuary of political discourse, a province carefully guarded by men both North and South. Second, her argument had called for equality among the races, at least socially and politically, and the fears this doctrine inspired among white Americans both north and south of the Mason-Dixon line were to keep segregation alive in the United States well into the mid-twentieth century. It took a Supreme Court decision, *Brown v. the Board of Education (of Topeka, Kansas)*, to terminate the Jim Crow segregation practices of public school systems both North and South, long after arguments for educational civil rights had been advanced by educators and civil rights activists.

Associated with the antislavery movement of the early nineteenth century were prominent New England names, both conservative and moderate, radical and militant, who now stand out as luminaries in a firmament of change that on reflection looks extremely moral and right. However, it is important to remember that in the 1820s to 1840s, some of these figures were considered a radical, even dangerous, fringe element, and that they were often regarded as violent insurrectionists. For example, Henry David Thoreau, author of "Civil Disobedience" and *Walden* (1850) and a proponent of nonviolent change and leadership by example, nevertheless also penned essays like "Slavery in Massachusetts" and "A Plea for Captain John Brown," in which Thoreau compared Brown to Jesus Christ, a martyr in the universal cause of eternal freedom for mankind. This was more than a hyperbolic association; Thoreau's essay was written between October and December 1859, when Brown was scheduled to be hanged for the violent insurrection at Harpers Ferry, Virginia, and Thoreau argued openly for reevaluation of John Brown as a national hero rather than an abolitionist martyr.

It is also important to remember that the period of intense abolitionist debate, 1820–1865, was also the period when scientific theories of evolution were regularly challenging the doctrines of the Bible concerning the creation of man and the origin of species, as Charles Darwin would later title his 1859 treatise. Darwin was a relative latecomer to the race-theory debates that were raging in both Europe and the United States during the early decades of the nineteenth century, and modern readers should consider that the abolitionists were confronted by extremely hostile racial doctrines that were pseudoscientifically developed by leading biologists from universities like Oxford, Cambridge, and Harvard. Monogenesis, an argument that all people were evolved from a single pair of original parents, as described in the Book of Genesis, suited the antislavery advocates, while polygenesis, the belief that humanity was descended from multiple original sources, better suited the proslavery view. For Garrison, Phillips, Child, Weld, and Walker, this would mean taking extremely unpopular and often confrontational stands against slavery and race prejudice (which the Garrisonians saw as inextricably linked). It would also mean taking significant physical risks and exposing one's home and family to retaliation by the often violent opposing groups. William Lloyd Garrison was nearly lynched by an angry Boston mob who opposed his racial-equality doctrines, and in 1830 he was convicted of libel and imprisoned. These antebellum slavery debates were not abstractions; they were frequently heated confrontations that erupted into violent interaction between the proslavery and antislavery camps.

Antislavery doctrines were often embraced by theologians (especially in New England) who argued a monogenic racial theory of evolution, i.e., that all human beings were derived from a unique, created original, Adam and Eve, and that differences among us today are cultural and ethnic but not essential. Though not all abolitionists were also proponents of full, natural equality between the races, many embraced this monogenic view and argued for full social and political equality for Africans. Opposing this view was that of polygenesis, which argued that humankind was evolved from several original creations, and that the contemporary differences in ethnic and racial composition were the result of an intentional separation of the races at the time of creation. Proslavery advocates like Josiah Nott, who published *Types of Mankind, or Ethnological Researches* in 1843, were vigorously opposed by abolitionists such as the theologian Alexander McLeod, the clergyman James Freeman Clarke, the journalists William Lloyd Garrison and Wendell Phillips, and the slave narrator Frederick Douglass.

The most prominent vehicles for this confrontation were the abolitionist newspaper and the sermonic tract, combined with the powerful oratory of the lyceum or speaker's platform. Wendell Phillips was particularly well regarded as a prominent abolitionist speaker, and he and Garrison became the leading speaker and writer of the antebellum abolitionist cause. They were joined by leading black abolitionists such as Frederick Douglass and David Walker, and by early feminist advocates and abolitionists like Lydia Maria Child, Angelina Grimké Weld, and Sarah M. Grimké, the two sisters from South Carolina who embraced abolitionism and became extremely vocal opponents of America's national sin. Characterizing slavery as "wrong" and "sinful" had long been an argument of antislavery thinkers; now the more contemporary rights of women and the scientific arguments that developed around the theory of evolution were engaged in the slavery debates.

Slavery thus became associated with the pseudoscientific arguments of the polygenesis school, and with the biblical proslavery arguments of ministers who used their Bibles to establish a precedent in ancient history by which the "peculiar institution" was justified in Scripture by God himself. The abolitionists vigorously opposed this view, and they joined the moral suasion of earlier antislavery advocates to the more militant and aggressive arguments of crusaders like Garrison and Phillips.

The examination of history by way of the lives of prominent participants is not a new phenomenon. The Bible itself focuses on life writing as a way of exploring the history of Israel's leaders, such as Moses and David; and a transcendentalist opponent of slavery, Ralph Waldo Emerson, wrote that "there is properly no history, only biography." Emerson wrote in the tradition of New England Puritanism, which also composed its history as the lives of eminent leaders, and Cotton Mather's *Magnalia Christi Americana* (1702) contains the lives of sixty-four New England leaders from 1620 to 1698. Thus the abolitionist movement in antebellum America should be reviewed through the writings of two prominent groups. The first group comprised the white, militant antislavery advocates like Garrison, Wendell Phillips, John Brown, Henry David Thoreau, Lydia Maria Child, and Harriet Beecher Stowe, who penned the most powerful and successful antislavery document of all in her 1852 novel, *Uncle Tom's Cabin.*

The second group was composed of African American abolitionists, represented in this volume by Frederick Douglass, David Walker, Alexander Crummell, and James McCune Smith. But readers should also consider the widely available slave narratives by Douglass, Jupiter Hammond, William Wells Brown, Josiah Henson, Henry Bibb, and Harriet Jacobs, who told the story of the hardships, injustices, oppression, and horrors of slavery from a first-person perspective, from an "insider's point of view." The voices that appear in these slave narratives, which should be read in conjunction with the abolitionist documents contained in this vol-

ume, differ markedly from the demanding, hostile, and often uncompromising tone of some of the white abolitionist writing, such
as Garrison's first editorial for *The Liberator,* January 1, 1831. The
slave narrators told an intensely personal story, often filled with
pathos, but always focused on the dual objective of attaining personal freedom and achieving emancipation and equality for all
African Americans. This contrast may be seen clearly by comparing
any of the Garrison texts or Lydia Maria Child's 1833 *Appeal in Favor of That Class of Americans Called Africans* with the tone and
style of Douglass's first of three autobiographical accounts, *A
Narrative of the Life of an American Slave, Frederick Douglass,
Written by Himself* (1845) or Harriet Jacobs's autobiographical narrative, *Linda: Incidents in the Life of a Slave Girl* (1861).

Although a full historical treatment of this movement lies out-
side the scope of this introduction to abolitionism, the story of
those unsung heroes of the Underground Railroad organization,
who risked imprisonment and even their lives to provide security
and safety to escaped slaves who were making their way from the
plantation South to the Promised Land of Northern freedom, is
central to antislavery history. The Fugitive Slave Law of 1850, part
of the Compromise of 1850, was specifically designed to curtail the
work of the Underground Railroad and to placate Southern politicians in Congress, who were being asked to approve the bill, and
this unjust law required that all escaped slaves be returned as property to their rightful owners in the South, regardless of the conviction of the Northern antislavery sympathizers. Thus it became a
federal crime punishable by fines and jail sentences to harbor an escaped slave or to participate in the work of the Underground Railroad. Lane Seminary in Cincinnati and Oberlin College, also in
Ohio, were two institutional targets of the Fugitive Slave Law, and
despite this federal injunction, many workers continued to assist escaped slaves either into safe sanctuary in the North or into further
escape into Canada.

Finally, the abolitionists represented in this volume were opposed to the objectives of the American Colonization Society,
which had been organized in 1817 with the goal of removing the
Africans in America to Africa, specifically Liberia, over a gradual
course of emancipation that would also include immediate depor-
tation to Africa. The abolitionists opposed colonization for two

primary reasons. First, it was clear from the outset that the "colonization societies" were all white, all male, and had no intention of consulting the victims of slavery themselves about their wishes concerning removal to Africa. The first reason derives from the second, that the colonizationists were usually race theorists who considered the African inferior to the white. As historian John Thomas put it,

> Some Southern planters supported the American Colonization Society in the hope that exporting free Negroes would strengthen the institution of slavery, while Northern philanthropists endorsed colonization in the equally futile expectation that it would purify American democracy by ridding the country of slaves. Thus colonization embraced two irreconcilable points of view. On one crucial issue, however, both Northern and Southern colonizationists were agreed—the Negro was inherently inferior to the white man and had no place in a democratic society. It was precisely this sweeping assumption of inferiority and unfitness which the pioneer abolitionists rejected. Their argument proved devastatingly simple: slavery was a sin and a crime, a sin because it denied to the Negro the status of a human being, a crime because it violated the natural rights to life, liberty, and the pursuit of happiness guaranteed in the Declaration of Independence. These two beliefs—in the spiritual equality of all believers and the political equality of all Americans—served as the chief moral weapons in the attack on slavery. (John L. Thomas, introduction to *Slavery Attacked: The Abolitionist Crusade* [Englewood Cliffs, N.J.: Prentice-Hall, 1963], p. 1)

It was this crucial issue that brought the abolitionists of the 1830s and 1840s together with the early feminists. "The principle of absolute human equality was the basic philosophical premise that American feminism borrowed from Garrisonian abolitionism. Because the abolitionists' target was northern racial prejudice and their goal the development of white empathy for the suffering of the slave, the core of their argument was the essential unity of whites with blacks. Although many Garrisonians believed in biological differences between the races, their politics ignored physical, cultural, and historical characteristics that might distinguish blacks from whites. They stressed instead the common humanity and the moral identity of the races. They expressed this approach as a moral

abstraction, a first principle, but its basis was the very concrete demands of the agitational task they faced." (Ellen Dubois, "Women's
Rights and Abolition: The Nature of the Connection," in *Feminism
and Suffrage, 1848–1869* ([Ithaca, N.Y.: Cornell University Press,
1978], pp. 245–46) The task of overcoming race prejudice and a fundamental belief in the inequality of the races politically, socially,
and biologically was always hard work for the Garrisonians, whose
camp had led the way in militant opposition to the United States
Constitution, which they viewed as a proslavery document. Even
Abraham Lincoln, when running for the United States Senate in
1858, argued for the inequality of the races in his debates with
Stephen Douglas. As difficult as it may be to believe, Lincoln, who
would five years later author the Emancipation Proclamation and
the Gettysburg Address, spoke these words:

> "While I was at the hotel today an elderly gentleman called upon me
> to know whether I was really in favor of producing a perfect equality
> between the negroes and white people. [great laughter] While I had
> not proposed to myself on this occasion to say much on the subject,
> yet as the question was asked me I thought I would occupy perhaps
> five minutes in saying something in regard to it. I will say then that I
> am not, nor ever have been, in favor of bringing about in any way the
> social and political equality of the white and black races. [ap-
> plause]—that I am not nor ever have been in favor of making voters
> or jurors of negroes, nor of qualifying them to hold office, nor to in-
> termarry with white people; and I will say in addition to this that
> there is a physical difference between the white and black races
> which I believe will forever forbid the two races living together on
> terms of social and political equality. And inasmuch as they cannot
> so live, while they do remain together there must be the position of
> superior and inferior, and I as much as any other man am in favor of
> having the superior position assigned to the white race. I say upon
> this occasion I do not perceive that because the white man is to have
> the superior position the negro should be denied everything. I do not
> understand that because I do not want a negro woman for a slave I
> must necessarily have her for a wife. [cheers and laughter] My under-
> standing is that I can just let her alone. I am now in my fiftieth year,
> and I certainly never have had a black woman for either a slave or a
> wife. So it seems to me quite possible for us to get along without
> making either slaves or wives of negroes." Louis Ruchames, ed.,

Racial Thought in America from the Puritans to Abraham Lincoln
[Amherst: University of Massachusetts Press, 1963], pp. 380–81)

These perspectives were widely shared by citizens of the United States, both North and South, during the antebellum decades. Lincoln's opinions were voiced during the Lincoln-Douglas debates of 1858, and they show the political pressure on the candidate to produce viewpoints that would not offend the constituency, even though by 1858, the race-theory arguments had been voiced repeatedly and the abolitionists had responded with their own arguments for full racial equality, especially in Garrison's *Liberator* editorials and in Lydia Maria Child's *Appeal*. As late as 1863, Abraham Lincoln considered colonization as a resolution to the slavery issue, which he perceived as the cause of disunion and a clear threat to a restoration of the Union at the conclusion of the Civil War.

It is difficult today to understand the opposition to emancipation and full equality that was encountered by the abolitionists of the 1830s, 1840s, and 1850s, partly because modern readers are so aware of the enormous success of Harriet Beecher Stowe's abolitionist novel *Uncle Tom's Cabin*. First published in 1852, by 1860 the novel had sold over 4 million copies in the United States, primarily to Northern readers, since the book was banned in the Southern slaveholding states and the slaves themselves, some 4.5 million of them, were prohibited from learning to read and write by the laws of those states. (In a reading population of only 15 million literate souls, Mrs. Stowe's novel had sold one copy for every three people who were able to read its contents.) The militant abolitionists of the crusade from 1830 to 1865 were a serious threat to the political and social order of the United States, especially for those Southern states whose economy depended almost entirely on slave labor. By 1850, "King Cotton" was the leading export of the United States, and a disruption of this production was rightly feared to threaten the larger economy of the country.

But for the abolitionists, the two decades preceding the publication of *Uncle Tom's Cabin* were crucial, and they divided along the watermark year of 1840. John Thomas notes that "by 1840, the Abolitionists were engaged in a civil war of their own, with both political abolitionists and Garrisonians struggling for control of the nearly moribund national society. . . . Thus the year 1840 marked a turning point in the Abolitionist crusade. Its institutional phase was over. Although Garrison's 'Old Organization' (as his followers called themselves) and the secessionist 'New Organization' (as they contemptuously referred to their opponents) continued to agitate for immediate emancipation, an effective national organization ceased to exist after 1840." (Thomas, *Slavery Attacked*, pp. 3–4) By 1840, both moderate antislavery advocates and militant abolitionists were calling for immediate emancipation, but Garrison's camp had declared war on the U.S. Constitution itself, labeling it a proslavery document and a "compact with Satan," an alliance with hell itself. Garrison had early called for "no union with slaveholders," effectively declaring that the North should secede from the South. By the late 1850s, it appeared that the South might indeed secede from the North, and imminent disunion was an enormous threat to politicians like Lincoln, who sought to preserve the Union at all costs, even at the cost of making appeals to slaveholders and Southern politicians. But in 1840 the abolitionists were severely divided, and a new political party was formed out of one wing of the controversy. The Liberty Party selected James Birney and Thomas Earle, a Philadelphia Quaker, as the candidates for president and vice president. With the Garrisonians still calling for "no union with slaveholders," the concept of party politics within the Union was inconceivable. As Louis Ruchames put it:

A decisive event in Abolitionist history was Garrison's decision, in 1843, that slavery could not be eliminated as long as the North remained in the Government of the United States and thereby cooperated with the South, under the Constitution, in the maintenance of slavery. The Constitution, Garrison came to believe, assumed the existence of slavery, gave the institution its sanction, and could not be changed without the consent of a considerable portion of the slave states themselves, which therefore made the abolition of slavery by constitutional means impossible. The Constitution, he concluded, was—in the words of the prophet Isaiah whom he quoted—"a covenant with death and an agreement with hell." Indeed, the "free states," by upholding the Constitution, "are guardians and essential supports of slavery. We are the jailers and constables of the institution." The only moral and just course for the North was disunion or secession, which would ultimately result in the fall of slavery. (Louis

Ruchames, *The Abolitionists* [New York: G. P. Putnam's Sons, 1960], p. 23)

Thus William Lloyd Garrison distanced himself from those very charter documents the abolitionist movement had sought to reconcile with current events through a vigorous debate over slavery and freedom. After all the water had settled and the Civil War was at an end, after the Emancipation Proclamation had been written and the Thirteenth Amendment to the Constitution debated, Abraham Lincoln paid high tribute to Garrison in a public statement on April 5, 1865: "I have been only an instrument," he said. "The logic and moral power of Garrison and the anti-slavery people of the country and the Army, have done all." (Ruchames, *The Abolitionists*, p. 24)

The abolitionist crusade was led by Garrison and Wendell Phillips, who were joined by the Quaker poet John Greenleaf Whittier and the Boston writer Lydia Maria Child. Garrison founded the New England Antislavery Society in 1831 and the American Antislavery Society in 1833, when factionalism within the New England group threatened to compromise his militant demands for immediate and unconditional emancipation and full racial equality. Frederick Douglass, the escaped former slave who had joined the group in 1841, attended an abolitionist gathering on Nantucket, where he was asked to speak of his life as a slave, and from 1841 to 1848 Douglas was a staunch Garrisonian abolitionist. However, his association with Garrison soured when he independently founded his own newspaper, *The North Star,* later to be called *Frederick Douglass's Paper.* This dispute over control of the media for the abolitionist crusade continued throughout their careers, and each man contributed mightily to the cause from wholly different perspectives. The lives and writings of these individual abolitionists are crucial to understanding their differing philosophies and the history of the antislavery struggle in the antebellum United States.

Garrison was internationally famous, and extended his radical influence by joining forces with Sarah and Angelina Grimké to espouse the linked causes of abolition and women's rights. Lydia Maria Child joined his organization in 1833, and her *An Appeal in Favor of That Class of Americans Called Africans* showed Garrison's influence on her own positions, particularly in its urgency and demand for full racial equality. Women's rights and emancipation of the slaves were thus joined, so the abolitionist movement energized both components of the reform work. Garrison was also very controversial; the state of Georgia placed a price on his head, and established a reward of five thousand dollars (a huge sum in those days) for his arrest and conviction. In 1832 Garrison penned *Thoughts on African Colonization*, in which he opposed the racial paternalism of the American Colonization Society's ambitious plan to deport all Africans from the United States to Liberia. In 1830, quite early in his career, he was sued for libel and forced to spend forty-nine days in a Baltimore jail, and in 1835 he was dragged through the streets of Boston with a noose around his neck in what might have been an antiabolitionist lynching had it not been for Boston mayor Theodore Lyman, who placed him in the Leverett Street jail for a night of safekeeping.

Like Frederick Douglass and Wendell Phillips, Garrison sought radical change in America's social and political structure. He argued for a complete overhaul of the democratic form of government to include African Americans as full citizens, and he espoused doctrines of full racial equality, a position which some of his fellow abolitionists, like Theodore Parker, were not prepared to accept. Primarily, however, it was his opposition to the United States Constitution that made him controversial, even among his abolitionist followers. For example, on Independence Day, 1854, at an abolitionist celebration in Framingham, Massachusetts, Garrison publicly burned the Constitution of the United States, crying out, "So perish all compromises with tyranny." (See Henry Mayer, *All on Fire: William Lloyd Garrison and the Abolition of Slavery* [New York: St. Martin's, 1998], chps. 1–3.) Garrison was a strident and sometimes monotonous speaker, unlike Wendell Phillips, who had the oratorical skills of an evangelical minister. But his message was always clear: "I hate slavery as I hate nothing else in this world. It is not only a crime, but the sum of all criminality." His personal anger and sense of outrage were often less balanced and controlled than Douglass's or Phillips's, even though Douglass had scars on his back from youthful floggings and suffered his entire life the discrimination practiced against Negroes in nineteenth-century America. Thus Garrison was a highly controversial leader of the abolitionist movement when viewed from a public perspective.

Abraham Lincoln's tribute to his genius and determination shows how highly regarded he was by the president, even though he was not invited to the White House, as Douglass was, nor did he serve in public offices as a reward for his work in the emancipation process. However, he did hold together the militant wing of the abolitionist crusade for three decades by continuous weekly publication of *The Liberator* and by denouncing slavery at every opportunity.

Wendell Phillips (1811–1884) was perhaps the most eloquent orator of the abolitionist lecture circuit, although Frederick Douglass was easily his rival. Phillips was a Boston Brahmin, attended the Boston Latin School and Harvard Law School, and could trace his heritage back to the founding of the Massachusetts Bay Colony in 1630. He married a wealthy woman and never developed much of a law practice, but spent his hours fighting against slavery. In 1837, at a meeting in Faneuil Hall, site of Revolutionary War gatherings of the first patriots, Phillips denounced the murder of Elijah Lovejoy, an abolitionist editor in Alton, Illinois, and the first white man to be martyred for supporting black slaves. Phillips's speeches were "passionate and eloquent," and "caught the imagination of his audience," according to the *Dictionary of American Biography*. At age twenty-six, like his colleague Garrison, Phillips had found his calling.

He became an ally of Garrison and often wrote for *The Liberator*. He "followed Garrison in his refusal to link Abolitionism with the program of any political party and like Garrison, he condemned the Constitution of the United States because of its compromise with the slavery issue" (*Dictionary of American Biography*). The center of abolitionist activity in the 1840s, after the fragmentation of the American movement into warring factions, was not New England, but Great Britain, and both Garrison and Phillips were delegates to the World Antislavery Convention held in London in 1840. Both men denounced the Constitution of the United States as a proslavery compact, and following Garrison's twenty-seven years as president of the American Antislavery Society, Phillips succeeded his friend and colleague. Like Garrison, Phillips linked the issues of women's rights and abolition, but he was not as radical a thinker or as passionate a critic as his mentor, and his writings lack the invective that characterizes Garrison's tracts and the rhetorical strategies that give Douglass's writings so much power.

Frederick Douglass (1818–1895) was born into slavery, the mulatto son of a slave mother and a white man, possibly his mother's master. He was originally named Frederick Augustus Washington Bailey. He would later take the name "Douglass" from a character of Sir Walter Scott whom he admired. His adolescent years were miserable ones, with much suffering as a plantation hand, and he was early separated from his mother, who worked as a field hand some twelve miles distant. His recollection of the few meetings he ever had with his mother are some of the most moving lines of his *Narrative of the Life of Frederick Douglass,* the first of his three autobiographical accounts. Douglass was not only an accomplished orator in the abolitionist cause; he was also a skilled author. He held audiences spellbound, and his speeches reveal a sense of personal identity with his audience. (See, e.g., the use of direct address and the personal pronouns "you" and "your" in his "What to the Slave Is the Fourth of July?" [1852], represented in this volume as a late response to Jefferson's Declaration of Independence and a critique of America's renunciation of these fundamental principles.) He also had a clear sense of the dramatic force of his delivery. Once, during the opening moments of a lecture in London, an audience expressed hostile disbelief in his past as a chattel slave because his oratory and elocution were so powerful. (It was well known that slaves were held in illiteracy and ignorance as a means of control.) Without speaking another word, Douglass promptly stripped off his shirt and turned his flayed back to the incredulous audience to show the scars of his floggings. The veracity of his testimony was authenticated by the exposure of his body as a textual testimony to his slave past.

In this volume, the slave narrators are represented by Douglass, but none of his autobiographical writings are excerpted here because they deserve to be read in full and are readily available in paperback. In addition to the 1845 *Narrative,* one should consult *My Bondage and My Freedom* (1855) and *The Life and Times of Frederick Douglass, Written by Himself* (1881). The repeated phrase "written by himself" is critical in these Douglass titles, as veracity and credibility were serious problems for slave narrators as abolitionists, whose credentials, literacy, and truth telling were often questioned by skeptical reading audiences.

He was twice married, first to Anna Murray Douglass, who had assisted in planning his escape from Maryland to the North, and finally to Helen Pitts Douglass, a white woman, about whom Douglass remarked that he had married his first wife in honor of his mother, and his second in honor of his (white) father, whom he did not know. Douglass and William Wells Brown were the two most prominent slave narrators who participated in the abolitionist movement, and it is significant that Douglass developed a keen political instinct, which governed his publishing and speaking about the relationships between slavery and the United States government, women's rights, and the United States Constitution. For example, unlike the Garrisonians, with whom he broke not only over the independence of his own newspaper, but also over fidelity to the Constitution, Douglass professed belief in the Constitution as an antislavery document which, when properly amended, would allow emancipation. Douglass was, however, powerfully radical in his critique of America's hypocrisy concerning the Declaration of Independence. In this volume, Douglass's critique, "What to the Slave Is the Fourth of July?," is presented not only as a response to the Declaration of Independence, but also as a wake-up call to an errant nation that had abandoned its charter principles and had allowed slavery to coexist with annual proclamations and celebrations of individual rights. Douglass was invited to give the Fourth of July oration for 1852 by the Rochester, New York, Antislavery Society. He refused. But he did give this powerful address on July 5, 1852, to a large audience. The hypocrisies and inconsistencies of American democratic government are castigated severely.

It is also important that at the first American women's-rights convention, held at Seneca Falls, New York, in 1848, a year of revolution throughout Europe, Douglass was a prominent speaker to the women assembled, who also critiqued the founding documents of the United States in the convention's "Declaration of Sentiments." On the day of his death, February 20, 1895, Douglass had just spoken at a women's-rights meeting. He was politically very influential if not powerful. He regularly wrote for the *Washington Evening Star*, *Harper's Weekly*, *Woman's Journal*, and the *London Times*, in addition to editing *Frederick Douglass's Paper* and the *National Era*, which had originally published Harriet Beecher Stowe's *Uncle Tom's Cabin* serially. Like Garrison, Douglass was a man of strong principles, and he voiced his opinions freely and powerfully. He fought most of his life for the emancipation of the slaves, then turned to related issues, including opposition to the migration of freed blacks to the North. He was the friend and confidant of several presidents, including Abraham Lincoln, and in 1889 he was appointed by President Benjamin Harrison to be consul general to the Republic of Haiti. Under President Grover Cleveland, he was given charge of the Office of Recorder of Deeds. The political-patronage appointments and public appearances made Douglass what we would call today a "public intellectual"; however, Douglass never abandoned his abolitionist rhetoric, and at the signing of the Emancipation Proclamation in 1863, he pronounced that "the work of freedom is not here concluded; it has only begun."

William Wells Brown (1814–1884) was another slave narrator who, like Douglass, espoused the abolitionist cause and articulated its connection with women's rights. His autobiographical slave narrative, *Narrative of William W. Brown, a Fugitive Slave, Written by Himself* (1847) was complemented by a literary work, *Clotel, or, The President's Daughter: Narrative of Slave Life in the United States* (1853). He also authored a refutation of the pseudoscience of "polygenesis" that was prominent among proslavery advocates, called *The Black Man: His Antecedents, His Genius, and His Achievements* (1863). Brown was often compared to Douglass, and while Douglass controlled the journalistic and political end of the ex-slave abolitionist spectrum, Brown was a prominent contributor to its literature. *Clotel* was reissued in 1860 as *Miralda, or the Beautiful Quadroon*. Brown spent his adult life as a fugitive slave, escaped from bondage, in the service of the abolitionist movement as a speaker and writer.

Brown's popular works joined Harriet Beecher Stowe's *Uncle Tom's Cabin* as "non-fiction novels" that dramatized the damning effects of slavery on both the owners and the slaves. In 1894, Mark Twain would also publish such a novel, *Pudd'nhead Wilson*, long after emancipation had been achieved but at the height of Jim Crow segregation legislation. This was the era of *Plessy v. Ferguson*, the Supreme Court decision that allowed "separate but equal" accommodations for whites and blacks in housing, transportation, and education. As Stowe's work clearly shows, and as *Clotel* also argues, the institution of slavery is the "demonic other" that must be ended; individual characters, both oppressed and oppressor, are subordinated in these novels to the pervasive evils of the "system," that "peculiar institution" that threatened the very fabric of American democracy.

Ultimately, Stowe was the most powerful of the literary abolitionists, for her narrative argues eloquently against the evils of slavery and utilizes several antecedent traditions to reach an extremely wide audience, including the slave narrative, the Puritan evangelical sermon tradition, and the literature of sentimentality and domesticity, with which her reading audiences were extremely familiar. Stowe's novel was an immediate success. Some 150,000 copies were in circulation by the end of 1852, and by the outbreak of the Civil War in 1861 it had been translated into sixteen languages (the figure was sixty-eight as of 1995, including Welsh and Bengali) and had sold over 4 million copies in English in the United States alone. Abraham Lincoln did not exaggerate much when he reportedly greeted Mrs. Stowe at the White House in 1863 by saying, "So this is the little lady who started this great big war." Stowe maintained close contacts with Frederick Douglass and other abolitionist writers throughout her career, though she was a much more private person than the public and political Douglass, Phillips, and Garrison. In this volume, Stowe's masterpiece is represented by the "Concluding Remarks," a brief chapter in which she used the mode of direct address and challenging invective to attack the hypocrisy of the United States in sermonic and biblical terms, showing clearly that the day of reckoning was near even as she prophesied that God would punish the nation for the sin of slavery.

To survey the abolitionist movement as a collection of eminent lives and the writings of those figures may seem peculiar to some readers. Historians, for example, might stress the internecine wars of the 1840s in which Garrison opposed certain types of political actions among his followers who established a "New Organization" in opposition to his more radical leadership. There were also some serious differences that developed between the two most prominent black and white leaders of the abolitionist cause, Douglass and Garrison. These disputes have been amply treated in scores of historical studies about antebellum antislavery activity, the most prominent of which are listed in the "Suggestions for Further Reading." They are represented here by primary texts authored by the

leading figures of the Garrisonian wing of the abolitionist movement, and by some of the more moderate voices that also struck out
against chattel slavery. What is important, it seems, is that both
black and white Americans were obsessively dedicated to the abolition of chattel slavery in the United States, and that two of these
spokesmen, Douglass and Garrison, were sufficiently united in
their opposition to the sanction of slavery by the federal government and the endorsement of the Fugitive Slave Act of 1850 by that
government to cry out against this national disgrace. They were
joined by the nonfiction novelists William Wells Brown and Harriet Beecher Stowe and by the slave narrators Douglass and Harriet
Jacobs in a crusade that not only emancipated the slaves but also
paved the way for the Civil Rights Act of 1875, the civil rights
movement of the 1960s, and the continued crusade of Dr. Martin
Luther King, Jr., who inherited the mantle of "civil disobedience"
from these early leaders.

As John Thomas has shown, the abolitionists relied almost exclusively on moral persuasion and aggressive rhetorical strategies to
develop their arguments and spread their beliefs. "To destroy the
power of slavery the Abolitionists relied on the equally simple
strategy of conversion. In the beginning, they tried to change the
minds of slaveholders and gain sympathizers by appealing directly
to the individual conscience. They broadcast their indictment in
their own press, organized societies and wrote pamphlets, compiled
statistics and circulated petitions, all with the purpose of bringing
their moral argument directly to bear on the presumed guilt of the
American people. The American Antislavery Society functioned
chiefly as a clearinghouse for a huge propaganda campaign mounted
by agents and agitators who looked to moral suasion for their
power. Its program, however variously interpreted in later years,
originally called for moral agitation directed at individual citizens in
both sections of the country to make them see and feel the sinfulness of slavery. Change people's hearts, they believed, and the people would soon change their habits." (John Thomas, ed., *Slavery
Attacked: The Abolitionist Crusade* [Englewood Cliffs, N.J.:
Prentice-Hall, 1963], pp. 1–2) The Garrisonians embraced "moral
suasion" in the early years, but later separated from those abolitionists who sought reform from within the system by public debate
and constitutional amendments. They added potent tactics to the

rhetoric of moral reform. "A smaller but more militant group of abolitionists—led by William Lloyd Garrison and Wendell Phillips, took another and—so they believed—a higher road to emancipation. Insisting that proscription and repression branded the American church and state as hopelessly corrupt, they demanded that abolitionists have 'no union with slaveholders.' They refused to seek office, vote for antislavery candidates, or in any way support the political abolitionists whom they denounced as traitors to the cause of moral suasion. With their intransigent 'come outer' beliefs, the Garrisonians carried moral suasion to its limits in Christian nonresistance and women's rights. The logic of their position, if not all of their activities, pointed toward secession." (Thomas, *Slavery Attacked*, p. 3) Indeed, Garrison was an early voice in the secessionist argument, stating firmly that there should be "no union with slaveholders," a position that placed the North clearly in the position of seceding from the slaveholding South.

Finally, emancipation required all the forces drawn together, if not working together, to bring an end to the national disgrace of chattel slavery. As Ken Burns's effective Public Broadcasting System series entitled *The Civil War* has shown, one cannot understand the history of the United States without having some grasp of the issues that preceded the coming of the most devastating conflict in our nation's history, one where some 620,000 lives were lost on both sides, more than have been lost in all the other American wars combined.

Historians have argued endlessly whether "slavery" or "the right to secede from the Union by the Confederacy" caused the Civil War; however, there can be little doubt that Alexis de Tocqueville was correct when, in the 1830s, he predicted that the success or failure of American democracy would rest entirely on how effectively the relationships between African Americans and white Americans were developed. The problems that Tocqueville cited are still present in American society, and while the issue of slavery is no longer a subject of political debate, the subtle and pernicious legacy of race prejudice, which Garrison clearly saw as the root cause of slavery in the first place, remains unresolved. As we enter the twenty-first century, and as the United States takes its place in a global political system, the issue of race prejudice will continue to plague Americans precisely because the crucial articulation of principle developed by the founding fathers declared that "all men are created equal." The documents that follow trace the history of that Enlightenment doctrine through the turbulent antebellum period when Americans were seeking a new identity as a nation founded on principles of equality and brotherhood rather than caste and inherited position. These documents show the passion of liberators like Garrison, Child, and Douglass, who sought to reform the American system of government to reflect those ideological principles with which the foundations had been laid from 1776 to 1787. With the flexibility of the Constitution's amendment system, and the doctrine of free speech protected by the First Amendment to the Constitution, the abolitionists set about changing the United States forever, by eradicating the ideological inconsistency of chattel slavery in a republic founded on Enlightenment doctrines of individual freedom and inalienable rights.

"Suggestions for Further Reading" contains both primary materials and secondary critical works, most of which are readily available. The primary source recommendations are of course taken from the antebellum period of American history and thought; however, recent editions of these texts are available and have been cited below.

Acknowledgments

By dedicating this volume to Dr. Arthur Banks, the first African American Ph.D. in political science (Johns Hopkins University) and professor at Morehouse College, and to the memory of Louise Jackson, granddaughter of slaves, who contributed more to this volume than can ever be repaid, the editor wishes to acknowledge his years as an instructor at Morehouse College, 1964–1967. I am also indebted to David Blight, professor of history at Amherst College, colleague and friend, who has read, advised, and encouraged throughout the course of this project. Ruth Jones of Amherst and Georgia Barnhill of the American Antiquarian Society supplied the graphics.

Mason Lowance, Jr.
University of Massachusetts, Amherst
March 1999

SUGGESTIONS FOR FURTHER READING

Abzug, Robert. *Cosmos Crumbling: American Reform and the Religious Imagination.* New York: Oxford University Press, 1994.

———. *Passionate Liberator: Theodore Dwight Weld and the Dilemma of Reform.* New York: Oxford University Press, 1980.

Allison, Robert J. *The Interesting Narrative of the Life of Olaudah Equiano, Written by Himself.* Boston: Bedford Books of St. Martin's Press, 1995.

Ammons, Elizabeth, ed. *Uncle Tom's Cabin.* New York: W. W. Norton Critical Edition, 1994.

Andrews, William L. *To Tell a Free Story: The First Century of Afro-American Autobiography, 1760–1865.* Urbana: University of Illinois Press, 1986.

———, ed. *Critical Essays on Frederick Douglass.* Boston: G. K. Hall, 1991.

———, ed. *The Frederick Douglass Reader.* New York: Oxford University Press, 1996.

Aptheker, Herbert. *Abolitionism: A Revolutionary Movement.* Boston: Twayne Publishers for G. K. Hall, 1971.

Baker, Houston. *Long Black Song: Essays in Black American Literature and Culture.* Charlottesville: University Press of Virginia, 1972.

Bartlett, Irving. *Wendell and Ann Phillips: The Community of Reform, 1840–1880.* New York: W. W. Norton, 1979.

Berlin, Ira. *Many Thousands Gone: The First Two Centuries of Slavery in North America.* Cambridge, Mass.: Belknap Press of Harvard University Press, 1998.

Beyan, Amos J. *The American Colonization Society and the Creation of the Liberian State: A Historical Perspective, 1822–1900.* Lanham, Mich.: University Press of America, 1991.

Blassingame, John. *The Slave Community: Plantation Life in the Antebellum South.* New York: Oxford University Press, 1979.

Blight, David W. *Frederick Douglass's Civil War: Keeping Faith in Jubilee.* Baton Rouge: Louisiana State University Press, 1989.

———, ed. *Narrative of the Life of Frederick Douglass, an American Slave, Written by Himself.* Boston: Bedford Books of St. Martin's Press, 1993.

Blockson, Charles L. *The Underground Railroad.* New York: Prentice-Hall Press, 1987.

Bloom, Harold, ed. *Modern Critical Interpretations: Frederick Douglass's Narrative of the Life of Frederick Douglass, an American Slave.* New York: Chelsea House, 1988.

Brown, William Wells (1814–1884). *The Travels of William Wells Brown, including the Narrative of William Wells Brown, a Fugitive Slave, and The American Fugitive in Europe.* Edited by Paul Jefferson. New York: M. Weiner, 1991.

Burns, Roger, ed. *Am I Not a Man and a Brother: The Antislavery Crusade of Revolutionary America, 1688–1788.* New York: Chelsea House, 1977.

Cain, William E., ed. *William Lloyd Garrison and the Fight Against Slavery: Selections from* The Liberator. Boston: Bedford Books of St. Martin's Press, 1995.

Ceplair, Larry, ed. *The Public Years of Sarah and Angelina Grimké: Selected Writings, 1835–1839.* New York: Columbia University Press, 1989.

Chesebrough, David B. *Frederick Douglass: Oratory from Slavery.* Westport, Conn.: Greenwood Press, 1998.

Child, Lydia Maria (1802–1880). *An Appeal in Favor of that Class of Americans Called Africans.* Edited with introduction by Carolyn Karcher. Amherst: University of Massachusetts Press, 1996.

———. *A Lydia Maria Child Reader.* Edited by Carolyn Karcher. Durham, N.C.: Duke University Press, 1997.

Commager, Henry Steele. *Theodore Parker: An Anthology.* Boston: Beacon Press, 1960.

Cott, Nancy F. *The Bonds of Womanhood: Woman's Sphere in New England, 1780–1835.* New Haven, Conn.: Yale University Press, 1977.

Countryman, Edward. *How Did American Slavery Begin?* Boston: Bedford Books of St. Martin's Press, 1999.

Davis, Charles T., and Henry Louis Gates Jr., eds. *The Slave's Narrative.* New York: Oxford University Press, 1985.

Davis, David Brion. *From Homicide to Slavery: Studies in American Culture.* New York: Oxford University Press, 1986.

———. *The Problem of Slavery in Western Culture.* New York: Oxford University Press, 1966.

Delaney, Martin Robinson (1812–1885). *Blake or the Huts of America: A Novel.* Edited with an introduction by Floyd J. Miller. Boston: Beacon Press, 1970.

Dictionary of Afro-American Slavery. Edited by Randall Miller and John David Smith. New York: Greenwood Press, 1988.

Dillon, Merton L. *The Abolitionists: The Growth of a Dissenting Minority.* Dekalb: Northern Illinois University Press, 1974.

Douglass, Frederick (1818–1895). *The Frederick Douglass Papers.* Edited by John W. Blassingame. New Haven, Conn.: Yale University Press, 1979.

———. *The Life and Times of Frederick Douglass: his early life as a slave, his escape from bondage, and his complete history, written by Himself.* Edited with a new introduction by Rayford W. Logan. New York: Bonanza Books, 1972.

———. *My Bondage and My Freedom.* Edited with an introduction by William Andrews. Urbana: University of Illinois Press, 1987.

Dubois, Ellen. "Women's Rights and Abolition: The Nature of the Connection." In *Feminism and Suffrage: The Emergence of an Independent Women's Movement in America, 1848–1869.* Ithaca, N.Y.: Cornell University Press, 1978.

Du Bois, W. E. B. *Writings of W. E. B. Du Bois.* New York: Literary Classics of the United States, Viking Press, 1986.

Dumond, Dwight Lowell. *Antislavery: The Crusade for Freedom in America.* Ann Arbor: University of Michigan Press, 1961.

———. *Antislavery Origins of the Civil War in the United States.* Ann Arbor: University of Michigan Press, 1964.

———. *A Bibliography of Antislavery in America.* Ann Arbor: University of Michigan Press, 1961.

Elkins, Stanley. *Slavery: A Problem in American Institutional and Intellectual Life.* Chicago: University of Chicago Press, 1959–79.

Essays and Pamphlets on Antislavery. Westport, Conn.: Negro Universities Press, 1970.

Faust, Drew Gilpin. *Mothers of Invention: Women of the Slaveholding South in the American Civil War.* Chapel Hill: University of North Carolina Press, 1996.

Filler, Louis. *The Crusade Against Slavery, 1830–1860.* New York: Harper and Row, 1960.

———. *Wendell Phillips on Civil Rights and Freedom.* Washington: University Press of America, 1982.

Finkleman, Paul, ed. *Articles on American Slavery: An Eighteen-Volume Set Collecting Nearly Four Hundred of the Most Important Articles on Slavery in the United States.* New York: Garland Publishing, 1989.

———, ed. *Dred Scott v. Sandford: A Brief History with Documents.* Bedford Books: Boston, 1997.

Fitzhugh, George. *Cannibals All! or, Slaves without Masters.* Edited by C. Vann Woodward. Cambridge, Mass.: Harvard University Press, 1964.

Fogel, Robert William. *Without Consent or Contract: The Rise and Fall of American Slavery.* New York: W. W. Norton, 1989.

Foner, Eric. *Nothing but Freedom: Emancipation and Its Legacy.* Baton Rouge: Louisiana State University Press, 1983.

———. *Slavery, the Civil War, and Reconstruction.* Washington, D.C.: American Historical Association, 1990.

Foner, Philip. *Three Who Dared: Prudence Crandall, Margaret Douglass, Myrtilla Miner: Champions of Antebellum Black Education.* Westport, Conn.: Greenwood Press, 1984.

Fox-Genovese, Elizabeth. *Within the Plantation Household: Black and White Women of the Old South.* Chapel Hill: University of North Carolina Press, 1988.

Franklin, John Hope. *From Slavery to Freedom: A History of Negro Americans.* New York: Alfred A. Knopf, 1968.

Fredrickson, George M. *The Arrogance of Race: Historical Perspectives on Slavery, Racism, and Social Inequality.* Middletown, Conn.: Wesleyan University Press, 1988.

———. *The Black Image in the White Mind: The Debate on Afro-American Character and Destiny, 1817–1914.* New York: Harper and Row, 1971.

Freehling, William W. *The Reintegration of American History: Slavery and the Civil War.* New York: Oxford University Press, 1994.

Garfield, Deborah, and Rafia Zafar, eds. *Harriet Jacobs and "Incidents in the Life of a Slave Girl": New Critical Essays.* New York: Cambridge University Press, 1996.

Genovese, Eugene D. *From Rebellion to Revolution: Afro-American Slave Revolts in the Making of the Modern World.* Baton Rouge: Louisiana State University Press, 1979.

———. *Roll, Jordan, Roll: The World the Slaveholders Made.* New York: Random House, 1974.

Gougeon, Len. *Emerson's Antislavery Writings.* Athens: University of Georgia Press, 1988.

———. *Virtue's Hero: Emerson, Antislavery, and Reform.* Athens: University of Georgia Press, 1990.

Greenberg, Kenneth S. *The Confessions of Nat Turner and Related Documents*. Boston: Bedford Books of St. Martin's Press, 1996.

Hansen, Debra Gold. *Strained Sisterhood: Gender and Class in the Boston Female Antislavery Society*. Amherst: University of Massachusetts Press, 1993.

Harrold, Stanley. *The Abolitionists and the South, 1831–1861*. Lexington: University of Kentucky Press, 1995.

Hawkins, Hugh, and Lawrence Goodheart, eds. *The Abolitionists: Means, Ends, and Motivations*. Lexington, Mass.: D.C. Heath and Co., 1995.

Helper, Hinton Rowan (1829–1909). *The Impending Crisis of the South: How to Meet It*. Edited by George Fredrickson. Cambridge, Mass.: Harvard University Press, 1968.

Hildreth, Richard. *Despotism in America: An Inquiry into the Nature, Results, and Legal Basis of the Slave-Holding System in the United States*. 1854. New York: Augustus Kelley, 1970.

Hinks, Peter P. *To Awaken My Afflicted Brethren: David Walker and the Problem of Antebellum Slave Resistance*. University Park: Pennsylvania State University Press, 1996.

Horton, James, and Lois Horton. *In Hope of Liberty*. New York: Oxford University Press, 1997.

Huggins, Nathan Irvin. *Black Odyssey: The Afro-American Ordeal in Slavery*. New York: Pantheon Books, 1977.

Jacobs, Harriet A. (1813–1897). *Incidents in the Life of a Slave Girl, Written by Herself*. Edited by Lydia Maria Child. Newly edited with a new introduction by Jean Fagan Yellin. Cambridge, Mass.: Harvard University Press, 1987.

Johannsen, Robert Walter. *Lincoln, the South, and Slavery: The Political Dimension*. Baton Rouge: Louisiana State University Press, 1991.

Jones, Howard. *Mutiny on the "Amistad": The Saga of a Slave Revolt and Its Impact on American Abolition, Law, and Diplomacy*. New York: Oxford University Press, 1987.

Jordan, Winthrop. *White Over Black: American Attitudes Toward the Negro, 1550–1812*. New York: W. W. Norton, 1968.

Karcher, Caroline. *First Woman of the Republic: A Biography of Lydia Maria Child*. Durham, N.C.: Duke University Press, 1998.

Kemble, Fanny (1809–1893). *Journal of a Residence on a Georgian Plantation in 1838–1839*. Edited with introduction by John A. Scott. New York: Alfred A. Knopf, 1970.

Kolchin, Peter. *American Slavery, 1619–1877*. New York: Hill and Wang, 1995.

Kraditor, Aileen S. *Means and Ends in American Abolitionism: Garrison and His Critics on Strategy and Tactics, 1834–1850.* New York: Pantheon Books, 1960.

Lacy, Dan. *The Abolitionists.* New York: McGraw-Hill, 1978.

Lane, Ann J., ed. *The Debate over Slavery: Stanley Elkins and His Critics.* Urbana: University of Illinois Press, 1971.

Leary, Lewis. *John Greenleaf Whittier.* New Haven, Conn.: College and University Press, 1961.

Lloyd, Arthur Young. *The Slavery Controversy, 1831–1860.* Chapel Hill: University of North Carolina Press, 1939.

Lowance, Mason I. "Biography and Autobiography in Early America." In *The Columbia Literary History of the United States,* edited by Emory Elliott. New York: Columbia University Press, 1988.

———. "Frederick Douglass." In *African American Writers,* edited by Lea Bacheler and A. Walton Litz. New York: Charles Scribner's Sons, 1991.

———. "The Slave Narrative in American Literature." In *African-American Writers,* edited by Lea Bacheler and A. Walton Litz. New York: Charles Scribner's Sons, 1991.

———. "Spirituals." In *Encyclopedia of American Poetry.* Chicago: Fitzroy-Dearborn, 1998.

Lowance, Mason, et al., eds. *The Stowe Debate: Rhetorical Strategies in Uncle Tom's Cabin.* Amherst: University of Massachusetts Press, 1994.

Lowell, James Russell (1819–1891). *James Russell Lowell's The Biglow Papers, First Series, a Critical Edition.* Edited by Thomas Wortham. Dekalb: Northern Illinois University Press, 1977.

Martin, B. Edmon. *All We Want Is Makes Us Free: La Amistad and the Reform Abolitionists.* Lanham, Mich., and New York: University Press of America, 1986.

Martin, Waldo E. *The Mind of Frederick Douglass.* Chapel Hill: University of North Carolina Press, 1984.

Mayer, Henry. *All on Fire: William Lloyd Garrison and the Abolition of Slavery.* New York: St. Martin's Press, 1998.

McFeely, William S. *Frederick Douglass.* New York: W. W. Norton, 1991.

McInerney, Daniel John. *The Fortunate Heirs of Freedom: Abolition and Republican Thought.* Lincoln: University of Nebraska Press, 1994.

McKitrick, Eric. *Slavery Defended: The Views of the Old South.* Englewood Cliffs, N.J.: Prentice-Hall, 1963.

McPherson, James M. *The Struggle for Equality: Abolitionists and the Ne-*

gro in the Civil War and Reconstruction. Princeton, N.J.: Princeton University Press, 1964.

Miller, William Lee. *Arguing About Slavery: The Great Battle in the United States Congress.* New York: Alfred A. Knopf, 1995.

Moore, Wilbert Ellis. *American Negro Slavery and Abolition: A Sociological Study.* New York: Third Press, 1971.

Nelson, Truman, ed. *Documents of Upheaval: Selections from William Lloyd Garrison's* The Liberator, *1831–1865.* New York: Hill and Wang, 1966.

New Perspectives on Race and Slavery in America: Essays in Honor of Kenneth M. Stampp. Edited by Robert Abzug and Stephen E. Maizlish. Lexington: University Press of Kentucky, 1986.

Nichols, Charles H. *Many Thousands Gone: The Ex-Slaves' Account of Their Bondage and Freedom.* New York: Athenaeum, 1974.

Parish, Peter J. *Slavery: History and Historians.* New York: Harper and Row, 1989.

Parker, Theodore. *The Slave Power.* New York: Arno Press and New York Times, 1969.

Patterson, Orlando. *The Ordeal of Integration: Progress and Resentment in America's Racial Crisis.* New York: Civitas/Counterpoint, 1998.

Pease, Jane, and William Pease. *The Antislavery Argument.* Indianapolis: Bobbs-Merrill, 1965.

———. *Bound with Them in Chains: A Biographical History of the Antislavery Movement.* Westport, Conn.: Greenwood Press, 1972.

———. *They Who Would Be Free: Blacks Search for Freedom, 1830–1861.* New York: Athenaeum Press, 1974.

Perry, Lewis. *Radical Abolitionism: Anarchy and Government of God in Antislavery Thought.* Ithaca, N.Y.: Cornell University Press, 1973.

Perry, Lewis, and Michael Fellman. *Antislavery Reconsidered: New Perspectives on the Abolitionists.* Baton Rouge: Louisiana State University Press, 1979.

Quarles, Benjamin. *The Black Abolitionists.* New York: Oxford University Press, 1969.

Richards, Leonard. *Gentlemen of Property and Standing: Anti-Abolition Mobs in Jacksonian America.* New York: Oxford University Press, 1970.

Ripley, C. Peter, et al., eds. *The Black Abolitionist Papers: The United States.* 5 vols. Chapel Hill: University of North Carolina Press, 1991.

Rose, Willie Lee Nichols. *Slavery and Freedom.* Edited by William Freehling. New York: Oxford University Press, 1982.

Ruchames, Louis, ed. *The Abolitionists: A Collection of Their Writings.* New York: G. P. Putnam's Sons, 1960.

Seelye, John. *Memory's Nation: The Place of Plymouth Rock.* Chapel Hill: University of North Carolina Press, 1998.

Sekora, John, and Darwin Turner, eds. *The Art of the Slave Narrative: Original Essays in Criticism and Theory.* Macomb: Western Illinois University Press, 1982.

Smith, John David. *An Old Creed for the New South: Proslavery Ideology and Historiography, 1865–1918.* Athens: University of Georgia Press, 1991.

Smith, Valerie. *Self-Discovery and Authority in Afro-American Narrative.* Cambridge, Mass.: Harvard University Press, 1987.

Snay, Mitchell. *The Gospel of Disunion: Religion and Separatism in the Antebellum South.* New York: Cambridge University Press, 1993.

———. *Religion and the Antebellum Debate over Slavery.* Athens: University of Georgia Press, 1998.

Sorin, Gerald. *Abolitionism: A New Perspective.* New York: Praeger, 1972.

Stampp, Kenneth M. *The Peculiar Institution: Slavery in the Antebellum South.* New York: Alfred A. Knopf, 1961.

Stepto, Robert B. *From Behind the Veil: A Study of Afro-American Narrative.* Urbana: University of Illinois Press, 1979.

Stewart, James B. *Holy Warriors and the Abolitionists and American Slavery.* New York: Hill and Wang, 1976.

———. *Wendell Phillips, Liberty's Hero.* Baton Rouge: Louisiana State University Press, 1986.

Stowe, Harriet Beecher (1811–1896). *Uncle Tom's Cabin.* New York: New American Library, 1981.

Strane, Susan. *A Whole-Souled Woman: Prudence Crandall and the Education of Black Women.* New York: W. W. Norton, 1990.

Stuckey, Sterling. *Slave Culture: Nationalist Theory and the Foundations of Black America.* New York: Oxford University Press, 1987.

Sumner, Charles (1811–1874). *The Selected Letters of Charles Sumner.* Edited by Beverly Wilson Palmer. Boston: Northeastern University Press, 1990.

Sundquist, Eric, ed. *Frederick Douglass: New Literary and Historical Essays.* New York: Cambridge University Press, 1990.

————. *To Wake the Nations: Race in Nineteenth-Century American Literature.* Cambridge, Mass.: Harvard University Press, 1986.

Takaki, Ronald. *From Different Shores: Perspectives on Race and Ethnicity in America.* New York: Oxford University Press, 1987.

————. *Iron Cages: Race and Culture in Nineteenth-Century America.* New York: Alfred A. Knopf, 1979.

————. *Lewis Tappan and the Evangelical War Against Slavery.* Cleveland: Case Western Reserve Press, 1969.

Thomas, John L. *The Liberator: William Lloyd Garrison, a Biography.* Boston: Little, Brown, 1963.

————, ed. *Slavery Attacked: The Abolitionist Crusade.* Englewood Cliffs, N.J.: Prentice-Hall, 1963.

Tise, Larry E. *Proslavery: A History of the Defense of Slavery in America, 1700–1740.* Athens: University of Georgia Press, 1987.

Tracy, Susan J. *In the Master's Eye: Representations of Women, Blacks, and Poor Whites in Antebellum Southern Literature.* Amherst: University of Massachusetts Press, 1995.

Tragle, Henry Irving. *The Southampton Slave Revolt of 1831: A Compilation of Source Material.* Amherst: University of Massachusetts Press, 1971.

Tung-Hsun Sun. *Historians and the Abolitionist Movement.* Taipei: Institute of American Culture, Academia Sinica, 1976.

Underground Railroad. Produced by the Division of Publications, National Park Service, Department of the Interior, Washington, D.C., 1998. This book is available through the Government Printing Office, Washington, D.C.

Ven Deburg, William L. *Slavery and Race in American Popular Culture.* Madison: University of Wisconsin Press, 1984.

Walker, Peter F. *Moral Choices: Memory, Desire, and Imagination in Nineteenth-Century American Abolition.* Baton Rouge: Louisiana State University Press, 1978.

Walters, Ronald G. *The Antislavery Appeal: American Abolitionism After 1830.* Baltimore: Johns Hopkins University Press, 1976.

Weinstein, Allen, and Frank O. Gatell. *American Negro Slavery: A Modern Reader.* New York: Oxford University Press, 1968.

White, Deborah. *Ain't I a Woman: Female Slaves in the Plantation South.* New York: W. W. Norton, 1985.

Wish, Harvey, ed. *Antebellum Writings of George Fitzhugh and Hinton Rowan Helper on Slavery.* New York: Capricorn Books, 1960.

———. *Slavery in the South: A Collection of Contemporary Accounts of the System of Plantation Slavery in the Southern United States in the Eighteenth and Nineteenth Centuries.* New York: Farrar, Straus and Giroux, 1964.

Witness for Freedom: African-American Voices on Race, Slavery, and Emancipation. Edited by Peter Ripley. Chapel Hill: University of North Carolina Press, 1993.

Wood, Betty. *The Origins of American Slavery: Freedom and Bondage in the English Colonies.* New York: Hill and Wang, 1997.

Yellin, Jean F. *Women and Sisters: The Antislavery Feminists in American Culture.* New Haven, Conn.: Yale University Press, 1989.

———, ed. *Linda: Incidents in the Life of a Slave Girl, Harriet Jacobs.* Cambridge: Harvard University Press, 1985.

Yellin, Jean F., and John Van Horne, eds. *The Abolitionist Sisterhood: Women's Political Culture in Antebellum America.* Ithaca, N.Y.: Cornell University Press, 1994.

THE HISTORICAL BACKGROUND FOR
ANTEBELLUM ABOLITIONISM,
1700–1830

INTRODUCTION

The general introduction has shown how the abolitionist crusade of 1830–1865 grew out of an earlier antislavery movement that was largely religious in origin and character and that lacked the aggressive, demanding resolve of William Lloyd Garrison, Lydia Maria Child, Frederick Douglass, and Wendell Phillips. The documents that follow include representative texts from this antislavery debate during the years 1700–1800, when Judge Samuel Sewall penned *The Selling of Joseph*, an antislavery pamphlet that criticized American chattel slavery by invoking biblical precedents. The final documents included here are Thomas Jefferson's Declaration of Independence (1776), Phillis Wheatley's "On Being Brought from Africa to America" (1773), and Frederick Douglass's "What to the Slave is the Fourth of July?" (1852), a critique of Jefferson's assertion that "all men are created equal" in the context of chattel slavery for African Americans.

The antebellum slavery debates intensified early in the nineteenth century, particularly following the formation of the New England Antislavery Society in 1831 and the American Antislavery Society in 1833. The publication of David Walker's *Appeal* in 1830 and the commencement of William Lloyd Garrison's *The Liberator* on January 1, 1831, marked a new era in abolitionist rhetoric and thought. The early antislavery advocates had generally argued for "gradualism," a deliberate evolutionary change in American society that would require the prohibition of the importation of slaves but would allow the gradual abolition of slavery through attrition and even colonization. In the eighteenth century, the religious and moral arguments that were mounted against slavery used scriptural texts to counter the biblical precedents of the Old Testament which proslavery advocates had used to support the institution. Garrisonians called for immediate and unconditional emancipation of the slaves, with no compensation for the slaveowners.

The moral and religious arguments were advanced well before the abolitionist crusade of the 1830s, but these pioneering voices were often, like John the Baptist's, "voices crying in the wilderness," speaking out in a society that was either opposed to any form of emancipation or simply indifferent to the moral ramifications of the issue. Prior to 1776, when Jefferson's Declaration of Independence argued the equality of mankind, a natural-rights principle that grew out of Enlightenment doctrine, the antislavery arguments were primarily developed out of scriptural texts or religious doctrine. The Enlightenment had effectively challenged the monarchies of Europe with a radically new view of humanity that disabled essentialist arguments concerning the nature of man, and these natural-rights views were fused with antislavery biblical reasoning to advance an early argument for emancipation. Ironically, it was this very biblical precedent, particularly the Old Testament practices of enslaving captured enemies or the practice of holding polygamous female slaves during the Age of the Patriarchs (Genesis), that gave nineteenth-century proslavery advocates examples from Scripture to use against the abolitionists who demanded an immediate end to chattel slavery in the United States. The charter documents of the new nation set individual freedoms and human rights as the highest priority; biblical precedent included not only Christ's humane teachings but also the Old Testament slavery precedents and Saint Paul's letter to Philemon, in which certain forms of slavery are clearly condoned. Moreover, several prominent Founding Fathers, including George Washington and Thomas Jefferson, who were architects of the new government and authors of these charter documents were themselves slaveholders, creating an inconsistency between theory and practice that plagued the nineteenth-century Congress as well as the framers of the Constitution.

For example, at the age of eleven, George Washington inherited ten slaves when his father died. Until the Revolutionary War, Washington really did not question slavery; there is no record of his having protested its existence or having written anything in opposition to it. He continued to hold slaves at Mount Vernon after his inauguration as president of the United States, and Martha Washington's dowry included slaves. Like most Southern plantation owners, Washington needed slave labor to develop his landholdings. When he was only nineteen years old, he already owned over fourteen hundred acres of Virginia farmland west of the Blue Ridge Mountains because he had received much of this land in lieu of payment for his services as a land surveyor. Washington was paternalistic toward his slaves. He often referred to them as "my family" and considered Mount Vernon, his palatial Potomac estate, as their home. He even saw to their health maintenance and the care of their teeth, not only because this was "good business" and would protect the investment in his property, but because he considered himself the patriarch of a large plantation family. It is significant that Washington did not participate in the selling of slaves, although he did purchase slaves for his estate. After the Revolution, Washington came to hate slavery and wrote, "it being among my first wishes to see some plan adopted by the Legislature by which slavery in this Country may be abolished by slow, sure, and imperceptible degrees."

This "gradualist" approach to the termination of slavery was prominent in the tracts produced in the eighteenth century, such as *An Oration upon the Moral and Political Evil of Slavery, and the Free Relief of Negroes, and Others Unlawfully Held in Bondage* (1793) by George Buchanan (1763–1808). The antislavery writers of the seventeenth and eighteenth centuries included here used moral suasion and the Bible in different ways, but primarily to establish a moral position against the inhumanity of slavery as a societal institution. For example, Samuel Sewall argued that "manstealing" was morally wrong, a violation of God's ordinances, and he cited Exodus 21.16, which reads, "He that Stealeth a man and Selleth him, or if he be found in his hand, he shall surely be put to Death."

Similarly, Cotton Mather argued the Christian value of the Negro, his capacity for salvation, and the urgency for slaveholders to redeem themselves by Christianizing their slaves. "Who can tell but that this Poor Creature may belong to the Election of God! Who can tell but that God may have sent this Poor Creature into my hands, so that one of the Elect may by my means be called; by my Instruction be made wise unto Salvation! The Glorious God will put an unspeakable glory upon me, if it may be so! The Consideration that would move you, to Teach your Negroes the Truths of the Glorious Gospel, as far as you can, and bring them, if it may be, to live according to those Truths, a Sober, and a Godly life . . ." The Mathers owned slaves in Massachusetts before the new state outlawed slavery in 1783; Cotton Mather here essentially argued that Christian slaves would make better slaves for their having been introduced to the principles of the Christian faith.

In 1754, the Quaker John Woolman returned to the religious argument for the humane treatment of Africans, and writing some fifty years after Sewall and Mather, he argued for the emancipation of slaves if not for the equality of blacks and whites. "Why should it seem right to honest Men to make Advantage by the People more than by others? Others enjoy Freedom, receive wages, equal to their work, at, or near such Time as they have discharged these equitable Obligations they are under to those who educated them. These have made no Contract to serve; been more expensive in raising up than others, and many of them appear as likely to make a right use of freedom as other People; which Way then can an honest man withhold from them that Liberty, which is the free Gift of the Most High to His rational creatures?" Woolman argued the humanity of the Negro, a conventional eighteenth-century Enlightenment doctrine which was challenged in the early nineteenth century by scientific and pseudoscientific theories about the natural inferiority of the black race.

Woolman concluded: "Negroes are our fellow creatures, and their present condition amongst us requires our serious Consideration. We know not the time when those Scales, in which Mountains are weighed, may turn. The Parent of Mankind is gracious; His Care is over the smallest Creatures; and Multitudes of Men escape not this. . . ." Thomas Jefferson, like John Woolman, was troubled greatly by the obvious inhumanity of chattel slavery. However, Jefferson was also a product of his times, and, like George Washington, owned a large Virginia plantation which required labor to maintain. His *Notes on the State of Virginia* (1782) reveals that he was deeply divided over the slavery issue. On the one hand, he argued that slavery was wrong and that emancipation should be gradually adopted in the United States. Although he did not emancipate his own slaves until after his death, when some of his slaves were manumitted by the terms of his will, and although he is now known to have sired a child by the female slave Sally Hemmings, his argument in *Notes on the State of Virginia* reflects an ambivalence toward the institution because of its inhuman practices.

Still, Jefferson also outlined the racial differences between blacks and whites in *Notes,* and he concluded that these differences are immutable and eternal. Jefferson's recapitulation of contemporary race-theory arguments was not unusual. Henri Gregoire, a French scientist, countered Jefferson's essentialist position in 1808, in his *On the Cultural Achievement of Negroes*. The British anthropologist James Pritchard articulated widely influential views on race classification, by which a hierarchy of races was established, and in Germany, Johann Friedrich Blumenbach (1742–1840) argued that there were five basic racial types, placing the Anglo-Saxon at the pinnacle of the polygenic chain, and the African Negro at the bottom.

This development was, in retrospect, extremely important in establishing the European conception of the African. The eighteenth-century Age of Enlightenment had embraced theories of race that stressed the unity of humanity while recognizing that there were vast differences between specific persons, including racial differences. But these differences were perceived as being variations or mutations on a common origin, and all humans were regarded to be developing progressively. Until the late eighteenth century, it was not difficult to establish the "humanity" of the Negro, even if it was problematic to establish his equality with the European. But with the rise of scientific reasoning and "race classification," and the methodology of nineteenth-century researchers like Samuel Morton, J. B. Turner, Josiah Nott, George R. Gliddon, J. H. Van Evrie, and O. S. Fowler, serious challenges to the notion that "all men are created equal" were authoritatively advanced, and a hierarchy of races was established not only in the scientific literature, but also in the popular cultural assumptions about race.

Politically and socially, these perceived differences stripped the African of his freedom in chattel slavery, and among free blacks, of his right to vote and, in some instances, to own property, which was a precondition for enjoying the franchise. These historical debates about the "rightness" and "wrongness" of slavery would continue until the Civil War and the Thirteenth Amendment to the Constitution abolished slavery forever; however, the debates concerning the biological, social, and political equality of the African in America continued during Reconstruction and late into the nineteenth century, in such literary works as Mark Twain's *Pudd'nhead Wilson* (1894) and into the twentieth century in such studies as Herrnstein and Murray's *The Bell Curve* (1993).

Finally, it is important to be aware of some of the facts and figures concerning slavery between 1700 and 1865. According to the census of 1790, there were 697,647 slaves out of a total population of 3,929,827. By 1800, there were 896,849 slaves out of a total population of 5,305,925. In 1808, the United States Congress outlawed the importation of slaves to the United States and abolished the slave trade. Still, slaves were illegally smuggled into the states through Southern ports, and natural breeding and population growth accounted for a rapid increase in the slave population throughout the South. In 1810, there were 1,191,364 slaves in a population of 7,289,314, and by 1820, there were 1,538,064 slaves in a total population of 9,638,181. By 1830, this figure had risen to 2,010,436 slaves in a population of 12,856,407. Hence, it appears that according to the ratio of increase between 1820 and 1830, there must have been, in 1835, no fewer than 2,245,144 slaves in the United States. These figures are found in *Stroud's Compendium on Slavery* (1843), an encyclopedia of information on slavery in the Southern states compiled early in the nineteenth century and reprinted and revised frequently.

These figures mean little unless they can be established in a historical context and interpreted in social and political terms. As political forces in a democracy are determined by population and the voting power of certain groups, it is significant that in 1856, the free states in the North had 144 members in the U.S. House of Representatives, while the slave states of the South had 90 members. This means that one Northern, free-state representative represented 91,958 white men and women while one Southern, slave-state representative represented 68,725 white men and women. The Southern "Slave Power" was a function of congressional representation, and the Southern members of Congress exercised this power regularly to perpetuate the institution of slavery on which the Southern economy was dependent.

Similarly, in the United States Senate in 1856, the sixteen free states in the North had a white population of 13,243,000 and had thirty-two senators. The fifteen slave states in the South, with a population of only 6,185,248, held thirty Senate seats. This translates into an unfavorable ratio for the Northern free voting citizens: 413,813 free men of the North enjoyed the same privilege in the Senate given to only 206,175 proponents of slavery. The geographical area of the fifteen slave states was 851,508 square miles, while the geographical area of the free Northern states was 612,597.

The following chart is a summary of the number of slave voyages taken to the Americas between 1595 and 1867.

Summary information contained in the consolidated data of the history of the Atlantic slave trade, as of 23 April 1997.

Number of slave voyages, 1595-1867, in the data-set:	26,807 voyages
Of this total are known:	
Places of ship departure:	19,899 voyages
Places of trade on the African coast: [Only intended locations reported]:	14,904 voyages [4,079] voyages
Thus, some indication of African places of trade for:	18,983 voyages
Places of trade in the Americas:	18,259 voyages
Places of trade both Africa and Americas:	13,803 voyages
Numbers of Africans embarked on Coast: average per slave ship	8,550 voyages 330
Numbers of Africans disembarked in Americas: average per slave ship	15,181 voyages 284
At least one owner known:	16,177 voyages

SOURCE NOTE: Atlantic Slave-Trade Project, W. E. B. Du Bois Institute, Harvard University.

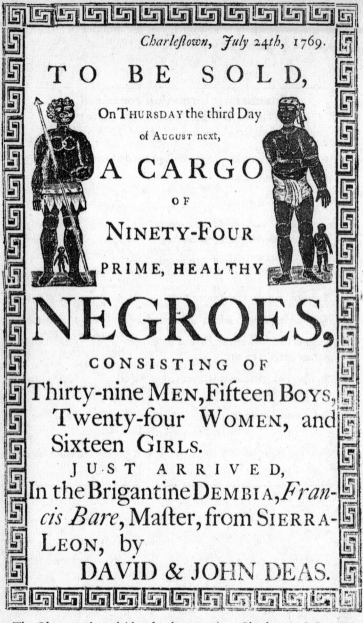

Charlestown, July 24th, 1769.

TO BE SOLD,

On THURSDAY the third Day of AUGUST next,

A CARGO

OF

NINETY-FOUR

PRIME, HEALTHY

NEGROES,

CONSISTING OF

Thirty-nine MEN, Fifteen BOYS, Twenty-four WOMEN, and Sixteen GIRLS.

JUST ARRIVED,

In the Brigantine DEMBIA, *Francis Bare*, Master, from SIERRA-LEON, by

DAVID & JOHN DEAS.

The *Chapman* broadside of a slave auction, Charleston, S.C., 1769.
[By permission of the American Antiquarian Society.]

Samuel Sewall (1652–1730)

Samuel Sewall was not only one of the Massachusetts Bay Colony's most distinguished jurists and lawyers; he was also a successful merchant and an early American political figure. His prominence was also controversial. In 1692, he participated actively in the Salem witchcraft trials that sent many victims to the gallows, and in 1696, Sewall had the courage to recant his actions four years earlier in a public confession, while his colleagues and fellow jurists remained silent. The following excerpts are from his tract *The Selling of Joseph*, which was published in Boston on June 12, 1700, and stands as one of the first antislavery pamphlets printed in America. (A Quaker document protesting the slave trade had appeared as early as 1687.) The full text of *The Selling of Joseph* shows clearly that Sewall condemned chattel slavery; however, it also reveals a writer who was familiar with contemporary race theory and who accepted the inherent inferiority of the Negro to the white. Modern readers should consider what Sewall meant when he regarded the African in America as a type of "extravasat Blood," or separate biological group within the "Body Politick." Sewall is best remembered for his full confession of error for the Salem witchcraft trials; however, *The Selling of Joseph* sets out the arguments not only about slavery as an institution, but also concerning full racial equality, that would be debated throughout the nineteenth century. The *Diary of Samuel Sewall* was published by the Harvard University Press, in 1973; in 1963, Ola E. Winslow authored *Samuel Sewall: A Life,* which is the standard biography.

THE SELLING OF JOSEPH:
A MEMORIAL (1700)

FORASMUCH AS LIBERTY *is in real value next unto*
LIFE: *None ought to part with it themselves, or deprive others
of it, but upon most mature Consideration.*

The Numerousness of Slaves at this day in the Province, and the Uneasiness of them under their Slavery, hath put many upon thinking whether the Foundation of it be firmly and well laid; so as to sustain the Vast Weight that is built upon it. It is most certain that all Men, as they are the Sons of *Adam*, are Coheirs; and have equal Right unto Liberty, and all their outward Comforts of Life. God *hath given the Earth* [with all its Commodities] *unto the Sons of Adam, Psal.* 115.16. *And hath made of One Blood, all Nations of Men, for to dwell on all the face of the Earth, and hath determined the Times before appointed and the bounds of their habitation; That they should seek the lord. Forasmuch then as we are the Offspring of* God. *Act* 17.26, 27, 29. Now although the Title given by the last ADAM, doth infinitely better Men's Estates, respecting GOD and themselves; and grants them a most beneficial and inviolable Lease under the Broad Seal of Heaven, who were before only Tenants at Will; Yet through the Indulgence of GOD to our First Parents after the Fall, the outward Estate of all and every of their Children, re-mains the same, as to one another. So that Originally, and Natu-rally, there is no such thing as Slavery. *Joseph* was rightfully no more a Slave to his Brethren, than they were to him: and they had no more Authority to *Sell* him, than they had to *Slay* him. And if *they* had nothing to do to Sell him; the *Ishmaelites* bargaining with them, and paying down Twenty pieces of Silver, could not make a Title. Neither could *Potiphar* have any better Interest in him than the *Ishmaelites* had. *Gen.* 37.20, 27, 28 . . .

And seeing GOD hath said, *He that Stealeth a man and Selleth him, or if he be found in his hand, he shall surely be put to Death. Exod.* 21.16. This Law being of Everlasting Equity, when Man Stealing is ranked amongst the most atrocious of the Capital Crimes: What louder Cry can there be made of that Celebrated Warning. *Caveat Emptor* . . .

And all things considered, it would conduce more to the Welfare of the Province, to have Slaves for Life. Few can endure to hear of a Negro's being made free; and indeed they can seldom use their free-dom well; yet their continual aspiring after their forbidden Liberty, renders them Unwilling Servants. And there is such a disparity in their Conditions, Colour & Hair, that they can never embody with us, and grow up into orderly Families, to the Peopling of the Land: but still remain in our Body Politick as a kind of extravasat Blood . . .

Moreover it is too well known what Temptations Masters are under, to connive at the Fornication of their Slaves; lest they should be obligated to find them Wives, or pay their Fines.

It is likewise most lamentable to think, how in taking Negroes out of *Africa,* and Selling of them here, That which GOD ha's joined together men do boldly rend asunder; Men from their Country, Husbands from their Wives, Parents from their Children. How horrible is the Uncleanness, Mortality, if not Murder, that the ships are guilty of that bring great Crouds of the miserable men, and Women. Methinks, when we are bemoaning the barbarous usage of our Friends and Kinsfolk in *Africa:* it might not be unseasonable to enquire whether we are not culpable in forcing the *Africans* to become Slaves amongst our selves . . .

Obj. 1. *These Blackamores are of the Posterity of Cham, and therefore are under the Curse of Slavery.* Gen. 9.25, 26, 27.

Answ. Of all Offices, one would not beg this; *viz.* Uncalled for, to be Executioner of the Vindictive Wrath of God; the extent and duration of which is to us uncertain. If this ever was a Commission; How do we know but that it is long since out of Date? Many have found it to their Cost, that a Prophetical Denunciation of Judgment against a Person or People, would not warrant them to inflict that evil. If it would *Hazel* might justify himself in all he did against his Master, and the *Israelites,* from 2 *Kings* 8.10, 12 . . .

But it is possible that by cursory reading, this Text may have been mistaken. For *Canaan* is the person Cursed three times over, without the mentioning of *Cham.* Good expositors suppose the Curse entailed on him, and that this Prophesie was accomplished in the Extirpation of the *Canaanites* . . .

Obj. 2. *The* Nigers *are brought out of Pagan Country, into places where the Gospel is Preached.*

Answ. Evil must not be done, that good may come of it. The extraordinary and comprehensive Benefit accruing to the Church of God, and to *Joseph* personally, did not rectify his brethrens Sale of him . . .

Obj. 3. *The* Africans *have Wars one with another; Our ships bring lawful Captives taken in those Wars.*

Answ. For ought is known, their Wars are much such as were between *Jacob's* Sons and their Brother *Joseph.* An Unlawful War can't make lawful Captives. And by Receiving, we are in danger to promote, and partake in their Barbarous Cruelties. *Therefor all things whatsoever ye would that men should do to you, do ye even to them: for this is the Law and the Prophets.* Matt. 7.12 . . .

Obj. 4. Abraham *had Servants bought with his Money, and born in his House.*

Answ. Until the Circumstance of *Abraham's* purchase be recorded, no Argument can be drawn from it. In the mean time, Charity obliges us to conclude that he knew it was lawful and good . . .

It is Observable that the *Israelites* were strictly forbidden the buying, or selling one another for Slaves. *Levit.* 25.39, 56. *Jer.* 34.8 . . . 22. And GOD gaged His Blessing in lieu of any loss they might conceit they suffered thereby. *Deut.* 15.18. And since the partition Wall is broken down, inordinate Self love should likewise be demolished. GOD expects that Christians should be of a more Ingenuous and benign frame of spirit. Christians should carry it to all the World, as the *Israelites* were to carry it towards another. And for men obstinately to persist in holding their Neighbors and Brethren under the Rigor of perpetual Bondage, seems to be no proper way of gaining Assurance that God ha's given them Spiritual Freedom . . .

SOURCE NOTE: Louis Ruchames, *Racial Thought in America from the Puritans to Abraham Lincoln* (Amherst: University of Massachusetts Press, 1964), with permission of Bruce Wilcox, Director. Originally printed by Bartholomew Green and John Allen, June 12, 1700.

John Saffin

John Saffin was Samuel Sewall's contemporary, and he was also a vocal critic of Sewall's position on slavery. He was a successful merchant, a slave dealer and trader, and in 1701, at the time of his writing a response to Sewall's *The Selling of Joseph*, he was a member of the same judicial court as Sewall. Sewall condemned Saffin privately, and Saffin replied publicly to Sewall in *A Brief Candid Answer to a Late Printed Sheet, Entitled,* The Selling of Joseph. Saffin's document is one of the earliest printed defenses of the institution of slavery on record. It had been lost until George H. Moore discovered a copy and published it in an appendix to his *Notes on the History of Slavery in Massachusetts.* The most comprehensive account of the controversy is Lawrence W. Towner's "The Sewall-Saffin Dialogue on Slavery," in the *William and Mary Quarterly* 21 (January 1964), pp. 40–52. See also Louis Ruchames, *Racial Thought in America from the Puritans to Abraham Lincoln* (Amherst: University of Massachusetts Press, 1964).

A BRIEF CANDID ANSWER TO A LATE PRINTED SHEET, ENTITLED, THE SELLING OF JOSEPH (1701)

That Honourable and Learned Gentleman, the Author of a Sheet, Entitled, *The Selling of Joseph*, A Memorial, seems from thence to draw this conclusion, that because the Sons of *Jacob* did very ill in selling their Brother *Joseph* to the *Ishmaelites*, who were Heathens, therefore it is utterly unlawful to Buy and Sell Negroes, though among Christians; which Conclusion I presume is not well drawn from the Premises, nor is the case parallel; for it was unlawful for the *Israelites* to sell their Brethren upon any account, or pretence whatsoever during life. But it was not unlawful for the Seed of *Abraham* to have Bond men, and Bond women either born in their House, or bought with their Money, as is written of *Abraham, Gen.* 14.14 & 21.10 & *Exod.* 21.16 & *Levit.* 25.44, 45, 46 *v.* After the giving of the Law: And in *Josh.* 9.23. That famous Example of the Gibeonites is a sufficient proof where there [is] no other . . .

So God hath set different Orders and Degrees of Men in the World, both in Church and Common weal. Now, if this Position of parity should be true, it would then follow that the ordinary Course of Divine Providence of God in the World should be wrong, and unjust (which we must not dare to think, much less to affirm) and all the sacred Rules, Precepts and Commands of the Almighty which he hath given the Son of Men to observe and keep in their respective Places, Orders and Degrees, would be to no purpose; which unaccountably derogate from the Divine Wisdom of most High, who hath made nothing in vain, but hath Holy Ends in all his Dispensation to the Children of men . . .

Our Author doth further proceed to answer some Objections of his own framing, which he supposes some might raise.

Object. 1. *That these Blackamores are of the Posterity of* Cham *and therefore under the Curse of Slavery. Gen.* 9.25, 26, 27. The which the Gentleman seems to deny, saying, *they were the Seed of the Canaan that were Cursed.*

Answ. Whether they were so or not, we shall not dispute: this may suffice, that not only the seed of *Cham* or *Canaan,* but any lawful Captives of other Heathen Nations may be made Bond men as hath been proved . . .

Object. 2. *That the Negroes are brought out of Pagan Countreys into places where the Gospel is Preached.* To which he Replies, *that we must not doe Evil that good may come of it.*

Answ. To which we answer, That it is no Evil thing to bring them out of their own Heathenish Country, where they may have the Knowledge of the True God, be Converted and Eternally saved . . .

Obj. 3. *The* Africans *have* Wars *one with another;* our Ships bring lawful Captives taken in those Wars.

To which our Author answer Conjecturally, and Doubtfully, *for ought we know,* that may or may not be; which is insignificant and proves nothing. He also compares the Negroes with another, with the Wars between *Joseph* and his Brethren. But where doth he read of any such War?

By all which it doth evidently appear both by Scripture and Reason, the practice of the People of God in all Ages, both before and after the giving of the Law, and in the times of the Gospel, that there were Bond men, Women and Children commonly kept by holy and good men, and improved in Service: and therefore by the Command of God, *Lev.* 25.44, and their venerable Example, we may keep Bond men, and use them in our Service still; yet with all candour, moderation and Christian prudence, according to their state and condition consonant to the Word of God . . .

THE NEGROES CHARACTER

Cowardly and cruel are those Blacks *Innate,*
Prone to Revenge, Imp of inveterate hate.
He that exasperates them, soon espies
Mischief and murder in their very eyes.
Libidinous, Deceitful, False and Rude,
The Spume Issue of the Ingratitude.
The Premeses consider'd, all may tell,
How near good Joseph *they are parallel . . .*

SOURCE NOTE: Louis Ruchames, *Racial Thought in America from the Puritans to Abraham Lincoln* (Amherst: University of Massachusetts Press, 1964), with permission of Bruce Wilcox, Director.

Cotton Mather (1663–1728)

Cotton Mather was the son of Increase Mather, who served as the president of Harvard College and minister of the Old North Church in Boston in the late seventeenth and early eighteenth centuries. Remembered today as the quintessential Puritan, Cotton Mather authored over four hundred printed volumes during his adult life, including the *Magnalia Christi Americana* (1702), or "the Wonderful Works of Christ in America." He was wide ranging in his interests and advocated the smallpox inoculation for the colonists. Graduated from Harvard College in 1678, Mather was later made a fellow of the Royal Society of London for his work on early American medicine, *The Angel of Bethesda*. Active in the Salem witchcraft trials of 1692, Mather argued against "spectral evidence," the practice of condemning as witches those persons who had appeared to the bewitched as "spectres"; but he also wrote *The Wonders of the Invisible World* in 1693, which is a defense of the view that satanic powers can occupy the natural world. Though he was critical of the use of spectral evidence in the trials of 1692, Mather did not publicly disclaim the actions of the court, as did Samuel Sewall. Born in 1663 in Boston, he died in 1728 only a few years after his illustrious father, Increase Mather, had died.

Modern readers recall the name "Cotton Mather" as the most representative Puritan divine, largely because of his prolific writing. During his lifetime, however, Mather served as assistant minister in his father's church, and his personal life was tragic. Two of his three wives predeceased him, and the third suffered from mental illness. Of his fifteen children, only two survived him, and he presided at all of their funerals. Although he was considered as a possible replacement for his father as president of Harvard, he was never offered the position. Mather's family context is established in Robert Middlekauff's *The Mathers: Three Generations of Puritan Intellectuals* (1971). The standard biography is *The Life and Times of Cotton Mather,* for which Kenneth Silverman won the Pulitzer Prize in 1984.

THE NEGRO CHRISTIANIZED:
AN ESSAY TO EXCITE AND ASSIST
THAT GOOD WORK, INSTRUCTION
OF NEGRO-SERVANTS IN
CHRISTIANITY (1706)

Truly, to Raise a *Soul*, from a dark State of Ignorance and Wickedness, to the Knowledge of GOD, and the Belief of CHRIST, and the practice of our Holy and Lovely RELIGION; 'Tis the noblest Work, that ever was undertaken among the Children of men.

It is come to pass by the *Providence* of God, without which there comes nothing to pass, that Poor NEGROES are cast under your Government and protection. You take them into your *Families;* you look on them as part of your *Possessions:* and you Expect from their Service, a Support, and perhaps an Increase, of your other *Possessions.*

Who can tell but that this Poor Creature may belong to the Election of God! Who can tell, but that God may have sent this Poor Creature into My hands, so that One of the Elect may by my means be Called; by my Instruction be made Wise unto Salvation! The glorious God will put an unspeakable Glory upon me, if it may be so! The Consideration that would move you, To Teach your *Negroes* The *Truths* of the Glorious Gospel, as far as you can, and bring them, if it may be, to live according to those *Truths*, a *Sober* and a *Righteous*, and a *Godly* Life . . .

The *condition* of your *Servants* does loudly solicit your pains to *Christianize* them; and you cannot but hear the cry of it, if you have not put off all *Christian Compassion*, all Bowels of *Humanity*. When you see how laboriously, how obsequiously your *Negroes* apply themselves, to serve you, to content you, to enrich you, What? Have you abandoned all principles of Gratitude, or Generosity?

The State of your *Negroes* in the World, must be low, and mean, and abject; a State of servitude. No *Great Things* in this World, can be done for them. Something then, let there be done, towards their welfare in the *World to Come* . . . *Every one of us shall give account of himself to God* . . .

Yea the pious *Masters*, that have instituted their *Servants* in

Christian Piety, will even in this Life have a sensible *Recompence.* The more *Serviceable,* and Obedient and obliging Behaviour [of] their Servants unto them, will be a sensible & a notable *Recompence.* Be assured, Syrs; your Servants will be the *Better Servants,* for being made *Christian Servants.* To *Christianize* them aright, will be to *fill them with all Goodness. Christianity* is nothing but a very Mass of Universal *Goodness.* Were your *Servants* well tinged with the spirit of *Christianity,* it would render them exceeding *Dutiful* unto their *masters,* exceeding *Patient* under their *Masters,* exceeding faithful in their Business, and afraid of speaking or doing any thing that may justly displease you . . .

The way is now cleared for the work that is proposed: that excellent WORK, THE INSTRUCTION OF THE NEGROES IN THE CHRISTIAN RELIGION . . .

SOURCE NOTE: Louis Ruchames, *Racial Thought in America from the Puritans to Abraham Lincoln* (Amherst: University of Massachusetts Press, 1964), with permission of Bruce Wilcox, Director.

John Woolman (1720–1772)

John Woolman was born in Burlington County, New Jersey, near Mount Holly, a settlement of Quakers. Woolman attended school in Mount Holly, and he was deeply influenced by the Quaker doctrines of nonviolence and passive resistance. He rejected the Calvinist concept of "innate depravity" or "original sin" and the doctrines of "election" or "predestination." Instead, Woolman's simple theology advocated universal redemption through Christ and a belief in the "inner light" through which individual believers might come to know God.

Like Quakers throughout history, Woolman found his conscience in conflict with the theocracy of New England Puritanism, and he was uncomfortable as a businessman because of the profit motive and particularly because one commodity was slaves. Woolman was essentially self-educated, and practiced surveying early in his adult life; then he became a scrivener in a lawyer's office, where he was responsible for the drafting of wills, indentures, and bills of sale. His *Journal* was first published in 1774, and it is a deeply sensitive and personal account of the struggles of his conscience, from the killing of a robin when he was quite young to his later distress over having drafted an indenture for the sale of a slave, a task he resolved never to repeat.

The latter action resulted in a resolution that would govern his later life, namely, that he would never again participate in the institution of slavery and that he would work to end the practice. Woolman was an extremely popular writer because of his intensely personal style; his *Journal* was accompanied by his midcentury publication, *Some Considerations on the Keeping of Negroes,* in which he argued that "the Colour of a Man avails nothing, in Matters of Right and Equity." The manuscript of this book was completed by 1747, but it was not published until 1754. Critical studies include Daniel Shea, *Spiritual Autobiography in Early America* (Princeton, N.J.: Princeton University Press, 1968) and Mason Lowance, "Biography and Autobiography in Early America," in Emory Elliott, ed., *The Columbia Literary History of the United States* (New York: Columbia University Press, 1988).

SOME CONSIDERATIONS ON
THE KEEPING OF NEGROES
(1754 AND 1762)

To consider mankind otherwise than Brethren, to think Favours are peculiar to one Nation, and exclude others, plainly supposes a Darkness in the Understanding: For as God's Love is universal, so where the Mind is sufficiently influenced by it, it begets a Likeness of itself, and the Heart is enlarged towards all Men . . .

Through the Force of long Custom, it appears needful to speak in Relation to Colour—Suppose a white Child, born of Parents of the meanest Sort, who died and left him an Infant, fall into the Hands of a Person, who endeavours to keep him a Slave, some Men would account him an unjust Man in doing so, who yet appear easy while many Black People of honest Lives, and good Abilities, are enslaved, in a Manner more shocking than the case here supposed. This is owing chiefly to the Idea of Slavery being connected with the Black Colour, and Liberty with the White:—And where false Ideas are twisted into our Minds, it is with Difficulty we get fairly disentangled . . .

The Colour of a Man avails nothing, in Matters of Right and Equity. Consider Colour in Relation to Treaties; by such Disputes betwixt nations are sometimes settled. And should the Father of us all so dispose Things, that Treaties with black Men should sometimes be necessary, how then would it appear amongst the Princes and Ambassadors, to insist on the Prerogative of the white Colour?

The Blacks seem far from being our Kinsfolks, and did we find an agreeable Disposition and sound Understanding in some of them, which appeared as a good Foundation for a true Friendship between us, the Disgrace arising from an open Friendship with a Person of so vile a Stock, in the common Esteem, would naturally tend to hinder it . . .

So that, in their present Situation, there is not much to engage the Friendship, or move the Affection of selfish Men: But such who live in the Spirit of true Charity, to sympathise with the Afflicted in the lowest Stations, is a Thing familiar to them . . .

Though there were Wars and Desolations among *Negroes,* before the *Europeans* began to trade there for Slaves, yet now the Calamities are greatly increased, so many Thousands being annually brought from thence; and we, by purchasing them, with Views of self-interest, are become Parties with them, and accessary to that Increase.

In the present Case, relating to Home-born *Negroes,* whose Understandings and Behaviour are as good as common among other People, if we have any Claim to them as Slaves, that Claim is grounded on their being the Children or Offspring of Slaves, who, in general, were made such through Means as unrighteous, and attended with more terrible Circumstance than the Case here supposed . . .

Why should it seem right to honest Men to make Advantage by these People more than by others? Others enjoy Freedom, receive Wages, equal to their Work, at, or near, such Time as they have discharged these equitable Obligations they are under to those who educated them—These have made no Contract to serve; been no more expensive in raising up than others, and many of them appear as likely to make a right Use of Freedom as other People; which Way then can an honest Man withhold from them that Liberty, which is the free Gift of Most High to his rational Creatures?

The *Negroes* who live Plunder, and the Slave-Trade, steal poor innocent Children, invade their Neighbours Territories, and spill much Blood to get these Slaves: And can it be possible for an honest Man to think that, with View to Self-interest, we may continue Slavery to the Offspring of these unhappy Sufferers, merely because they are the Children of Slaves, and not have a Share of this Guilt . . .

Negroes are our Fellow Creatures, and their present Condition amongst us requires our serious Consideration. We know not the Time when those Scales, in which Mountains are weighed, may turn. The parent of Mankind is gracious: His Care is over his smallest Creatures; and a Multitude of Men escape not his Notice: and though many of them are trodden down, and despised, yet he remembers them: He seeth their Affliction, and looketh upon the spreading increasing Exaltation of the Oppressor . . . And wherever gain is preferred to Equity, and wrong Things Publickly encouraged to that Degree, that Wickedness takes Root, and spreads wide amongst the Inhabitants of a Country, there is real Cause for Sorrow to all such, whose Love to Mankind stands on a true Principle, and wisely consider the End and Event of Things.

SOURCE NOTE: Louis Ruchames, *Racial Thought in America from the Puritans to Abraham Lincoln* (Amherst: University of Massachusetts Press, 1964), with permission of Bruce Wilcox, Director.

Phillis Wheatley (1753–1784)

The story of Phillis Wheatley is a remarkable one. She was born sometime in 1753 in Africa, and was transported across the Atlantic on the "middle passage" in the slave ship *Phillis,* arriving in Boston in 1761. Only eight or nine years old, she was fortunately purchased by John Wheatley, a Boston tailor, and his wife, Susannah. Typically, she was given their surname; in addition, she was given the Christian name of the vessel on which she had crossed. The Wheatleys treated her as a child of their own, and she was given an exceptional education for a woman of her time, let alonea slave woman. John Milton and Alexander Pope were her most admired English poets, and she also learned Latin and was well versed in the Bible. In 1773, she traveled to England and presented for publication her *Poems on Various Subjects, Religious and Moral,* which was published later that year. These verses made Phillis Wheatley an instant celebrity, particularly in Boston, where the Wheatleys and other prominent Bostonians gave much recognition to this slave girl turned poet who brought to their attention some of the feelings of African Americans concerning the inconsistencies between the condition of American slaves and the Enlightenment principles of the American Revolution. In dedicating her verses to William Lege, the earl of Dartmouth, for example, she argues:

> Should you, my lord, while you peruse my song,
> Wonder from whence my love of Freedom sprung,
> Whence flow these wishes for the common good,
> By feeling hearts best understood,
> I, young in life, by seeming cruel fate
> Was snatched from Afric's fancied happy seat:
> What pangs excruciating must molest,
> What sorrows labor in my parent's breast?
> Steeled was that soul and by no misery moved
> That from a father seized his babe beloved:
> Such, such my case. And can I then but pray
> Others may never feel tyrannic sway?

This suggested correlation between abduction from Africa for the slave and the tyranny of Britain over the colonies was one of Phillis Wheatley's most prominent themes. However, much of her verse is neoclassical celebratory poetry, such as "To the University, in New England," "On the Death of the Rev. Mr. George Whitefield, 1770," and "To His Excellency General Washington." Wheatley was deeply religious and wrote not only the eulogy to George Whitefield, an evangelical minister who toured New England with Jonathan Edwards and conducted the revival movement now known as the Great Awakening, but also the celebratory poem "Thoughts on the Works of Providence," which betrays her persistent voice of protest against slavery and the oppression of the colonies by Great Britain. "Almighty, in these wond'rous works of Thine, / What Power, what Wisdom, and what Goodness shine! / And are Thy wonders, Lord, by men explored, / And yet creating glory unadored!" is a passage that contains none of the irony and even the bitterness of her expression of anguish over the condition of herself and her fellow Africans who had been made slaves in America. One brief poem represents her many views on this subject, and it is one of her best known, "On Being Brought from Africa to America":

> Twas mercy brought me from my pagan land,
> Taught my benighted soul to understand
> That there's a God, that there's a Savior too:
> Once, I redemption neither sought nor knew.
> Some view our sable race with scornful eye.
> "Their color is a diabolic dye."
> Remember, Christians, Negroes, black as Cain,
> May be refined, and join the angelic train.

Here, Wheatley ironically expresses one of the most prominent antebellum proslavery arguments, i.e., that Christianizing the barbarous pagans of Africa justified the institution of chattel slavery, without which the African would never have known Christian redemption. The final couplet here makes clear Wheatley's rejection of this doctrine, and her assertion of the equality of the races socially, culturally, biologically, and certainly theologically. Throughout her short life, she presented these veiled views on the condition of her people, and the tragedy of her marriages and the deaths of two of her three children, who predeceased her. At the time of her death in 1784, her third child was also dying, and passed away soon after Wheatley.

SOURCE NOTE: Julian D. Mason, ed., *The Poems of Phillis Wheatley* (1989), as cited by Louis Ruchames, *Racial Thought in America from the Puritans to Abraham Lincoln* (Amherst: University of Massachusetts Press, 1964), with permission of Bruce Wilcox, Director.

Thomas Jefferson (1743–1826)

Thomas Jefferson, the third president of the United States, was primary author of the Declaration of Independence, 1776. His famous phrase, "all men are created equal," long stood as a challenge to American democratic principles in the nineteenth century.

A DECLARATION BY THE REPRESENTATIVES OF THE UNITED STATES OF AMERICA, IN GENERAL CONGRESS ASSEMBLED (1776)

When, in the course of human events, it becomes necessary for one people to dissolve the political bands which have connected them with another, and assume among the powers of the earth the separate and equal station to which the laws of nature and of nature's God entitle them, a decent respect to the opinions of mankind requires that they should declare the causes which impel them to the separation.

We hold these truths to be self evident: that all men are created equal; that they are endowed by their Creator with inherent and inalienable rights; that among these are life, liberty, and the pursuit of happiness; that to secure these rights, governments are instituted among men, deriving their just powers from the consent of the governed; that whenever any form of government becomes destructive of these ends, it is the right of the people to alter or to abolish it, and to institute new government, laying its foundation on such principles, and organizing its powers in such form, as to them shall seem most likely to effect their safety and happiness . . . But when a long train of abuses and usurpations, begun at a distinguished period and pursuing invariably the same object, evinces a design to reduce them under absolute despotism, it is their right, it is their duty to throw off such government, and to provide new guards for their future security . . .

SOURCE NOTE: Mason Lowance and Georgia Bumgardner, eds., *Massachusetts Broadsides of the American Revolution* (Amherst: University of Massachusetts Press, 1976), p. 46.

Joseph Story (1779–1845)

The abolitionist text that follows is unusual because of its early date, 1820. Two New Englanders, Joseph Story (1779–1845) and Daniel Webster (1782–1852), were early-nineteenth-century critics of slavery, and both practiced law in Massachusetts, though Webster was born in Salisbury, New Hampshire. In 1820—the year of the Missouri Compromise by which that state was admitted to the Union as a slave state while territories west of the Mississippi were to be admitted as free states—both men argued publicly against slavery.

1820 was also the bicentennial year of the Pilgrims' landing at Plymouth, and celebrations of this event were particularly important in New England, although Plymouth Rock had by this time become a national symbol, an icon of freedom and the "new beginning" experienced by those first settlers. Daniel Webster was chosen to deliver the bicentennial oration at Plymouth in December of that year, exactly two hundred years after the Pilgrims had landed. For a short time, early in the century, Webster had practiced law in Portsmouth, New Hampshire, at a bar where Joseph Story was a prominent figure. However, the inextricable link between the two men was less personal than it was ideological. Their opposition to slavery was declared in these two public addresses in 1820, and the power of their rhetoric signaled the beginning of the slavery debates that would continue through the Emancipation Proclamation to the ratification of the Thirteenth Amendment to the Constitution in 1865.

Webster's speech was essentially a celebration of Plymouth Rock, its long and significant history, its value as a national symbol of freedom, and its meaning to Americans. However, Webster's speech was delivered in December 1820, and he was familiar with Justice Story's "Charge," which had been delivered on May 8 of the same year. What Webster did was to challenge Americans at the beginning of their new century to espouse the values of the Puritan forefathers and to terminate the institution of chattel slavery. Historian John Seelye put it this way:

"It was against this dark background that Webster, toward the end of his Plymouth oration . . . finally admitted that the long and shining record of American progress did have one blot upon it, caused by the 'traffic' whose 'contamination' inspired the 'revolt' of every 'feeling of humanity . . .

I mean the African slave trade.' He called upon 'all the true sons of New-England, to cooperate with the laws of man, and the justice of heaven. If there be, within the extent of our knowledge or influence, any participation in this traffic, let us pledge ourselves here, upon the Rock of Plymouth, to extirpate and destroy it. It is not fit, that the land of the Pilgrims, should bear the shame longer.' . . . Indeed, one of Webster's major themes in his oration was a generic map tracing the evolution of 'liberty,' from the 'love of religious liberty' associated with the Pilgrims to a love of 'freedom' in its most exalted form, which gives men of 'conscience' the courage to resist the 'hand of power' when it becomes restrictive: 'Nothing can stop it, but to give way to it; nothing can check it, but indulgence.' " (John Seelye, *Memory's Nation: The Place of Plymouth Rock* [Chapel Hill, N.C.: University of North Carolina Press, 1998], p. 81) Clearly, Webster had received inspiration from Story's "Charge," and he went on to demand that the slave trade be eradicated "from the land of the Pilgrims." Suggesting that contemporary America had lost some of the innocence of early New England, he argued, "[L]et that spot be purified, or let it cease to be of New England. Let it be purified, or let it be set aside from the Christian world; let it be put out of the circle of human sympathies and human regards, and let civilized man henceforth have no communion with it." (Seelye, p. 83) The language here is uncompromising and forceful, foreshadowing the insistent demands of William Lloyd Garrison over the following decades. It was a landmark performance, as John Seelye has convincingly argued, and together with Justice Story's "Charge" gave rise to increasing demands for the termination of slavery in the land of the free and the home of the brave.

Justice Story's "Charge" was a different type of document from Webster's acclaimed public address. The state of Maine was newly minted in 1820, and it was admitted to the Union as a free state in part to balance the admission of Missouri as a slave state, under the terms of the Missouri Compromise. Story's "Charge" is technically a speech to the first grand jury assembled in the new state, but its publication and its rhetorical force gave it added exposure and influence. One of the most prominent features of Story's challenge to the grand jury is a long and graphic narrative account of the infamous "middle passage" on board slave ships crossing the Atlantic from Africa to the West Indies and the east coast of the United States. This description is provided here, and it echoes the account written in 1782 by Olaudah Equiano, or Gustavas Vassa, whose slave narrative is one of the few to include a full account of the "middle passage." Story's recounting of the African's transatlantic voyage to the new world is moving and disturbing, not only for its recapitulation of the horrors suffered on board those slave ships, but also for the power of its language to move readers to action. It concludes with some rhetorical terms that would become very familiar in the emerging arguments for abolition in the decades to come: "Our constitutions of government have declared that all men are born free and equal, and have certain unalienable rights, among which are the right of enjoying their lives, liberties and property, and of seeking and obtaining their own safety and happiness. May not the miserable African ask, 'Am I not a man and a brother?' " (See Seelye, pp. 81–82)

A CHARGE DELIVERED TO THE GRAND JURY OF THE CIRCUIT OF THE UNITED STATES . . . FOR THE JUDICIAL DISTRICT OF MAINE, MAY 8, 1820

The circumstances under which I address you at the present moment are perhaps without a parallel in the annals of the other quarters of the world. This District has just been admitted into the union as a free, sovereign and independent state, possessing in common with all the others an equality of national rights and honors, and protected by an excellent constitution framed, by its own deliberations, upon principles of justice and equity.

And in what manner has this been accomplished? Not by the course, in which the division of empires has been usually sought and obtained—by civil dissension and warfare—by successful resistance wading through the blood of friends and foes to its purpose— or by the terror of the sword, whose brightness has been stained by the sacrifice of innocence, or rusted by the tears of suffering and conquered virtue. Unhappily for mankind, a change of government has rarely taken place without involving evils of the most serious nature. It has been but the triumph of tyranny in the overthrow of liberties of the people; or the sudden reaction of popular resentment, indignant at wrongs and stimulated to criminal excesses.

Here a different scene—a scene of peace and good order has been presented. The separation has been the result of cool deliberation and cautious examination of the interests of both parties. It has been conducted in a spirit of mutual conciliation and friendship, with an anxious desire to promote the real happiness and prosperity of the people . . .

Nor let us indulge the vain hope that we shall escape a like fate, if we neglect to preserve those institutions in their purity, which sustain the great interests of society. If we grow indifferent to the progress of vice; if we silently wink at violations of the laws; if we habitually follow the current of public opinion without pausing to consider its directions; if we cherish a sullen irreverent disregard of the constitution of government, under which we live, or resign ourselves to factious discontent under the exercise of its legitimate power; the time is not far distant when we shall be separated into rival states, engaged in furious contests for paltry objects, and ultimately become the prey of some unprincipled chieftain, who will first arrive at power by flattering popular prejudices, and then secure his bad eminence by the destruction of the liberties of his country . . .

But there are other acts, which the laws of the United States have declared piracy—which are punishable as such only when committed on board of American ships, or by persons who are justly amenable to our criminal jurisdictions . . .

2. A second declared piracy by our Laws, is the piratically and feloniously running away with any ship or vessel or any goods or merchandise to the value of fifty dollars, or the voluntarily yielding up any ship or vessel to any pirate . . .

3. A third act of piracy by our laws is the laying of violent hands by any seaman upon his commander, thereby to hinder and prevent his fighting in defence of his ship or the goods committed to his trust . . .

4. A fourth act of piracy by our laws is the making of a revolt by a mariner on board of the ship to which he belongs.

It is not easy to enumerate all the various circumstances, which constitute a "revolt," a word which in this clause is used in the sense of mutiny or rebellion—a mere act of disobedience to the lawful commands of the officers of the ship by the crew does not of itself constitute a revolt. But if there be a general combination of the crew to resist the lawful commands of their officers to usurp their authority on board of the ship; and any overt acts are done by the crew in the pursuance of such design; such as the confinement of their officers, or depriving them of the control and management of the ship, these and the like acts seem properly to constitute a revolt.

From this clause it is apparent how deeply involved in guilt are those of our citizens who enlist themselves in the armed ships of foreign states, and commit hostilities upon their countrymen, or plunder their property, since the law declares that they shall be "adjudged and taken to be pirates, felons, and robbers," and shall on conviction suffer death . . .

And in the next place, gentlemen, let me call your attention to that most detestable traffic, the *Slave Trade*.

The existence of Slavery under any shape is so repugnant to the natural rights of man and the dictates of justice, that it seems difficult to find for it any adequate justification. It undoubtedly had its origin in times of barbarism, and was the ordinary lot of those who were conquered in war. It was supposed that the conqueror had a right to take the life of his captive, and by consequence might well bind him to perpetual servitude. But the position itself on which this supposed right is founded, is not true. No man has a right to kill his enemy except in cases of absolute necessity; and this absolute necessity ceases to exist even in the education of the conqueror himself, when he has spared the life of his prisoner . . .

It is also made an offence for any citizen or other person as master, owner, or factor, to build, fit, equip, load, or otherwise prepare any vessel in any of our ports, or to cause any vessel to sail from any port whatsoever for the purpose of procuring any negro, mulatto, or person of color from any foreign country to be transported to any port or place whatsoever, to be held, sold or disposed of, as a slave, or *to be held to service or labor.* It is also made an offence for any citizen or *other person resident within our jurisdiction* to take on board, receive or transport in any vessel from the Coast of Africa or any other foreign country, or from sea, any negro, mulatto or person of color not an inhabitant of, or held to service in the United States, for the purpose of holding, selling or disposing of such person as a slave, or to be held to service or labor . . .

And, Gentlemen, how can we justify ourselves or apologize for an indifference to this subject? Our constitutions of government have declared that all men are born free and equal, and have certain unalienable rights, among which are the right of enjoying their lives, liberties and property, and of seeking and obtaining their own safety and happiness. May not the miserable African ask, "Am I not a man and a brother?" . . .

We believe in the Christian religion. It commands us to have good will to all men; to love our neighbors as ourselves, and to do unto all men as we would they should do unto us. It declares our accountability to the Supreme God for all our actions, and holds out to us a state of future rewards and punishments as the sanction by which our conduct is to be regulated. And yet there are men calling themselves Christians who degrade the negro by ignorance to a level with the brutes, and deprive him of all the consolations of religion. He alone of all the rational creation, they seem to think, is to be at once accountable for his actions, and yet his actions are not to be at his own disposal; but his mind, his body, and his feelings are to be sold to perpetual bondage.—To me it appears perfectly clear that the slave trade is equally repugnant to the dictates of reason and religion and is an offence equally against the laws of God and man . . .

I have called this an *inhuman* traffic, and, gentlemen, with a view to enlist your sympathies as well as your judgments in its suppression, permit me to pass from those cold generalities to some of those details, which are the ordinary attendants upon this trade. Here indeed there is no room for the play of imagination. The records of the British Parliament present us a body of evidence on this subject, taken with the most scrupulous care while the subject of the abolition was before it; taken too from persons who had been engaged in, or eye witnesses of the trade; taken too, year after year in the presence of those whose interests or passions were most strenuously engaged to oppose it . . .

The number of slaves taken from Africa in 1768 amounted to one hundred and four thousand; and though the numbers somewhat fluctuated in different years afterwards, yet it is in the highest degree probable that the average, until the abolition, was not much below 100,000 a year. England alone in the year 1786, employed 130 ships, and carried off about 42,000 slaves . . .

The whole number transported, consists of *kidnapped people.*— This mode of procuring them includes every species of treachery and knavery. Husbands are stolen from their wives, children from their parents, and bosom friends from each other . . .

The second class of slaves, and that not *inconsiderable,* consists of those, whose villages have been depopulated for obtaining them. The parties employed in these predatory expeditions go out at night, set fire to the villages, which they find, and carry off the wretched inhabitants, thus suddenly thrown into their power, as slaves . . .

The third class of slaves consists of such persons as are said to have been convicted of crimes, and are sold on this account for the benefit of their kings . . .

The fourth class includes prisoners of war captured sometimes in ordinary wars, and sometimes in wars originated for the very purposes of slavery.

The fifth class comprehends those who are slaves by birth; and some traders on the coast make a practice of breeding from their own slaves, for the purpose of selling them, like cattle, when they are arrived at a suitable age.—The sixth class comprehends such as have sacrificed their liberty to the spirit of gaming . . .

They are sold immediately upon their arrival on the rivers or coasts, either to land-factors at *depots* for that purpose, or directly to the ships engaged in the trade.—They are then carried in boats to the various ships whose captains have purchased them. The men are immediately confined two and two together either by the neck, leg, or arm, with fetters of solid iron.—They are then put into their apartments, the men occupying the fore part, the women the after part, and the boys the middle of the vessel. The tops of these apartments are grated for the admission of light and air; and the slaves are stowed like any other lumber, occupying only an allotted portion of room.—Many of them while the ships are waiting for their full lading in sight of their native shore, manifest great appearance of distress and oppression; and some instances have occurred where they have sought relief by suicide, and others where they have been afflicted with delirium and madness.—In the day time, if the weather be fine they are brought upon deck for air.—They are placed in a long row of two and two together, on each side of the ship, a long chain is then made to pass through the shackles of each pair, and by this means each row is secured to the deck. In this state they eat their miserable meals, consisting of horse-beans, rice and yams, with a little pepper and palm oil.—After their meals, it is a custom to make them jump for exercise as high as their fetters will allow them; and if they refuse they are whipped until they comply. This the slave merchants call dancing, and it would seem literally to be the dance of death.

When the number of slaves is completed, the ships begin what is called the middle passage, to transport the slaves to the colonies.— The height of the apartments in the ships is different according to the size of the vessel, and is from six feet to three feet, so that it is impossible to stand erect in most of the vessels, and in some scarcely to sit down in the same posture. In the best regulated ships, a grown person is allowed but sixteen inches in width, thirty-two inches in height, and five feet eleven inches in length, or to use the expressive language of a witness, not so much room as a man has in his coffin.—They are indeed so crowded below that it is almost impossible to walk through the groups without treading on some of them; and if they are reluctant to get into their places they are compelled by the lash of a whip.—And here their situation becomes wretched beyond description. The space between decks, where they are confined, often becomes so hot that persons who have visited them there have found their shirts so wetted with perspiration that water might be wrung from them; and the steam from their confined bodies comes up through the gratings like a furnace.—The bad effects of such confinement and want of air are soon visible in the weakness and faintness which overcomes the unhappy victims . . .

When the scuttles in the ship's side are shut in bad weather, the gratings are not sufficient for airing the room; and the slaves are then seen drawing their breath with all that anxious and laborious effort for life, which we observe in animals subjected to experiments in foul air or in an exhausted receiver of an air pump.—Many of them expire in this situation crying out in their native tongue "we are dying."—During the time that elapses from the slaves being put on board on the African coast to their sale in the colonies about one fourth part, or twenty-five thousand per annum are destroyed—a mortality which may be easily credited after the preceding statement.

At length the ship arrives at her destined port, and the unhappy Africans who have survived the voyage are prepared for sale. Some are consigned to Brokers who sell them for the ships at private sale. With this view they are examined by the planters, who want them for their farms, and in the selection of them, friends and relations are parted without any hesitation; and when they part with mutual embraces they are severed by a lash . . .

The scenes which I have described are almost literally copies from the most authentic and unquestionable narratives published under the highest authority. They present a picture of human wretchedness and human depravity, which the boldest imagination would hardly have dared to portray, and from which (one should think) the most profligate would shrink with horror. Let it be considered that this wretchedness does not arise from the awful visitations of providence in the shape of plagues, famines or earthquakes, the natural scourges of mankind; but is inflicted by man on man from the accursed love of gold.—May we not justly dread the displeasure of that Almighty being, who is the common father of us all, if we do not by all means within our power endeavor to suppress such infamous cruelties . . .

I make no apology, Gentlemen, for having detained you so long upon this interesting subject. In vain shall we expend our wealth in missions abroad for the promotion of Christianity; in vain shall we rear at home magnificent temples to the service of the most High; if we tolerate this traffic, our charity is but a name, and our religion little more than a faint and delusive shadow.

SOURCE NOTE: Joseph Story, *A Charge Delivered to the Grand Jury of the Circuit Court of the United States at Its First Session in Portland for the Judicial District of Maine, May 8, 1820, and Published at the Unanimous Request of the Grand Jury and of the Bar* (Portland, 1820).

Frederick Douglass (1818–1895)

Frederick Douglass is best remembered for his three autobiographical narratives—*Narrative of the Life of Frederick Douglass, an American Slave, Written by Himself* (1845), *My Bondage and My Freedom* (1855), and *The Life and Times of Frederick Douglass* (1881)—and for his eloquence on the abolitionist speaking circuit, which he joined soon after his escape to the North from slavery on a plantation near Baltimore, Maryland. As his three autobiographies make clear, Douglass had little genealogy to display at the opening of his narratives, even though they were modeled on the *Autobiography* of Benjamin Franklin, another self-made American, but one who could trace his genealogy back to English ancestors. Rather, the Douglass story is the account of one person's rise from abject misery in slavery, a moment where he had bottomed out, and confessed that the "peculiar institution," which he loathed with every fiber of his being, had won the day. By the end of his life in 1895, he had been an adviser to three presidents, including Abraham Lincoln, and had served his country as consul general to Haiti. Frederick Douglass was, by any measurement, an authentic American hero, one of Ralph Waldo Emerson's "Representative Men." When he was invited to address the Antislavery Society in Rochester, New York, for the Fourth of July oration of 1852, he requested that the date of the talk be changed to July 5, as he did not wish to participate in the celebration of hypocrisy and could not join the festivities recalling the Declaration of Independence. This was an important personal and political statement; as in all of Douglass's writing, there are two narrative agendas. First, he always sought to tell his own story in personal and intimate detail, which engrossed the reader in the account of his remarkable rise from the misery of slavery to significant public renown. Second, his writings always "universalize" his personal experience to include the wider suffering of his brothers and sisters who remain in bondage, so that the autobiographies are essentially political as well as personal documents. "What to the Slave Is the Fourth of July?," another title for the Rochester speech, is an angry attack on American hypocrisy, and as such, should be juxtaposed with David Walker's *Appeal* (1829). But the Douglass speech is also one of his most rhetorically powerful and effective abolitionist addresses, and much of its secret lies in the speaker's ability to make direct contact with his audience, through persuasive, direct statements to those who heard his appeal. What follows are excerpts from the July 5, 1852, address.

WHAT TO THE SLAVE IS THE
FOURTH OF JULY? (1852)

. . . The fact is, ladies and gentlemen, the distance between this platform and the slave plantation, from which I escaped, is considerable—and the difficulties to be overcome in getting from the latter to the former are by no means slight. That I am here today is, to me, a matter of astonishment as well as of gratitude. You will not, therefore, be surprised if in what I have to say I evince no elaborate preparation, nor grace my speech with any high sounding exordium. With little experience and with less learning, I have been able to throw my thoughts hastily and imperfectly together; and trusting to your patient and generous indulgence, I will proceed to lay them before you.

This, for the purpose of this celebration, is the Fourth of July. It is the birthday of your National Independence, and of your political freedom. This to you is what the Passover was to the emancipated people of God. It carries your minds back to the day, and to the act of your great deliverance; and to the signs, and to the wonders, associated with that act, and that day. This celebration also marks the beginning of another year of your national life; and reminds you that the Republic of America is now 76 years old. I am glad, fellow-citizens, that your nation is so young. Seventy-six years, though a good old age for a man, is but a mere speck in the life of a nation. Three score and ten is the allotted time for individual men; but nations number their years by thousands. According to this fact, you are, even now, only in the beginning of your national career, still lingering in the period of childhood. I repeat, I am glad this is so. There is hope in the thought, and hope is much needed, under the dark clouds which lower above the horizon. The eye of the reformer is met with angry flashes, portending disastrous times; but his heart may well beat lighter at the thought that America is still young, and that she is still in the impressible stage of her existence . . . Were the nation older, the patriot's heart might be sadder, and the reformer's brow heavier. Its future might be shrouded in gloom, and the hope of its prophets go out in sorrow . . .

Fellow Citizens, I am not wanting in respect for the fathers of this republic. The signers of the Declaration of Independence were brave men. They were great men, too—great enough to give frame to a great age. It does not often happen to a nation to raise, at one time, such a number of truly great men . . . They were statesmen, patriots, and heroes, and for the good they did, and the principles they contended for, I will unite with you to honor their memory. They loved their country better than their own private interests; and, though this is not the highest form of human excellence, all will concede that it is a rare virtue, and that when it is exhibited it ought to command respect . . . They were peace men; but they preferred revolution to peaceful submission to bondage. They were quiet men; but they did not shrink from agitation against oppression. They showed forbearance; but they knew its limits. They believed in order; but not in the order of tyranny. With them, nothing was settled that was not right. With them, justice, liberty and humanity were "final"; not slavery and oppression. You may well cherish the memory of such men. They were great in their day and generation. Their solid manhood stands out the more as we contrast it with these degenerate times . . . Would to God, both for your sakes and ours, that an affirmative answer could be truthfully returned to these questions! . . . But such is not the state of the case. I say it with a sad sense of the disparity between us. I am not included within the pale of this glorious anniversary! Your high independence only reveals the immeasurable distance between us. The blessings in which you, this day, rejoice, are not enjoyed in common. The rich inheritance of justice, liberty, prosperity, and independence, bequeathed by your fathers, is shared by you, not by me. The sunlight that brought light and healing to you, has brought stripes and death to me. This Fourth of July is **yours, not mine.** You may rejoice, I must mourn. To drag a man in fetters into the grand illuminated temple of liberty, and call upon him to join you in joyous anthems, were inhuman mockery and sacrilegious irony. Do you mean, citizens, to mock me, by asking me to speak today? If so, there is a parallel to your conduct. And let me warn you that it is dangerous to copy the example of a nation whose crimes, towering up to heaven, were thrown down by the breath of the Almighty, burying that nation in irrecoverable ruin! I can today take up the plaintive lament of a peeled and woe-smitten people. "By the rivers of Babylon, there we sat down. Yea! We wept in the midst thereof. For there, they that carried us away captive, required of us a song; songs of Zion. How can we sing the Lord's song in a strange land? If I forget thee, O Jerusalem, let my right hand forget her cunning. If I do not remember thee, let my tongue cleave to the roof of my mouth." (Psalm 137.1–6) . . . Would you have me argue that man is entitled to liberty? that he is the rightful owner of his own body? You have already declared it. Must I argue the wrongfulness of slavery? Is that a question for Republicans? . . . How should I look today, in the presence of Americans, dividing, and subdividing a discourse, to show that men have a natural right to freedom? . . .

What, am I to argue that it is wrong to make men brutes, to rob them of their liberty, to work them without wages, to keep them ignorant of their relations to their fellow men, to beat them with sticks, to flay their flesh with the lash, to load their limbs with irons, to hunt them with dogs, to sell them at auction, to sunder their families, to knock out their teeth, to burn their flesh, to starve them into obedience and submission to their masters? **Must I argue that a system thus marked with blood, and stained with pollution, is wrong?**

. . . What, then, remains to be argued? Is it that slavery is not divine, that God did not establish it; that our doctors of divinity are mistaken? There is blasphemy in the thought. That which is inhuman, cannot be divine!! Who can reason on such a proposition? They that can, may; I cannot. The time for such argument has passed. At a time like this, scorching irony, not convincing argument, is needed. O! had I the ability, and could reach the nation's ear, I would, today, pour out a fiery stream of biting ridicule, blasting reproach, withering sarcasm, and stern rebuke. For it is not light that is needed, but fire, it is not a gentle shower, but thunder. We need the storm, the whirlwind, and earthquake. The feeling of the nation must be quickened; the conscience of the nation must be roused; the propriety of the nation must be startled; the hypocrisy of the nation must be exposed; and its crimes against God and man must be proclaimed and denounced.

What, to the American slave, is *your* Fourth of July? I answer: a day that reveals to him, more than all other days in the year, the gross injustice and cruelty to which he is the constant victim. To him, your celebration is a sham; your boasted liberty, an unholy license; your national greatness, swelling vanity; your sounds of rejoicing are empty and heartless; your denunciation of tyrants, brass fronted impudence; your shouts of liberty and equality, hollow mockery; your prayers and hymns, your sermons and thanksgivings, with all your religious parade and solemnity, are, to him, mere bombast, fraud, deception, impiety, and hypocrisy—a thin veil to cover up crimes which would disgrace a nation of savages. **There is not a nation on the earth guilty of practices more shocking and bloody than are the people of the United States, at this very hour.**

. . . But a still more inhuman, disgraceful, and scandalous state of things remains to be presented. By an act of the American Congress [the Fugitive Slave Law of 1850], not yet two years old, slavery has been nationalized in its most horrible and revolting form. By that act, Mason and Dixon's line has been obliterated; New York has become Virginia; and the power to hold, hunt, and sell men, women, and children, as slaves, remains no longer a mere state institution, but is now an institution of the whole United States. The power is co-extensive with the Star-spangled Banner, and American Christianity. Where these go, may also go the merciless slave-hunter. Where these are, man is not sacred. He is a bird for the sportsman's gun. By the most foul and fiendish of all human decrees, the liberty and person of every man are put in peril. Your broad republican domain is hunting ground for me, not for thieves and robbers, enemies of society, but for men guilty of no crime. Your lawmakers have commanded all good citizens to engage in this hellish sport . . . I take this law to be one of the grossest infringements of Christian Liberty, and, if the churches and ministers of our country were not stupidly blind, or most wickedly indifferent, they, too, would so regard it. At the very moment that they are thanking God for the enjoyment of civil and religious liberty, and for the right to worship God according to the dictates of their own consciences, they are utterly silent in respect to a law which robs religion of its chief significance and makes it utterly worthless to a world lying in wickedness . . . The fact that the church of our country (with fractional exceptions) does not esteem the Fugitive Slave Law as a declaration of war against religious liberty, implies that the church regards religion simply as a form of worship, an empty ceremony, and not a vital principle, requiring active benevolence, justice, love, and good will towards man . . . But the church of this country is not only indifferent to the wrongs of the slave, it actually takes sides with the oppressors. It has made itself the bulwark of American slavery, and the shield of American slave hunters. Many of its most eloquent Divines, who stand as the very lights of the church, have shamelessly given the sanction of religion and the Bible to the whole slave system. They have taught that man may, properly, be a slave; that the relation of master and slave is ordained of God; that to send back an escaped bondman to his master is clearly the duty of all the followers of the Lord Jesus Christ; and this horrible blasphemy is palmed off upon the world for Christianity! For my part, I would say, welcome infidelity! welcome atheism! They convert the very name of religion into an engine of tyranny and barbarous cruelty, and serve to confirm more infidels, in this age, than all the infidel writings of Thomas Paine, Voltaire, and Bolingbroke put together have done! . . . In prosecuting the antislavery enterprise, we have been asked to spare the church, to spare the ministry; but how, we ask, could such a thing be done? We are met on the threshold of our efforts for the redemption of the slave, by the church and ministry of the country, in battle arrayed against us; and we are compelled to fight or flee. From what quarter, I beg to know, has proceeded a fire so deadly upon our ranks, during the last two years, as from the Northern pulpit? As the champions of oppressors, the chosen men of American theology have appeared, men honored for their so-called piety, and their real learning . . . My spirit wearies of such blasphemy; and how such men can be supported, as the standing types and representatives of Jesus Christ, is a mystery which I leave others to penetrate . . . Noble men may be found, scattered all over these Northern States, of whom Henry Ward Beecher, of Brooklyn, Samuel J. May, of Syracuse, and my esteemed friend, Rev. R. R. Raymond, on the platform, are shining examples, and let me say further, that, upon these men lies the duty to inspire our ranks with high religious faith and zeal, and to cheer us on in the great mission of the slave's redemption from his chains.

Fellow citizens, I will not enlarge further on your national inconsistencies. The existence of slavery in this country brands your Republicanism as a sham, your humanity as a base pretense, and your Christianity as a lie. It destroys your moral power abroad; it corrupts your politicians at home. It saps the foundation of religion; it makes your name a hissing and a byword to a mocking earth. It is the antagonistic force in your government; the only thing that seriously disturbs and endangers your Union. It fetters your progress; it is the enemy of improvement; the deadly foe of education; it fosters pride; it breeds insolence; it promotes vice; it shelters crime; it is a curse to the earth that supports it; and yet you cling to it as if it were the sheet anchor of all your hopes. Oh! be warned! be warned! a horrible reptile is coiled up in your nation's bosom; the venemous creature is nursing at the tender breastful republic; **for the love of God, tear away, and fling from you the hideous monster, and let the weight of twenty millions crush and destroy it forever!** . . . In the fervent aspirations of William Lloyd Garrison, I say, and let every heart join in saying it:

> *God speed the year of jubilee*
> *The wide world o'er!*
> *When from their galling chains set free,*
> *Th' oppres'd shall vilely bend the knee,*
> *And wear the yoke of tyranny*
> *Like brutes no more.*
> *That year will come, and freedom's reign,*
> *To man his plundered rights again Restore.*
>
> *God speed the day when human blood*
> *Shall cease to flow!*
> *In every clime be understood,*
> *The claims of human brotherhood,*
> *And each return for evil, good,*
> *Not blow for blow;*
> *That day will come all feuds to end,*
> *And change into a faithful friend*
> *Each foe.*
>
> *God speed the hour, the glorious hour,*
> *When none on earth*
> *Shall exercise a lordly power,*

Nor in a tyrant's presence cower;
But to all manhood's stature tower,
By equal birth!
That hour will come, to each, to all,
And from his prison-house, to thrall
Go forth!

Until that year, day, hour, arrive,
With head, and heart, and hand I'll strive,
To break the rod, and rend the gyve,
The spoiler of his prey deprive—
So witness heaven!
And never from my chosen post,
Whate'er the peril or the cost,
Be driven.

SOURCE NOTE: "What to the Slave Is the Fourth of July? Speech at Rochester, New York, July 5, 1852," in *Frederick Douglass's Paper*, July 19, 1852.

THE BIBLICAL ANTISLAVERY
ARGUMENTS

INTRODUCTION

There are five documents in this section, and they share several characteristics in common. First, all use the Bible as a source for the development of antislavery arguments, often critiquing the same texts used by proslavery advocates to advance the opposite cause. Second, all five are relatively free from the exacting scriptural exegetical habits of mind that are found in proslavery sermons on the Bible. While abolitionists and antislavery advocates both used the Bible as an antislavery resource, they were less able to turn to Scripture for precedent and example than the proslavery writers because the Old Testament, and some parts of the New Testament, offer historical precedents for the divine sanction for slavery.

Proslavery ministers used the traditional Protestant sermon form, very popular among the New England Puritans and the fundamentalists of the antebellum South, whereby the minister would commence his sermon with a text, out of which he would derive a doctrine, and following a lengthy exegesis of this text and doctrine, he would apply the lessons of the doctrine and exegesis to his congregation in a well-delineated third section called the "application." Proslavery sermons tended to follow this format rather exactly because the "doctrine" often derived from the Old Testament text was that God approved of the practice of slavery. Just as the New England Puritans had sought to demonstrate that their "errand into the wilderness" was a recapitulation of the excursion from Egypt to the Promised Land by the Israelites of old, proslavery advocates, especially in the South, attempted to use the Old Testament as a precedent-setting text for the sanctioned practice of chattel slavery.

Antislavery advocates likewise followed the sermon format of text, doctrine, and application. However, their emphasis was less on the exegesis of text and more on the moral application of the spiritual principles inherent in the text to the social and political issue of slavery in America. For example, in James Freeman Clarke's Thanksgiving Day sermon of 1842, a special-occasion sermon that would have been attended by many more listeners than the usual

Sunday sermon, we find very little exegesis but long passages emphasizing the moral wrong of slavery. "First, the evils to the slave are very great. He is not always treated badly, but he is always *liable* to be so treated. He is entirely at the mercy of his master. If he is liable to be beaten, starved, over-worked, and separated from his family; and whoever knows human nature, knows that such cases will not be rare . . . I could tell you stories of barbarities which I knew of, which it would sicken you to hear, as it does me to think of them . . . A worse evil to the slave than the cruelties he sometimes endures, is the moral degradation which results from his condition. Falsehood, theft, licentiousness, are natural consequences of his situation. He steals,—why should he not?—he cannot, except occasionally, earn money; why should not he steal it?" Similarly, Joshua Burt, who also preached in 1842, used anecdotal moral examples rather than Scripture precedents to develop his antislavery argument: "Go to South Carolina and give a single child of oppression a single tract, on which is impressed God's First Commandment, 'Thou shalt have no other Gods before me,' and you are liable to arrest and imprisonment for the deed!!—but I cannot dwell on the detail of slavery's doings. It is a crushing system from beginning to end. Mental, moral and religious light, to a most fearful extent, it puts out. It is claimed, that all this severity, and all this cruelty, are necessarily incident to the system? Be it so. That fact shows what the system is; and is itself one of the most powerful arguments against it."

Of the texts that follow, the most conventional sermon was preached by Alexander McLeod. In *Negro Slavery Unjustifiable* (1802) the minister commences with a text taken from Exodus 21.16: "He that stealeth a man, and selleth him, or if he be found in his hand, he shall surely be put to death." "Manstealing" was indeed a capital crime in ancient Israel, but slaves were often not "stolen"; they were taken in battle. Nevertheless, McLeod immediately concludes, on the strength of his exegesis, that "the practice of buying, holding, or selling our unoffending fellow-creatures as slaves is immoral." Even here, where the minister has commenced with a textual allusion to the Old Testament and has followed the conventional format of the exegetical sermon, McLeod almost immediately turns to Enlightenment doctrine to prove his case rather than using the precedents of the Old Testament. "It is intended, in this discourse, to *confirm the doctrine of the proposition—to answer objections to it—and make some improvement of it . . . [that] to hold any of our fellow-men in perpetual slavery is sinful.* This appears from the inconsistency of the practice of holding slaves with the *natural rights of man.*" For scriptural evidence, McLeod turns to the "family of man" argument that he finds supported by New Testament texts. "The Bible is the criterion of doctrine and conduct. It represents the European and the Asiatic, the African and the American, as different members of the same great family—the different children of the same benign and universal parent. *God has made of one blood all nations of men for to dwell on all the face of the earth, and hath determined the bounds of their habitation,* Acts xvii. 26."

Theodore Dwight Weld also turns to the "manstealing" argument, showing the immorality of the law codes of Southern states, such as Louisiana, in the context of this scriptural prohibition against human bondage. "The giving of the law at Sinai, immediately proceed the promulgation of that body of laws and institutions, called the Mosaic system. Over the gateway of that system, fearful words were written by the finger of God—HE THAT STEALETH A MAN AND SELLETH HIM, OR IF HE BE FOUND IN HIS HAND, HE SHALL SURELY BE PUT TO DEATH. See Exodus, xxi. 16."

Robert Dale Owen's *The Wrong of Slavery* (1864) is a relatively late example of this reasoning process, by which the antislavery advocate would commence with a biblical text but depart from it quickly and advance instead a moral or philosophical argument based on the Enlightenment doctrine of universal human value.

These divergent approaches to Scripture were an inevitable result of the prominence of the Bible in the culture of antebellum America. While not total, the literacy rate was relatively high, particularly in the North, and among the slaves themselves, the Bible became a text that was heard orally if not always understood through reading. (The training of slaves to read and write was prohibited by law in most of the slaveholding Southern states.) Nevertheless, in Harriet Beecher Stowe's *Uncle Tom's Cabin,* the Bible is the staple of Tom's literary diet, and he regularly annotates his copy, which he reads to Eva as they share scriptural and moral lessons. Thus the

Bible became a pawn, routinely brokered by pro- and antislavery advocates to advance their side of the argument and to defeat the opposition. As it has served throughout its history, the Bible was a resource document for a wide and divergent variety of arguments concerning slavery and contemporary human behavior.

Theodore Dwight Weld (1803–1895)

Theodore Dwight Weld was born November 23, 1803, in Hamton, Connecticut. His youth was spent in revival meetings and reform gatherings, including the Oneida Institute in New York. He was deeply influenced by Lewis Tappan, and by 1830, while still in his twenties, he had become active in the abolitionist movement to which Tappan also belonged. There were two strong antislavery institutions in Ohio in the 1830s: Lane Seminary in Cincinnati and Oberlin College. Theodore Weld was active in both of them. Lane Seminary became the pulpit for President Lyman Beecher, father of Harriet Beecher Stowe, and it was there that Weld organized a series of antislavery debates between leading ministers and intellectuals who were brought to Lane for these confrontations. Always a disciple of the Tappans, who were militant abolitionists, calling for immediate and unconditional emancipation, Weld fell out of favor at Lane and moved to Oberlin, where he continued his work as an antislavery abolitionist. He authored two important antislavery works, *The Bible Against Slavery* (1837) and *Slavery As It Is: The Testimony of a Thousand Witnesses* (1839). Stowe credits the latter volume in her *Key to Uncle Tom's Cabin* (1853) as having inspired her to write the book, and she borrowed heavily from its "testimonies," or authentic examples clipped from newspapers and other firsthand sources, to create episodes in her novel. In 1838, Weld married Angelina Grimké, another militant abolitionist, and together they forged one of the most formidable antislavery alliances found in antebellum America. (Angelina Grimké is represented in this volume in the third section, "The Abolitionist Crusade, 1830–1865," with her "Letters to Catharine E. Beecher, in Reply to an Essay on Slavery and Abolitionism, Addressed to A. E. Grimké" (1838).

THE BIBLE AGAINST SLAVERY (1837)

If we would know whether the Bible is the charter of slavery, we must first determine *just what slavery is* . . .

That this is American slavery, is shown by the laws of slave states. Judge Stroud, in his *Sketch of the Laws relating to Slavery,* says, The cardinal principles of slavery, that the slave is not to be ranked among sentient beings, but among *things*—is an article of property, a chattel personal, obtains as undoubted law in all of these states (the slave states). The law of South Carolina thus lays down the principle, Slaves shall be deemed, held, taken, reputed, and adjudged in law to be *chattels personal* in the hands of their owners and possessors, and their executors, administrators, and assigns, to ALL INTENTS, CONSTRUCTIONS, AND PURPOSES WHATSOEVER. (*Brevard's Digest,* 229) In Louisiana, a slave is one who is in the power of a master to whom he *belongs;* the master may sell him, dispose of his *person, his industry, and his labor;* he can do nothing, possess nothing, nor acquire any thing, but what most belong to his master. *Civil Code of Louisiana,* Art. 35 . . .

This is American slavery. The eternal distinction between a person and a thing, trampled under foot—the crowning distinction of all others—their centre and circumference—the source, the test, and the measure of their value—the rational, immortal principle, embalmed by God in everlasting remembrance, consecrated to universal homage in a baptism of glory and honor, by the gift of His Son, His Spirit, His Word, His presence, providence, and power; His protecting shield, upholding staff, and sheltering wing; His opening heavens, and angels ministering, chariots of fire, and songs of morning stars, and a great voice in heaven, proclaiming eternal sanctions, and confirming the word with the signs following . . .

Having stated the *principle* of American slavery, we ask, DOES THE BIBLE SANCTION SUCH A PRINCIPLE? To the *law* and the *testimony.* First, the moral law, or the ten commandments. Just after the Israelites were emancipated from their bondage in Egypt, while they stood before Sinai to receive the law, as the trumpet waxed louder, and the mount quaked and blazed, God spoke the ten commandments from the midst of clouds and thunderings. *Two* of those shalt not take from another what belongs to him. All man's powers of body and mind are God's gift to *him* . . .

The eighth commandment *presupposes and assumes the right of every man to his powers, and their product.* Slavery robs of both . . .

The giving of the law at Sinai, immediately proceed the promulgation of that body of laws and institutions, called the Mosaic system. Over the gateway of that system, fearful words were written by the finger of God—HE THAT STEALETH A MAN AND

SELLETH HIM, OR IF HE BE FOUND IN HIS HAND, HE SHALL SURELY BE PUT TO DEATH. See Exodus, xxi. 16 . . .

No wonder that God, in a code of laws prepared for such a people at such a time, should light up on its threshold a blazing beacon to flash terror to slaveholders. *He that stealeth a man and selleth him, or if he be found in his hand, he shall surely be put to death.* Ex. xxi. 16. God's cherubim and flaming sword guarding the entrance to the Mosaic system! See also Deut. xxiv. 7 . . .

The crime specified is that of *depriving* SOMEBODY *of the ownership of a man.* Is this somebody a master? and is the crime that of depriving a *master* of his *servant*?

The crime, as stated in the passage, is three-fold—man *stealing, selling,* and *holding.* All are put on a level, and whelmed under one penalty—DEATH . . .

But in the case of stealing a *man*, the first act drew down the utmost power of punishment; however often repeated, or however aggravated the crime, human penalty could do no more. The fact that the penalty for *man*-stealing was death, and the penalty for *property*-stealing, the mere *restoration of double,* shows that the two cases were adjudicated on totally different principles . . .

Further, when *property* was stolen, the whole of the legal penalty was a compensation of the person injured. But when a *man* was stolen, no property compensation was offered . . .

If God permitted man to hold *man* as property, why did he punish for stealing *that* kind of property infinitely more than for stealing any *other* kind of property? Why did he punish with *death* for stealing a very little, perhaps not a sixpence worth, of *that* sort of property, and make a mere *fine,* the penalty for stealing a thousand times as much, of any other sort of property—especially if God did by his own act annihilate the difference between man and *property,* by putting him *on a level with it?* . . .

The incessant pains-taking throughout the Old Testament, in the separation of human beings from brutes and things, shows God's regard for the sacredness of his own distinction . . .

Objections Considered

The advocates of slavery are always at their wit's end when they try to press the Bible into their service. Every movement shows that they are hard-pushed. Their odd conceits and ever varying shifts, their forced constructions, lacking even plausibility, their bold assumptions, and blind guesswork, not only proclaim their *cause* desperate, but themselves. Some of the Bible defences thrown around slavery by ministers of the Gospel, do so torture common sense, Scripture, and historical fact, that it were hard to tell whether absurdity, fatuity, ignorance, or blasphemy, predominates, in the compound. Each strives so lustily for the mastery, it may be set down a drawn battle.

How often has it been set up in type, that the color of the negro is the *Cain-mark*, propagated downward. Doubtless Cain's posterity started an opposition to the ark, and rode out the flood with flying streamers! Why should not a miracle be wrought to point such an argument, and fill out for slaveholders a Divine title-deed, vindicating the ways of God to men?

OBJECTION 1. *Cursed be Canaan, a servant of servants shall he be unto his brethren.* Gen. I. 25.

This prophecy of Noah is the *vade mecum* of slaveholders, and they never venture abroad without it. It is a pocket-piece for sudden occasion—a keepsake to dote over—a charm to spell-bind opposition, and a magnet to attract whatsoever worketh abomination, or maketh a lie. But closely as they cling to it, cursed be Canaan is a poor drug to stupefy a throbbing conscience—a mocking lullaby, vainly wooing slumber to unquiet tossings, and crying. Peace, be still, where God wakes war, and breaks his thunders.

Those who plead the curse on Canaan to justify negro slavery, *assume* all the points in debate.

1. That the condition prophesied was slavery, rather than the mere *rendering of service* to others, and that it was the bondage of *individuals* rather than the condition of a *nation tributary* to another, and in *that* sense its *servant*.

2. That the *predication* of crime *justifies* it; that it grants absolution to those whose crimes fulfil it, if it does not transform the crimes into virtues. How piously the Pharaohs might have quoted God's prophecy to Abraham, *Thy seed shall be in bondage, and they shall afflict them for four hundred years.* And then, what *saints* were those that were crucified of the Lord of glory!

3. That the Africans are descended from Canaan. Whereas

Africa was peopled from Egypt and Ethiopia, and Mizraim settled Egypt, and Cush, Ethiopia? See Gen. x. 15–19, for the locations and boundaries of Canaan's posterity. So on the assumption that African slavery fulfills the prophecy, a curse pronounced upon one people, is quoted to justify its infliction upon another. Perhaps it may be argued that Canaan includes all Ham's posterity. Whereas the history of Canaan's descendants, for more than three thousand years, is a record of its fulfillment. First, they were made tributaries by the Israelites. Then Canaan was the servant of Shem. Afterward, by the Medes and Persians. Then Canaan was the servant of Japhet, mainly, and secondarily of the other sons of Ham. Finally, they were subjected by the Ottoman dynasty, where they yet remain. Thus Canaan is *now* the servant of Shem and Japhet and the other sons of Ham.

But it may still be objected, that though Canaan is the only one *named* in the curse, yet the 22d and the 23d verses show that it was pronounced upon the posterity of Ham in general. *And Ham, the father of the Canaan, saw the nakedness of his father, and told his two brethren without.* —Verse 22. In verse 23 Shem and Japhet cover their father with a garment. Verse 24, *And Noah awoke from his wine, and knew what his* YOUNGER *son had done unto him, and said,* &c.

It is argued that this *younger* son cannot be *Canaan*, as he was not the *son*, but the grandson of Noah, and therefore it must be *Ham*. We answer, whoever that *younger son* was, or whatever he did, *Canaan* alone was named in the curse. Besides, the Hebrew word *Ben*, signifies son, grandson, great-grandson, or *any one* of the posterity of an individual. Gen. xxix. 5, *And he said unto them, Know ye Laban the* SON *of Saul, came down to meet the king.* But Mephibosheth was the son of Jonathan, and the *grandson* of Saul. 2 Sam. ix. 6. So Ruth iv. 17. *There is a SON born to Naomi.* This was the son of Ruth, the daughter-in-law of Naomi. Ruth iv. 13,15. So 2 Sam. xxi. 6. *Let seven men of his (Saul's) SONS be delivered unto us,* &c. Seven of Saul's *grandsons* were delivered up. 2 Sam. xxi. 8, 9. So Gen. xxi. 28, *And hast not suffered me to kiss my* SONS *and my daughters;* and in the 55th verse, *And early in the morning Lan rose up and kissed his* SONS, &c. These were his *grandsons.* So 1 Kings ix. 20, *The driving of Jehu, the* SON *of Nimshi.* So 1 Kings

xix. 16. But Jehu was the *grandson* of Nimshi. 2 Kings ix. 2,14. Who will forbid the inspired writers to use the *same* word when speaking of *Noah's* grandson?

Further, if Ham were meant what propriety in calling him the *younger* son? The order in which Noah's sons are always mentioned, make Ham the *second,* and not the *younger* son. If it be said that Bible usage is variable, and that the order of birth is not always preserved in enumerations; the reply is, that, enumeration in the order of birth, is the rule, in any other order the *exception.* Besides, if the younger member of a family, takes precedence of older ones in the family record, it is a mark of pre-eminence, either in original endowments, or providential instrumentality. Abraham, though sixty years younger than his eldest brother, and probably the youngest of Terah's sons, stands first in the family genealogy. Nothing in Ham's history warrants the idea of his pre-eminence; besides, the Hebrew word *Hakkaton,* rendered *younger,* means as the *little, small.* The same word is used in Isaiah xl. 22. A LITTLE ONE *shall become a thousand.* Also in Isaiah xxii. 24. *All vessels of* SMALL *quantity.* So Psalms cxv. 13. *He will bless them that fear the Lord, both* SMALL *and great.* Also Exodus xvii. 22. *But every* SMALL *matter they shall judge.* It would be a perfectly literal rendering of Gen. ix. 24, if it were translated thus, when Noah knew what his little son, or grandson (Benno hakkaton) had done unto him, he said, cursed be Canaan.

Even if the Africans were the descendants of Canaan, the assumption that their enslavement is a fulfillment of this prophecy, lacks even plausibility, for, only a mere *fraction* of the inhabitants of Africa have at any one time been the slave of other nations. If the objector say in reply, that a large majority of the Africans have always been slaves *at home,* we answer, 1st. *It is false in point of fact,* though zealously bruited often to serve a turn. 2d. *If it were true,* how does it help the argument? The prophecy was, Cursed be Canaan, a servant of servants shall he be *unto his* BRETHREN, not unto himself!

SOURCE NOTE: Theodore Dwight Weld, *The Bible Against Slavery* (Boston, 1837).

Alexander Crummell (1819–1898)

Alexander Crummell was born in New York City on March 3, 1819, and he died on September 10, 1898. Crummell was a "freeman" or "free African" although his father, Boston Crummell, was at one time a slave. According to his biographer, Wilson J. Moses, Crummell was a "passionate man with a keen, acerbic wit, but he was also a dark, brooding, Miltonic figure. He was optimistic concerning the future of black people in America and what he called 'the destined superiority of the Negro.' But he was also pessimistic about human nature and spoke repeatedly of human degradation and depravity." (Wilson J. Moses, ed., *Selected Writings of Alexander Crummell, 1840–1898* [Amherst: University of Massachusetts Press, 1992], p. 5) This habit of mind is perhaps best seen in some of his sermons, such as "The Day of Doom," preached in 1854, in which he reminds his listeners of the approaching Judgment and the Apocalypse that awaits the world of sinners, not only the slave owners of the United States. "Crummell was a complex figure, whose significance cannot be understood so long as we cling to the standard cliches about African American culture or stereotypes concerning the black preacher. Crummell absolutely rejected the 'get-happy' philosophy of 'feel-good religion.' His writings illustrate the existence of a strenuous black Protestant ethic that was later to be manifested in the Puritanical discipline of the Nation of Islam under Elijah Muhammad and Malcolm X." (Moses, *Selected Writings*, p. 5) Crummell was celebrated by W. E. B. Du Bois in his classic work *The Souls of Black Folk: Essays and Sketches*, in an essay called "Of Alexander Crummell." Crummell was an exceptionally well educated man, and spent many years living in England, and in 1853 he received an earned, not an honorary, degree from Cambridge University. He traveled widely in Liberia and other parts of Africa, and returned to the United States to become pastor of Saint Luke's Episcopal Church in Washington, D.C., from 1879 to 1894. Crummell lived a very long life and contributed many essays to the literature of Reconstruction America, engaging in the same debates concerning the future of the African in America that would occupy Booker T. Washington and W. E. B. Du Bois at the turn of the century. For example, his speech "Our National Mistakes and the Remedy for Them" was an apologia for the United States government delivered before the Common Council and the Citizens of Monrovia, Liberia, West Africa, on July 26, 1870, which was the Liberian day of national independence. In another address, "The Destined Superiority of the Negro," Crummell preached a Thanksgiving sermon in November 1877 that critiqued the race-theory arguments of antebellum writers like Josiah Nott and George Gliddon, contending that the African Negro had in fact demonstrated, historically, a progress that was not characteristic of other oppressed races. "Wave after wave of a destructive tempest has swept over his head, without impairing in the least his peculiar vitality. Indeed, the Negro, in certain localities, is a superior man, today, to what he was three hundred years ago. With an elasticity rarely paralleled, he has risen superior to the dread inflictions of a prolonged servitude, and stands, today, in all the lands of his thraldom, taller, more erect, more intelligent, and more aspiring than any of his ancestors for more than two thousand years of a previous era." (Moses, *Selected Writings*, p. 200) In another postbellum speech, "The Black Woman of the South: Her Neglects and Her Needs," given before the Freedman's Aid Society of Ocean Grove, New Jersey, on August 15, 1883, Crummell fused the women's-rights agenda with the further emancipation of the African from the Jim Crow culture of Reconstruction.

The text that follows is excerpted from "An Address to the British and Foreign Anti-Slavery Society," published in *The Anti-Slavery Reporter*, June 2, 1851, pp. 87–89. Here, Crummell focuses on the injustices of chattel slavery as an institution and on the degradation of the Negro that has historically followed the enslavement of Africans in America.

AN ADDRESS TO THE BRITISH
ANTISLAVERY SOCIETY (1851)

Sir, it seems to me that the friends of the negroes in the United States, during the last fifteen or twenty years, have partially forgotten one great fact, namely, that the origin of slavery is not, perhaps, to be found so much in any particular laws, as in the weakness, the benightedness, and the degradation of that particular class brought into slavery. It is the disposition, on the part of the strong and selfish, to use and employ the weak and miserable part of creation as their own instruments. How is this to be remedied? I cannot ignore the other plans which have been proposed and enforced here this evening; for I regard each of them as good and feasible. Yet I think there is one other plan which should not be neglected . . . I do think, that if you wish to free a people from the effects of slavery, you must improve and elevate their character. And the Negro needs this improvement. I do not pretend to deny that the people to whom I belong in the United States are, as a whole, weak and degraded. How could it be otherwise? For upward of two centuries they have, for the most part, been deprived of all religious instruction; debarred from all the means and appliances of education; cut off from all participation in civil and political prerogatives; shut out beyond the pale of humanity! And what could be the result of such a regimen as this, but degradation and benightedness? Sir, it is one of the marvels of the world that they did preserve so many of the high instincts of humanity as they do—that they have not become, long ere this, thoroughly brutalized and demented! But, Sir, it is full time now to begin to instruct this people, to cultivate their minds, and to instill into them good moral and religious principles. Extend to them the means of improvement, and allow them full opportunity for the development of their capacities, and oppression could not withstand the influence and power thereof . . . But Sir, there are great difficulties in the way of the cultivation even of the free colored race in America. In the Southern States, it is forbidden by cruel and oppressive laws. In the Northern States, the prejudice of the whites prevents a full participation in the advantages of schools and colleges; while, on the other hand, the poverty of the colored people makes them unable to secure to themselves these advantages to a desirable extent. From these circumstances arises the necessity that the friends of the African in America should interest themselves in the educational interests of the colored race in America . . . [Opposing colonization, Crummell continues.] The idea that a colony, made up, as its advocates frequently assert, of ignorant, degraded, benighted slaves fresh from the slave-shambles and cotton plantations of the Southern States of America when once carried across the ocean, should become the hope of Africa! Sir, the idea is preposterous, upon their own showing, in the last degree that men, who have been degraded for centuries—that a people who have been made base and miserable by a most galling oppression—who had been almost brutalized, and kept almost godless; that these should be the men to lay the foundations of the great states on the coast of Africa, of dispelling the ignorance of the nations, and of propagating virtue. Where was there ever such a marvelous sight witnessed in all the history of the world? Take up the history of colonization, both ancient and modern, and on which of its many pages do you discover such a result, or can you find such a precedent? ... The Negro is an exception to the general facts. I have been noticing, Sir, that the middle passage alone is enough to destroy any people. It has not destroyed the vitality of the Negro!! They have increased in mental and moral importance, and have made themselves felt. Yes, Sir, they have made themselves so much felt, that they have made their cause and their interests matters of great importance to the nation enslaving them. In many cases they have worked out their emancipation—for emancipation has not been merely a boon. It has been, also, an achievement on the part of the black man ... When I notice the endurance of this race, their patience and hopefulness, their quiet perseverance and humility; when I contemplate their remarkable vitality and strong tenacity of life;— when I see their gradual rise from degradation and enslavement, and their transition in many quarters from a state of chattelism to manhood and freedom;—when I behold the capable men of this people coming forward to vindicate and redeem their brethren in Africa and in other lands;—when I observe the increased interest of the Christian world and especially of Christian England in Africa and the simultaneous interest of African chiefs and Africans in general, in the Gospel, and all the zealous efforts of the civilized world in behalf of this people—I cannot but think that all these are the concurrent Providences of God for good; that they are all tending to some great fact—some glorious manifestation of African development in the future—a Fact so high and lofty in its moral significance that it may justify claim to be the realization of the poet's prediction, "Time's noblest offspring is the last."

SOURCE NOTE: "An Address to the British and Foreign Anti-Slavery Society," by Alexander Crummell, in Wilson J. Moses, ed., *Destiny and Race: Selected Writings, 1840–1898, Alexander Crummell* (Amherst: University of Massachusetts Press, 1992), pp. 157–164.

James Freeman Clarke (1810–1888)

James Freeman Clarke was born in Hanover, New Hampshire, and graduated from Harvard College (1829) and the Harvard Divinity School (1833). He became a Unitarian minister, following the example of Ralph Waldo Emerson, who was his friend and mentor among the transcendentalists of Concord. He was active in the affairs of Harvard and served for a quarter century on its board of overseers while also occupying a Boston pulpit and teaching at the divinity school. He was an armchair abolitionist, but he wrote two extremely important antislavery books whose rhetorical powers are evident from the selection included here, *Slavery in the United States* (1843). He was an editor of the *Monthly Journal of the American Unitarian Association* and *The Christian World,* in addition to authoring numerous books and articles on Christian doctrine. He died in Boston on June 8, 1888.

SLAVERY IN THE UNITED STATES (1843)

You may say, *"we can do nothing to remorse the evils of slavery."* Will it do no good to look at great moral questions,—questions of right and wrong, toward which the intellect of the World is turning its attention? It will not do, when we stand before the judgment-seat of Christ, to say that two millions of our fellow beings were under a hard yoke, under a system of government which we were supporting, under laws which we were enacting, and that we would not so much as ask whether we could do any thing to abate the evil . . .

I feel somewhat qualified to speak of it,—if a seven years' residence in a slave-holding community can entitle one to claim some acquaintance with the facts,—if an intimate friendship with many slaveholders, and many obligations and kindnesses received at their hands, can vindicate one from any prejudice against the men,—and if a New England love for freedom, breathed in with her air in childhood, confirmed in youth, and I thank God never relinquished amid other influences in manhood, can prevent me from having imbibed an undue partiality for the system . . .

I. Let us look, then in the first place, at *the evils* of the system of slavery . . .

People have imagined that the slaves were being whipped and worked all the time, that they were dripping with blood, that their misery was constant and universal . . . Yet the *real* evils of slavery never have been, and hardly can be exaggerated. Some circumstances about it may be. There are many very kind masters,—very many . . .

There are also many pleasing features connected with the system. God has given alleviations and compensations to the worst institutions. There is often a strong attachment between the master and servant, very different from the mercenary relations which exist so much among ourselves between employer and domestic. The white child and black grow up together,—they play together on the floor when children, and as they grow up, the one feels the responsibility of a protector, and the other the affection which comes from respect and reliance. Evils, sufficiently enormous, remain, after all such abatements . . .

1. First the evils to the slave are very great. He is not always treated badly, but he is always *liable* to be so treated. He is entirely at the mercy of his master. If he is liable to be beaten, starved, overworked, and separated from his family; and whoever knows human nature, knows that such cases will not be rare . . .

I could tell you stories of barbarities which I knew of, which it would sicken you to hear, as it does me to think of them. But it would give you a false impression. It would be as if I should collect all the accounts of murders and other atrocities committed in this city. It is enough to know, that when men are trusted with irresponsible power they will often abuse it . . .

A worse evil to the slave than the cruelties he sometimes endures, is the moral degradation which results from his conditions. Falsehood, theft, licentiousness, are natural consequences of his situation. He steals,—why should he not?—he cannot, except occasionally, earn money; why should not he steal it? He lies,—it is the natural weapon of weakness against tyrant strength. He goes to excess in eating and drinking and animal pleasures,—for he has no access to any higher pleasures. And a man cannot be an animal without sinking below an animal,—a brutal man is worse than a brute. An animal cannot be more savage or more greedy than the law of his nature allows. But there seems to be no limit to the degradation of a man. Slavery is the parent of vice; it always has been, and always will be. Cowardice and cruelty, cunning and stupidity, abject submission and deadly vindictiveness, are now as they always have been the fruits of slavery . . .

The system of slavery, then, is a soul-destroying system . . .

. . . I have spoken of a few of the evils of the system of slavery to the slave himself. The evils to his master are, perhaps, nearly as great. This is admitted by intelligent slaveholders. It was admitted by Mr. Clay, when he said at a speech at Lexington, before he became the champion of the institution,—"that he considered the system as a curse to the master as well as a bitter wrong to the slave, and to be justified only by an urgent political necessity." It is an evil to the slaveholder every way . . .

There is no comfort, no cleanliness, no improvement with slaves in your family. It is perpetual annoyance and vexation. Society is poisoned in its roots by the system. The spirit, tone, and aim of society is incurably bad, wherever slavery is . . .

. . . The political evils of slavery form a distinct and important part of the argument,—but I cannot stop to dwell on them. I refer you to the speeches of John Quincy Adams, that noble old man who stood up alone in manly opposition to the encouragements of slavery, and bore the tumultuous and furious denunciations of its champion, when no Northern man had the courage to take a stand by his side. "Unshaken, unseduced, unterrified," he stood like the mountain, round which cluster and darken the black clouds and against whose summit they discharge fire and hail, but which emerges from the tumult serene and calm, while there broken, baffled wreaths of mist are driven down the wind . . .

II. Let us now examine the question of the *sinfulness* of slavery.

There are two theories on this subject which I think extreme,— one, of the Abolitionists who demand immediate emancipation,— the other, of the South Carolina party of slaveholders.

The first theory declares that to hold slaves, or to have anything to do with holding slaves, is always sinful, and to be repented of immediately,—that no slaveholder should be permitted commune in our churches, and that we should come out and be separate from this unclean thing as far as possible. They support this theory by the inconsistencies of slavery with the rights of man and the spirit of the gospel . . .

The other party, among who, I am sorry to say, are to be found ministers of the gospel at the South and the North, professors of moral philosophy in Southern colleges, and distinguished cities of the free States, declare slavery to be a system which is sanctioned by the Bible, has existed in all times and is necessary to the progress of the world in freedom and happiness. They speak much of the patriarchs of the Old Testament, and of the fact that while slavery, in atrocious forms, existed in the times of Christ and his Apostles, neither Jesus nor his Apostles were abolitionists, or rebuked it, but instead of commanding the masters to emancipate their slaves, or the slaves to run away, told the masters to be just kind, and the slaves to be obedient and faithful in the relations . . .

The answer of the Abolitionists to this is not satisfactory, because they wish to prove too much,—they denied that slavery did exist under Mosaic institutions; and they accuse their opponents of "torturing the pages of the blessed Bible." . . .

But what shall we say of those who attempt to justify the system, and would have us believe, that because Jesus did not denounce it he had approved of it,—that God ordained that Jesus approved a system that turns man into a brute,—degrades the soul, and makes it almost incapable of progress,—a system, then, which allowed the master to crucify his slave, and throw him into a fish pond to be eaten by carp, for breaking a glass dish,—that Jesus, who taught that we are to love our brethren as ourselves, did not disapprove of this system, or think it sinful? . . .

III. I must now say something on the third point,—*what are our duties in relation to slavery?*

OBJECTION 1. *"We ought to let the whole matter alone; we have nothing to do with it. It is a Southern matter, and should be left exclusively to the South."*

We have a good deal to do with slavery. We support it indirectly throughout the South. It is the strength of the Union which supports slavery, not the strength of the South. It is the power of the free States which upholds this system. If the Union between the free and slave States were dissolved, slavery could not last ten years . . .

Again, by the clause in the Constitution which declares that the slave, escaping North, shall be given up to his Southern master, Massachusetts becomes a hunting ground for the South. She is not wholly a free State,—not so free as Canada. The soil of Canada cannot tolerate the presence of a slave; the soil of New England can. The Southern bondman, flying North, and entering the limits of New England, is still a bondman. When he has passed through New England and crossed the Canada boundary, he has ceased to be a slave. His chains have fallen off from him. Slavery, then, can and does exist on our soil.

We ought not cease our efforts, wisely and earnestly conducted, for the abolition of slavery, till it can be said of New England as it could long ago be said of Old England, that a slave's foot cannot tread soil, a slave's breath taint her air . . .

But we ought to take higher ground. Have we nothing to do with slavery? Are we, then, Christians? Is not our neighbor the suffering man, at the pole or beneath the equator? Ought we not to love him as ourselves? Shall Mason and Dixon's line be an insurmountable barrier to our Christian sympathies? Shall we send missionaries to Africa or India, and help to Poland and Greece, and think nothing of the poor slaves in Georgia and Missouri? Or is political freedom so much more valuable a possession than personal, that it becomes a duty to interfere on behalf of a nation which is taxed without being represented, but criminal to interfere on behalf of a *man*, who is made chattel, and despoiled of all his rights? . . .

OBJECTION 2. *"But you can do nothing. The North cannot do anything for the slave. We cannot approach him. And if we could, the system is too deeply rooted, and too extensive to be overthrown by human efforts. We must leave it to the Providence of God."*

. . . There is every probability that in a few years Kentucky, Maryland and Virginia will emancipate their slaves and secede from the ranks of slavery.

These, and other facts, show that there are natural causes at work, under Providence, which indicate very certainly that slavery in the United States must terminate sooner or later. For there will always be a determined opposition made to every movement towards emancipation in the South, and to resist this, moral convictions are needed, and the influence of a sound public opinion at the North . . .

. . . however we may differ from some of the sentiments and

some parts of the course pursued by abolitionists, they deserve the credit of having been the first effectually of this great subject . . .

OBJECTION 4. *"They do not wish to be free. They are very happy as they are."*

So they [slaves] are, sometimes. Undoubtedly they are often satisfied with their lot. But not generally. I have generally found, on conversing with them, a strong desire for freedom deeply seated in their breasts. If they do not desire freedom, why are the southern newspapers constantly filled with advertisements of runaway negroes, and constantly decorated with a series of embellishments representing a black man, with a bundle on his shoulder, running? . . .

OBJECTION 5. *"But they are not intended to be free. They are an inferior race."*

It is a mistake to speak of the African as an inferior race to the Caucasian. It is doubtless *different* from this, just as this is also different from the Malay, the Indian, the Mongolian. There are many varieties in the human family. The Englishman, Welshman, Scotchman and Irishman are organically different—so are the Pawnee, the Mandan and the Winnebago Indians. But it will not do to say *now* that the African is inferior—he never has been tried. In some faculties he probably is inferior—in others probably superior. The colored man has not so much invention as the white, but more of the perceptive powers. The black child will learn to read and write as fast or faster than the white child, having equal advantages. The blacks have not the indomitable perseverance and will, which make the Caucasian, at least the Saxon portion of it, *masters* wherever they go—but they have a native courtesy, a civility like that from which the word "gentleman" has its etymological meaning, and a capacity for the highest refinement of character. More than all, they have almost universally, a strong religious tendency, and that strength of attachment which is capable of any kind of self-denial, and self-sacrifice. Is this an inferior race—so inferior as to be only fit for chains? . . .

What then is our duty? We ought to remember the bond as bound with them. In our thoughts and our prayers remember them . . .

We should make those whom we send to Congress feel that if they suffer the encroachments of slave power, that if they do not manfully uphold the rights of the North we shall hold them faithless and recreant, unworthy to have been born on the hills of New England. We ought to watch them . . .

What is needed more than anything else now, on this, and many other subjects, is a class of *independent* men—who will not join the abolitionists in their denunciations and their violence, nor join the South in their defence of slavery—who can be temperate without being indifferent—who can be moderate and zealous also—who can make *themselves felt* as a third power, holding the balance between violent parties, and compelling both to greater moderation and justice . . .

We can rebuke every man who truckles or bows to slavery, or who voluntarily offers himself as its instrument—rebuke him by refusing him our countenance or support as long as he shows this disposition. Finally, feeling that the Lord reigns, and that no evil can triumph forever, we can calmly look to him for aid, and rely on his Providence, yet doing ourselves also, whatever our hand finds to do working while the day lasts, knowing that the night cometh when no man can work . . .

SOURCE NOTE: James Freeman Clarke, *Slavery in the United States, a Sermon Delivered in Armory Hall, Thanksgiving Day, November 24, 1842* (Boston, 1843).

Alexander McLeod (1774–1833)

Alexander McLeod was, like Robert Dale Owen, a Scotsman by birth, but he emigrated to the United States at the age of eighteen and entered Union College in Schenectady, New York, where he also taught Greek. He was associated with the Reformed Presbyterian Church, and was always pressing his church to defend human rights, particularly with reference to slavery. He was pastor of the First Reformed Presbyterian Church of New York City and soon became a leading orator in the antislavery cause. His sermon excerpted here, *Negro Slavery Unjustifiable* (1802), is an early exegesis of Scripture in the cause of emancipation, and as in his other writings, McLeod offers his readers and congregation a reasoned, logical, methodical discourse that makes good moral sense. He was very active in promoting causes in New York City, and was a member of the American Society for Meliorating the Condition of the Jews and the New York Society for Instruction of the Deaf and Dumb. His early Scripture-based response to the proslavery arguments, also based on the Bible, is notable for its logical exposition and clear reasoning. This text should be contrasted with Josiah Priest's *The Bible Defense of Slavery* (1852) or Alexander McCaine's *Slavery Defended from Scripture Against the Attacks of the Abolitionists* (1842). McLeod was an early "gradualist," and was active in the American Colonization Society.

NEGRO SLAVERY UNJUSTIFIABLE (1846)

This sermon was preached and published in America in 1802, and unpublished in this country [England] in 1804.

The author was a Scotchman, the son of an eminent clergyman of the Established Church in Mull. He emigrated to America in early life, and, by his talents and character, rose to eminence and influence as a minister of the Gospel.

The principle upon which Dr. McLeod acted in refusing an invitation to the ministry and pastoral charge, till the community calling him was purged of the scandal of slave-holding, he never abandoned nor relaxed. He regarded the country of his adoption with what some, on his side of the water, may consider an over-weening partiality; but he was not blind to its evils. In a sermon which was published during the late war, in 1815, he lifted a faithful testimony against the immoralities of the Federal Government of the United States. "By the terms of the national compact," says he, "God is not at all acknowledged, and holding men in slavery is au-thorised. The constitution of our government recognises the prac-tice of holding *men*, without being convicted of any offence, in *perpetual slavery*. This evil, prohibited by the divine law, Exod. xxi. 16, is equally inconsistent with what is said in the declaration of American independence to be a self-evident truth: "We hold these truths to be self-evident—that all men are created equal—that they are endowed by the Creator with certain unalienable rights—that among these are life, liberty, and the pursuit of happiness—that to secure these rights governments are instituted among men." In di-rect opposition to these *self-evident* maxims, the constitution pro-vided for the continuance of the slave trade till the year 1808, and it still provides for the continuance of *slavery* in this *free* country. It even gives to the slave-holder an influence in legislation, propor-tioned to the number of his fellowmen he holds in bondage. For these national immoralities, I am bound, as a minister of the Gospel, who derives his politics from the Bible, to pronounce upon the Government the sentence—TEKEL, *thou art weighed in the bal-ances, and art found wanting.* Let me not be understood, however, as conveying the idea, that the other belligerent is not faulty in these respects. Great Britain set the example to her colonies of prosecut-ing the slave-trade. She still continues, in her numerous provinces, thousands in abject bondage. A few good men, after the repeated, the continued exertions of years in the British Parliament, obtained, at last, victory honourable to themselves, and to the cause of hu-manity, in finally abolishing the African trade; but these injured people, already in durance, have no hope of release for themselves or their offspring. Slavery is a black, a vile inheritance left to Amer-ica by her royal stepmother.

And we believe that the time is come for a decision, for the trumpet giving a certain sound, and for sending faithful and reiter-ated remonstrances to American Christians on the sin and danger of implication in the evil of slavery. We have strong views on this ne-cessity, and have pleasures and encouragement in the harmony and decision of sentiment on the subject in the documents appended. How can we read otherwise than with emotions of grief and indignation, as we did the other day in the advertising columns of an American newspaper, of date May 5, 1846—"SLAVES FOR SALE. A likely family of NEGROES, consisting of a MAN, twenty-seven years old, his wife twenty-three, and four children, from eight to two years old, raised in this climate, and fully guaranteed." And this stands among a considerable number of similar advertisements. What! shall families be knocked down to the highest bidder like herds and flocks? Shall the tenderest ties of nature be forcibly and unfeelingly ruptured? Shall husband and wife, in opposition to the strongest affections of the human heart, and in spite of the revealed law of Heaven, be torn asunder from one another? Shall the parents and offspring be cruelly and for ever separated? Shall rational beings be abandoned to ignorance and misery? Shall unoffending fellowmen be doomed to perpetual slavery, and to leave only this inheritance to their children? Shall immortal souls be left to be destroyed for ever for lack of knowledge? Reason, humanity, justice, mercy, interest, lift their indignant voices against all this; and high above them all, while in harmony with them, our holy and benevolent Christianity lifts its loudest protestations! How long shall such enormities be obtruded on the public eye?

The Practice of Holding Men
In Perpetual Slavery
Condemned
Exod. xxi. 16.

He that stealeth a man, and selleth him, or
if he be found in his hand, he shall surely be put to death.

The divine law declares this a crime, and prescribes the punishment. *He who stealeth a man, and selleth him, or if he be found in his hand, he shall surely be put to death.*

From the text, I consider myself authorised to lay before you the following proposition:

The practice of buying, holding, or selling our unoffending fellow-creatures as slaves is immoral.

The text will certainly support this proposition. According to the common principles of law, the receiver of stolen goods, if he know them to be such, is esteemed guilty as well as the thief. The slaveholder never had a right to force a man into his service, or to retain him, without an equivalent. To sell him, therefore, is to tempt another to sin, and to dispose of that, for money, to which he never had a right . . .

It is intended, in this discourse, to *confirm the doctrine of the proposition—to answer objections to it—and make some improvement of it.*

I. To hold any of our fellow-men in perpetual slavery is sinful.

1. This appears from the inconsistency of the practice of holding slaves with *natural rights of man.* This is a term which has been much abused. It is proper that accurate ideas should be annexed to it, otherwise its force, in the present argument, will not be perceptible. If man were a being, owing his existence to accident, and not a creature of God, his rights would indeed be negative. If he stood in a state of independency of his Maker, and not a subject of law, his rights could be determined only by the will of society. But he is *neither the son of chance* nor the *possessor of independency* . . .

2. If one man have a right to the services of another, without an equivalent, right stands opposite and contrary to right. This confounds the distinction between right and wrong. It destroys morality and justice between man and man, between nation and nation. I have a right to enslave and sell you. You have an equal right to enslave and sell me. The British have a right to enslave the French, and the French the British—the Americans the Africans, and the Africans the Americans. This would be to expel right from the human family—to resolve law into force, and justice into cunning. In the struggle of contending rights, violence would be the only arbiter. The decisions of reason would be perverted, and the sense of morality extirpated from the breast . . .

3. The practice of enslaving our fellow-men stands equally opposed to the general tenor of sacred scriptures.

    The Bible is the criterion of doctrine and conduct. It represents the European and the Asiatic, the African and the American, as different members of the same great family—the different children of the same benign and universal parent. *God has made of one blood all nations of men for to dwell on all the face of the earth, and hath determined the bounds of their habitation,* Acts xvii. 26. In relation to one another, they are equally bound to the exercise of benevolence, and are respected as naturally having no inequality of rights. Every man is bound to respect his fellow-man as his neighbour, and is commanded to love him as himself. Our reciprocal duties the divine Jesus summarily comprehends in that direction commonly called the golden rule: *Whatever ye would that men should do to you, do ye even so to them: for this is the law and the prophets.* This is the sum of the duties inculcated in the law of Moses . . .

4. The practice which I am opposing is a manifest violation of four precepts of the decalogue.

   If this can be shown, it will be an additional confirmation of the doctrine of the proposition. Revelation informs us, that whosoever offends in one point is guilty of all, James ii. 10. And the reason is added, because the same authority is wantonly opposed in that one point which gives sanction to the whole divine revelation. By inference, therefore, the whole decalogue is violated, but there is a direct breach of the fifth, the sixth, the eighth, and the tenth commandments.

   The *sixth* requires the use of all lawful means to preserve the lives of men. But ah! Slavery, how many hast thou murdered? Thou hast kindled wars among the miserable Africans. Thou hast carried the captive, who escaped death, into a still more miserable state. Thou hast brought down the grey hairs of an aged parent, with sorrow, to the grave. Thou hast hurried them on board the floating prisons, and hast chained them in holds, which have soon extinguished the remaining spark of life. The few who have escaped, thou hast deprived of liberty, dearer itself than life . . .

It debases a part of the human race, and tends to destroy their intellectual and active powers. The slave, from his infancy, is obliged implicitly to obey the will of another. There is no circumstance which can stimulate him to exercise. If he think or plan, his thoughts and plans must give way to those of his master. He must have less depravity of heart than his white brethren, otherwise he must, under this treatment, become thoughtless and sullen. The energies of his mind are left to slumber. Every attempt is made to smother them. It is not surprising that such creatures should appear deficient in intellect . . .

Their moral principles also suffer. They are never cultivated. They are early suppressed. While young, the little tyrants of their master's family rule over them with rigour. No benevolent tie can exist between them. The slave, as soon as he can exercise his judgment, observes laws to protect the life, the liberty, and the property of his master; but no law to procure these for him. He is private property. His master's will is his rule of duty. We have no right to expect morality or virtue from such an education and such examples.

Another evil consequence is the encouragement of licentiousness and debauchery.

The situation of the blacks is such as to afford every encouragement to a criminal intercourse. This is not confined to the blacks themselves, but frequently and shamefully exists between them and their masters. The lust of the master may be gratified and strengthened by intercourse with the slave, without fear of prosecution for the support of the offspring, or the character of the mother. The situation of these women admits of few guards to their chastity. Their education does not strengthen it. In the Southern States, illicit connection with a negro or mulatto woman is spoken of as quite a common thing. The number of mulattos in the Northern States prove that this evil is also prevalent among their inhabitants. It is usually a concomitant of slavery.

This leads to a fourth lamentable consequence—the destruction of natural affection.

An irregular intercourse renders it difficult for the father to ascertain his proper offspring. Among the slaves themselves marriage is a slender tie. The master sells the husband to a distance from his wife, and the mother is separated from her infant children. This is a common thing. It must destroy, in a great measure, natural affection. Nor is the evil confined to the slaves. Their master, in this instance, exceeds them in hardness of heart. He sees his slave nursing an infant resembling himself in colour and in features. Probably it is his child, his nephew, or his grand-child. He beholds such, however, not as relatives, but as slaves, and rejoices in the same manner that he does in viewing the increase of his cows or his horses.

O America, what hast thou to account for on the earth, didst commission thy delegates, in peace, and in security from the overawing menaces of a tyrant, or of factions, to form thy Constitution. Thou didst possess, in a peculiar sense, the light of reason, of science, of revelation, of past argumentation, and of past experience. Thou hadst thyself formerly condemned the principle, and, in the most solemn manner, made an appeal to heaven for the justice of thy cause. Heaven heard, and answered agreeably to thy wishes. Yet thou didst contradict a principle so solemnly asserted. Thou hast made provision of increasing the number, and continuing the bondage of thy slaves. Thy judgments may tarry, but they will assuredly come. Individuals are also in danger . . .

There is God; and while godliness continues to have *the promise of the life which now is, as well as that which is to come,* those who continue to practice the system of slavery may expect to suffer loss.

I have now finished what I designed to say in confirmation of the doctrine of the proposition and shall proceed.

II. To refute objections offered to the principle I have been defending.

OBJECTION I. "Nature has made a distinction between man and man. One has stronger intellectual powers than another. As physical strength prevails in the subordinate ranks of creation, let superiority of intellect preside among intelligent creatures. The Europeans and their descendants are superior in this respect to the Africans. These latter are, moreover, in their own country, miserable. Their state is not rendered worse by being enslaved. It is just for the more intelligent to rule over the more ignorant, and to make use of their services."

ANSWER. The distinctions which nature makes between man and man are probably not so great as those which owe their existence to adventitious circumstances.

The inferiority of the blacks to the whites has been greatly exaggerated. Let the fact, however, be granted, and yet inference a sense of tyranny. It is founded in false notions concerning the nature of man. You say, "a greater proportion of intellect gives a right to rule over the less intelligent." But you are to observe that man is not only a creature capable of intellectual exertion, but also one who possesses moral sentiments, and is a free agent. He has a right, from the constitution given by the Author of nature, to dispose of himself, and be his own master in all respects, except in violating the will of Heaven. He naturally acts agreeably to the motives presented to him, with a liberty of choice respecting them. He who argues a right to rule from natural endowments must have more than a superior understanding to show. He must evidence a superiority of moral excellence, and an investiture with authority; otherwise he can have no right to set aside the principle of self-government, and act in opposition to that freedom which is necessarily implied in personal responsibility to the Supreme Moral Governor. Consider the consequences which the objection, if granted, would involve. He who could, by cunning contrivance, reduce his innocent and more simple neighbour under his power, would be justifiable in enslaving him and his offspring for ever . . .

OBJECTION II. "The negroes are a different race of people from us. Their capacities, their shape, their colour, and their smell, indicate their procedure originally from a different pair. They are inferior to the white people in all these respects. This gives a right to the use of the other subordinate ranks of animated being."

ANSWER. This goes upon the footing of discrediting Scripture authority. In a discourse to professed Christians I might reject it without consideration. There may, however, be in my hearing a slaveholder who is an unbeliever of revelations. I would reason even with him, that, if possible, I may serve the cause of justice, of liberty, and of man. The use of sound reason and philosophy Christianity by no means discards.

The principle of your arguments is inadmissible; and if it were not, it would not serve your purpose.

1. It is inadmissible. Among the individuals of every species there is a difference. Nor more causes than are sufficient to account for any phenomenon are required by the rules of philosophizing. The action of the elements on the human body, the diet and the manners of men, are causes sufficient to account for that change in the organization of bodies which gives them a tendency to absorb the rays of light, to perspire more freely, and to put on that shape which is peculiar to the inhabitants of Guinea and their descendants. A single century will make a forcible distinction between the inhabitants of a northern and a southern climate, when the diet and manners are similar. A difference in this can make a distinction in the latitude. It is impossible to prove that twenty or thirty centuries, during which successive generations did not mingle with a foreign race, could not give to the African negro the peculiarity of bodily appearances which so stubbornly adheres to him when translated into another clime. A few years of a hot sun may produce a swarthiness of complexion which the mildest climate cannot, for years, exchange for a

rosy cheek. According to the laws for propagating the species, the offspring resembles the parent. It is not to be expected that a very apparent change should be wrought on the complexion of the offspring of negroes already in this country. Ten times the number of years which have passed over the heads of the successive generations on the coast of Guinea, may be necessary before the negroes can retrace the steps by which they have proceeded from a fair countenance to their present shining black. The causes of bodily variety in the human species which I have stated are known to exist. It is highly unphilosophical to have recourse to others which are only conjectural. Enmity to revelation makes many a one think himself a philosopher . . .

OBJECTION III. "I firmly believe the Scriptures. All the families of the earth are brethren. They are originally descended from Adam and secondarily from Noah. But the blacks are the descendants of Ham. They are under a curse, and a right is given to their brethren to rule over them. We have a divine grant, in Gen. ix. 25–27, to enslave the negroes."

ANSWER. This threatening may have extended to all the descendants of Ham. It is, however, to be noticed, that it is direct to Canaan, the son of Ham. In order to justify negro slavery from this prophecy, it will be necessary to prove four things. 1. That all the posterity of Canaan were devoted to suffer slavery. 2. That African negroes are really descended of Canaan. 3. That each of the descendants of Shem and Japheth has a moral right to reduce any of them to servitude. 4. That every slave-holder is really descended from Shem or Japheth. Want of proof in any one of these particulars will invalidate the whole objection. In a practice so contrary to the general principles of the divine law, a very express grant from the Supreme authority is the only sanction to us. But not one of the four facts specified as necessary can be supported with unquestionable documents. On each of them, however, we may spend a thought.

1. The threatening is general. It does not imply particular personal servitude as much as political inferiority and national degradation. It does not imply that every individual of that race should of right be kept in a state of slavery.

2. It is possible the negroes are descended from Ham. It is even probable. But it is almost certain that they are not the offspring of Canaan. The boundaries of their habitation are defined, Gen. x. 19. The Canaanish territory is generally known from subsequent history.

3. The supposition, however, that the curse fell on the negroes, may be granted with safety to the cause of those who are opposed to the system by which they are enslaved. It will not serve as a warrant for this practice. It is not to be considered as a rule of duty, but as the prediction of a future event. God has, in his providence, given many men over to slavery, to hardships, and to death. But this does not justify the tyrant and the murderer. Had it been predicted, in so many words, that the Americans should, in the beginning of the nineteenth century, be in possession of African slaves, we might argue from the fact the truth of the prophecy, but not the propriety of the slave-holder's conduct. It was foretold that Israel should be in bondage in Egypt, Gen. xv. 13. This did not justify the cruelty of Pharaoh. He was a vessel of wrath. Jesus, our God and Redeemer, was the subject of many predictions. According to ancient prophecy, and to satisfy divine justice, he was put to death. The characters who fulfilled this prediction were wicked to an extreme, Acts ii. 23.

4. Slave-holders are probably the descendants of Japheth, although it cannot be legally ascertained. And they may be fulfilling the threatening on Canaan, although they are not innocent. Be not afraid, my friends; prophecy shall be fulfilled, although, you should liberate your slaves. This prediction has had its accomplishments three thousand years ago. The descendants of Shem did, by divine direction, under the conduct of Joshua, subjugate the offspring of Canaan, when they took possession of the promised land.

This naturally leads us to consider another objection—the most plausible argument that can possibly be offered in defence of the unhallowed practice of holding our fellow men in perpetual bondage . . .

OBJECTION IV. "God permitted the ancient Israelites to hold their fellow creature in servitude. Men and women were bought and sold among them. The bond servant is called his master's money, Exod. xxi. 21. Had it been wrong in its nature to enslave any human being, God could not have granted the Hebrews a permission to do it. Negro slavery, stripped of some accidental cruelties, is not necessarily wicked."

ANSWER. This objection requires minute attention. The fact is granted Heaven did permit the Hebrews to purchase some of the human race for servitude. The general principle deduced from this fact is also granted. It is, in certain cases, lawful to enslave our fellow creatures. The application of it to justify the practice of modern nations is by no means admissible.

God is the Lord of the Universe. As the SUPREME GOVERNOR, he does what is right. His subjects have violated his law, abused their liberty, and rebelled against the majority of Heaven. They have forfeited to his justice the liberty and the life he gave them. These they must yield. They will, at the time appointed by the Judge, be enclosed in the grave. The sovereign has also a right to the use of whatever instrument he chooses in the execution of the sentence. He may choose the famine or the pestilence, the winds or the waves, wild beasts or human beings, to be the executioners.

Civil society has certain laws, to which its members, voluntarily claiming its privileges, have assented. A violation of these is the violation of a contract, and the penalty stipulated must be paid by the offender. When, by a person's licentiousness, justice is violated, or society endangered, it is just and necessary to enslave the criminal, we cheerfully grant; and shall now proceed to show that the objection does not apply to the doctrine which I have been endeavoring to establish.

You cannot argue conclusively, in defence of negro slavery, from the practice of the ancient Hebrews, unless you can prove, 1st, That the slavery into which they were permitted to reduce their fellow creatures was similar to that in which the negroes are held; and, 2dly, That you have the same permission which they had extended to you. If proof fails in *either* of these, the objection is invalid, and I undertake to show that *both* are without proof.

I. The servitude into which the Hebrews were permitted to reduce their fellow men was attended with such restrictions as rendered it essentially different from the negro slave-trade. It may be considered. 1. With reference to the brethren; 2. As it respected strangers . . .

SOURCE NOTE: Alexander McLeod, *Negro Slavery Unjustifiable* (London, 1846).

Robert Dale Owen (1801–1877)

Robert Dale Owen was a relative latecomer to the abolitionist cause, writing his most important work, *The Wrong of Slavery*, in 1864. However, he was a social reformer from a very early age, and the son of Robert Owen, a Scottish reformer, who developed in his son theories of social reform and labor welfare that easily transferred to the antislavery cause. Owen traveled widely in reform circles in Britain and Europe, and knew William Godwin, Jeremy Bentham, and Mary Wollstonecraft Shelley. In the United States, Owen edited *The Free Enquirer*, a reform publication. He also participated in the development of one of the popular Utopian communities in mid-nineteenth-century America, the commune at New Harmony, Indiana. A natural politician and reformer, he served in the Indiana state legislature and was a member of the U.S. House of Representatives from 1843 to 1847. He was largely responsible for legislation that founded the Smithsonian Institution in Washington, D.C., and he wrote an important letter to President Abraham Lincoln in 1862 that apparently had some influence on the president's decision to emancipate the slaves one year later. Owen died at Lake George, New York, June 24, 1877. (See *Dictionary of American Biography*.)

THE WRONG OF SLAVERY (1864)

From the Preface

It is little more than three years since the first insurgent gun was fired against Fort Sumter: three years, as we reckon time; a generation, if we calculate by the stirring events and far-reaching upheavals that have been crowded into the eventful months.

Things move fast in days like these. War changes the legal relations of the combatants. War, in its progress, presents unlooked-for aspects of affairs, brings upon us necessities, opens up obligations. The rebellion—creator and teacher as well as scourge and destroyer—confers new rights, discharges from old bonds, imposes bounden duties.

Great questions come to the surface—questions of national policy, demanding solution. In deciding some of these, we find little aid from precedent; for our condition as a nation is, to a certain extent, unprecedented.

We have been trying an experiment that never was tried in the world before. We have been trying to maintain a democratic government over thirty millions of people, of whom twenty millions existed under one system, industrial and social, ten millions under another. The twenty millions, chiefly one race, carried out among themselves a Declaration made eighty-eight years ago touching the equal creation and the inalienable rights of man. The ten millions consisted in nearly equal portions, of two races—one the descendants of voluntary emigrants who came hither seeking freedom and happiness in a foreign land; the other deriving their blood from ancestors against whom was perpetrated a terrible wrong, who came in chains and were sold as chattels. From these forced emigrants and their descendants were taken away almost all human rights, the right of life and of perpetuating a race of bondsmen excepted. Laws denied to them the rights of property, of marriage, of family, of education, of self-defense. The master-race sought to live by their labor.

The experiment we have been trying for more than three-quarters of a century was, whether, over social and industrial elements thus discordant, a republican government, asserting freedom in thought, in speech, in action, can be peacefully maintained.

Grave doubts, gloomy apprehensions, touching the nation's Future, have clouded the hopes of our wisest public men in days past. Even the statesmen of the Revolution saw on the horizon the cloud no bigger than a man's hand. Gradually it rose and spread and darkened. The tempest burst upon us at last.

Then some, faint-hearted and despairing of the Republic, prophesied that the good old days were gone, never to return. Others, stronger in hope and faith, recognized, through the gloom, the correcting and reforming hand of God. They acknowledged that the experiment had failed; but they confessed also that it ought never to have succeeded. In adversity men look into their hearts, there to read lessons which prosperity had failed to teach them.

The experiment ought never to have succeeded, because it involved a grievous offense against Humanity and Civilization. In peace, before the act of slaveholders made them public enemies, we scrupled to look this offense in the face, seeing no remedy. But war, which has its mission, opened our eyes and released our hands. Times disturbed and revolutionary bring their good as well as their evil. In such times abuses ripen rapidly; their consequences mature, their ultimate results become apparent. We are reminded of their transitory character. We are reminded that, although for the time and in a certain stage of human progress some abuses may have their temporary use, and for this, under God's economy, may have been suffered to continue, yet all abuses have but a limited life: the Right only is eternal. Great, under such circumstances, are our responsibilities; momentous are the issues, for good or for evil, that hang upon our decisions.

. . . In briefly tracing, from its inception in this hemisphere, the rise and progress of the great wrong which still threatens the life of the nation, I have followed the fortunes of a vast multitude, equal in number to the population, loyal and disloyal, black and white, of these United States. I have sketched, by the light of authentic documents, the dismal history of that multitude through three centuries and a half; seeking out their representatives, and inquiring into the numbers and the condition of these, at the present day. In so doing, I have arrived at conclusions which, to those who have never looked closely into the subject, may seem too marvelous for belief.

. . . In concluding this branch of the subject, I have spoken of Emancipation as a solemn national duty which, now that the constitutional obstacle has been removed, we cannot, consistently with what we owe to God and man, neglect or postpone. I have shown that our faith is pledged, and cannot be broken without bringing upon us the contempt of the civilized world.

Finally, after having traced the connection of the two races in the past, and set forth the duty of one race towards the other in the present, I have sought to look forward and inquire how they are likely, when both shall be free, to live together in the future; whether we shall have a race among us unwilling or unable to support itself; whether admixture of the races, both being free, is probable or desirable; whether without admixture, the reciprocal social influence of the races on each other promises good or evil; what are the chances that a base prejudice of race shall diminish and disappear;

and, lastly, whether, in case the colored man shall outlive that prejudice, disgraceful to us and depressing to him, and shall be clothed by law with the same rights in search of which we sought this Western World, there will be any thing in connection with his future in these United States to excite regret or inspire apprehension.

SOURCE NOTE: Robert Dale Owen, *The Wrong of Slavery, the Right of Emancipation and the Future of the African Race in the United States* (Philadelphia: J. B. Lippincott, 1864).

THE ABOLITIONIST CRUSADE,
1830–1865

INTRODUCTION

"I am in earnest, I will not equivocate, I will not excuse, I will not retreat a single inch, and I will be heard." (1831)

"I hate slavery as I hate nothing else in this world. It is not only a crime, but the sum of all criminality." (1865)

—WILLIAM LLOYD GARRISON

The general introduction to this volume emphasizes the power of the abolitionist movement from 1830 to 1865, when "gradualism" was replaced with an aggressive form of protest that led to the abolition of slavery with the Thirteenth Amendment to the Constitution in 1865. The two pronouncements above characterize the rhetorical strategies not only of William Lloyd Garrison but of all the abolitionists of this final phase of the antislavery movement. With the former slave Frederick Douglass, the Boston writer Lydia Maria Child, and the orator Wendell Phillips, Garrisonians led the movement to protest the very foundations of the government of the new nation, the Constitution itself. In 1826, at the age of twenty-one, Garrison became the editor of *The Free Press,* a journal in which he published the early poems of John Greenleaf Whittier, a Quaker poet with whom Garrison maintained a close friendship throughout his life.

Garrison's opposition to slavery was foremost in his reform activities, but he also opposed other injustices, including the oppression of women, which would later splinter his abolitionist following because many conservative abolitionists did not favor women's suffrage. Garrison and Wendell Phillips were the mainstays of the New England and the American Antislavery Societies, and they exerted a continuous pressure on the Congress for "immediate and unconditional emancipation of the slaves, with no compensation to slaveowners." An early protest demonstrator, Garrison publicly burned the Constitution on July 4, 1854, declaring, "So perish all compromises with tyranny!" These outbursts were accompanied by his call for disunion, a Northern version of secession which would sever the Union ties with the slaveholding South. Phillips authored *The Constitution a Proslavery Compact* (1845), which declared the Constitution, which had made no specific provisions concerning slavery and thus was viewed by the more militant abolitionists to be a charter document that permitted and tolerated slavery, "a covenant with death and an agreement with hell." Garrison attacked Daniel Webster, a United States senator from Massachusetts who had supported the Compromise of 1850 with its Fugitive Slave Law because he believed that disunion was even worse than the evil of slavery, and his assault on Webster's politics of compromise was accompanied by James Russell Lowell's essay "Daniel Webster," which is excerpted in this volume. Garrison suffered ill health throughout his life, including respiratory infections and kidney disease, and his highly controversial outbursts occasionally led to violence against him. The state of Georgia offered a five-thousand-dollar reward for Garrison's arrest and conviction, and in 1830 he and Benjamin Lundy, his coeditor at *The Genius of Universal Emancipation,* were sued for libel; Garrison was found guilty and spent seven weeks in a Baltimore jail. Similarly, Lydia Maria Child's early novels, which were immensely successful, were dropped by her publisher after 1833, when she published *An Appeal in Favor of That Class of Americans Called Africans.* Not only did the sales of her earlier works abruptly cease; she was also ostracized by her own family, and lost all of her social friends in Boston because of her insistence not only on unconditional emancipation, but on the full racial equality of blacks and whites.

Garrison, Child, and Phillips held together the "abolitionist crusade" of the 1830s and 1840s, which suffered internecine warfare and several factional divisions, including the formation of the Liberty Party in the 1840s, with its own presidential candidate and political platform. Garrison's personal life was tragic; never economically strong, he was the father of seven children, two of whom predeceased him, and his wife suffered a long illness which left her a permanent invalid. Nevertheless, Garrison led the antebellum abolitionist movement through its several phases of growth, from the gradualist principles of colonization, which he briefly embraced when very young, to his denunciation of colonization in his disagreement with Edward Everett, to his consistent opposition to the Constitution and the Compromise of 1850, with its abhorrent Fugitive Slave Law. On the Commonwealth Mall in Boston, there is a larger-than-life statue of Garrison, seated, calm, and deliberate, with the immortal words cited above engraved on its marble base. Garrison was indeed "larger than life," and his enduring principles of emancipation and the equality of the races were unusual in antebellum America, where even powerful antislavery advocates like Harriet Beecher Stowe and Abraham Lincoln could also embrace elements of contemporary race theory.

Garrison and his followers in the abolitionist crusade were highly controversial, leading historians to view them as extremists who voiced unpopular opinions concerning slavery and who were unable to attract a sufficiently large following to form an effective political alliance for emancipation legislation. Throughout Reconstruction and well into the twentieth century, the "extremist" perception of the Garrisonians persisted. They are now being reassessed as a necessary and crucial element in the entire antislavery enterprise, whose vituperation was needed to prompt a reluctant nation to do the right thing and to confront the essential contradiction of the Constitution and the Declaration of Independence when slavery was still tolerated by both state and federal governments. The papers of William Lloyd Garrison and the writings of Lydia Maria Child and Wendell Phillips are held in the Boston Public Library Rare Book Room and in the collections of the Boston Athenaeum, 10 Beacon Street, Boston, 02116. However, many of Garrison's most important editorials for *The Liberator* have been reprinted in William Cain, ed., *William Lloyd Garrison and the Fight Against Slavery: Selections from* The Liberator (Boston: Bedford Books of St. Martin's Press, 1995). Readers should also consult Edward Countryman, *How Did American Slavery Begin?* (Boston: Bedford Books of St. Martin's Press, 1999). Suggestions for further reading follow the Lydia Maria Child section here, and critical studies of Frederick Douglass and Wendell Phillips are listed in the "Suggestions for Further Reading" that follows the general introduction to this volume.

Our Country is the World, our Countrymen are all Mankind.

The masthead of William Lloyd Garrison's newspaper,
The Liberator, showing a slave auction within sight of the Capitol.
[Courtesy of Ruth Owen Jones.]

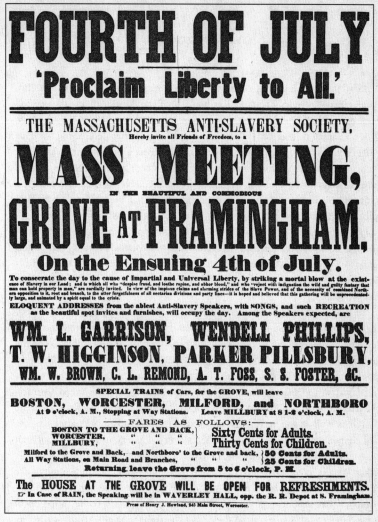

FOURTH OF JULY

'Proclaim Liberty to All.'

THE MASSACHUSETTS ANTI-SLAVERY SOCIETY,

Hereby invite all Friends of Freedom, to a

MASS MEETING,

IN THE BEAUTIFUL AND COMMODIOUS

GROVE at FRAMINGHAM,

On the Ensuing 4th of July.

To consecrate the day to the cause of Impartial and Universal Liberty, by striking a mortal blow at the existence of Slavery in our Land; and to which all who "despise fraud, and loathe rapine, and abhor blood," and who "reject with indignation the wild and guilty fantasy that man can hold property in man," are cordially invited. In view of the impious claims and alarming strides of the Slave Power, and of the necessity of combined Northern opposition to it, root and branch, to the utter forgetfulness of all sectarian divisions and party lines—it is hoped and believed that this gathering will be unprecedentedly large, and animated by a spirit equal to the crisis.

ELOQUENT ADDRESSES from the ablest Anti-Slavery Speakers, with SONGS, and such RECREATION as the beautiful spot invites and furnishes, will occupy the day. Among the Speakers expected, are

WM. L. GARRISON, WENDELL PHILLIPS, T. W. HIGGINSON, PARKER PILLSBURY, WM. W. BROWN, C. L. REMOND, A. T. FOSS, S. S. FOSTER, &C.

SPECIAL TRAINS of Cars, for the GROVE, will leave

BOSTON, WORCESTER, MILFORD, and NORTHBORO

At 9 o'clock, A. M., Stopping at Way Stations. Leave MILLBURY at 8 1-2 o'clock, A. M.

———— FARES AS FOLLOWS:————

BOSTON TO THE GROVE AND BACK, } Sixty Cents for Adults.
WORCESTER, " " " } Thirty Cents for Children.
MILLBURY, " " "

Milford to the Grove and Back, and Northboro' to the Grove and back, } 50 Cents for Adults.
All Way Stations, on Main Road and Branches, " " " } 25 Cents for Children.

Returning, leave the Grove from 5 to 6 o'clock, P. M.

The HOUSE AT THE GROVE WILL BE OPEN FOR REFRESHMENTS.

☞ In Case of RAIN, the Speaking will be in WAVERLEY HALL, opp. the R. R. Depot at S. Framingham.

Press of Henry J. Howland, 245 Main Street, Worcester.

Announcement of an abolitionist meeting in Framingham
starring Wendell Phillips and William Lloyd Garrison.
[By permission of the American Antiquarian Society.]

William Lloyd Garrison (1805–1879)

William Lloyd Garrison, possibly the most important of the antebellum abolitionists, certainly the most influential of the American antislavery advocates, was born in Newburyport, Massachusetts, on December 10, 1805. When Garrison was only three years old, his father left home and his mother was forced into wage-slavery servitude as a domestic servant. The family was divided when William was only seven, and he became a voracious reader, though he was largely self-educated. He worked as a printer's apprentice and learned the newspaper trade so that by 1826, when he was only twenty-one, he purchased the *Essex Courant* and named it the *Newburyport Free Press.* Thus began one of the most politically and socially important journalistic careers in American history. A few years later, Garrison became associated with antislavery and abolitionism through his position as coeditor, with Benjamin Lundy, of *The Genius of Universal Emancipation.*

In that same year, Garrison made one of the most important antislavery speeches of his career. In the "Address to the American Colonization Society," he tentatively embraced the principles of colonization but rejected the gradualist notion that progress in emancipation would come at a relatively slow pace, if moral suasion was used rather than political upheaval and social discord. In this speech, excerpted below, Garrison announced a principle that he would embrace throughout his entire career, namely, that the North as well as the South was implicated in the custom of chattel slavery, and that it was illogical to argue that slavery was exclusively a "Southern problem." He wrote: "I assume, as distinct and defensible propositions, . . . [t]hat, as the free states—by which I mean non-slaveholding States—are constitutionally involved in the guilt of slavery, by adhering to a national compact that sanctions it; and in the danger, by liability to be called upon for aid in case of insurrection; they have the right to remonstrate against its continuance, and it is their duty to assist in its overthrow." Two related Garrisonian principles are contained in this assertion, principles which again would reappear throughout his career as a leading abolitionist. First, Garrison was very outspoken in his criticism of the United States Constitution, which he perceived to be a "proslavery compact," an agreement with Satan, and a violation of the very principles for which the American

Revolution had been fought. Constitutional arguments concerning slavery are regularly contrasted with the principles of the Declaration of Independence in Garrison editorials. Second, Garrison actually became an early "secessionist," arguing that the North should break away from the South and purify itself of the sin of slavery rather than enter into further complicity in the propagation of slavery.

These arguments appear regularly in the editorials Garrison wrote for his own abolitionist newspaper, *The Liberator,* which was published from January 1, 1835, to 1865, at the end the Civil War he had helped to start. The first editorial he wrote for *The Liberator,* also excerpted here, ends with a verse that states the central themes of the abolitionist movement from 1830 to 1865:

> *Oppression! I have seen thee, face to face,*
> *And met thy cruel eye and cloudy brow,*
> *But thy soul-withering glance I fear not now—*
> *For dread to prouder feelings doth give place*
> *Of deep abhorrence! Scorning the disgrace*
> *Of slavish knees that at thy footstool bow*

> *I also kneel—but with far other vow,*
> *Do hail thee and thy hord of hirelings base:—*
> *I swear, while life-blood warms thy throbbing veins,*
> *Still to oppose and thwart, with heart and hand,*
> *Thy brutalising sway—till Afric's chains*
> *Are burst, and Freedom rules the rescued land,—*
> *Trampling Oppression and his iron rod:*
> Such is the vow I take—**SO HELP ME GOD!**

AN ADDRESS TO THE AMERICAN COLONIZATION SOCIETY (1829)

When Garrison delivered the following address, he was only twenty-four years old. This is a remarkable achievement for anyone that age, but it was especially important given Garrison's limited formal education. Largely self-educated, he read much in American history and especially American political history, and he was thoroughly familiar with the American Revolution and the founding documents, such as the Declaration of Independence and the U.S. Constitution. Although Garrison would later repudiate the concept of colonization, by which free African Americans would be returned to Africa gradually, thus ensuring freedom for all and removing the issue of slavery from the United States, he does temporarily embrace colonization in this early speech. However, the address is important in the canon of his writings not so much for its immediate political stance, as for Garrison's articulation of several principles which would remain constants of his abolitionist arguments throughout his career. Never far away in a Garrison document is the contrast between what is and what ought to be in the American experiment known as democracy. Here, Garrison points out the hypocrisy of the presence of slavery in a new nation dedicated to the fundamental principle that "all men are created equal," as Thomas Jefferson had put it. Also present here is Garrison's vehement attack on specific institutions of American civilization, such as the churches for their failure to address the slavery problem directly, and the federal government for its willingness to allow slavery, under the evasive language of the Constitution, as part of the fabric of American life. Finally, Garrison's directness, his style of immediate and direct confrontation, would also mark his speeches and tracts throughout his career.

Fifty-three years ago, the Fourth of July was a proud day for our country. It clearly and accurately defined the rights of man; it made no vulgar alterations in the established usages of society; it presented a revelation adapted to the common sense of mankind; it vindicated the omnipotence of public opinion over the machinery of kingly government; it shook, as with the voice of a great earthquake, thrones which were seemingly propped up with Atlantean pillars; it gave an impulse to the heart of the world, which yet thrills to its extremities.

It may be profitable to inquire, whether the piety which founded, and the patriotism which achieved our liberties, remain unimpaired in principle, undiminished in devotion. Possibly our Samson is sleeping in the lap of Delilah, with his locks shorn and his strength departed. Possibly his enemies have put out his eyes, and bound him with fetters of brass, and compelled him to grind in the prison-house; and if, in his rage and blindness, he find the pillars of the fabric, woe to those for whose sport he is led forth!

For many years, the true friends of their country have witnessed the return of this great jubilee with a terror, that no consolation could remove, and with a grief, that no flattery could assuage. They have seen, that, instead of being distinguished for rationality of feeling and purity of purpose, it has exhibited the perversion of reason and the madness of intemperance. Patriotism has degenerated into mere animal indulgence; or, rather, into the most offensive personalities. Liberty has gone hand in hand with licentiousness—her gait unsteady, her face bloated, her robe bedraggled in the dust. It seems as if men had agreed, by common consent, that an act, which on any other day, would impeach a fair reputation, on this, should help enlarge that reputation. The love of country has been tested by the exact number of libations poured forth, the most guns fired, the greatest number of toasts swallowed, and the loudest professions of loyalty to the Union, uttered over the wine-cup.

Indeed, so dear is Liberty to many, that they cannot make too free with her charms: they owe her so much, that they owe the Most High nothing. It would shock their sensibility, and tarnish their reputation as patriots, to be caught at a religious celebration of our national anniversary. The day, they argue, should be properly appreciated; and, unless a man gets gloriously inebriated, either at home or in the streets, at his own or a public table, in digesting his own good sayings or those of others—unless he declaims roundly in praise of freedom, and drinks perdition to tyrants—it shows that he is either a monarchist or a bigot . . .

It is this fatal delusion, which so terrifies men of reflection and foresight; which makes the Christian shudder at the prospect before us, and the Patriot weep in despair; which, unless the mercy of God interpose, seals the doom of our country . . .

I speak not as a partisan or an opponent of any man or measures, when I say, that our politics are rotten to the core. *We* boast of our freedom, who go shackled to the polls, year after year, by tens, and hundreds, and thousands! *We* talk of free agency, who are the veriest machines—the merest automata—in the hands of unprincipled jugglers! *We* prate of integrity, and virtue, and independence, who sell our birthright for office, and who, nine times in ten, do not get Esau's bargain—no, not even a mess of pottage! Is it republicanism to say, that the majority can do no wrong? Then I am not a republican. Is it aristocracy to say, that the people sometimes shamefully abuse their high trust? Then I am an aristocrat. Rely upon it, the republic does not bear a charmed life: our prescriptions, administered through the medium of the ballot-box—the mouth of the political body—may kill or cure, according to the nature of the disease, and our wisdom in applying the remedy. It is possible that a people may bear the title of freemen, who execute the work of slaves. To the dullest observer of the signs of the times, it must be apparent, that we are rapidly approximating to this condition . . .

But there is another evil, which, if we had to contend against nothing else, should make us quake for the issue. It is a gangrene preying upon our vitals—an earthquake rumbling under our feet—a mine accumulating materials for a national catastrophe. It should make this a day of fasting and prayer, not of boisterous merriment and idle pageantry—a day of great lamentation, not of congratulatory joy. It should spike every cannon, and haul down every banner. Our garb should be sackcloth—our heads bowed in the dust—our supplications, for the pardon and assistance of Heaven . . .

I stand up here in a more solemn court, to assist in a far greater cause; not to impeach the character of one man, but of a whole people—not to recover the sum of a hundred thousand dollars, but to obtain the liberation of two millions of wretched, degraded beings, who are pining in hopeless bondage—over whose sufferings scarcely an eye weeps, or a heart melts, or a tongue pleads either to God or man. I regret that a better advocate had not been found, to enchain your attention, and to warm your blood. Whatever fallacy, however, may appear in the argument, there is no flaw in the indictment; what the speaker lacks, the cause will supply.

Sirs, I am not come to tell you that slavery is a curse, debasing in its effect, cruel in its operation, fatal in its continuance. The day and the occasion require no such revelation. I do not claim the discovery as my own, 'that all men are born equal,' and that among their inalienable rights are 'life, liberty, and the pursuit of happiness.' Were I addressing any other than a free and Christian assembly, the enforcement of this truth might be pertinent. Neither do I intend to analyze the horrors of slavery for your inspection, not to freeze your blood with authentic recitals of savage cruelty. Nor will time allow me to explore even a furlong of that immense wilderness of suffering, which remains unsubdued in our land. I take it for granted that the existence of these evils is acknowledged, if not rightly understood. My object is to define and enforce our duty, as Christians and Philanthropists.

On a subject so exhaustless, it will be impossible, in the moiety of an address, to unfold all the facts which are necessary to its full development. In view of it, my heart wells up like a living fountain, which time cannot exhaust, for it is perpetual. Let this be considered as the preface of a noble work, which your inventive sympathies must elaborate and complete.

I assume, as distinct and defensible propositions,

I. That the slaves of this country, whether we consider their moral, intellectual or social condition, are pre-eminently entitled to the prayers, and sympathies, and charities of the American people; and that their claims for redress are as strong as those of any Americans could be, in a similar condition.

II. That, as the free States—by which I mean non-slaveholding States—are constitutionally involved in the guilt of slavery, by adhering to a national compact that sanctions it; and in the danger, by liability to be called upon for aid in case of insurrection; they have the right to remonstrate against its continuance, and it is their duty to assist in its overthrow.

III. That no justificative plea for the perpetuity of slavery can be found in the condition of its victims; and no barrier against our righteous interference, in the laws which authorize the buying, selling and possessing of slaves, nor in the hazard of a collision with slaveholders.

IV. That education and freedom will elevate our colored population to a rank with the whites—making them useful, intelligent and peaceable citizens.

In the first place, it will be readily admitted, that it is the duty of every nation primarily to administer relief to its own necessities, to cure its own maladies, to instruct its own children, and to watch over its own interests. He is 'worse than an infidel,' who neglects his own household, and squanders his earnings upon strangers; and the policy of that nation is unwise, which seeks to proselyte other portions of the globe at the expense of its safety and happiness. Let me not be misunderstood. My benevolence is neither contracted nor selfish. I pity that man whose heart is not larger than a whole continent. I despise the littleness of that patriotism which blusters only for its own rights, and, stretched to its utmost dimensions, scarcely covers its native territory; which adopts as its creed, the right to act independently, even to the verge of licentiousness, without restraint, and to tyrannize wherever it can with impunity. This sort of patriotism is common. I suspect the reality, and deny the productiveness of that piety, which confines its operations to a particular spot—if that spot be less than the whole earth; nor scoops out, in every direction, new channels for the waters of life. Christian charity, while it 'begins at home,' goes abroad in search of misery. It is as copious as the sun in heaven. It does not, like the Nile, make a partial inundation, and then withdraw; but it perpetually overflows, and fertilizes every barren spot. It is restricted only by the exact number of God's suffering creatures. But I mean to say, that, while we are aiding and instructing foreigners, we ought not to forget our own degraded countrymen; that neither duty nor honesty requires us to defraud ourselves, that we may enrich others.

The condition of the slaves, in a religious point of view, is deplorable, entitling them to a higher consideration, on our part, than any other race; higher than the Turks or Chinese, for they have the privileges of instruction; higher than the Pagans, for they are not dwellers in a gospel land; higher than our red men of the forest, for we do not bind them with gyves, nor treat them as chattels.

And here let me ask, what has Christianity done, by direct effort, for our slave population? Comparatively nothing. She has explored the isles of the ocean for objects of commiseration; but, amazing stupidity! she can gaze without emotion on a multitude of miserable beings at home, large enough to constitute a nation of freemen, whom tyranny has heathenized by law. In her public services, they are seldom remembered, and in her private donations they are forgotten. From one end of the country to the other, her charitable societies form golden links of benevolence, and scatter their contributions like rain-drops over a parched heath; but they bring no sustenance to the perishing slave. The blood of souls is upon her garments, yet she heeds not the stain. The clankings of the prisoner's chains strike upon her ear, but they cannot penetrate her heart.

I have said, that the claims of the slaves for redress are as strong as those of any Americans could be, in a similar condition. Does any man deny the position? The proof, then, is found in the fact, that a very large proportion of our colored population were born on our soil, and are therefore entitled to all the privileges of American citizens. This is their country by birth, not by adoption. Their children possess the same inherent and unalienable rights as ours; and it is a crime of the blackest dye to load them with fetters.

Every Fourth of July, our Declaration of Independence is produced, with a sublime indignation, to set forth the tyranny of the mother country, and to challenge the admiration of the world. But what a pitiful detail of grievances does this document present, in comparison with the wrongs which our slaves endure! In the one case, it is hardly the plucking of a hair from the head; in the other, it is the crushing of a live body on the wheel; the stings of the wasp contrasted with the tortures of the inquisition. Before God, I must say, that such a glaring contradiction, as exists between our creed and practice, the annals of six thousand years cannot parallel. In view of it, I am ashamed of my country. I am sick of our unmeaning declamation in praise of liberty and equality; of our hypocritical cant about the unalienable rights of man. I could not, for my right hand, stand up before a European assembly, and exult that I am an American citizen, and denounce the usurpations of a kingly government as wicked and unjust; or, should I make the attempt, the recollection of my country's barbarity and despotism would blister my lips, and cover my cheeks with burning blushes of shame . . .

It may be objected, that the laws of the slave States form insurmountable barriers to any interference on our part.

Answer. I grant that we have not the right, and I trust not the disposition, to use coercive measures. But do these laws hinder our prayers, or obstruct the flow of our sympathies? Cannot our charities alleviate the condition of the slave, and perhaps break his fetters? Can we not operate upon public sentiment, (the lever that can move the moral world,) by way of remonstrance, advice, or entreaty? Is Christianity so powerful, that she can tame the red men of our forests, and abolish the Burman caste, and overthrow the gods of Paganism, and liberate lands over which the darkness of Superstition has lain for ages; and yet so weak, in her own dwelling-place, that she can make no impression upon her civil code? Can she contend successfully with cannibals, and yet be conquered by her own children?

Suppose that, by a miracle, the slaves should suddenly become white. Would you shut your eyes upon their sufferings, and calmly talk of constitutional limitations? No; your voice would peal in the ears of the taskmasters like deep thunder; you would carry the

Constitution by force, if it could not be taken by treaty; patriotic assemblies would congregate at the corner of every street; the old Cradle of Liberty would rock to a deeper tone than ever echoed therein at British aggression; the pulpit would acquire new and unusual eloquence from our holy religion. The argument, that these white slaves are degraded, would not then obtain. You would say, it is enough that they are white, and in bondage, and they ought immediately to be set free. You would multiply your schools of instruction, and your temples of worship, and rely upon them for security.

But the plea is prevalent, that any interference by the free States, however benevolent or cautious it might be, would only irritate and inflame the jealousies of the South, and retard the cause of emancipation.

If any man believes that slavery can be abolished without a struggle with the worst passions of human nature, quietly, harmoniously, he cherishes a delusion. It can never be done, unless the age of miracles return. No; we must expect a collision, full of sharp asperities and bitterness. We shall have to contend with the insolence, and pride, and selfishness, of many a heartless being. But these can be easily conquered by meekness, and perseverance, and prayer.

It is often despondingly said, that the evil of slavery is beyond our control. Dreadful conclusion, that puts the seal of death upon our country's existence! If we cannot conquer the monster in his infancy, while his cartilages are tender and his limbs powerless, how shall we escape his wrath when he goes forth a gigantic cannibal, seeking whom he may devour? If we cannot safely unloose two millions of slaves now, how shall we bind upwards of TWENTY MILLIONS at the close of the present century? But there is no cause for despair. We have seen how readily, and with what ease, that horrid gorgon, Intemperance, has been checked in its ravages. Let us take courage. Moral influence, when in vigorous exercise, is irresistible. It has an immortal essence. It can no more be trod out of existence by the iron foot of time, or by the ponderous march of iniquity, than matter can be annihilated. It may disappear for a time; but it lives in some shape or other, in some place or other, and will rise with renovated strength. Let us, then, be up and doing. In the simple and stirring language of the stout-hearted LUNDY, 'all the friends of the cause must go to work, keep to work, hold on, and never give up.'

Years may elapse before the completion of the achievement; generations of blacks may go down to the grave, manacled and lacerated, without a hope for their children; the philanthropists, who are now pleading in behalf of the oppressed, may not live to witness the dawn which will precede the glorious day of universal emancipation; but the work will go on—laborers in the cause will multiply—new resources will be discovered—the victory will be obtained, worth the desperate struggle of a thousand years. Or, if defeat follow, woe to the safety of this people! The nation will be shaken as if by a mighty earthquake. A cry of horror, a cry of revenge, will go up to heaven in the darkness of midnight, and re-echo from every cloud. Blood will flow like water—the blood of guilty men, and of innocent women and children. Then will be heard lamentations and weeping, such as will blot out the remembrance of the horrors of St. Domingo. The terrible judgments of an incensed God will complete the catastrophe of republican America.

And since so much is to be done for our country; since so many prejudices are to be dispelled, obstacles vanquished, interests secured, blessings obtained; since the cause of emancipation must progress heavily, and meet with much unhallowed opposition, why delay the work? There must be a beginning, and now is a propitious time—perhaps the last opportunity that will be granted us by a long-suffering God. No temporising, lukewarm measures will avail aught. We must put our shoulder to the wheel, and heave with our united strength. Let us not look coldly on, and see our southern brethren contending single-handed against an all-powerful foe—faint, weary, borne down to the earth. We are all alike guilty. Slavery is strictly a national sin. New-England money has been expended in buying human flesh; New-England ships have been freighted with sable victims; New-England men have assisted in forging the fetters of those who groan in bondage.

I call upon the ambassadors of Christ every where to make known this proclamation: 'Thus saith the Lord God of the Africans, Let this people go, that they may serve me.' I ask them to 'proclaim liberty to the captives, and the opening of the prison to them that are bound'—to light up a flame of philanthropy, that shall burn till all Africa be redeemed from the night of moral death, and the song of deliverance be heard throughout her borders.

I call upon the churches of the living God to lead in this great enterprise. If the soul be immortal, priceless, save it from redeemless woe. Let them combine their energies, and systematize their plans, for the rescue of suffering humanity. Let them pour out their supplications to heaven in behalf of the slave. Prayer is omnipotent: its breath can melt adamantine rocks—its touch can break the stoutest chains. Let anti-slavery charity-boxes stand uppermost among those for missionary, tract and educational purposes. On this subject, Christians have been asleep; let them shake off their slumbers, and arm for the holy contest.

I call upon our New-England women to form charitable associations to relieve the degraded of their sex. As yet, an appeal to their sympathies was never made in vain. They outstrip us in every benevolent race. Females are doing much for the cause at the South; let their example be imitated, and their exertions surpassed, at the North. [Here, Garrison states a theme that will reappear as a leit-motif throughout his abolitionist career: the oppression of women parallels the oppression of slaves, and both need to be emancipated urgently and immediately. Garrison was active in his support for women's rights and wrote frequently on the subject, including an editorial for *The Liberator,* January 12, 1838, excerpted in this volume. In the brief statement above, he also acknowledges the fusion of moral power in women and antislavery sentiment, a theme which would also reappear in Stowe's *Uncle Tom's Cabin* (1852). See Ann Douglas, "Introduction" to *Uncle Tom's Cabin* (New York: Penguin Classics, 1981).]

I call upon the great body of newspaper editors to keep this subject constantly before their readers; to sound the trumpet of alarm, and to plead eloquently for the rights of man. They must give the tone to public sentiment. One press may ignite twenty; a city may warm a State; a State may impart a generous heat to a whole country.

I call upon the American people to enfranchise a spot, over which they hold complete sovereignty; to cleanse that worse than Augean stable, the District of Columbia, from its foul impurities. I conjure them to select those as Representatives, who are not too ignorant to know, too blind to see, nor too timid to perform their duty.

I will say, finally, that I tremble for the republic while slavery exists therein. If I look up to God for success, no smile of mercy or forgiveness dispels the gloom of futurity; if to our resources, they are daily diminishing; if to all history, our destruction is not only possible, but almost certain. Why should we slumber at this momentous crisis? If our hearts were dead to every throb of humanity; if it were lawful to oppress, where power is ample; still, if we had any regard for our safety and happiness, we should strive to crush the Vampyre which is feeding upon our life-blood. All the selfishness of our nature cries aloud for a better security. Our own vices are too strong for us, and keep us in perpetual alarm; how, in addition to these, shall we be able to contend successfully with millions of armed and desperate men, as we must eventually, if slavery do not cease?

SOURCE NOTE: *Selections from the Writings and Speeches of William Lloyd Garrison, with an Appendix* (Boston: R. F. Walcut, 1852), pp. 45–61; see also Wendell Phillips and Francis Jackson Garrison, *William Lloyd Garrison, 1805–1879: The Story of His Life Told by His Children*, 4 vols. (Boston: Houghton Mifflin, 1885–1889), vol. 1, pp. 127–137, as cited in William E. Cain, ed., *William Lloyd Garrison and the Fight Against Slavery* (Boston: Bedford Books of St. Martin's Press, 1995), pp. 61–70.

COMMENCEMENT OF
THE LIBERATOR (1831)

Garrison regularly preached the immediate, unconditional, uncompensated abolition of slavery from the commencement of his public career at the age of twenty-four through the Civil War and the signing of the Emancipation Proclamation. His tenacity and determined efforts to end the "peculiar institution" were rewarded after thirty-five long years of extremely hard work as an editor and a public speaker, public disapprobation, and a lawsuit for libel in 1829 for which he was jailed for forty-nine days. In 1831, the Georgia legislature placed a five-thousand-dollar bounty on Garrison's head, offering a reward for his capture and imprisonment. Like his contemporary and colleague in the abolitionist movement, Lydia Maria Child, Garrison suffered enormous social discrimination in Boston; neither of these abolitionist leaders was accepted by Boston society after their outspoken criticism of the Constitution and their demand for immediate and unconditional emancipation. Child's 1833 *An Appeal in Favor of that Class of Americans Called Africans* followed closely the arguments of the black abolitionist David Walker, whose own *Appeal* (1830) was treated to a hostile reception both North and South. These pioneering attempts to change the system through reasoned discourse ultimately influenced the divisions between proslavery and antislavery advocates in both regions of the United States, setting up the ideological origins of the Civil War. Meanwhile, their proponents, Child, Garrison, and Walker, suffered a wide range of opposition, including the disapproval of family members. Thus the youthful but thoughtful protest of Garrison in 1831 is all the more meaningful; with extremely limited social reinforcement and with a determination and conviction about the "sin of slavery," he set out the principles of abolitionism in ideological and personal terms by articulating, in the opening editorial of *The Liberator,* January 1, 1831, the urgency of his message. These words have now become permanently associated with Garrison's career and beliefs; they are inscribed, in marble, on the base of his larger-than-life monument, which resides on the Commonwealth Avenue Mall in Boston's Back Bay. At twenty-six, Garrison had the courage to stand against the majority of his countrymen and declare:

> *I am in earnest, I will not equivocate, I will not excuse, I will not retreat a single inch, and **I will be heard**.*

Garrison's 1831 editorial continued with a full recantation of his Park Street address two years earlier: "Assenting to the 'self-evident truth' maintained in the American Declaration of Independence, 'that all men are created equal, and endowed by their Creator with certain inalienable rights—among which are life, liberty, and the pursuit of happiness,' I shall strenuously contend for the immediate enfranchisement of our slave population. In Park-Street Church, on the Fourth of July, 1829, in an address on slavery, I unreflectingly assented to the popular but pernicious doctrine of gradual abolition. I seize this opportunity to make a full and unequivocal recantation, and thus publicly to ask pardon of my God, of my country, and of my brethren the poor slaves, for having uttered a sentiment so full of timidity, injustice and absurdity."

TRUISMS (1831)

One of Garrison's most effective rhetorical strategies was the assumption that his speeches and writings were being directed to reasonable people, whose rational minds would respond intelligently to the logic of his arguments. Another strategy was the emotional appeal to common humanity, by which the reader, or listener, would feel compassion or sympathy for the plight of the oppressed slave and contempt for the slaveholder. A third strategy, which he regularly used, was the ironic observation or statement, the staple of good satirical writing from Lucian to Jonathan Swift. For example, an editorial for the January 8, 1831, *Liberator* carried a list of principles which were purported to be the central arguments of slaveholders and proslavery advocates. A selection from this "list" follows, illustrating clearly Garrison's penchant for satirical and ironic understatement, and the resulting clarity with which the true meaning of each statement is revealed. These entries also show Garrison's double message, his advocacy of immediate and unconditional emancipation, and his belief that slavery and racism were inseparable from one another, that the enslavement of another human being was by definition an admission of one's belief in his essential inferiority, a view which Garrison vehemently opposed.

> *Of all men living, an American citizen who is the owner of slaves is the most despicable; he is a political hypocrite of the very worst description.—I stain the star-spangled banner that was never struck down in battle.*
>
> —O'CONNELL

1. All men are born equal, and entitled to protection, excepting those whose skins are black and hair wooly; or, to prevent mistake, excepting Africans, and their descendants.

2. If white men are ignorant and depraved, they ought freely to receive the benefits of education; but if black men are in this condition, common sense dictates that they should be held in bondage, and never instructed.

3. He who steals a sheep, or buys one of a thief, deserves severe punishment. He who steals a Negro, or buys him of a kidnapper, is blameless. Why? Because a sheep can be eaten, and a negro cannot; because he has a black fleece, and it a white one; because the law asserts that this distinction is just, and law, we all know, is founded in equity, and because pure benevolence actuates in the one case, and downright villainy in the other.

4. The color of the skin determines whether a man has a soul or not. If white, he has an immortal essence; if black, he is altogether beastly. Mulattoes, however, derive no benefit from this rule.

5. The blacks ought to be held in fetters, because they are too stupid to take care of themselves; at least, we are not so stupid as to suffer them to make the experiment.

6. To kidnap children on the coast of Africa is a horrid crime, deservedly punishable with death; but he who steals them, in this country, as soon as they are born, performs not merely an innocent but a praiseworthy act.

7. In Africa, a man who buys or sells another, is a monster of hell. In America, he is an heir of heaven.

8. A man has a right to heap unbounded execration upon the foreign slave trade and the abettors thereof; but if he utter a sentiment derogatory to the domestic traffic, or to those who assist in the transportation of victims, he is to be imprisoned for publishing a libel, and sentenced to pay a fine of not less than one thousand dollars.

9. He who calls American slaveholders tyrants is a fool, a fanatic, or a madman; but if he apologize for monarchial governments, or an hereditary aristocracy, set him down as a tory, and a traitor to his country.

10. There is not the least danger of a rebellion among the slaves; and even if they should revolt *enmasse* what could they do? Their united physical force would be utterly contemptible.

11. None but fanatics or idiots desire immediate abolition. If the slaves were liberated at once, our throats would be cut, and our houses pillaged and burnt.

12. Our slaves must not be educated for freedom. Our slaves must never learn the alphabet, because knowledge would teach them to throw off their yoke.

13. People at the North have no right to alleviate physical suffering, or illumine spiritual darkness, at the South. But they have a right to assist the Greeks, or the Hindoos, or any foreign nation.

15. A white man, who kills a tyrant, is a hero, and deserves a monument. If a slave kills his master, he is a murderer, and deserves to be burnt.

16. The slaves are kept in bondage for their own good. Liberty is a curse to the free people of color—their condition is worse than that of their slaves! Yet it would be very wicked to bind them with fetters for their good.

17. The slaves are contented and happy. If sometimes they are so ungrateful or deluded as to abscond, it is pure philanthropy that induces their masters to offer a handsome reward for their detection.

18. Blacks have no intellect. The laws, at the South, which forbid their instruction, were not enacted because it was supposed these brutes had brains, or for the sake of compliment, but are owing simply to an itch for superfluous legislation.

19. Slaves are held as property. It is the acme of humanity and justice, therefore, in the laws, to recognize them also as moral agents, and punish them in the most aggravated manner, if they perpetrate a crime; though they cannot read, and have neither seen or known the laws!

20. It is foolish and cruel for an individual to denounce slavery; because the more he disturbs the security of the masters, the more vindictive will be their conduct toward the slaves. For the same reason, we ought to prefer the products of slave labor to those of free; as the more wealthy masters become, the better they will be enabled to feed and clothe their menials.

21. To deny that a man is a christian or republican, who holds slaves and dooms their children to bondage, is most uncharitable and inconsistent.

22. To say that a clerical slave is bound to follow his own precepts, or to obey the seventh and tenth commandments, is preposterous.

23. To doubt the religious vitality of a church, which is composed of slaveholders, is the worst species of infidelity.

24. The Africans are our slaves—not because we like to oppress, or to make money unjustly—but because Noah's curse must be fulfilled, and the scriptures obeyed.

SOURCE NOTE: *The Liberator,* ed. William Lloyd Garrison, January 8, 1831. Boston Public Library and Neilson Library, Smith College, Northampton, Mass.

HENRY CLAY'S
COLONIZATION ADDRESS (1830)

In these selections concerning Henry Clay and the Clay "Colonization Address," Garrison enters the antebellum debate concerning race theory, discussed elsewhere in this volume. Especially in the first selection, where the abolitionist declares the "absurdity" of a doctrine of racial inequality, he mounts an argument that conflicted with the prevailing sentiment of many white Americans, including abolitionists. Like Wendell Phillips and Lydia Maria Child, Garrison called for "full racial equality" and an end to racial discrimination as a foundation for emancipation and full, equal citizenship for the African American.

February 12, 1830

There are few individuals, I am persuaded, who cherish a higher regard for Henry Clay, or who look forward to his ultimate elevation to the Presidency with more satisfaction than I do . . .

In reviewing his recent address before the Colonization Society of Kentucky, it is more than probable that I shall have occasion to differ widely from his views of slavery—perhaps to be somewhat personal, even pointedly so—and therefore I have deemed it necessary to avow my partiality, in order to escape the charges of political hostility . . .

. . . I find, therein, many liberal concessions relative to the evils of slavery—many hearty desires to see our country free from this foul blemish—something about expediency, and safety, and gradual manumission—but no where do I see the claims of justice enforced with becoming fearlessness or candor—no personal application— no direct allusion to the awful guilt of debasing the physical, and defiling the moral workmanship of the great God—creatures made a little lower than the angels, and capable of the highest intellectual attainments—not a word—Therefore my dissatisfaction.

The episode, at the commencement of the address, relative to the persecuted Indians, is replete with tenderness, truth, humanity, justice—spoken at an eventful crisis, and calculated to unite many discordant views. One cannot help remarking how much more freely Mr. Clay breathes in defending these poor red men, than in speaking of the Africans. Yet his notion about the *natural* physical and intellectual superiority of the whites over the Indians, is unphilosophical and absurd. *I deny the postulate, that God has made, by an irreversible decree, or any inherent qualities, one portion of the human race superior to another.* No matter how many breeds are amalgamated—no matter how many shades of color intervene between tribes or nations—give them the same chances to improve, and a fair start at the same time, and the result will be equally brilliant, equally productive, equally grand . . .

But let these wandering tribes be universally reclaimed, and civilization pour in upon them its renovating light, and the "glorious gospel of the blessed God" dispel the mist of superstition, and who shall put limits to their progress in knowledge, in virtue, in the arts and sciences, or in any moral or intellectual improvement?

February 19, 1830

It is morally impossible, I am convinced, for a slaveholder to reason correctly on the subject of slavery. His mind is warped by a thousand prejudices, and a thick cloud rests upon his mental vision. He was really taught to believe, that a certain class of beings were born for servitude, whom it is lawful to enthrall, and over whom he is authorized—not merely by the law of his native state, but by Jehovah himself—to hold unlimited dominion. His manhood, perhaps, may detect the absurdity of the doctrine, but interest weakens the force of conviction, and he is never at a loss to find palliatives for his conduct. He discourses eloquently, it may be, upon the evils of the system—deprecates its continuance as a curse upon the country—shudders when he contemplates individual instances of barbarity—and rejoices in gradual emancipation. Interrogate him relative to his own practices, and you touch the apple of his eye. If not disposed to resent your freedom, he takes shelter in the ignorance and helplessness of his slaves; and, dexterously relinquishing the authority of an oppressor, assumes the amiableness of a philanthropist! "The poor creatures are penniless—benighted—without a home! Freedom would be a curse, rather than a blessing to them—they are happy now—why should I throw them upon an unpitying world?" Will a christian reason in this manner? Yes—if a christian can be a slaveholder—but the two characters differ so widely, that I know not how they can unite in one man. Yet this wicked cant obtains as readily at the north as the south and with many it is as impregnable as the rock of Gibraltar. Does not every tyrant make the welfare of his subjects a plea for his conduct?

What evidence—besides mere words—does that slaveholder give me or the world, that his benevolence is sincere? Have not his slaves toiled early and late, through summer's heat and winter's cold, faithfully, steadily, year after year, for his own aggrandizement? Yes. What recompense have they received? A bare maintenance. To whom does the property, in equity, belong? To those who accumulated it—the slaves. If the account were fairly adjusted, who would be penniless? The master. *Let him, then, at least divide his substance.* But the blacks are ignorant, and cannot safely be liberated! Then is moral degradation a crime! Then is slavery eternal! Did that *benevolent* and *christian* master ever strive to elevate their minds—to illuminate their understandings—or lead their souls to God? Never! Is he now, in the copiousness of his sympathy, teaching them the way to heaven, or preparing them to enjoy the blessing of liberty? No—they are scarcely more intelligent than his cattle. But they are happy! Horrible perversion of the term! Mockery of Mockeries! And by an American—a Christian, too!

March 5, 1830

Although Mr. Clay deeply laments the existence of slavery as an evil of gigantic size, and sympathizes with the unfortunate beings who groan in bondage, yet he says:

> If the question were submitted, whether there should be either immediate or gradual emancipation of all the slaves in the United States, without their removal or colonization, painful as it is to express the

opinion, I have no doubt that it would be unwise to emancipate them.

I can hardly credit my senses that this is the language of Henry Clay. The alternative here presented is shocking. It would lead to the most disastrous consequences. It would make slavery eternal. For, be it remembered, Mr. Clay believes Africa to be the only feasible, safe and proper spot on which to colonize our colored population. Now, talk as we may of the abilities of government—of colonization societies, and charitable donations, and facilities of transportation, and our multitude of ships—the scheme is as delusive and hopeless as any that was ever projected by a civilized people. Mr. Clay, it is true, thinks otherwise: but, if it fail, he would prohibit *gradual* emancipation. In his sight, a free black is a nuisance—and a community of slaves more tolerable than a community of colored freemen. He consults nothing but policy, and forgets that justice should be first interrogated.

I do not place myself in a hostile attitude to this Society, neither do I choose to rank among its warmest advocates. Its policy or impolicy—its good or evil, in the aggregate, is a question which has constantly agitated but never satisfied my mind, and which time alone can solve. On a few points, however, my judgment is clear.

. . . What has the Society accomplished? Much, unquestionably, for a single association, engaged in a hazardous enterprise, and supported by the uncertain charities of the public. But has it, in any degree, sustained its high pretensions? or made good one of its numberless and extravagant proclamations? or taken away a fraction from the "sum total"? or made any visible impression upon the growth of slavery? Assuredly not.

It has been in existence about thirteen years—a term amply sufficient to test its capacity and usefulness. Its annual transportation to Liberia, I believe, has averaged *one hundred* souls. During this same period, the *increase* of the colored population has amounted to upwards of *five hundred thousand.* And yet such is the colonization mania—such the implicit confidence reposed in the operations of the Society—that no demonstration of its inefficiency, however palpable, can shake the faith of its advocates.

Let me be understood. I would not utterly discard the Colonization Society, as an auxiliary in the cause of African emancipation.

My complaint is, that its ability is overrated to a disastrous extent—
that this delusion is perpetuated by the conduct and assurances of
those who ought to act better—the members of the Society. I com-
plain, moreover, that the lips of these members are sealed up on the
subject of slavery, who, from their high standing and extensive influence, ought to expose its flagrant enormities, and actively assist
in its overthrow. But they dare not lead to the onset—and if they
shrink from the battle, "by whom shall the victory be won?"

. . . My views on the subject of slavery have been very imperfectly developed in the *Genius* [*of Universal Emancipation*]—the
cares and perplexities of the establishment having occupied a large
share of my time and attention. Every pledge, however, that I have
made to the public, shall be fulfilled. My pen cannot remain idle,
nor my voice be suppressed, nor my heart cease to bleed, while two
millions of my fellow beings wear the shackles of slavery in my
guilty country.

In all my writings, I have used strong, indignant, vehement language, and direct, pointed, scorching reproof. I have nothing to recall. Many have censured me for my severity—but, Thank God!
none have stigmatized me with luke-warmness. "Passion is reason—transport, temper here."

SOURCE NOTE: *Selections from the Writings and Speeches of William Lloyd Garrison,
with an Appendix* (Boston: R. F. Wallcut, 1852), microfilm in Neilson Library,
Smith College, Northampton, Mass., and in the collections of the Boston Public
Library. All of the references to Henry Clay may be found there.

THE GREAT
[CONSTITUTIONAL] CRISIS (1832)

Garrison was from the beginning of his career an opponent of the U.S.
Constitution, primarily because he believed it to be a proslavery document.
He was consistent in his opposition to the Constitution, and his outspoken
critique led him to recommend secession, the North from the South, the
free states from the slave states. One of his favorite rhetorical strategies was
to contrast the struggle for liberty in the American Revolution with the oppression of Africans who were engaged in their own struggle for liberty,
even in the context of the United States' attempt to reconcile its charter
documents concerning freedom with the "peculiar institution" that

blighted its democracy. In a speech on March 5, 1858, Garrison attacked the hypocrisy of the United States in allowing slavery while commemorating such events as the Boston Massacre, which had occurred on March 5, 1770. Here, at Faneuil Hall, just a few yards from the site of the Boston Massacre, Garrison abused the Constitution and once again called for disunion. "We shall be told that this is equivalent to a dissolution of the Union. Be it so! Give us Disunion with liberty and a good conscience, rather than Union with slavery and moral degradation. What! shall we shake hands with those who buy, sell, torture, and horribly imbrute their fellow-creatures, and trade in human flesh! God forbid! Every man should respect himself too much to keep such company. We must break this wicked alliance with men-stealers, or all is lost. By all the sacred memories of the past—by all that was persistent, courageous, unconquerable in the great struggle for American Independence . . . let us here renew our solemn pledge, that, come what may, we will not lay down our arms until liberty is proclaimed throughout all the land, to all the inhabitants thereof."

This kind of anticonstitutional rhetoric had alienated Garrison from many of his white countrymen, and from some fellow abolitionists, including the escaped slave Frederick Douglass, who came to view the Constitution as an antislavery document. Both Wendell Phillips and Garrison critiqued the Constitution as a hypocritical charter for white freedom, and this firm stand, coupled with the ambition of Frederick Douglass to break off from Garrison and to begin his own antislavery newspaper, led to a severe breach between the two abolitionists in 1851. As William Cain put it, "Garrison wished Douglass well when *The North Star* became *Frederick Douglass's Paper* in 1851. But by then he was emphasizing his disagreement with Douglass's new, antislavery interpretation of the Constitution (*Liberator,* July 4, 1851). And to hammer home his point, he published a letter from Reverend Samuel May . . . that slammed Douglass's alliance 'with slaveholders and slave-traders as voluntary supporters of one Constitution and Government.' It was not the rival paper as much as the shift in Douglass's thinking about the Constitution that thrust him and Garrison apart. The final break came at the meeting of the American Antislavery Society in May 1851, when Douglass repudiated Garrison's proslavery interpretation of the Constitution." (William Cain, ed., *William Lloyd Garrison and the Fight Against Slavery* [Boston, 1995], p. 47) Garrison's vituperative critique of American hypocrisy over the issue of individual freedom appears throughout his writing, particularly in texts written when he was incensed over injustice, as, for example, when he viewed the Dred Scott decision of

1857. When the Supreme Court of the United States ruled that Dred Scott, a slave from Missouri who had lived for years with his former master in two free states, Illinois and Wisconsin, would forever remain a slave even on the death of his former master, abolitionists and antislavery advocates voiced vigorous opposition. Garrison engaged in direct, confrontational attack, leaving nothing to the reader's imagination. "We are here to enter our indignant protest against the Dred Scott decision—against the infamous Fugitive Slave Law—against all unjust and oppressive enactments, with reference to complexional distinctions—against the alarming aggressions of the Slave Power upon the rights of the people of the North—and especially against the existence of the slave system at the South, from which all these have naturally sprung, as streams of lava from a volcano. We are here to reiterate the self-evident truths of the Declaration of Independence, and to call for their practical enforcement throughout our land. We are here to declare that the men who, like Crispus Attucks [an African American who was killed March 5, 1770, during the Boston Massacre], were ready to lay down their lives to secure American Independence, and the blessings of liberty—who, in every period of our history, at all times, and in all parts of the country, on the land and on the sea, have ever been prompt in the hour of peril to fill the deadly imminent breach, pour out their blood like water, and repel the minions of foreign tyranny from our shores—are not the men to be denied the claims of human nature, or the rights of citizenship. Alas! what have they reaped for all their patriotic toils and sufferings, but contumely, proscription, ostracism? O, shame on this cruelly unjust and most guilty nation! I trust in God that no colored men will ever again be found ready to fight under its banner, however great the danger that may menace it from abroad, until their rights are first secured, and every slave be set free." (William Cain, ed., *William Lloyd Garrison and the Fight Against Slavery* [Boston, 1995], p. 149)

This consistent anticonstitutional argument was perhaps best articulated in Garrison's early editorial in *The Liberator*, December 29, 1832, where he openly declared war on this most sacred of American charter documents and recommended disunion with slaveholders. His argument was always, "Immediate emancipation is the duty of the master, and the right of the slave . . . No Union with Slaveholders, religiously or politically." These declarative speech acts cost Garrison the support of moderate abolitionists, but they served to clarify the factions among the abolitionists, and set the Garrisonians such as Lydia Maria Child and Wendell Phillips off from both nonmilitant antislavery advocates and the more moderate wing of the abolitionist societies.

There is much declamation about the sacredness of the compact which was formed between the free and slave states, on the adoption of the Constitution. A sacred compact, forsooth! We pronounce it the most bloody and heaven-daring arrangement ever made by men for the continuance and protection of a system of the most atrocious villainy ever exhibited on earth. Yes—we recognize the compact, but with feelings of shame and indignation; and it will be held in everlasting infamy by the friends of justice and humanity throughout the world. It was a compact formed at the sacrifice of the bodies and souls of millions of our race, for the sake of achieving a political object—an unblushing and monstrous coalition to do evil that good might come. Such a compact was, in the nature of things and according to the law of God, null and void from the beginning. No body of men ever had the right to guarantee the holding of human beings in bondage . . . By the infamous bargain which they made between themselves, they virtually dethroned the Most High God, and trampled beneath their feet their own solemn and heaven-attested Declaration, that all men are created equal, and endowed by their Creator with certain inalienable rights—among which are life, liberty and the pursuit of happiness. They had no lawful power to bind themselves, or their posterity, for one hour—for one moment,—by such an unholy alliance. It was not valid then—it is not valid now. Still they persisted in maintaining it—and still do their successors, the people of Massachusetts, of New-England, and of the twelve free States, persist in maintaining it. A sacred compact! a sacred compact! What, then, is wicked and ignominious? This, then, is the relation in which we of New-England stand to the holders of slaves at the south, and this is virtually our language toward them: "Go on, most worthy associates, from day to day, from month to month, from year to year, from generation to generation, plundering two millions of human beings of their liberty and the fruits of their toil—driving them into the fields like cattle—starving and lacerating their bodies—selling the husband from his wife, the wife from her husband, and children from their parents—spilling their blood—withholding the bible from their hands and all knowledge from their minds—and kidnapping annually sixty thousand infants, the offspring of pollution and shame! Go on, in these practices,—we do not wish nor mean to interfere, . . . although we know that by every principle of law which does not utterly disgrace us by assimilating us to pirates, that they have as good and as true a right to the equal protection of the law as we have . . . We pledge to you our physical strength, by the sacredness of the national compact—a compact by which we have enabled you already to plunder, persecute, and destroy two millions of slaves, who now lie beneath the sod; and by which we now give you the same piratical license to prey upon a much larger number of victims and all their posterity. Go on—and by this sacred instrument, the Constitution of the United States, dripping as it is with human blood, we solemnly pledge you our lives, our fortunes, and our sacred honor, that we will stand by you to the last."

People of New-England, and of the free States! is it true that slavery is no concern of yours? Have you no right even to protest against it, or to seek its removal? Are you not the main pillars of its support? How long do you mean to be answerable to God and the world, for spilling the blood of the poor innocents? Be not afraid to look the monster Slavery boldly in the face. He is your implacable foe—the vampyre who is sucking your life-blood—the ravager of a large portion of your country, and the enemy of God and man. Never hope to be a united, or happy, or prosperous people while he exists. He has an appetite like the grave—a spirit as malignant as that of the bottomless pit—and an influence as dreadful as the corruption of death. Awake to your danger! the struggle is a mighty one—it cannot be avoided—it should not be, if it could.

It is said that if you agitate this question, you will divide the Union. Believe it not; but should disunion follow, the fault will not be yours. You must perform your duty, faithfully, fearlessly and promptly, and leave the consequences to God: that duty clearly is to cease from giving countenance and protection to southern kidnappers. Let them separate, if they can muster courage enough—and the liberation of their slaves is certain. Be assured that slavery will very speedily destroy this Union, *if it be let alone;* but even if the Union can be preserved by treading upon the necks, spilling the blood, and destroying the souls of millions of your race, we say it is not worth a price like this, and that it is in the highest degree criminal for you to continue the present compact. Let the pillars thereof fall—let the superstructure crumble into dust—if it must be upheld by robbery and oppression.

SOURCE NOTE: From *The Liberator,* Saturday, December 29, 1832, ed. William Lloyd Garrison, in collections of Neilson Library, Smith College, Northampton, Mass. (microfilm).

AMERICAN COLORPHOBIA (1847)

Garrison's anticonstitutional arguments may have isolated him from more moderate abolitionists and from many Northern whites, but his claims for Negro equality—politically, socially, and biologically—placed him in an extreme position even among militant abolitionists. Gerrit Smith, Wendell Phillips, Frederick Douglass, and Lydia Maria Child may have shared some of his views on racial equality, but his outspoken positions on race had the double effect of alienating some of his supporters while clearly defining the racism even among the abolitionists. When defending Frederick Douglass when he was attacked for his friendship with a white woman, Garrison argued:

There is nothing which excites more unfeigned astonishment in the old world, than the prejudice which dogs the footsteps of the man of color in this pseudo republic. True, there are many absurd, criminal, aristocratic distinctions abroad, which ought to cease; but there are also found, to a great extent, in the United States, and have been common to all countries, and in every age. They originate in the pride of wealth, in successful enterprise, in educational superiority, in official rank, in civil, military, and ecclesiastical rule. For these, there may be framed some plausible excuses. But to enslave, brutalize, scorn and insult human beings solely on account of the hue of the skin which it has pleased God to bestow on them; to pronounce them accursed, for no crime on their part; to treat them substantially alike, whether they are virtuous or vicious, refined or vulgar, rich or poor, aspiring or grovelling; to be inflamed with madness against them in proportion as they rise in self-respect, and improve in their manners and morals; this is an act so unnatural, a crime so monstrous, a sin so God-defying, that it throws into the shade all other distinctions known among mankind. Thank God, it is confined to a very small portion of the globe; though, strange to tell, it is perpetrated the most grossly, and in a spirit the most ferocious and inexorable, in a land claiming to be the pattern-land of the world—the most enlightened, the most democratic, the most Christian. Complexional caste is tolerated no where excepting in the immediate vicinage of slavery. It has no foundation in nature, reason, or universal custom. But, as the origin of it is to be traced to the existence of slavery, so its utter eradication is not to be expected until that hideous system be overthrown. Nothing but the removal of the cause can destroy the effect. That, with all its desperate efforts to lengthen its cords and strengthen its stakes, the Slave Power is continually growing weaker, is most clearly demonstrated in the gradual abatement of the prejudice which we have been deploring; for strong and terrible as that prejudice now is, it has received a very perceptible check within the last ten years, especially in New England.

No one can blame the intelligent and virtuous colored American for turning his back upon the land of his nativity, and escaping from it with the precipitancy that marked the flight of Lot out of Sodom. To remain in it is to subject himself to continual annoyance, persecution, and outrage. In fifteen, or twenty days, he can place his feet on the shores of Europe—in Great Britain and Ireland—where, if he cannot obtain more food or better clothing, he can surely find that his complexion is not regarded as a crime, and constitutes no barrier to his social, intellectual, or political advancement. He who, with this powerful temptation to become an exile before him, in resolved to remain at home, and take his lot and portion with his down-trodden brethren—to lay his comfort, reputation and hopes on the altar of freedom—exhibits the true martyr spirit, and is deserving of a world's sympathy and applause. Such a man, in an eminent degree, is FREDERICK DOUGLASS. Abroad, beloved, honored, admitted to the most refined circles, and eulogised by the Jerrolds, the Howitts, and a host of Britain's brightest intellects;—at home, not without numerous friends and admirers, it is true, yet made the object of popular contumely, denied the customary rights and privileges of a man, and surrounded by an atmosphere of prejudice which is enough to appal the stoutest heart, and to depress the most elastic spirit. Such is the difference between England and America; between a people living under a monarchical form of government, and a nation of boasting republicans!— O what crimes are perpetrated under the mask of democratic liberty! what outrages are consummated under the profession of Christianity!

> 'Fleecy locks and dark complexion
>   Cannot forfeit Nature's claim;
> Skins may differ, but affection
>   Dwells in white and black the same.'
> (Garrison, *The Liberator*, June 11, 1847)

DECLARATION OF THE NATIONAL ANTISLAVERY CONVENTION (1833)

Always critical of American values and especially of the hypocrisy embodied in the Constitution of the United States, Garrison set forth positive principles of belief and action in several statements drafted for antislavery societies. For example, in 1833, Garrison drafted the first principles of abolitionism in stating the objectives of the American Antislavery Society at its meeting in December of that year. Although these principles were debated at the convention, Garrison is usually credited with writing much of the text, which included the following:

Therefore we believe and affirm—

That there is no difference, *in principle*, between the African slave trade and American slavery;

That every American citizen, who retains a human being in involuntary bondage, is [according to Scripture] a MAN-STEALER;

That the slaves ought instantly to be set free, and brought under the protection of law;

That if they had lived from the time of Pharaoh down to the present period, and had been entailed through successive generations, their right to be free could never have been alienated, but their claims would have constantly risen in solemnity;

That all those laws which are now in force, admitting the right of slavery, are therefore before God utterly null and void; being an audacious usurpation of the Divine prerogative, a daring infringement on the law of nature, a base overthrow of the very foundations of the social compact, a complete extinction of all the relations, endearments and obligations of mankind, and a presumptuous transgression of all the holy commandments—and that therefore they ought to be instantly abrogated.

We further believe and affirm—

That all persons of color who possess the qualifications which are demanded of others, ought to be admitted forthwith to the enjoyment of the same privileges, and the exercise of the same prerogatives, as others; and that the paths of preferment, of wealth, and of intelligence, should be opened as widely to them as to persons of a white complexion.

We maintain that no compensation should be given to the planters emancipating their slaves—

Because it would be a surrender of the great fundamental principle that man cannot hold property in man;

Because SLAVERY IS A CRIME, AND THEREFORE IT IS NOT AN ARTICLE TO BE SOLD;

Because the holders of slaves are not the just proprietors of what they claim;—freeing the slaves is not depriving them of property, but restoring it to the right owner;—it is not wronging the master, but righting the slave—restoring him to himself;

Because immediate and general emancipation would only destroy nominal, not real property: It would not amputate a limb or break a bone of the slaves, but by infusing motives into their breasts, would make them doubly valuable to the masters as free laborers; and

Because if compensation is to be given at all, it should be given to the outraged and guiltless slaves, and not to those who have plundered and abused them.

We regard, as delusive, cruel and dangerous, any scheme of expatriation which pretends to aid, either directly or indirectly, in the emancipation of the slaves, or to be a substitute for the immediate and total abolition of slavery.

We fully and unanimously recognise the sovereignty of each State, to legislate exclusively on the subject of the slavery which is tolerated within its limits. We concede that Congress, *under the present national compact,* has no right to interfere with any of the slave States, in relation to this momentous subject.

But we maintain that Congress has a right, and is solemnly bound, to suppress the domestic slave trade between the several States, and to abolish slavery in those portions of our territory which the Constitution has placed under its exclusive jurisdiction.

We also maintain that there are, at the present time, the highest obligations resting upon the people of the free States, to remove slavery by moral and political action, as prescribed in the Constitution of the United States. They are now living under a pledge of their tremendous physical force to fasten the galling fetters of tyranny upon the limbs of millions in the southern States;—they are liable to be called at any moment to suppress a general insurrection of the slaves;—they authorise the slave owner to vote for three-fifths of his slaves as property, and thus enable him to perpetuate his oppression;—they support a standing army at the south for its protection;—and they seize the slave who has escaped into their territories, and send him back to be tortured by an enraged master or a brutal driver.

This relation to slavery is criminal and full of danger: IT MUST BE BROKEN UP.

These are our views and principles—these, our designs and measures. With entire confidence in the overruling justice of God, we plant ourselves upon the Declaration of our Independence, and upon the truths of Divine Revelation, as upon the EVERLASTING ROCK.

We shall organize Anti-Slavery Societies, if possible, in every city, town and village of our land.

We shall send forth Agents to lift up the voice of remonstrance, of warning, of entreaty and rebuke.

We shall circulate, unsparingly and extensively, anti-slavery tracts and periodicals.

We shall enlist the PULPIT and the PRESS in the cause of the suffering and the dumb.

We shall aim at a purification of the churches from all participation in the guilt of slavery.

We shall encourage the labor of freemen over that of the slaves, by giving a preference to their productions;—and

We shall spare no exertions nor means to bring the whole nation to speedy repentance.

Our trust for victory is solely in GOD. *We* may be personally defeated, but our principles never. TRUTH, JUSTICE, REASON, HUMANITY, must and will gloriously triumph. Already a host is coming up to the help of the Lord against the mighty, and the prospect before us is full of encouragement.

SOURCE NOTE: "Declaration of the National Antislavery Convention," in Garrison, ed., *The Liberator*, December 14, 1833. Microfilm in Neilson Library, Smith College.

SPEECH AT THE FOURTH NATIONAL
WOMEN'S RIGHTS CONVENTION (1853)

Finally, it is important to note that both Frederick Douglass and Garrison were strong supporters of the rights of women as well as fighters for the emancipation of the slaves. Douglass was a speaker at the Seneca Falls Convention of 1848, where the Declaration of Sentiments, an expression of the rights of women, was drafted. Although Garrison is best remembered for his vigorous lifelong crusade against the "peculiar institution" of chattel slavery, he was also committed to emancipating women from the oppressive conditions forced upon them by a society that denied them voting rights, educational opportunity, and property-ownership privileges. Garrison's attacks on the Constitution, on Southern politicians like John C. Calhoun and Henry Clay, and on legislation such as the Compromise of 1850 have long been recognized; however, his editorials in favor of women's rights are less heralded. Like Frederick Douglass, Garrison also spoke at meetings where women's rights held center stage, and at the Fourth Annual National Women's Rights Convention held in Cleveland, Ohio, in October 1853, he introduced the following resolutions:

1. *Resolved*, That by Human Rights we mean Natural Rights, in contradistinction to conventional usages, and because woman is a human being, she therefore has Human Rights.

2. *Resolved*, That because woman is a human being and man is no more, she has, by virtue of her constitutional nature, equal rights with man, and that state of society must necessarily be wrong,

which does not, in its usages and institutions, afford equal opportunities for the enjoyment and protection of those Rights.

3. *Resolved,* That it is the coolest assumption for man to claim the prerogative of determining the sphere of woman; and that he is adding insult to injury, when he denounces her as unwomanly, and condemns her as 'unsexing herself' if she ventures to pass over the limit he assigns her.

4. *Resolved,* That the Common Law, by giving to the husband the custody of his wife's person, does virtually place her on a level with criminals, lunatics and fools, since these are the only classes of adult persons over whom the law-makers have thought it necessary to place keepers.

5. *Resolved,* That if it be true, in the language of John C. Calhoun, 'that he who digs the money out of the soil has a right to it against the Universe,' then the law which gives to the husband the power to use his wife's earnings, makes robbery, and is as mean as it is unjust.

6. *Resolved,* That woman will soonest free herself from the legal disabilities she now suffers by securing the right to the elective franchise, thus becoming herself a law-maker; and that to this end we will petition our respective State Legislatures to call conventions, to amend their constitutions so that the right of the franchise shall not be limited by the word 'male.'

7. *Resolved,* That there is neither justice nor sound policy in the present arrangements of society restraining woman to so comparatively narrow a range of employments; excluding them from those which are most lucrative; and even in those to which they are admitted, awarding them a compensation less generally one-half or two-thirds than is paid to men for an equal amount of service rendered.

8. *Resolved,* That although the question of intellectual strength and attainments of women has nothing to do with the settlement of their rights yet in reply to the oft-repeated inquiry, 'Have women by nature the same force of intellect with men?' we will say, this inquiry never can be answered till women shall have such training as shall give their physical and intellectual powers as full opportunities for development by being as heavily taxed and all their resources as fully called forth as are those of men.

On Wednesday evening, Wm. Lloyd Garrison presented the following series of resolutions to the Convention:—

1. *Resolved,* That the natural rights of one human being are those of every other; in all cases equally sacred and inalienable; hence, the boasted 'Rights of Man,' about which we hear so much, are simply the 'Rights of Woman,' about which we hear so little; or, in other words, they are the Rights of Humankind, neither affected by or dependent upon sex or condition.

2. *Resolved,* That those who deride the claims of woman to a full recognition of her civil rights and political equality, exhibit the spirit which tyrants and usurpers have displayed in all ages towards the mass of mankind—strike at the foundation of all truly free and equitable government—contend for a sexual aristocracy, which is as irrational and unjust in principle, as that of wealth or hereditary descent—and show their appreciation of liberty to be wholly one-sided and supremely selfish.

3. *Resolved,* That for the men of this land to claim for themselves the elective franchise, and the right to choose their own rulers, and enact their own laws, as essential to their freedom, safety and welfare, and then to deprive all the women of all these safe guards, solely on the ground of a difference of sex, is to evince the pride of self-esteem, the meanness of usurpation, and the folly of a self-assumed superiority.

4. *Resolved,* That woman, as well as man, has a right to the highest mental and physical development—to the most ample educational advantages—to the occupancy of whatever position she can reach in Church and State, in science and art, in poetry and music, in painting and sculpture, in civil jurisprudence and political economy, and in the varied departments of human industry, enterprise and skill—to the elective franchise—and to a voice in the administration of justice and the passage of laws for the general welfare.

5. *Resolved,* That to pretend that the granting of these claims would tend to make woman less amiable and attractive, less regardful of her peculiar duties and obligations as wife and mother, a wanderer from her proper sphere, bringing confusion into domestic life, and strife into the public assembly, is the cant of Papal Rome, as to the discordant and infidel tendencies of the right of private judgment in matters of faith—is the outcry of legitimacy of the incapacity of the people to govern themselves—is the false allegation which

selfish and timid conservatism is ever making against every new measure of Reform—and has no foundation in reason, experience, fact or philosophy.

6. *Resolved,* That the consequences arising from the exclusion of woman from the possession and exercise of her natural rights and the cultivation of her mental faculties have been calamitous to the whole human race—making her servile, dependent, unwomanly—the victim of a false gallantry on the one hand, and of tyrannic subjection on the other—obstructing her mental growth, crippling her physical development, and incapacitating her for general usefulness, and thus inflicting an injury upon all born of woman; and cultivating in man a lordly and arrogant spirit; a love of dominion, a disposition to lightly disregard her comfort and happiness, all of which have been indulged in to a fearful extent, to the curse of his own soul, and the desecration of her nature.

7. *Resolved,* That so long as the most ignorant, degraded and worthless men are freely admitted to the ballot-box, and practically acknowledged to be competent to determine who shall be in office, and how the government shall be administered, it is preposterous to pretend that women are not qualified to use the elective franchise, and that they are fit only to be recognized, politically speaking, as *non compos mentis.*

SOURCE NOTE: *The Liberator,* October 28, 1853, ed. William Lloyd Garrison, in collections of Neilson Library, Smith College, Northampton, Mass. (microfilm).

NO COMPROMISE WITH SLAVERY (1854)

The text that follows is one of Garrison's most important statements concerning the "peculiar institution" of slavery. By 1854, he was already widely known as a militant abolitionist, and the public expected from *The Liberator* regular editorials concerning the evils of slavery and the necessity of immediate and unconditional emancipation. Further, the Garrisonians, as they were called, demanded that there by no compensation for slaveholders, as this would be tantamount to admitting that human beings could be purchased and sold in a system of illicit trade. In "No Compromise with Slavery," Garrison outlines his principles emphatically and reaches great oratorical and rhetorical heights. The address was subsequently published by the American Antislavery Society, from which this text was taken, and sections of the speech were also published in *The Liberator*.

Of necessity, as well as of choice, I am a "Garrisonian" Abolitionist—the most unpopular appellation that any man can have applied to him, in the present state of public sentiment; yet, I am more than confident, destined ultimately to be honourably regarded by the wise and good. Representing then, that phase of Abolitionism which is the most contemned—to the suppression of which, the means and forces of the Church and the State are most actively directed—I am here to defend it against all its assailants as the highest expediency, the soundest philosophy, the noblest patriotism, the broadest philanthropy, and the best religion extant. To denounce it as fanatical, disorganizing, reckless of consequences, bitter and irreverent in spirit, infidel in heart, deaf alike to the suggestions of reason and the warnings of history, is to call good evil, and evil good. Let me define my positions, and at the same time challenge anyone to show wherein they are untenable.

I. I am a believer in that portion of the Declaration of Independence in which it is set forth, as among self-evident truths, "that all men are created equal; that they are endowed by their Creator with certain inalienable rights; that among these are life, liberty, and the pursuit of happiness." Hence, I am an Abolitionist. Hence, I cannot but regard oppression in every form—and most of all, that which turns a man into a thing—with indignation and abhorrence. Not to cherish these feelings would be recreancy to principle. They who desire me to be dumb on the subject of Slavery, unless I will open my mouth in its defence, ask me to give the lie to my professions, to degrade my manhood, and to stain my soul. I will not be a liar, a poltroon, or a hypocrite, to accommodate any party, to gratify any sect, to escape any odium or peril, to save any interest, to preserve any institution, or to promote any object. Convince me that one man may rightfully make another man his slave, and I will no longer subscribe to the Declaration of Independence. Convince me that liberty is not the inalienable birthright of every human being, of whatever complexion or clime, and I will give that instrument to the consuming fire. I do not know how to espouse freedom and slavery together. I do not know how to worship God and Mammon at the same time. My crime is, that I will not go with the multitude to do evil. My singularity is, that when I say that Freedom is of God, and Slavery is of the devil, I mean just what I say. My fanaticism is, that I insist on the American people abolishing Slavery, or ceasing to prate of the rights of man.

II. Notwithstanding the lessons taught us by Pilgrim Fathers and Revolutionary Sires, by Plymouth Rock, on Bunker Hill, at Lexington, Concord, and Yorktown; notwithstanding our Fourth of July celebrations, and ostentatious displays of patriotism; in what European nation is personal liberty held in such contempt as in our own? Where are there such unbelievers in the natural equality and freedom of mankind? **Our slaves outnumber the entire population of the country at the time of our revolutionary struggle.** In vain do they clank their chains, and fill the air with their shrieks, and make their supplications for mercy. In vain are their sufferings portrayed, their wrongs rehearsed, their rights defended. For one rebuke of the man-stealer, a thousand denunciations of the Abolitionists are heard. For one press that bears a faithful testimony against Slavery, a score are ready to be prostituted to its service. For one pulpit that is not "recreant to its trust," there are ten that openly defend slaveholding as compatible with Christianity, and scores that are dumb. For one church that excludes the human enslaver from its communion table, multitudes extend to him the right hand of religious fellowship. I have expressed the belief that, so lost to all self-respect and all ideas of justice have we become by the corrupting presence of Slavery, in no European nation is personal liberty held at such a discount, as a matter of principle, as in our own. See how clearly this is demonstrated. The reasons adduced among us in justification of slaveholding, and therefore against personal liberty, are multitudinous. I will enumerate only a dozen of these.

1. "The victims are black."
2. "The slaves belong to an inferior race."
3. "Many of them have been fairly purchased."
4. "Others have been honestly inherited."
5. "Their emancipation would impoverish their owners."
6. "They are better off as slaves than they would be as freemen."

7. "They could not take care of themselves if set free."
8. "Their simultaneous liberation would be attended with great danger."
9. "Any interference in their behalf will excite the ill-will of the South, and thus seriously affect Northern trade and commerce."
10. "The Union can be preserved only by letting Slavery alone, and that is of paramount importance."
11. "Slavery is a lawful and constitutional system, and therefore not a crime."
12. "Slavery is sanctioned by the Bible; the Bible is the word of God; therefore God sanctions Slavery, and the Abolitionists are wise above what is written."

Here then, are twelve reasons which are popularly urged in all parts of the country, as conclusive against the right of a man to himself. If they are valid, in any instance, what becomes of the Declaration of Independence?

III. The Abolitionism which I advocate is as absolute as the Law of God, and as unyielding as His throne. It admits of no compromise. Every slave is a stolen man; every slaveholder is a man-stealer. By no precedent, no example, no law, no compact, no purchase, no bequest, no inheritance, no combination of circumstances, is slaveholding right or justifiable. While a slave remains in fetters, the land must have no rest. Whatever sanctions his doom must be pronounced accursed. The law that makes him a chattel is to be trampled under foot; the compact that is formed at his expense, and cemented with his blood, is null and void; the church that consents to his enslavement is horribly atheistical; the religion that receives to its communion the enslaver is the embodiment of all criminality. Such, at least, is the verdict of my own soul, on the supposition that I am to be the slave; that my wife is to be sold from me for the vilest purposes; that my children are to be torn from my arms, and disposed of to the highest bidder, like sheep in the market. And who am I but a man? What right have I to be free, that another man cannot prove himself to possess by nature? No man is to be injured in his person, mind, or estate. He cannot be, with benefit to any other man, or to any state of society. Whoever would sacrifice him for any purpose is both morally and politically insane. Every man is equivalent to every other man. Destroy the equivalent, and what is left? "So God created man in his own image—male and female created he them." This is a death-blow to all claims of superiority, to all charges of inferiority, to all usurpation, and to all oppressive dominion. No man can show that I have taken one step beyond the line of justice, or forgotten the welfare of the master, in my anxiety to free the slave . . . But, then, if they are men; if they are to run the same career of immortality with ourselves; if the same law of God is over them as over all others; if they have souls to be saved or lost; if Jesus included them among those for whom he laid down his life; if Christ is within many of them "the hope of glory," then, when I claim for them all that we claim for ourselves, because we are created in the image of God, I am guilty of no extravagance, but am bound, by every principle of honour, by all the claims of human nature, by obedience to the Almighty God, to remember them that are in bonds as bound with them, and **to demand their immediate and unconditional emancipation.**

How has the slave system grown to its present enormous dimensions? Through compromise. How is it to be exterminated? Only by an uncompromising spirit. This is to be carried out in all the relations of life—social, political, religious. Whatever may be the guilt of the South, the North is still more responsible for the existence, growth, and extension of Slavery. In her hand has been the destiny of the Republic from the beginning. She could have emancipated every slave, long ere this, had she been upright in heart and free in spirit. She has given respectability, security, and the means of sustenance and attack to her deadliest foe. She has educated the whole country, and particularly the Southern portion of it, secularly, theologically, religiously; and the result is, three millions and a half of slaves, increasing at the appalling rate of one hundred thousand a year, three hundred a day, and one every five minutes, the utter corruption of public sentiment, and general skepticism as to the rights of man. The pulpits, with rare exceptions, filled with men as careful to consult the popular will as though there were no higher law, and now, the repeal of the Missouri Compromise, and the consecration of five hundred thousand square miles of free territory forever to the service of the Slave Power!

And what does all this demonstrate? That the sin of this nation is not geographical—is not specially Southern—but deep seated and Universal. "The whole head is sick, and the whole heart faint." **If it** would be a damning sin for us to admit another Slave State into the Union, why is it not a damning sin to permit a Slave State to remain in the Union? . . . Not a single slaveholder will I allow to enjoy repose on any other condition than instantly ceasing to be one. Not a single slave will I leave in his chains, on any conditions, or under any circumstances . . . The Scriptural injunction is to be obeyed: "Resist the devil, and he will flee from you." My motto is, "No union with slaveholders, religiously or politically." Their motto is, "Slavery forever."

While the present union exists, I pronounce it hopeless to expect any repose, or that any barrier can be effectually raised, against the extension of Slavery. With two-thousand million dollars' worth of property in human flesh in its hands, to be watched and wielded as one vast interest for all the South, with forces never divided, and purposes never conflictive, with a spurious, Negro hating religion universally diffused, and everywhere ready to shield it from harm, with a selfish, sordid, divided North, long since bereft of its manhood, to cajole, bribe and intimidate, with its foot planted on two-thirds of our vast national domains, and there unquestioned, absolute and bloody in its sway, with the terrible strength and boundless resources of the whole country at its command, it cannot be otherwise than that the Slave Power will consummate its diabolical purposes to the uttermost . . . In itself, Slavery has no resources and no strength. Isolated and alone, it could not stand an hour; and, therefore, further aggression and conquest would be impossible . . .

What then, is to be done? Friends of the slave, the question is not whether by our efforts we can abolish Slavery, speedily or remotely, for duty is ours, the result with God; but whether we will go with the multitude to do evil, sell our birthright for a mess of pottage, cease to cry aloud and spare not, and remain in Babylon when the command of God is, "Come out of here, my people . . ."

SOURCE NOTE: "No Compromise with Slavery: An Address, Delivered in the Broadway Tabernacle," New York, February 14, 1854, by William Lloyd Garrison (New York: American Antislavery Society, 1854).

David Walker (1785–1830)

Garrison was an early militant voice of protest against chattel slavery in the United States, but he was quickly joined by other abolitionist voices, including those of a rising tide of black abolitionist writers. One of the most influential of these black writers was David Walker, who in 1829 authored a pamphlet of some seventy pages which vigorously attacked the hypocrisy of the United States. According to Garrison's biographer, Henry Mayer, Walker attributed the slaves' misery to four basic causes: "the barbarity of slavery, a cringing and servile attitude—even among free blacks—that perpetuated ignorance, the indifference of the Christian clergy, and the colonization scheme that insulted black citizenship and aspirations." And, Mayer writes, "Walker explicitly attacked Thomas Jefferson's racist assertions about black inferiority and he urged black men to give *Notes on the State of Virginia* to their sons to inspire their anger. He deplored submissiveness among blacks, contended for their right of self-defense, and raised a prophetic voice for a rebellion in the name of the Lord's justice . . . the pamphlet was published in September, 1829, and went through two more editions over the next six months." (Mayer, *All on Fire: William Lloyd Garrison and the Abolition of Slavery* [New York: St. Martin's Press, 1998], p. 83) David Walker's *Appeal* would have a significant influence on the abolitionist writer Lydia Maria Child, whose 1833 treatise *An Appeal in Favor of that Class of Americans Called Africans* would acknowledge a large debt to David Walker's inspiration. Walker and Henry Highland Garnet were early African abolitionists whose works broadened the spectrum of abolitionist sentiment during the first decade of militant abolitionism, 1830–1840. No longer the province of New England evangelical Christians and Quaker antislavery rhetoricians, the movement was enlarged to embrace black writers and escaped slaves themselves, like Frederick Douglass, who not only became one of the leading speakers for the abolitionist cause through New England, but also carried the message to England in person and argued his case throughout the world by way of his autobiographical *A Narrative of the Life of Frederick Douglass: an American Slave* (1845), the first of three such autobiographical documents he would write.

Very little is known of Walker's life. He was born in Wilmington,

North Carolina, September 28, 1785. His mother was a free woman, and according to *Stroud's Compendium of the Laws of Slavery,* the condition of the mother determined the condition of the child, whether slave or free. Thus Walker grew up surrounded by African slaves in the slaveholding South. At a very early age, Walker developed a hatred of slavery and the "peculiar institution" that would inform his rhetoric throughout his short life. He argued, while still living in North Carolina, "If I remain in this bloody land, I will not live long. As true as God reigns, I will be avenged for the sorrow which my people have suffered. This is not the place for me—no, no. I must leave this part of the country. It will be a great trial for me to live on the same soil where so many men are in slavery; certainly I cannot remain where I must hear their chains continually, and where I must encounter the insults of their hypocritical enslavers. God, I must." And go he did. Walker made his way to New England and settled permanently in Boston, where he opened a secondhand-clothing store and became an abolitionist reformer. His major work, the *Appeal,* was published in 1829, and it went through several printings during the following two years. Southern slaveholders attempted, unsuccessfully, to suppress it. So they responded by enacting harsher laws and penalties designed to prevent Negro slaves from learning to read, so that seditious literature like Walker's *Appeal* would have little impact on the very group it was designed to inspire. The book is divided into four sections, or "articles," and the essential elements are summarized in the first section of each article. Throughout the work, Walker, who was entirely self-educated, alludes to the Bible, citing many references to slavery in Egypt and to the emancipation of the Israelites through Moses' leadership. He used his Bible effectively, for his readership, both black and white, would have been steeped in biblical folklore and the Judeo-Christian tradition, a tradition that David Walker and William Lloyd Garrison would use effectively as rhetorical strategies for their inspirational and motivational appeals to moral conscience. David Walker was threatened for his seditious writing, and a reward was offered for him, dead or alive. One thousand dollars was posted for the return of his body, but ten thousand was offered if he were captured and delivered alive. One can only speculate why the larger amount was posted for his capture. The *Appeal* was Walker's most important work, partly because he lived only to the age of forty-five. He died at his home, and at the time there was speculation, now discounted, that he had been murdered. (Mayer, p. 87)

AN APPEAL TO THE COLORED CITIZENS
OF THE WORLD (1829)

Preamble

I am fully aware, in making this appeal to my much afflicted and suffering brethren, that I shall not only be assailed by those whose greatest earthly desires are, to keep us in abject ignorance and wretchedness, and who are of the firm conviction that heaven has designed us and our children to be slaves and beasts of burden to them and their children . . . Can our condition be any worse? Can it be more mean and abject? If there are any changes, will they not be for the better, though they may appear for the worse at first? Can they get us any lower? Where can they get us? They are afraid to treat us worse, for they know well, the day they do it they are gone . . . I appeal to heaven for my motive in writing, who knows that my object is, if possible, to awaken in the breasts of my afflicted, degraded and slumbering brethren, a spirit of enquiry and investigation respecting our miseries and wretchedness in this *Republican Land of Liberty*!!!! . . . And as the inhuman system of slavery, is the source from which most of our miseries proceed, I shall begin with that curse to nations; which has spread terror and devastation through so many nations of antiquity, and which is raging to such a pitch at the present day in Spain and in Portugal . . . The fact is, the labor of slaves comes so cheap to the avaricious usurpers, and is, as they think, of such great utility to the country where it exists, that those who are actuated by sordid avarice only, overlook the evils, which will as sure as the Lord lives, follow after the good. In fact, they are so happy to keep in ignorance and degradation, and to receive the homage and the labor of the slaves, they forget that God rules in the armies of heaven and among the inhabitants of the earth, having his ears continually open to the cries, tears, and groans of his oppressed people; and being a just and holy Being will at one day appear fully in behalf of the oppressed, and arrest the progress of the avaricious oppressors; for although the destruction of the oppressors God may not effect by the oppressed, yet the Lord our God will bring other destructions upon them—for not infrequently will he cause them to rise up one against another, to be split and divided, and to oppress each other, and sometimes to open hostilities with sword in hand . . . Their destruction may indeed be procrastinated a while, but can it continue long while they are oppressing the Lord's people? Has He not the hearts of all men in His hand? Will he suffer one part of his creatures to go on oppressing another like brutes always, with impunity? And yet those avaricious wretches are calling for Peace!!! I declare it does appear to me, as though some nations think God is asleep, or that he made the Africans for nothing else but to dig their mines and work their farms, or they cannot believe history, sacred or profane. I ask every man who has a heart and is blessed with the privilege of believing—Is not God a God of justice to all his creatures? Do you say he is? Then if he gives peace and tranquility to tyrants, and permits them to keep our fathers, our mothers, ourselves, and our children in eternal ignorance, and wretchedness to support them and their families, would he be to us a God of Justice?? I ask, O ye Christians!! who hold us and our children, in the most abject ignorance and degradation, that ever a people were afflicted with since the world began—I say, if God gives you peace and tranquility, and suffers you thus to go on afflicting us and our children, who have never given you the least provocation, Would he be to us a God of Justice? If you will allow that we are men, who feel for each other, does not the blood of our fathers and of us their children, cry aloud to the Lord of Sabaoth against you, for the cruelties and murders with which you have, and do continue to afflict us . . .

Article I.

I promised to demonstrate to the satisfaction of the most incredulous, that we, the colored people of these United States of America, are the most wretched, degraded, and abject set of beings that ever lived since the world began, and that the white Americans having reduced us to the wretched state of slavery, treat us in that condition more cruelly (they being an enlightened and christian people) than any heathen nation did any people whom it had reduced to our condition . . . To prove farther that the condition of the Israelites was better under the Egyptians than ours is under the whites, I call upon the professing christians, I call upon the philanthropist, I call upon the very tyrant himself, to show me a page of history, either sacred or profane, on which a verse can be found, which maintains, that the Egyptians heaped the insupportable insult upon the children of Israel by telling them that they were not of the human family. Can the whites deny this charge? Have they not, after having reduced us to the deplorable condition of slaves under their feet, held us up as descending originally from the tribes of Monkeys and Orang-Outangs? O! my God! I appeal to every man of feeling—is not this unsupportable? Is it not heaping the most gross insult upon our miseries, because they have got us under their feet and we cannot help ourselves? . . . Has not Mr. Jefferson declared to the world, that we are inferior to the whites, both in the endowments of our bodies and of minds? It is indeed surprising, that a man of such great learning, combined with such excellent natural parts, should speak so of a set of men in chains . . . Here, let me ask Mr. Jefferson (but he is gone, to answer at the bar of God, for the deeds done in his body while living), therefore I ask the whole American people, had I not rather die, or be put to death than to be a slave to any tyrant, who takes not only my own, but my wife and children's lives by inches? Yea, I would meet death with avidity far in preference to such servile submission to the murderous hands of tyrants. Mr. Jefferson's very severe remarks on us have been so extensively argued upon by men whose attainments in literature, I shall never be able to reach, that I would not have meddled with it, were it not to solicit each of my brethren, who has the spirit of a man, to buy a copy of Mr. Jefferson's "Notes on Virginia," and put it in the hand of his son. For let no one of us suppose that the refutations which have been written by our white friends are enough—they are *whites*—we are *blacks* . . . The whites have always been an unjust, jealous, unmerciful, avaricious and blood thirsty set of beings, always seeking after power and authority . . . In fact, take them as a body, they are ten times more cruel, avaricious and unmerciful than ever [the heathens] were; for while they were heathens they were bad enough it is true, but it is positively a fact that they were not quite so audacious as to go and take vessel loads of men, women, and children, and in cold blood and through devilishness, throw them into the sea and murder them in all kinds of ways. While they were heathens, they were too ignorant for such barbarity. But being christians, enlightened and sensible, they are now completely prepared for such hellish cruelties . . . The whites have had the essence of the gospel as it was preached by my master and his apostles—the Ethiopians have not . . . the Lord will give it to them to their satisfaction . . .

Article II. Our Wretchedness in Consequence of Ignorance.

Ignorance, my brethren, is a mist, low down into the very dark and almost impenetrable abyss of which, our fathers for many centuries have been plunged. The christians, and enlightened of Europe, and some of Asia, seeing the ignorance and consequent degradation of our fathers, instead of trying to enlighten them, by teaching them that religion and light with which God had blessed them, they have plunged them into wretchedness ten thousand times more intolerable, than if they had left them entirely to the Lord, and to add to their miseries, deep down into which they have plunged them, tell them, that they are an inferior and distinct race of beings . . . The whites want slaves, and want us for their slaves, but some of them will curse the day they ever saw us. As true as the sun ever shone in its meridian splendor, my colour will root some of them out of the very face of the earth. They shall have enough of making slaves of, and butchering, and murdering us in the manner which they have. No doubt some may say that I write with a bad spirit, and that I being a black, wish these things to occur. Whether I write with a bad or good spirit, I say if these things do not occur in their proper time, it is because the world in which we live does not exist, and we are deceived with regard to its existence . . . I should like to see the whites repent peradventure God may have mercy on them, some however, have gone so far that their cup must be filled. Ignorance and treachery, one against the other—a servile and abject submission to the lash of tyrants, we see plainly, my brethren, are not the natural elements of the blacks, as the Americans try to make us believe; but these are misfortunes which God has suffered our fathers to be enveloped in for so many ages, no doubt in consequence of their disobedience to their Maker and which do, indeed, reign at this time among us, almost to the destruction of all other principles, for I must truly say, that ignorance, the mother of treachery and deceit, gnaws into our very vitals. Ignorance, as it now exists among us, produces a state of things, O my Lord! too horrible to present to the world. Any man who is curious to see the full force of igno-rance developed among the colored people of the United States of America, has only to go into the southern and western states of this confederacy, where, if he is not a tyrant, but has the feelings of a human being, who can feel for a fellow creature, he may see enough to make his very heart bleed! He may see there, a son take his mother, who bore almost the pains of death to give him birth, and by the command of a tyrant, strip her as naked as she came into the world, and apply the cow-hide to her, until she falls a victim to death in the road! He may see a husband take his dear wife, not un-frequently in a pregnant state, and perhaps far advanced, and beat her for an unmerciful wretch, until his infant falls a lifeless lump at her feet! Can the Americans escape God Almighty? If they do, can he be to us a God of Justice? . . .

How can, Oh! how can those enemies but say that we and our children are not of the Human Family, but were made by our cre-ator to be an inheritance to them and theirs forever? How can the slave-holders but say that they can bribe the best coloured person in the country, to sell his brethren for a trifling sum of money, and take that atrocity to confirm them in their avaricious opinion, that we were made to be the slaves of them and their children?

How could Mr. Jefferson but say, "I advance it therefore as a suspicion only, that the blacks, whether originally a distinct race, or made distinct by time and circumstances, are *inferior to the whites in the endowments both of body and mind*? It is not against experi-ence to suppose that different species of the same genus, or varieties of the same species, may possess different qualifications. [Here, my brethren, listen to him.] Will not a love of natural history then, one who views the gradations in all the races of animals with the eye of philosophy, excuse any effort to keep those in the department of man as distinct as nature has formed them? . . . This unfortunate difference of colour, and perhaps of faculty, is a powerful obstacle to the emancipation of these people. Many of their advocates, while they wish to vindicate the liberty of human nature are anxious also to preserve its dignity and beauty. Some of these, embarrassed by the question, 'What further is to be done with them?' join them-selves in opposition with those who are actuated by sordid avarice only." . . . For my part, I am glad that Mr. Jefferson has advanced his position for your sake; for you will either have to contradict or confirm him by your own actions and not by what our friends have said or done for us; for those things are other men's labors and do not satisfy the Americans who are waiting for us to prove to them ourselves that we are men before they will be willing to admit the fact . . .

Men of colour, who are also of sense, for you particularly is my appeal designed. Our more ignorant brethren are not liable to penetrate its value. I call upon you therefore to cast your eyes upon the wretchedness of your brethren and to do your utmost to enlighten them—*go to work and enlighten your brethren*—Let the Lord see you doing what you can to rescue them and yourselves from degradation . . . There is a great work for you to do, as trifling as some of you may think of it. You have to prove to the Americans and the world, that we are men, and not brutes as we have been represented, and by millions treated. **Remember, to let the aim of your labours among your brethren, and particularly the youths, be the dissemination of education and religion.** It is lamentable, that many of our children go to school, from four until they are eight or ten, and sometimes fifteen years of age, and leave school knowing but a little more about the grammar of their language than a horse does about handling a musket, and not a few of them are really so ignorant, that they are unable to answer a person correctly, general questions in geography, and to hear them read would only be to disgust a man who has a taste for reading . . . Some few of them, may make out to scribble tolerably well, over half a sheet of paper, which I believe has hitherto been a powerful obstacle in our way, to keep us from acquiring knowledge . . . The cause of this almost universal ignorance amongst us, I appeal to our school-masters to declare. Here is a fact, which I take from the mouth of a young coloured man, who has been in Massachusetts nearly nine years, and who knows grammar this day, nearly as well as he did the day he first entered the school-house, under a white master. This young man says—"my master would never allow me to study grammar." I asked him why? "The school committee forbid the colored children learning grammar, they would not allow any but the white children to study grammar." It is a notorious fact that the major part of the white Americans have, ever since we have been among them, tried to keep us ignorant and make us believe that God made us and our children to be the slaves to them and theirs. **Oh! My God, have mercy on Christian Americans!**

Article III. Our Wretchedness in Consequence of the Preachers of the Religion of Jesus Christ.

[Walker turns his critical eye to the hypocrisy he sees in the Christian church throughout history, with particular emphasis on contemporary nineteenth-century evangelical Christianity, which had all but abandoned the cause of emancipation both North and South. There were, of course, exceptions to these generalizations, and several are cited in the "Biblical Antislavery Arguments" section of this volume. However, Walker was correct in his indictment of the church for its hypocrisy in relation to the teachings of Jesus, particularly the Sermon on the Mount, found in the Book of Matthew. Of the fifty-five proslavery sermons preached and published during the decade of the 1830s, thirty-seven were authored by Northern ministers.—Ed.]

Religion, my brethren, is a substance of deep consideration among all nations of the earth . . . But pure, and undefiled religion, such as was preached by Jesus Christ and his apostles, is hard to be found in all the earth . . . Indeed, the way in which religion was and is conducted by the Europeans and their descendants, one might believe it was a plan fabricated by themselves and the devils to oppress us!

The wicked and ungodly, seeing their preachers treat us with so much cruelty, they say: our preachers, who must be right, if any body are, treat them like brutes, and why cannot we?—They think it is no harm to keep them in slavery and put the whip to them, and why cannot we do the same!—They being preachers of the gospel of Jesus Christ, if it were any harm, they would surely preach against their oppression and do their utmost to erase it from the country; not only in one or two cities, but one continual cry would be raised in all parts of this confederacy and would cease only with the complete overthrow of the system of slavery, in every part of the country. But how far the American preachers are from preaching against slavery and oppression, which have carried their country

to the brink of a precipice; . . . Can the American preachers appeal
unto God, the Maker and Searcher of hearts, and tell him, with the
Bible in their hands, that they make no distinction on account of
men's colour? Can they say, O God! thou knowest all things—thou
knowest that we make no distinction between thy creatures to
whom we have to preach thy Word? . . . I believe you cannot be so
wicked as to tell him that his Gospel was that of *distinction* . . .
What right, then, has one of us, to despise another and to treat him
cruel, on account of his colour, which none but the God who made
it can alter? Can there be a greater absurdity in nature, and particularly in a free republican country? But the Americans, having introduced slavery among them, their hearts having become almost
seared, as with an hot iron, and God has nearly given them up to
believe a lie in preference to the truth!!! and I am awfully afraid that
this pride, prejudice, avarice and blood, will, before long, prove the
final ruin of this happy republic, or land of liberty!!! Can anything
be a greater mockery of religion than the way in which it is conducted by the Americans?

Article IV. Our Wretchedness in Consequence of the Colonization Plan.

[Walker here summarizes Henry Clay's colonization scheme, which he
satirically critiques as he quotes from it, and uses it to further illustrate the
cruelty of white Americans to the Africans they have enslaved.—Ed.]

Says he, "That class of the mixt population of our country
(coloured people) was peculiarly situated; they neither enjoyed the
immunities of freemen, nor were they subjected to the incapacities
of slaves, but partook, in some degree, of the qualities of both."
From their condition, and the unconquerable prejudices resulting
from their colour, they never could amalgamate with the free whites
of this country. It was desirable, therefore, as it respected them, and
the residue of the population of the country, to drain them off. Various schemes of colonization had been thought of, and a part of our
continent, it was supposed by some, might furnish a suitable establishment for them. But, for his part, Mr. Clay said, he had a decided
preference for some part of the coast of Africa. There, ample provi-

sion might be made for the colony itself, and it might be rendered instrumental in the introduction into that extensive quarter of the globe, of the arts, civilization, and Christianity. [Here, I ask Mr. Clay, what kind of Christianity? Did he mean such as they have among the Americans—distinction, whip, blood, and oppression? I pray the Lord, Jesus Christ, to forbid it.]

[Colonization was indeed proposed in various forms, from Thomas Jefferson through the middle of the century. It was temporarily embraced by a variety of antislavery and abolitionist thinkers, including William Lloyd Garrison and Abraham Lincoln. However, its association with "gradualism"—the slow removal of slavery as an institution from American soil, the popular form of emancipation theory before the emergence of Garrison, Walker, Child, Phillips, and the militant abolitionist advocates who called for immediate and unconditional emancipation of all slaves in the United States—led to its decline. Even Harriet Beecher Stowe shows how George Harris, a character modeled on the fugitive slave and abolitionist Frederick Douglass, eventually makes his way from the South to the North through Canada to Liberia. Walker's contempt for any form of colonization theory results from his understanding that colonizationists usually embraced contemporary race theory, in which blacks were deemed to be inferior to whites.—Ed.]

Man, in all ages, and all nations of the earth, is the same. Man is a peculiar creature—he is the image of his God, though he may be subjected to the most wretched condition upon earth, yet that spirit and feeling which constitute the creature man, can never be entirely erased from his breast, because the God who made him after his own image, planted it in his heart; he cannot get rid of it. The whites knowing this, they do not know what to do; they are afraid that we, being men, and not brutes, will retaliate, and woe will be to them; therefore, that dreadful fear, together with an avaricious spirit, and the natural love in them to be called masters, bring them to the resolve that they will keep us in ignorance and wretchedness, as long as they possibly can . . . Do the colonizationists think to send us off without first being reconciled to us? . . . Methinks colonizationists think they have a set of brutes to deal with, sure enough. Do they think to drive us from our country and homes, after having enriched it with our blood and tears, and keep back millions of our dear brethren, sunk in the most barbarous wretchedness, to dig up gold and silver for them and their children?

Now Americans, I ask you candidly, was your sufferings under Great Britain one hundredth part as cruel and tyrannical as you have rendered ours under you? Some of you, no doubt, believe that we will never throw off your murderous government, and "provide new guards for our future security." . . . Some of the whites are ignorant enough to tell us, that we ought to be submissive to them, that they may keep their feet on our throats. And if we do not submit to be beaten to death by them, we are bad creatures and of course must be damned. If any man wishes to hear this doctrine openly preached to us by the American preachers, let him go into the Southern and Western sections of this country. I do not speak from hearsay, what I have written, is what I have seen and heard myself. No man may think that my book is made up of conjecture, I have travelled and observed nearly the whole of those things myself, and what little I did not get by my own observation, I received from those among the whites and blacks, in whom the greatest confidence may be placed. The Americans may be as vigilant as they please, but they cannot be vigilant enough for the Lord, neither can they hide themselves, where he will not find and bring them out.

[David Walker's *Appeal* is an angry document. Its author had witnessed the brutal mistreatment of his "brethren" in the South and the race prejudices against Negroes in the North. Like Frederick Douglass and William Lloyd Garrison, he understood the linkage between race theory and slavery, the connection between a belief in the inferiority of one race and the superiority of another and the institution of chattel slavery. But he also believed that these views were learned, that they were social and political, and not "essential," and certainly not biological in origin. At the conclusion of the *Appeal*, an olive branch is held out to white America, coupled with an implicit threat, which is one of the reasons the book was so inflammatory.—Ed.]

Remember Americans, that we must and shall be free, and enlightened as you are, will you wait until we shall, under God, obtain our liberty by the crushing arm of power? Will it not be dreadful for you? I speak Americans for your good. We must and shall be free I say, in spite of you . . . Throw away your fears and prejudices then, and enlighten us and treat us like men, and we will like you more than we do now hate you, and tell us no more about colonization, for America is as much our country, as it is yours. Treat us like men, and there is no danger but we will all live in peace and happiness together. For we are not like you, hard hearted, unmerciful and unforgiving. What a happy country this will be, if the whites will listen. What nation under heaven, will be able to do anything with us, unless God gives us up into his hand? But Americans, I declare to you, while you keep us in bondage, and treat us like brutes, to make us support you and your families, we cannot be your friends. You do not look for it, do you? Treat us then like men, and we will be your friends.

SOURCE NOTE: *David Walker's Appeal; With a Brief Sketch of His Life*, by Henry Highland Garnet, *and also Garnet's Address to the Slaves of the United States of America* (New York: J. H. Tobitt, 1848), reprinted for the *New York Times* by the Arno Press (New York: 1969).

John Greenleaf Whittier (1807–1892)

Whittier, a beloved nineteenth-century American poet and close friend of Garrison, became a poet laureate of the abolitionist movement. His poem "The Slave Ships" highlighted the cruelties of the "middle passage," and his long poem "Massachusetts to Virginia" (1843) critiqued the decline in moral force in the "Old Dominion" of Virginia since its seventeenth-century founding on principles of human rights and liberty. Though less well known than his contemporary Henry Wadsworth Longfellow, Whittier wrote moral verse that was consistently critical of the institution of chattel slavery. He was a Quaker and espoused the antislavery doctrines of the Society of Friends.

MASSACHUSETTS TO VIRGINIA (1843)

The blast from Freedom's Northern hills, upon its
    Southern way,
Bears greeting to Virginia from Massachusetts Bay:
No word of haughty challenging, nor battle bugle's
    peal,
Nor steady tread of marching files, nor clang of
    horsemen's steel.

5   No trains of deep-mouthed cannon along our highways
    go;
Around our silent arsenals untrodden lies the snow;
And to the land-breeze of our ports, upon their errands
    far,
A thousand sails of commerce swell, but none are
    spread for war.

We hear thy threats, Virginia! thy stormy words and
    high,
10   Swell harshly on the Southern winds which melt along
    our sky;
Yet, not one brown, hard hand forgoes its honest labor
    here,

No hewer of our mountain oaks suspends his axe in
    fear.

Wild are the waves which lash the reefs along St.
    George's bank;
Cold on the shore of Labrador the fog lies white and
    dank;
15   Through storm, and wave, and blinding mist, stout are
    the hearts which man
The fishing-smacks of Marblehead, the sea-boats of
    Cape Ann.

The cold north light and wintry sun glare on their icy
    forms,
Bent grimly o'er their straining lines of wrestling with
    the storms;
Free as the winds they drive before, rough as the waves
    they roam,
20   They laugh to scorn the slaver's threat against their
    rocky home.

What means the Old Dominion? Hath she forgot the
    day
When o'er her conquered valleys swept the Briton's
    steel array?
How side by side, with sons of hers, the Massachusetts
    men
Encountered Tarleton's charge of fire, and stout
    Cornwallis, then?

25   Forgets she how the Bay State, in answer to the call
Of her old House of Burgesses, spoke out from Faneuil
    Hall?
When, echoing back her Henry's cry, came pulsing on
    each breath
Of Northern winds, the thrilling sounds of "Liberty or
    Death!"

What asks the Old Dominion? If now her sons have
    proved
30   False to their fathers' memory, false to the faith they
    loved;

If she can scoff at Freedom, and its great charter spurn,
Must we of Massachusetts from truth and duty turn?

We hunt your bondmen, flying from Slavery's hateful
    hell;
Our voices, at your bidding, take up the blood-hound's
    yell;
35 We gather, at your summons, above our fathers' graves,
From Freedom's holy altar-horns to tear your wretched
    slaves!

Thank God! not yet so vilely can Massachusetts vow;
The spirit of her early time is even with her now;
Dream not because her Pilgrim blood moves slow and
    calm and cool,
40 She thus can stoop her chainless neck, a sister's slave
    and tool!

All that a sister State should do, all that a free State
    may,
Heart, hand, and purse we proffer, as in our early day;
But that one dark loathsome burden ye must stagger
    with alone,
And reap the bitter harvest which ye yourselves have
    sown!

45 Hold while ye may, your struggling slaves, and burden
    God's free air
With woman's shriek beneath the lash, and manhood's
    wild despair;
Cling closer to the "cleaving curse" that writes upon
    your plains
The blasting of Almighty wrath against a land of
    chains.

Still shame your gallant ancestry, the cavaliers of old,
50 By watching round the shambles where human flesh is
    sold;
Gloat o'er the new-born child, and count his market
    value, when

The maddened mother's cry of woe shall pierce the
    slaver's den!

Lower than plummet soundeth, sink the Virginia name;
Plant, if ye will, your fathers' graves with rankest weeds
    of shame,
55   Be, if ye will, the scandal of God's fair universe;
We wash our hands forever of your sin and shame and
    curse.

A voice from lips whereon the coal from Freedom's
    shrine hath been,
Thrilled, as but yesterday, the hearts of Berkshire's
    mountain men:
The echoes of that solemn voice are sadly lingering still
60   In all our sunny valleys, on every wind-swept hill.

And when the prowling man-thief came hunting for his
    prey
Beneath the very shadow of Bunker's shaft of gray,
How, through the free lips of the son, the father's
    warning spoke;
How, from its bonds of trade and sect, the Pilgrim city
    broke!

65   A hundred thousand right arms were lifted up on high,
A hundred thousand voices sent back their loud reply;
Through the thronged towns of Essex the startling
    summons rang,
And up from bench and loom and wheel her young
    mechanics sprang!

The voice of free, broad Middlesex, of thousands as of
    one,
70   The shaft of Bunker calling to that of Lexington;
From Norfolk's ancient villages, from Plymouth's
    rocky bound
To where Nantucket feels the arms of ocean close her
    round;
From rich and rural Worcester, where through the calm
    repose

Of cultured vales and fringing woods the gentle Nashua
  flows,
75   To where Wachusett's wintry blasts the mountain
  larches stir,
Swelled up to Heaven the thrilling cry of "God save
  Latimer!"

And sandy Barnstable rose up, wet with the salt sea
  spray;
And Bristol sent her answering shout down
  Narragansett Bay!
Along the broad Connecticut old Hampden felt the
  thrill,
80   And the cheer of Hampshire's woodsmen swept down
  from Holyoke Hill.

The voice of Massachusetts! Of her free sons and
  daughters,
Deep calling unto deep aloud, the sound of many
  waters!
Against the burden of that voice what tyrant power
  shall stand?
No fetters in the Bay State! No slave upon her land!

85   Look to it well, Virginians! In calmness we have borne,
In answer to our faith and trust, your insult and your
  scorn;
You've spurned our kindest counsels; you've hunted
  for our lives;
And shaken round our hearths and homes your
  manacles and gyves!

We wage no war, we lift no arm, we fling no torch
  within
90   The fire-damps of the quaking mine beneath your soil
  of sin;
We leave ye with your bondmen, to wrestle, while ye
  can,
With the strong upward tendencies and godlike soul of
  man!

But for us and for our children, the vow which we have
    given
For freedom and humanity is registered in heaven;
95   No slave-hunt in our borders,—no pirate on our
    strand!
No fetters in the Bay State,—no slave upon our land!

SOURCE NOTE: (1) John Greenleaf Whittier, *The Complete Poetical Works of John Greenleaf Whittier,* Cambridge edition (Boston: Houghton-Mifflin, 1894); and (2) John Greenleaf Whittier, *Anti-Slavery Poems: Songs of Labor and Reform,* reprint of 1888 edition (New York: Arno Press, 1969).

JUSTICE AND EXPEDIENCY:
OR SLAVERY CONSIDERED WITH
A VIEW TO ITS RIGHTFUL AND
EFFECTUAL REMEDY, ABOLITION (1833)

John Greenleaf Whittier was also a close friend of William Lloyd Garrison and an early member of the abolitionist societies that Garrison founded. He was, with Garrison, a prominent founder of the American Antislavery Society. His treatise demands immediate and unconditional emancipation of the slaves, and this commitment places him squarely within the Garrison camp of reformers and abolitionists. According to Louis Ruchames, the pamphlet was first published in only five hundred copies; however, it was soon reprinted in a much larger edition of five thousand copies by the abolitionist Arthur Tappan.

. . . And what is this system which we are thus protecting and upholding? A system which holds two millions of God's creatures in bondage, which leaves one million females without any protection save their own feeble strength, and which makes the exercise of that strength in resistance to outrage punishable with death! which considers rational, immortal beings as articles of traffic, vendible commodities, merchantable property—which recognizes no social obligations, no natural relations—which tears without scruple the infant child from the mother, the wife from the husband, the parent from the child . . .

I come now to the only practicable, the only just scheme of emancipation: Immediate abolition of slavery; and immediate acknowledgment of the great truth, that man cannot hold property in man; an immediate surrender of baneful prejudice to Christian love; an immediate practical obedience to the command of Jesus Christ: "Whatsoever ye would that men should do unto you, do ye even so to them." . . . The term immediate is used in contrast with that of gradual. Earnestly as I wish it, I do not expect, no one expects, that the tremendous system of oppression can be instantaneously overthrown. The terrible and unrebukable indignation of a free people has not yet been sufficiently concentrated against it . . .

Let them at once strike off the grievous fetters. Let them declare that man shall no longer hold his fellow-man in bondage, a beast of burden, an article of traffic, within the governmental domain . . . If our fathers intended that slavery should be perpetual, that our practice should forever give the lie to our professions, why is the great constitutional compact so guardedly silent on the subject of human servitude? . . .

What, then, is our duty?

To give effect to the spirit of our Constitution; to plant ourselves upon the great declaration and declare in the face of all the world that political, religious, and legal hypocrisy shall no longer cover as with loathsome leprosy the features of American freedom; to loose at once the bands of wickedness; and to undo the heavy burdens, and let the oppressed go free . . .

I deny the right of the slave-holder to impose silence on his brother of the North in reference to slavery. What! Compelled to maintain the system, to keep up the standing army which protects it, and yet be denied the poor privilege of remonstrance! Ready, at the summons of the master to put down the insurrections of his slaves, the outbreaking of that revenge which is now, and has been, in all nations, and all times, the inevitable consequence of oppression and wrong, and yet like automata to act but not to speak! Are we to be denied even the right of a slave, the right to murmur? . . .

The slave-holding states are not free. The name of liberty is there, but the spirit is wanting. They do not partake of its invaluable blessings. Wherever slavery exists to any considerable extent, with the exception of some recently settled portions of the country and which have not yet felt in a great degree the baneful and deterioriating influences of slave labor, we hear at this moment the cry of suffering . . . A moral mildew mingles with and blasts the economy of nature. It is as if the finger of the everlasting God had written upon the soil of the slave-holder the language of His displeasure. Let, then, the slave-holding states consult their present interest by beginning without delay the work of emancipation . . . Let the cause of insurrection be removed, then, as speedily as possible. Cease to oppress. "Let him that stole steal no more." Let the laborer have his hire. Bind him no longer by the cords of slavery, but with those of kindness and brotherly love. Watch over him for his good. Pray for him; instruct him; pour light into the darkness of his mind. Let this be done and the horrible fears which now haunt the slumbers of the slave-holder will depart. Conscience will take down its racks and gibbets, and his soul will be at peace. His lands will no longer disappoint his hopes. Free labor will renovate them.

Historical facts; the nature of the human mind; the demonstrated truths of political economy; the analysis of cause and effect, all concur in establishing:

1. That immediate abolition is a safe and just and peaceful remedy for the evils of the slave system.
2. That free labor, its necessary consequence, is more productive, and more advantageous to the planter than slave labor.

In proof of the first proposition it is only necessary to state the undeniable fact that immediate emancipation, whether by an individual or a community, has in no instance been attended with violence and disorder on the part of the emancipated; but that on the contrary, it has promoted cheerfulness, industry, and laudable ambition in the place of sullen discontent, indolence, and despair . . . Because slave labor is the labor of mere machines; a mechanical impulse of body and limb, with which the mind of the laborer has no sympathy, and from which it constantly and loathingly revolts. Because slave labor deprives the master altogether of the incalculable benefit of the negro's will. That does not cooperate with the forced toil of the body. This is but the necessary consequence of all labor which does not benefit the laborer. It is a just remark of that profound political economist, Adam Smith, that "a slave can have no other interest than to eat and waste as much, and work as little, as he can." . . .

The conflicting interests of free and slave labor furnish the only ground for fear in relation to the permanency of the Union. The line of separation between them is day by day growing broader, and deeper; geographically and politically united, we are already, in a moral point of view, a divided people. But a few months ago we were on the very verge of civil war, a war of brothers, a war between the North and the South, between the slave-holder and the free laborer. The danger has been delayed for a time; this bolt has fallen without mortal injury to the Union, but the cloud from whence it came still hangs above us, reddening with the elements of destruction . . .

To counteract the dangers resulting from a state of society so utterly at variance with the great Declaration of American freedom should be the earnest endeavor of every patriotic statesman. Nothing unconstitutional, nothing violent, should be attempted; but the true doctrine of the rights of man should be steadily kept in view; and the opposition to slavery should be inflexible and constantly maintained. The almost daily violations of the Constitution in consequence of the laws of some of the slave states, subjecting free colored citizens of New England and elsewhere, who may happen to be on board one of our coasting vessels, to imprisonment immediately on their arrival in a Southern port, should be provided against. Nor should the immediate imprisonment of the free colored citizens of the Northern and Middle states, on suspicion of being runaways, subjecting them, even after being pronounced free, to the costs of their confinement and trial, be longer tolerated; for if we continue to yield to innovations like these upon the Constitution of our fathers, we shall erelong have the name only of a free government left us.

Dissemble as we may, it is impossible for us to believe, after fully considering the nature of slavery, that it can much longer maintain a peaceable existence among us. A day of revolution must come, and it is our duty to prepare for it. Its threatened evil may be changed into a national blessing. The establishment of schools for the instruction of the slave children, a general diffusion of the lights of Christianity, and the introduction of a sacred respect for the social obligations of marriage and for the relations between parents and children, among our black population, would render emancipation not only perfectly safe, but also of the highest advantage to the country. Two millions of freemen would be added to our population, upon whom in the hour of danger we could safely depend; "the domestic foe" would be changed into a firm friend, faithful, generous, and ready to encounter all dangers in our defence. It is well known that during the last war with Great Britain, wherever the enemy touched upon our Southern coast, the slaves in multitudes hastened to join them. On the other hand, the free blacks were highly serviceable in repelling them. So warm was the zeal of the latter, so manifest their courage in the defense of Louisiana, that the present Chief Magistrate of the United States publicly bestowed upon them one of the highest eulogiums ever offered by a commander to his soldiers . . .

An intense and powerful feeling is working in the mighty heart of England; it is speaking through the lips of Brougham and Buxton and O'Connell [British abolitionists], and demanding justice in the name of humanity according to the righteous law of God. The immediate emancipation of eight hundred thousand slaves is demanded with an authority which cannot much longer be trifled with. That demand will be obeyed; justice will be done; the heavy burdens will be unloosed; the oppressed set free. It shall go well for England.

And when the stain on our own escutcheon shall be seen no more; when the Declaration of Independence and the practice of our people shall agree; when truth shall be exalted among us; when love shall take the place of wrong; when all the baneful pride and prejudice of caste and color shall fall forever; when under one common sun of political liberty the slave-holding portions of our republic shall no longer sit, like the Egyptians of old, themselves mantled in thick darkness, while all around them is glowing with the blessed light of freedom and equality, then, and not till then, shall it go well for America!

SOURCE NOTE: *The Prose Works of John Greenleaf Whittier* (Boston, 1892), vol. 3, pp. 9–57.

Lydia Maria Child (1802–1880)

Lydia Maria Child was a prominent early feminist as well as an abolitionist. Like her contemporary Frederick Douglass, she linked the dual issues of emancipation and women's suffrage, and throughout her adult life promoted both causes. The poet John Greenleaf Whittier once said that "she was wise in counsel; and men like Charles Sumner, [William Ellery] Channing, [Thomas Wentworth] Higginson, Salmon Chase, Henry Wilson, and Governor Andrews availed themselves of her foresight and sound judgment of men and measures." (*Dictionary of American Biography*, p. 68) Although she wrote poetry and novels for much of her life, she is best remembered for her antislavery work, especially for the text excerpted here, *An Appeal in Favor of that Class of Americans Called Africans* (1833), and for her practical works designed for women, *The Frugal Housewife* (1829) and *The Mother's Book* (1831). Her early novels, *Hobomok* (1824) and *The Rebels, or, Boston Before the Revolution* (1825), are currently enjoying a revival as important contributions to American literary history; however, it is her reform works that place her centrally in the antebellum abolitionist camp.

Born February 11, 1802, she received little formal education but enjoyed the stimulation of her brother, a professor at Harvard Divinity School, and later, the partnership in antislavery work with her husband, David L. Child, a Boston attorney and her partner in their lifetime dedication to the abolitionist crusade. *An Appeal in Favor of That Class of Americans Called Africans* was an extremely radical declaration for its time in that it called not only for immediate rather than gradual emancipation of the slaves, but also argued for full racial equality. The *Appeal* caused a sensation everywhere it was read. It argued the moral urgency of emancipation and the cruel inhumanity of slavery, winning her "converts" among the abolitionists like Channing and Sumner, but alienating more conservative Bostonians and Southern proslavery advocates. The *Appeal*'s radical miscegenation argument recapitulates the plot of her earlier novel *Hobomok*, in which a Puritan woman marries an Indian man, and it anticipates the plot of her 1867 novel *A Romance of the Republic*, which presents interracial marriage as a solution to America's race problem. Reaction to the *Appeal*'s argument for biological equality and interracial relationships was extreme and punitive. Child had authored two earlier and extremely popular domestic manuals, *The Frugal Housewife* and *The Mother's Book*, and she was author of numerous children's pieces published in the *Juvenile Miscellany*. However, these popular successes were eclipsed by the storm of criticism that deluged publication of the *Appeal*. Because the book indicted both Northern and Southern racial prejudice, the Childs were instantly ostracized by Boston society, and friends and family members abandoned the revolutionary couple, who continued their dedicated work in the abolitionist movement. According to her biographer, Carolyn Karcher, "[Lydia's] elder brother, James, who had named his daughters Lydia Maria and Mary Conant (after the heroine of Child's *Hobomok*), turned hostile; a Jacksonian Democrat, he could not stomach either 'niggers' or 'nigger-lovers.' Her father, though he sympathized warmly with her abolitionist principles, did not extend the same sympathy toward David, but instead blamed his son-in-law for the heavy financial price of the couple's antislavery activism." (Karcher, chapter 8) Although Garrison and Phillips and the more militant abolitionists, some of whom also argued for full racial equality, continued to support Lydia Child's *Appeal,* she lost the friendship of many and was ostracized by Harvard professors and contemporary novelists like Catharine Maria Sedgwick, with whom she broke off a relationship because of abolitionism and racial views. "In addition to the pain of broken friendships, Child bore the cost of professional blacklisting as her erstwhile patrons among the Boston aristocracy mobilized against her. Former admirers like Harvard professor George Ticknor slammed their doors in her face, cut her dead in the street, and enforced a policy of ostracism toward anyone who violated the ban against her." (Karcher, chapter 8) While she was engaged in research for her book called *The History of the Condition of Women,* the Boston Athenaeum withdrew her free library privileges (Karcher, p. xlv). "Most damagingly, readers boycotted her writings and parents cancelled their subscriptions to the *Juvenile Miscellany. The Mother's Book,* which had been reissued five times in two years, promptly went out of print; the *Miscellany,* though beloved by its broad juvenile audience, folded; even sales of her most commercially successful work, *The Frugal Housewife,* then in its thirteenth printing, plummeted, reducing Child's already meager income to a pittance." (Karcher, p. xlv) Her literary popularity and social position in Boston were swiftly destroyed. But she joined Garrison and Phillips in moving forward the abolitionist cause and in provoking reactions among both Northern and Southern readers.

Although her text, excerpted here, did little to provide sources for her examples of slave cruelty—in contrast to Theodore Dwight Weld's *American Slavery As It Is* (1839), which detailed the newspapers and journals from which its evidence was taken—the moral force of her argument was so powerful that the book immediately set the terms of antislavery discourse for the next decade. Biblical examples would now be used in the service of a moral argument against slavery, and the Constitution and Declaration of Independence, so critical to Wendell Phillips and Lysander Spooner, who examined in minute detail the legal foundation for slavery, were muted voices compared to her irrefutable declarations that slavery was morally wrong and opposed to all conceptions of natural rights. As the Canadian historian Margaret Kellow put it, "Her *Appeal* mounted a searching critique of American slavery and race relations and articulated Child's growing concern about the threat slavery posed to the well-being of the Republic. Recognizing that slavery and race prejudice were grounded in a presumption of the inherent inferiority of African Americans, Child argued that the perceived inferiority of Black Americans was a consequence of enslavement. Only Emancipation would permit a fair assessment of the capacities of African Americans, a test in which Child was convinced African Americans would acquit themselves well. To subjugate an entire race on categorical grounds flew in the face of Child's beliefs about individualism and opportunity. Thus Child's views on racism and sexism flowed from the same source, her commitment to individual liberty." (Kellow, unpublished article manuscript, p. 4)

Perhaps her most lasting contribution to reform activities in antebellum America was this fusion of antislavery sentiment with concern for women's rights. Although Child contributed little oratory or essay writing to the specific cause of women's suffrage—which as early as 1848, with the Seneca Falls Convention and the "Declaration of Sentiments," had charted a course for equality for women—she managed in her antislavery writing to link the two causes together so that the moral force of one arena supported the other. Child did not argue for "identical exactness" between men and women, or indeed between blacks and whites; rather, "like Sarah Grimké and Lucretia Mott, Child grounded her commitment to women's rights solidly in the same commitment to egalitarianism which underwrote her commitment to antislavery. Child did not believe men and women were identical, but such differences as existed between them did not justify the subordination of women in antislavery or anywhere else." (Kellow, p. 5)

Lydia Maria Child edited the text of and authored the introduction to Harriet Jacobs's *Linda: Incidents in the Life of a Slave Girl* (1861), recently edited by Jean Fagan Yellin for the Harvard University Press. This introduction shows clearly the fusion of antislavery and women's rights, as does the Jacobs document itself.

Critical reaction to Child's *Appeal* in the 1830s was swift and harsh, but the written reviews were only the beginning of her decline in popularity. Her arguments for immediate emancipation had already been prominently advanced by William Lloyd Garrison through *The Liberator*, and her views on racial equality were also known, especially in Europe. "The distinctiveness of the *Appeal* lies not in the particular arguments it advances, but in its all-encompassing synthesis of facts and arguments from an unprecedented array of sources. Among Child's precursors, the British abolitionist Thomas Clarkson had detailed the horrors of the slave trade. The American legal scholar George Stroud had exhaustively studied southern slave laws and demonstrated their harshness. David Walker and Garrison had dissected colonizationist ideology and exposed its racism and illogicality. The Abbe Gregoire of the French Amis des Noirs had vindicated blacks against charges of inferiority by amassing examples of their achievements in science, art, and literature." (Karcher, p. xxxvii) But the power of her book is its capacity to focus the dual arguments of immediate emancipation and racial equality on a particular contemporary political problem, namely, the colonization movement.

According to Carolyn Karcher, the colonizationists, who argued for gradual emancipation and the eventual removal of all Africans from the United States to Africa, expressed the most visible form of resistance to David and Lydia Child's form of abolitionism. The *Appeal* focused on these dual problems and concentrated both of them into the attack on colonization. Karcher critiques the content thus:

In her pivotal chapter, "Colonization Society, and Anti-Slavery Society," placed at the center of the book, Child examines the two parties' opposing solutions to the problem of slavery: gradual emancipation accompanied by repatriation to Africa versus immediate emancipation followed by the bestowal of 'equal civil and political rights and privileges with the whites.' Since the principal point at issue between Colonizationists and abolitionists is whether prejudice against blacks can and should be overcome, she devotes the rest of the book to answering that question. Chapters 6 and 7, "Intellect of Negroes," and "Moral Character of Negroes," demolish the rational for prejudice—the myth of the Negro's biological inferiority and savage past—by resurrecting accounts of Africa's ancient civilizations and recalling numerous modern instances of blacks who have distinguished themselves by their talents. The final chapter, "Prejudices against People of Color, and Our Duties in Relation to This Subject," condemns racial discrimination and urges Americans to repudiate attitudes and practices inconsistent with the republican creed. Although the *Appeal* violates the prevailing norms of feminine discourse by its very engagement in political controversy, as well as by its authoritative display of erudition and its preoccupation with such matters as law, economics, and congressional apportionment, it simultaneously presents a woman's perspective on slavery. Repeatedly, Child focuses on the special ways in which slavery victimizes women and makes a mockery of the domestic ideology glorifying "true womanhood." In the process, she pointedly reveals the limitations on her own freedom as a woman that link her to her sisters in bonds. (Karcher, p. xxv)

Lydia Maria Child thus advanced an argument for the fusion of women's rights and the emancipation of the slaves, which, in 1833, was an extremely radical position to take. By 1848, the escaped slave Frederick Douglass, who had won respect as an abolitionist thinker and writer, was invited to speak at the Seneca Falls Convention, where the major issues of women's rights were addressed and where the charter document of the women's movement in the United States, the "Declaration of Sentiments," was ratified by the fewer than one thousand women who attended. But in 1833, the abolitionists like Garrison and Phillips were primarily focused on the harshness of chattel slavery, making Child's argument in the *Appeal* an important fusion of horizons for these important reform movements. Child died on October 20, 1880, at her home in Wayland, Massachusetts.

SUGGESTIONS FOR FURTHER READING

Child, Lydia Maria, ed. *The Antislavery Standard* (1841–49), a weekly antislavery newspaper published in New York.

———. *An Appeal in Favor of That Class of Americans Called Africans.* Ed. Carolyn Karcher. Amherst: University of Massachusetts Press, 1997.

———. *Correspondence between Lydia Maria Child and Gov. Wise and Mrs. Mason of Virginia.* 1860.

————. *The Duty of Disobedience to the Fugitive Slave Act: An Appeal to the Legislators of Massachusetts.* Boston: American Anti-Slavery Society, 1860.

————. *The Freedman's Book.* 1865.

————. "Introduction." *Linda: Incidents in the Life of a Slave Girl.* 1861. Edited by Jean Fagan Yellin. Cambridge, Mass.: Harvard University Press, 1987.

————. *Lydia Maria Child: Selected Letters, 1817–1880.* Edited by Milton Meltzer, Patricia G. Holland, and Francine Krasno. Amherst: University of Massachusetts Press, 1982.

————. *The Patriarchal Institution, As Described by Members of Its Own Family.* New York: American Anti-Slavery Society, 1860.

————. *A Romance of the Republic.* Boston: Ticknor and Fields, 1867.

Clifford, Deborah Pickman. *Crusader for Freedom: A Life of Lydia Maria Child.* Boston: Beacon Press, 1992.

Dubois, Ellen Carol. *Feminism and Suffrage: The Emergence of an Independent Women's Movement in America, 1848–1869.* Ithaca, N.Y.: Cornell University Press, 1978.

Ginzberg, Lori. *Women and the Work of Benevolence: Morality, Politics and Class in the Nineteenth-Century United States.* New Haven, Conn.: Yale University Press, 1990.

Karcher, Carolyn L. *The First Woman in the Republic: A Cultural Biography of Lydia Maria Child.* Durham, N.C.: Duke University Press, 1994.

Matthews, Glenna. *The Rise of Public Woman: Woman's Power and Woman's Place in the United States, 1630–1970.* New York: Oxford University Press, 1992.

Mills, Bruce. *Cultural Reformations: Lydia Maria Child and the Literature of Reform.* Athens: University of Georgia Press, 1994.

Osborne, William S. *Lydia Maria Child.* Boston: Twayne, 1980.

Smith-Rosenberg, Carroll. *Disorderly Conduct: Visions of Gender in Victorian America.* New York: Oxford University Press, 1985.

White, Deborah Gray. *Ar'n't I a Woman? Female Slaves in the Plantation South.* New York: W. W. Norton, 1985.

Yellin, Jean Fagan. *Women and Sisters: The Antislavery Feminists in American Culture.* New Haven, Conn.: Yale University Press, 1989.

AN APPEAL IN FAVOR OF THAT CLASS OF
AMERICANS CALLED AFRICANS (1833)

I beseech you not to throw down this volume as soon as you have glanced at the title ...

I am fully aware of the unpopularity of the task I have undertaken; but though I *expect* ridicule and censure, it is not in my nature to *fear* them ...

In almost all great evils there is some redeeming feature—*some* good results, even where it is not intended: pride and vanity, utterly selfish and wrong in themselves, often throw money into the hands of the poor, and thus tend to excite industry and ingenuity, while they produce comfort. But slavery is *all* evil—within and without—root and branch,—bud, blossom and fruit!

In order to show how dark it is in every aspect—how invariably injurious both to nations and individuals,—I will select a few facts from the mass of evidence now before me ...

In the first place, its effects upon *Africa* have been most disastrous ...

There are green and sheltered valleys in Africa,—broad and beautiful rivers,—and vegetation in its loveliest and most magnificent forms.—But no comfortable houses, no thriving farms, no cultivated gardens;—for it is not safe to possess permanent property, where each little state is surrounded by warlike neighbors, continually sending out their armed bands in search of slaves. The white man offers his most tempting articles of merchandise to the negro, as a price for the flesh and blood of his enemy; and if we, with all our boasted knowledge and religion, are seduced by money to do such grievous wrong to those who have never offended us, what can we expect of men just emerging from the limited wants of savage life, too uncivilized to have formed any habits of steady industry, yet earnestly coveting the productions they know not how to earn!

Villages are set on fire, and those who fly from the flames, rush upon the spears of the enemy. Private kidnapping is likewise carried on to a great extent, for he who can catch a neighbor's child is sure to find a ready purchaser; and it sometimes happens that the captor and his living merchandise are both seized by the white slave-trader. Houses are broken open in the night, and defenceless women and children carried away into captivity. If boys, in the unsuspecting innocence of youth, come near the white man's ships, to sell vegetables or fruit, they are ruthlessly seized and carried to slavery in a distant land . . .

In African legislation, almost all crimes are punished with slavery; and thanks to the white man's rapacity, there is always very powerful motive for finding the culprit guilty . . .

When the slave-ships are lying on the coast of Africa, canoes well armed are sent into the inland country, and after a few weeks they return with hundreds of negroes, tied fast with ropes. Sometimes the white men lurk among the bushes, and seize the wretched beings who incautiously venture from their homes; sometimes they paint their skins as black as their hearts, and by this deception suddenly surprise the unsuspecting natives; at other times the victims are decoyed on board the vessel, under some kind pretence or other, and then lashed to the mast, or chained in the hold. Is it not very natural for the Africans to say "devilish white"?

Treachery, fraud and violence desolate the country, rend asunder the dearest relations, and pollute the very fountains of justice. The history of the negro, whether national or domestic, is written in blood . . .

Having thus glanced at the miserable effects of this system on the condition of Africa, we will now follow the poor *slave* through his wretched wanderings, in order to give some idea of his physical suffering, his mental and moral degradation . . .

The following account is given by Dr. Walsh, who accompanied Viscount Strangford, as chaplain, on his embassy to Brazil. The vessel in which he sailed chased a slave ship . . .

Doctor Walsh was an eyewitness of the scene he describes; and the evidence given, at various times, before [the] British House of Commons, proves that the frightful picture is by no means exaggerated . . .

"The vessel had taken in, on the coast of Africa, three hundred and thirty-six males, and two hundred and twenty-six females, making in all five hundred and sixty-two: she had been out seventeen days, during which she had thrown overboard fifty-five. They were all enclosed under grated hatchways, between decks. The space was so low, and they were stowed so close together, that there was no possibility of lying down, or changing their position, night or day. The greater part of them were shut out from light and air; and this when the thermometer, exposed to the open sky, was standing, in the shade on our deck, at eighty-nine degrees . . .

The space between decks was divided into two compartments, three feet three inches high. Two hundred and twenty-six women and girls were thrust into one space two hundred and eighty-eight feet square; and three hundred and thirty-six men and boys were crammed into another space eight hundred feet square; giving the whole an average of twenty-three inches; and to each of the women not more than thirteen inches; though several of them were in a state of health, which peculiarly demanded pity.—As they were shipped on account of different individuals, they were branded like sheep, with the owner's marks of different forms; which, as the mate informed me with perfect indifference, had been burnt in with red-hot iron. Over the hatch way stood a ferocious looking fellow, the slave-driver of the ship, with a scourge of many-twisted thongs in his hand; whenever he heard the slightest noise from below, he shook it over them, and seemed eager to exercise it . . .

The heat of these horrid places was so great, and the odor so offensive, that it was quite impossible to enter them, even had there been room . . .

The officers insisted that the poor, suffering creatures, should be admitted on deck to get air and water. This was opposed by the mate of the slaver . . .

The officers, however, persisted and the poor beings were all turned out together. It is impossible to conceive the effect of this eruption—five hundred and seventeen fellow-creatures, of all ages and sexes, some children, some adults, some old men and women, all entirely destitute of clothing, scrambling out together to taste the luxury of a little fresh air and water. They came swarming up, like bees from a hive, till the whole deck was crowded to suffocation from stem to stern; so that it was impossible to imagine where they could all have come from, or how they could have stowed away . . .

After enjoying for a short time the unusual luxury of air, some water was brought; it was then that the extent of their sufferings was exposed in a fearful manner. They all rushed like maniacs towards it . . .

There is nothing from which slaves in the mid-passage suffer so much as want of water . . .

When the poor creatures were ordered down again, several of them came, and pressed their heads against our knees, with looks of the greatest anguish, with the prospect of returning to the horrid place of suffering below . . .

It was dark when we separated, and the last parting sounds we heard from the unhallowed ship, were the cries and shrieks of the slaves, suffering under some bodily infliction . . ."

Arrived at the place of destination, the condition of the slave is scarcely less deplorable. They are advertised with cattle; chained in droves, and driven to market with a whip; and sold at auction, with the beasts of the field. They are treated like brutes, and all the influences around them conspire to make them brutes . . .

Some are employed as domestic slaves, when and how the owner pleases; by day or by night, on Sunday or other days, in any measure or degree, with any remuneration or with none, with what kind or quantity of food the owner of the human beast may choose. Male or female, young or old, weak or strong, may be punished with or without reason, as caprice or passion may prompt . . .

From the moment the slave is kidnapped, to the last hour he draws his miserable breath, the white man's influence directly cherishes ignorance, fraud, treachery, theft, licentiousness, revenge, hatred, and murder. It cannot be denied that human nature thus operated upon, *must* necessarily yield, more or less, to all these evils.—And thus do we dare to treat beings, who, like ourselves, are heirs of immortality!

And now let us briefly inquire into the influences of slavery on the *white man's* character; for in this evil there is a mighty reaction . . .

The effect produced upon *slave-captains* is absolutely frightful. Those who wish to realize it in all its awful extent, may find abundant information in Clarkson's History of Slavery . . .

Of cruelties on board slave-ships, I will mention but a few instances; though a large volume might be filled with such detestable anecdotes perfectly well authenticated . . .

A child on board a slave-ship, of about ten months old took sulk and would not eat; the captain flogged it with a cat-o'-nine-tails;

swearing that he would make it eat, or kill it. From this, and other ill-treatment, the limbs swelled. He then ordered some water to be made hot to abate the swelling. But even his tender mercies were cruel. The cook, on putting his hand into the water, said it was too hot. Upon this the captain swore at him, and ordered the feet to be put in. This was done. The nails and skin came off. Oiled cloths were then put around them. The child was at length tied to a heavy log. Two or three days afterwards, the captain caught it up again, and repeated that he would make it eat, or kill it. He immediately flogged it again, and in a quarter of an hour it died. And after the babe was dead whom should the barbarian select to throw it over-board, but the wretched mother! In vain she tried to avoid the of-fice. He beat her, till he made her take up the child and carry it to the side of the vessel. She then dropped it into the sea, turning her head the other way, that she might not see it . . .

It may seem incredible to some that human nature is capable of so much depravity. But the confession of pirates show how habitual scenes of blood and violence harden the heart of man; and history abundantly proves that despotic power produces a fearful species of moral insanity . . .

Even in the slaveholding states it is deemed disreputable to asso-ciate with a professed slave-trader, though few perhaps would think it any harm to bargain with him . . .

Some of the advocates of this traffic maintained that the voyage from Africa to the slave-market, called the Middle Passage, was an exceedingly comfortable portion of existence. One went so far as to declare it "the happiest part of a negro's life." They aver that the Africans, on their way to slavery, are so merry, that they dance and sing. But upon a careful examination of witnesses, it was found that their singing consisted of dirge-like lamentations for the native land. After meals they jumped up in their irons for exercise. This was considered so necessary for their health, that they were whipped, if they refused to do it. And this was their dancing . . .

According to Clarkson's estimate, about two and a half of a hun-dred of human beings die annually, in the ordinary course of na-ture, including infants and the aged; but in an African voyage, where few babes and no old people are admitted, so that those shipped are at the firmest period of life, the annual mortality is forty-three in a hundred . . .

We next come to the influence of this diabolical system on the *slave-owner;* and here I shall be cautioned that I am treading on delicate ground, because our own country-men are slaveholders . . .

The following is the testimony of Jefferson, who had good opportunities for observation, and who certainly had no New-England prejudices: "There must, doubtless, be an unhappy influence on the manners of the people, produced by the existence of slavery among us. The whole commerce between master and slave is a perpetual exercise of the most boisterous passions; the most unremitting despotism on the one part, and degrading submission on the others. Our children see this and learn to imitate it; for man is an imitative animal. The parent storms; the child looks on, catches the lineaments of wrath, puts on the same airs in a circle of smaller slaves, gives loose to the worst of passions; and thus nursed, educated, and daily exercised in tyranny, cannot but be stamped by it with odious peculiarities. The man must be a prodigy, who can retain his morals and manners undepraved in such circumstances . . ."

In a community where all the labor is done by one class there must of course be another class who live in indolence; and we all know how much people that have nothing to do are tempted by what the world calls pleasures; the result is, that slaveholding states and colonies are proverbial for dissipation . . .

The following account was originally written by the Rev. William Dickey, of Bloomingsburg, to the Rev. John Rankin of Ripley, Ohio. It was published in 1826, in a little volume of letters, on the subject of slavery, by the Rev. Mr. Rankin, who assures us that Mr. Dickey was well acquainted with the circumstances he describes . . .

"In the country of Livingston, Kentucky, near the mouth of Cumberland river, lived Lilburn Lewis, the son of Jefferson's sister. He was the wealthy owner of a considerable number of slaves, whom he drove constantly, fed sparingly, and lashed severely. The consequence was, they would run away. Among the rest was an ill-grown boy, about seventeen, who having just returned from a skulking spell, was sent to the spring for water, and, in returning, let fall an elegant pitcher, which dashed to shivers on the rocks. It was night, and the slaves were all at home. The master had them collected into the most roomy negro-house, and a rousing fire made." (Reader, what follows is very shocking; but I have already said we must not allow our nerves to be more sensitive than our consciences. If such thing are done in our country, it is important that we should know of them, and seriously reflect upon them.) "The door was fastened, that none of the negroes, either through fear or sympathy, should attempt to escape; he then told them that the design of this meeting was to teach them to remain at home and obey his orders. All things being now in train, George was called up, and by the assistance of his younger brother, laid on a broad bench or block. The master then cut off his ankles with a broad axe. In vain the unhappy victim screamed. Not a hand among so many dared to interfere. Having cast the feet into the fire, he lectured the negroes at some length. He then proceeded to cut off his limbs below the knees. The sufferer besought him to begin with his head. It was in vain—the master went on thus, until trunk, arms, and head, were all in the fire. Still protracting the intervals with lectures, and threatenings of like punishment, in case any of them were disobedient, or ran away, or disclosed the tragedy they were compelled to witness. In order to consume the bones, the fire was briskly stirred until midnight . . .

The negroes were allowed to disperse, with charges to keep the secret, under the penalty of like punishment. When his wife asked the cause of the dreadful screams she had heard, he said that he had never enjoyed himself so well at a ball as he had enjoyed himself that evening . . .

N.B. This happened in 1811; if I be correct, it was on the 16th of December. It was on the Sabbath . . ."

In order to show the true aspect of slavery among us, I will state distinct propositions, each supported by the evidence of actually existing laws.

1. *Slavery is hereditary and perpetual, to the last moment of the slave's earthly existence, and to all his descendants, to the latest posterity.*
2. *The labor of the slave is compulsory and uncompensated; while the kind of labor, the amount of toil, and the time allowed for rest, are dictated solely by the master. No bargain is made, no wages given. A pure despotism governs the human brute; and even his covering and provender, both as to quantity and quality, depend entirely on the master's discretion.*
3. *The slave being considered a personal chattel, may be sold, or pledged, or leased, at the will of the master. He may be exchanged for marketable commodities, or taken in execution for the debts, or*

taxes, either of a living, or a deceased master. Sold at auction, "either individually, or in lots to suit the purchaser," he may remain with his family, or be separated from them for ever.

4. *Slaves can make no contracts, and have no legal right or any property, real or personal. Their own honest earnings, and the legacies of friends belong, in point of law, to their masters.*

5. *Neither a slave, nor free colored person, can be a witness against any white or free man, in a court of justice, however atrocious may have been the crimes they have seen him commit: but they may give testimony against a fellow-slave, or free colored man, even in cases affecting life.*

6. *The slave may be punished at his master's discretion—without trial—without any means of legal redress,—whether his offense be real, or imaginary: and the master can transfer the same despotic power to any person, or persons, he may choose to appoint.*

7. *The slave is not allowed to resist any free man under any circumstances: his only safety consists in the fact that his owner may bring suit, and recover, the price of his body, in case his life is taken, or his limbs rendered unfit for labor.*

8. *Slaves cannot redeem themselves, or obtain a change of masters, though cruel treatment may have rendered such a change necessary for their personal safety.*

9. *The slave is entirely unprotected in his domestic relations.*

10. *The laws greatly obstruct the manumission of slaves, even where the master is willing to enfranchise them.*

11. *The operation of the laws tends to deprive slaves of religious instruction and consolation.*

12. *The whole power of the laws is exerted to keep slaves in a state of the lowest ignorance.*

13. *There is in this country a monstrous inequality of law and right. What is a trifling fault in the white man, is considered highly criminal in the slave; the same offences which cost a white man a few dollars only, are punished in the negro with death.*

14. *The laws operate most oppressively upon free people of color.*

PROPOSITION 1.
—Slavery hereditary and perpetual.

In Maryland the following act was passed in 1715, and is still in force: "all negroes and other slaves, already imported, or hereafter to be imported into this province, and all children now born, or hereafter to be born, of such negroes and slaves, shall be slaves during their natural lives . . ."

PROPOSITION 3.—*Slaves considered personal chattels, liable to be sold, pledged, &c.*

The advertisements in the Southern papers furnish a continued proof of this; it is, therefore, unnecessary to go into the details of evidence. The power to separate mothers and children, husbands and wives, is exercised only in the British West Indies, and the *republic* of the United States!

PROP. 4.—*Slaves can have no legal claim to any property.*

The civil code of Louisiana declares: *all that a slave possesses belongs to his master*—he possesses nothing of his own, except his peculium, that is to say, the sum of money or moveable estate, which *his master chooses he should possess.*"—"Slaves are incapable of inheriting or transmitting property."—"Slaves cannot dispose of, or receive, by donation, unless they have been enfranchised conformably to law, or are expressly enfranchised by the act, by which the donation is made to them . . ."

In South Carolina "it is not lawful for any slave to buy, sell, trade, &c., without a license from his owner; nor shall any slave be allowed to keep any boat or canoe, for his own . . ."

In Georgia, a fine of thirty dollars a week is imposed upon any master who allows his slave to hire himself out, he is subject to a fine, from ten to twenty dollars; and it is lawful for any person, and the *duty* of the Sheriff, to apprehend the slave. In Maryland, the master, by a similar offence, except during twenty days at harvest time, incurs a penalty of twenty dollars per month . . .

In Mississippi, if a master allow his slave to cultivate cotton for his own use, he incurs a fine of fifty dollars; and if he license his slave to trade on his own account, he forfeits fifty dollars for each and every offence. Any person trading with a slave forfeits four times the value of the article purchased; and if unable to pay, he receives thirty-nine lashes, and pays the cost . . .

PROP. 5.—*No colored man can be evidence against a white man, &c.*

The master is merely obliged to take the precaution not to starve, or mangle, or murder his negroes, *in the presence of a white man.* No matter if five hundred colored people be present, they cannot testify to the fact . . .

The *Code Noir* merely allowed a slave's testimony to be heard by the judge, as a suggestion which might throw light on other evidence, without amounting of itself to any degree of legal proof . . .

PROP. 6.—*The master has absolute power to punish a slave, &c.*

The revised code of Louisiana declares: "The slave is entirely subject to the will of the master, who may correct and chastise him, though not with *unusual* rigor, nor so as to main or mutilate him, or to expose him to the danger of loss of life, or to cause his death." Who shall decide what punishment is *unusual* . . .

PROP. 7.—*The slave never allowed to resist a white man.*

It is enacted in Georgia, "If any slave shall presume to strike *any* white man, such slave, upon trial and conviction before the justice, shall for the *first* offence, suffer such punishment as the said justice thinks fit, not extending to life or limb; and for the second offence, *death.*" It is the same in South Carolina, excepting that death is there the punishment of the *third* offence . . .

PROP. 8.—*Slaves cannot redeem themselves or change masters.*

Stroud says, "as to the right of *redemption*, this proposition holds good in all the slaveholding States; and is equally true as it respects the right to compel a *change of master*, except in Louisiana. According to the new civil code of that State, the latter privilege may sometimes, perhaps, be obtained by the slave. But the master must first be *convicted* of cruelty—a task so formidable that it can hardly be ranked among possibilities . . ."

PROP. 9.—*Slave unprotected in his domestic relations.*

In proof of this, it is only necessary to repeat that the slave and his wife, and his daughters, are considered as the *property* of their owners, and compelled to yield implicit obedience—that he is allowed to give no evidence—that he must not resist *any* white man, under *any* circumstances which do not interfere with his *master's* interest . . .

PROP. 10.—*The laws obstruct emancipation.*

In nearly all slaveholding States, a slave emancipated by his master's will, may be seized and sold to satisfy *any debt*.

In Kentucky, Missouri, Virginia, and Maryland, greater facilities are afforded to emancipation. An instrument in writing, signed by two witnesses, or acknowledged by the owner of the slave in open court, is sufficient; the owner reserving the power to demand security for the maintenance of aged or infirm slaves. By the Virginia laws, an emancipated negro, more than twenty-one years old, is liable to be again reduced to slavery, if he remain in the State more than twelve months after his manumission . . .

PROP. 12.—*Whole power of the laws exerted to keep negroes in ignorance.*

The city of Savannah, in Georgia, a few years ago, passed an ordinance, by which "any person that teaches a person of color, slave or free, to read or write, or causes such persons to be so taught, is subjected to a fine of thirty dollars for each offence; and every person of color who shall teach reading or writing, is subject to a fine of thirty dollars or to be imprisoned ten days and whipped thirty-nine lashes . . ."

PROP. 13.—*There is a monstrous inequality of law and right.*

More than seven slaves walking or standing together in the road, without a white man, may receive twenty lashes each from any person . . .

PROP. 14.—*The laws operate oppressively on free colored people.*

Free people of color, like the slaves, are excluded by law from all means of obtaining the common elements of education . . .

A New-York paper, November, 1829, contains the following caution:

"*Beware of kidnappers!*—It is *well understood* that there is at present in this city, a gang of kidnappers, busily engaged in their vocation of stealing colored children for the Southern market! It is believed that three or four have been stolen within as many days . . ."

Chapter VII.

Moral Character of Negroes

The opinion that negroes are naturally inferior in intellect is almost universal among white men; but the belief that they are worse than other people, is, I believe, much less extensive: indeed, I have heard some, who were by no means admirers of the colored race, maintain that they were very remarkable for kind feelings, and strong affections. Homer calls the ancient Ethiopians "the most honest of men;" and modern travellers have given innumerable instances of domestic tenderness, and generous hospitality in the interior of Africa . . .

Chapter VIII.

Prejudices Against People of Color, and Our Duties in Relation to this Subject

There is another Massachusetts law, which an enlightened community would not probably suffer to be carried into execution under any circumstances; but it still remains to disgrace the statutes of this Commonwealth. It is as follows:

"No African or Negro, other than a subject of the Emperor of Morocco, or a citizen of the United States, (proved so by a certificate of the Secretary of the State of which he is a citizen,) shall tarry within this Commonwealth longer than two months; and on complaint a justice shall order him to depart in ten days; and if he do not then, the justice may commit such African or Negro to the House of Correction, there to be kept at hard labor; and at the next term of the Court of Common Pleas, he shall be tried, and if convicted of remaining as aforsesaid, shall be whipped not exceeding ten lashes; and if he or she shall not *then* depart, such process shall be repeated, and punishment inflicted, *toties quoties*." Stat. 1788, Ch. 54 . . .

The state of public feeling not only makes it difficult for the Africans to obtain information, but it prevents them from making profitable use of what knowledge they have. A colored man, however intelligent, is not allowed to pursue any business more lucrative than that of a barber, a shoe-black, or a waiter . . .

Every citizen ought to have a fair chance to try his fortune in any line of business, which he thinks he has ability to transact. Why should not colored men be employed in the manufactories of various kinds? If their ignorance is an objection, let them be enlightened, as speedily as possible. If their moral character is not sufficiently pure, remove the pressure of public scorn, and thus supply them with motives for being respectable. All this can be done. It merely requires an earnest wish to overcome a prejudice, which has "grown with our growth and strengthened with our strength," but which is in fact opposed to the spirit of our religion, and contrary to the instinctive good feelings of our nature . . .

It has been shown that no other people on earth indulge so strong a prejudice with regard to color, as we do. It is urged that negroes are civilly treated in England, because their numbers are so few. I could never discover any great force in this argument. Colored people are certainly not sufficiently rare in that country to be regarded as a great show, like a giraffe . . .

Mr. Garrison was the first person who dared to edit a newspaper, in which slavery was spoken of as altogether wicked and inexcusable. For this crime the Legislature of Georgia have offered five thousand dollars to any one who will "arrest and prosecute him to conviction *under the laws of that State.*" An association of gentlemen in South Carolina have likewise offered a large reward for the same object. It is, to say the least, a very remarkable step for one State in this Union to promulgate such a law concerning a citizen of another State, merely for publishing his opinions boldly . . .

Mr. Garrison is a disinterested, intelligent, and remarkably pure-minded man, whose only fault is that he cannot be moderate on a subject which it is exceedingly difficult for an honest mind to examine with calmness. Many who highly respect his character and motives, regret his tendency to use wholesale and unqualified expressions; but it is something to have the truth told, even if it be not in the mildest way. Where an evil is powerfully supported by the self-interest and prejudice of the community, none but an ardent individual will venture to meddle with it. Luther was deemed indiscreet even by those who liked him best . . .

Our books, our reviews, our newspapers, our almanacs, have all been silent, or exerted their influence on the wrong side. The negro's crimes are repeated, but his sufferings are never told. Even in our geographies it is taught that the colored race *must* always be degraded. Now and then anecdotes of cruelties committed in the slaveholding States are told by individuals who witnessed them; but they are almost always afraid to give their names to the public, because the Southerners will call them "a disgrace to the soil," and the Northerners will echo the sentiment . . .

We are told that the Southerners will of themselves do away with slavery, and they alone understand how to do it. But it is an obvious fact that all their measures have tended to perpetuate the system; and even if we have the fullest faith that they mean to do their duty, the belief by no means absolves us from doing ours. The evil is gigantic; and its removal requires every heart and head in the community . . .

I know a lady in Georgia who would, I believe, make any personal sacrifice to instruct her slaves, and give them freedom; but if she were found guilty of teaching the alphabet, or manumitting her slaves, fines and imprisonment would be the consequence; if she sold them, they would be likely to fall into hands less merciful than her own. Of such slave-owners we cannot speak with too much respect and tenderness. They are comparatively few in number, and stand in a most perplexing situation; it is a duty to give all our sympathy to *them*. It is mere mockery to say, what is so often said, that the Southerners as a body, really wish to abolish slavery. If they wished it, they certainly would make the attempt . . .

The strongest and best reason that can be given for our supineness on the subject of slavery, is the fear of dissolving the Union. The Constitution of the United States demands our highest reverence. Those who approve, and those who disapprove of particular portions, are equally bound to yield implicit obedience to its authority. But we must not forget that the Constitution provides for any change that may be required for the general good. The great machine is constructed with a safety-valve, by which any rapidly increasing evil may be expelled whenever the people desire it . . .

Under all circumstances, there is but one honest course; and that is to do right, and trust the consequences to Divine Providence. "Duties are ours; events are God's." Policy, with all her cunning can devise no rule so safe, salutary, and effective, as this simple maxim . . .

We cannot too cautiously examine arguments and excuses brought forward by those whose interest or convenience is connected with keeping their fellow creatures in a state of ignorance and brutality; and such we shall find in abundance, at the North as well as the South. I have heard the abolition of slavery condemned on the ground that New England vessels would not be employed to export the produce of the South, if they had free laborers of their own . . .

To "love our neighbor as ourselves," is, after all, the shrewdest way of doing business . . .

If we are not able to contribute to African schools, or do not choose to do so, we can least refrain from opposing them. If it be disagreeable to allow colored people the same rights and privileges as other citizens, we can do with our prejudice, what most of us often do with better feeling—we can conceal it . . .

Sixty thousand petitions have been addressed to the English parliament on the subject of slavery, and a large number of them were signed by women. The same steps here would be, with one exception, useless and injudicious; because the general government has not control over the legislatures of individual States. But the District of Columbia forms an exception to this rule. *There* the United States have power to abolish slavery; and it is the duty of the citizens to petition year after year, until a reformation is effected . . .

SOURCE NOTE: Lydia Maria Child, *An Appeal in Favor of That Class of Americans Called Africans* (1833), edited and with an introduction by Carolyn Karcher (Amherst: University of Massachusetts Press, 1996), by permission of Bruce Wilcox, Director.

William Ellery Channing (1780–1842)

William Ellery Channing was born in Newport, Rhode Island, on April 7, 1780. He died in Bennington, Vermont, on October 2, 1842. His career was vigorous and varied, including writings on the state of our national literary scene, *Remarks on a National Literature* (1830), numerous books of collected sermons, and three works on the slavery issue: *Slavery* (1835); *The Abolitionist* (1836); and *The Duty of the Free States* (1842). In 1803, he was made pastor of the Federal Street Congregational Church in Boston, which he turned into one of the most powerful pulpits of antebellum New England, just as the Episcopal minister Phillips Brooks would dominate the second half of the nineteenth century from another Boston pulpit, Trinity Church in Copley Square. Channing was the last great voice of the first wave of abolitionist thinkers, those who opposed slavery in principle but who were not committed to the Garrisonian ideal of immediate, unconditional, and total emancipation of the slaves. Also called "gradualists," the early abolitionists sought the emancipation of slaves through attrition, death, and colonization. Channing was regarded to be a theological liberal, and he became a New England leader of the Unitarian movement, the persuasion that deeply influenced Ralph Waldo Emerson, the Harvard literature professor Henry Wadsworth Longfellow, and the Supreme Court justice Oliver Wendell Holmes. His participation in the antislavery movement was largely effected through his writings, particularly the three books; and the excerpts here, taken from his 1835 work *Slavery,* show the clarity of his thinking and the power of his rhetoric. Like many abolitionists, Channing relied less on Scripture precedent for proof and more on the moral power of his argument, his appeal to feeling, intellect, and reason. Channing was a compromiser, a conciliatory thinker, and his position on the slavery issue was also one of compromise. Channing urged Northerners to extend a peace offering to the South, showing that their slavery was "your calamity, not your crime, and we will share with you the burden of putting an end to it." This reasoning was not to survive in the climate of militant abolitionism, led by William Lloyd Garrison and Wendell Phillips, who called for an immediate and unconditional end to slavery in the South.

SLAVERY (1835)

The first question to be proposed by a rational being is, not what is profitable, but what is Right. Duty must be primary, prominent, most conspicuous, among the objects of human thought and pursuit. If we cast it down from its supremacy, if we inquire first for our interests and then for our duties, we shall certainly err. We can never see the Right clearly and fully, but by making it our first concern. No judgment can be just or wise, but that which is built on the conviction of the paramount worth and importance of Duty. This is the fundamental truth, the supreme law of reason; and the mind, which does not start from this in its inquiries into human affairs, is doomed to great, perhaps fatal error.

The Right is the supreme good, and includes all other goods. In seeking and adhering to it, we secure our true and only happiness. All prosperity, not founded on it, is built on sand. If human affairs are controlled, as we believe, by Almighty Rectitude and Impartial Goodness, then to hope for happiness from wrong doing is as insane as to seek health and prosperity by rebelling against the laws of nature, by sowing our seed on the ocean, or making poison our common food. There is but one unfailing good; and that is fidelity to the Everlasting Law written on the heart, and rewritten and republished in God's Word.

Whoever places this faith in the everlasting law of rectitude must of course regard the question of slavery first and chiefly as a moral question . . .

The following remarks, therefore, are designed to aid the reader in forming a just moral judgment of slavery. Great truths, inalienable rights, everlasting duties, these will form the chief subjects of this discussion.

Of late our country has been convulsed by the question of slavery.

The consequence is, that not a few dread all discussion of the subject, and if not reconciled to the continuance of slavery, at least believe that they have no duty to perform, no testimony to bear, no influence to exert, no sentiments to cherish and spread, in relation to this evil.

There was never such an obligation to discuss slavery as at this moment, when recent events have done much to unsettle and obscure men's minds in regard to it.

Slavery ought to be discussed. We ought to think, feel, and write about it.

Slavery, indeed, from its very nature must be a ground of alarm wherever it exists. Slavery and security can by no device be joined together. But we may not, must not, by rashness and passion increase the peril. To instigate the slave to insurrection is a crime for which no rebuke and no punishment can be too severe. This would be to involve slave and master in common ruin. It is not enough to say, that the Constitution is violated by any action endangering the slave-holding portion of our country. A higher law than the Constitution forbids this unholy interference.

As men, as Christians, as citizens, we have duties to the slave, as well as to every other member of the community. On this point we have no liberty. The Eternal Law binds us to take the side of the injured; and this law is peculiarly obligatory, when we forbid him to lift an arm in his own defence.

This must triumph. It is leagued with God's omnipotence.

Slavery cannot stand before it. Great moral principles, pure and generous sentiments, cannot be confined to this or that spot.

They are divine inspirations, and partake of the omnipresence of their Author.

To increase this moral power is every man's duty. To embody and express this great truth is in every man's power; and thus every man can do something to break the chain of the slave.

The great teaching of Christianity is, that we must recognise and respect human nature in all its forms, in the poorest, most ignorant, most fallen. We must look beneath "the flesh," to "the spirit." The spiritual principle in man is what entitles him to our brotherly regard. To be just to this is the great injunction of our religion. To overlook this, on account of condition or color, is to violate the great Christian law.

To recognise our own spiritual nature and God's image in these humble forms; to recognise as brethren those who want all outward distinctions, is the chief way in which we are to manifest the spirit of Him, who came to raise the fallen and to save the lost.

He who cannot see a brother, a child of God, a man possessing all the rights of humanity under a skin darker than his own, wants the vision of a Christian . . .

These remarks are intended to show the spirit in which slavery ought to be approached, and the point of view from which it will be regarded in the present discussion.

1. I shall show that man cannot be justly held and used as Property.
2. I shall show that man has sacred and infallible rights, of which slavery is the infraction.
3. I shall offer some explanations to prevent misapplication of these principles.
4. I shall unfold the evils of slavery.
5. I shall consider the argument which the Scriptures are thought to furnish in favor of slavery.
6. I shall offer some remarks on the means of removing it.
7. I shall offer some remarks on abolitionism.
8. I shall conclude with a few reflections on the duties belonging to the times. In the first two sections I propose to show that slavery is a great wrong, but I do not intend to pass sentence on the character of the slave-holder. These two subjects are distinct. Men are not always to be interpreted by their acts or institutions. The same acts in different circumstances admit and even require very different constructions. I offer this remark, that the subject may be approached without prejudice or personal reference. The single object is to settle great principles. Their bearing on individuals will be a subject of distinct consideration . . .

Property

The slave-holder claims the slaves as his Property. The very idea of a slave is, that he belongs to another, that he is bound to live and labor for another, to be another's instrument, and to make another's will his habitual law, however adverse to his own.

A right, in a word, to use him as a tool, without contract, against will, and in denial of his right to dispose of himself or to use his power for his own good. "A slave," says the Louisiana Code, "is in the power of the master to whom he belongs."

Now this claim of property in a human being is altogether false, groundless. No such right of man in man can exist. A human being cannot be justly owned. To hold and treat him as property is to inflict a great wrong, to incur the guilt of oppression.

This position there is a difficulty in maintaining on account of its exceeding obviousness. It is too plain for proof. To defend it is like trying to confirm a self-evident truth.

The man, who, on hearing the claim to property in man, does not see and feel distinctly that it is a cruel usurpation, is hardly to be reached by reasoning, for it is hard to find any plainer principles than what he begins with denying.

As men we cannot justly be made slaves. Then no man can be rightfully enslaved . . .

A man cannot be seized and held as property, because he has Rights. This truth has never, I believe, been disputed. It is even recognised in the very codes of slave-legislation, which, while they strip a man of liberty, affirm his right to life, and threaten his murderer with punishment. Now, I say a being having rights cannot justly be made property; for this claim over him virtually annuls all his rights. It strips him of all power to assert them.

Another argument against property is to be found in the Essential Equality of men. I know that this doctrine, so venerable in the eyes of our fathers, has lately been denied. Verbal logicians have told us that men are "born equal," only in the sense of being equally born. They have asked whether all are equally born. They have asked whether all are equally tall, strong, or beautiful; or whether nature, Procrustes-like, reduces all her children to one standard of intellect and virtue.

Be it also remembered, that these diversities among men are as nothing in comparison with the attributes in which they agree, and it is this which constitutes their essential equality. All men have the same rational nature, and the same power of conscience, and all are equally made for indefinite improvement of these divine faculties, and for the happiness to be found in their virtuous use.

That a human being cannot be justly held and used as property is apparent from the very nature of property. Property is an exclusive, single right. It shuts out all claim but that of the possessor. What one man owns cannot belong to another.

Our laws know no higher crime than that of reducing a man to slavery. To steal or to buy an African on his own shore is piracy. In this act the greatest wrong is inflicted, the most sacred right violated. But if a human being cannot without infinite injustice be seized as property, then he cannot without equal wrong be held and used as such.

He cannot be property in the sight of God and justice, because he is a Rational, Moral, Immortal Being; because created in God's image, and therefore in the highest sense his child; because created to unfold Godlike faculties, and to govern himself by a Divine law written on his heart, and republished in God's Word. His whole nature forbids that he should be seized as property.

Such a being was plainly made for an End in Himself. He is a person, not a Thing. He is an End, not a mere Instrument or Means.

We have thus seen that a human being cannot rightfully be held and used as property. No legislation, not that of all countries or worlds, could make him so. Let this be laid down, as a first, fundamental truth. Let us hold it fast, as a most sacred, precious truth. Let us hold it fast against all customs, all laws, all rank, wealth, and power. Let it be armed with the whole authority of the civilized and Christian world.

What! is human legislation the measure of right? Are God's laws to be repealed by man's? Can government do no wrong? What is the history of human governments but a record of wrongs? How much does the progress of civilization consist in the substitution of just and humane, for barbarous and oppressive laws? Government, indeed, has ordained slavery, and to government the individual is in no case to offer resistance . . .

Rights

Man has rights by nature. The disposition of some to deride abstract rights, as if all rights were uncertain, mutable, and conceded by society, shows a lamentable ignorance of human nature. Whoever understands this must see in it an immovable foundation of rights. These are gifts of the Creator, not grants of society. In the order of things, they precede society, lie at its foundation, constitute man's capacity for it, and are the great objects of social institutions. The consciousness of rights is not a creation of human art, a conventional sentiment, but essential to and inseparable from the human soul.

Man's rights belong to him as a Moral Being, as capable of perceiving moral distinctions, as a subject of moral obligation.

It is said that in forming civil society the individual surrenders a part of his rights. It would be more proper to say that he adopts new modes of securing them . . .

How absurd is it to suppose, that by consenting to be protected by the state, and by yielding it the means, he surrenders the very rights which were the objects of his accession to the social compact!

In all ages the Individual has in one form or another been trodden in the dust. In monarchies and aristocracies he has been sacrificed to One or to the Few; who, regarding government as an heirloom in their families, and thinking of the people as made only to live and die for their glory, have not dreamed that the sovereign power was designed to shield every man, without exception, from wrong.

Let not the sacredness of individual man be forgotten in the feverish pursuit of property. It is more important that the Individual should respect himself, and be respected by others, than that the wealth of both worlds should be accumulated on our shores. National wealth is not the end of society. It may exist where large classes are depressed and wronged. It may undermine a nation's Spirit, institutions, and independence . . .

Slavery strips man of the fundamental right to inquire into, consult, and seek his own happiness. His powers belong to another, and for another they must be used. He must form no plans, engage in no enterprises, for bettering his condition. Whatever be his capacities, however equal to great improvements of his lot, he is chained for life by another's will to the same unvaried toil. He is forbidden to do for himself or others the work, for which God stamped him with his own best gifts.—Again, the slave is stripped of the right to acquire property. Being himself owned, his earnings belong to another. He can possess nothing but by favor.

Again, the slave is stripped of his right to his wife and children. They belong to another, and may be torn from him, one and all, at any moment, at his master's pleasure.—Again, the slave is stripped of the right to the culture of his rational powers. He is in some cases deprived by law of instruction, which is placed within his reach by the improvements of society and the philanthropy of the age. He is not allowed to toil, that his children may enjoy a better education than himself. The most sacred right of human nature, that of developing his best faculties, is denied.

He is subjected to the lash, by those whom he has never consented to serve, and whose claim to him as property we have seen to be a usurpation.

I will add but one more example of the violation of human rights by slavery. The slave virtually suffers the wrong of robbery, though with utter unconsciousness on the part of those who inflict it.

But it is not true that he owns nothing. Whatever he may be denied by man, he holds from nature the most valuable property, and that from which all other is derived, I mean his strength. His labour is his own, by the gift of that God who nerved his arm, and gave him intelligence and conscience to direct the use of it for his own and others' happiness. No possession is so precious as a man's force of body and mind.

The worth of articles of traffic is measured by the labor expended in their production.

To take by force a man's whole estate, the fruit of years of toil, would by universal consent be denounced as a great wrong; but what is this, compared with seizing the man himself, strength, and labor, by which all property is won and held fast? The right of property in outward things is as nothing, compared with the right to ourselves . . .

The Evils of Slavery

The first rank among the evils of slavery must be given to its Moral influence. This is throughout debasing.

The slave regarded and treated as property, bought and sold like a brute, denied the rights of humanity, unprotected against insult, made a tool, and systematically subdued, that he may be a manageable, useful tool, how can he help regarding himself as fallen below his race? How must his spirit be crushed! How can he respect himself? He becomes bound to Servility . . .

I proceed to consider its Intellectual influence, another great topic. God gave us intellectual power, that it should be cultivated; and a system which degrades it, and can only be upheld by its depression, opposes one of his most benevolent designs. Reason is

God's image in man, and the capacity of acquiring truth is among his best inspirations. To call forth the intellect is a principal purpose of the circumstances in which we are placed, of the child's connexion with the parent, and of the necessity laid on him in maturer life to provide for himself and others. The education of the intellect is not confined to youth; but the various experience of later years does vastly more than books and colleges to ripen and invigorate the faculties.

Now, the whole lot of the slave is fitted to keep his mind in childhood and bondage.

Should his eye chance to fall on "the Declaration of Independence," how would the truth glare on him, "that all men are born free and equal"! All knowledge furnishes arguments against slavery. From every subject light would break forth to reveal his inalienable and outraged rights . . .

I proceed, now, to the Domestic influences of slavery; and here we must look for a dark picture. Slavery virtually dissolves the domestic relations. It ruptures the most sacred ties on earth. It violates home. It lacerates the best affections. The domestic relations precede, and, in our present existence, are worth more than all our other social ties.

The most precious burden with which the heart can be charged, the happiness of the child, he must not bear. He lives not for his family, but for a stranger. He cannot improve their lot. His wife and daughter he cannot shield from insult. They may be torn from him at another's pleasure, sold as beasts of burden, sent he knows not whither, sent where he cannot reach them, or even interchange inquiries and messages of love. To the slave marriage has no sanctity. It may be dissolved in a moment at another's will. His wife, son, and daughter may be lashed before his eyes, and not a finger must be lifted in their defence. He sees the scar of the lash on his wife and child. Thus the slave's home is desecrated. Thus the tenderest relations, intended by God equally for all, and intended to be the chief springs of happiness and virtue, are sported with wantonly and cruelly.

And let it not be said that the slave has not the sensibilities of other men. Nature is too strong even for slavery to conquer. Even the brute has the yearnings of parental love . . .

Slavery produces and gives license to Cruelty. By this it is not meant that cruelty is the universal, habitual, unfailing result.

Slavery in this country differs widely from that of ancient times, and from which the Spaniards imposed on the aboriginals of South America. There is here an increasing disposition to multiply the comforts of the slaves, and in this let us rejoice. At the same time, we must remember, that, under the light of the present day, and in a country where Christianity and the rights of men are understood, a diminished severity may contain more guilt than the ferocity of darker ages . . .

Slavery, above all other influences, nourishes the passion for power and its kindred vices. There is no passion which needs a stronger curb. Men's worst crimes have sprung from the desire of being masters, of bending others to their yoke. And the natural tendency of bringing others into subjection to our absolute will is to quicken into fearful activity the imperious, haughty, proud, self-seeking propensities of our nature. Man cannot, without imminent peril to his virtue, own a fellow-creature, or use the word of absolute command to his brethren. God never delegated this power.

The slaveholder, indeed, values himself on his loftiness of spirit.

I approach a more delicate subject, and one on which I shall not enlarge. To own the persons of others, to hold females in slavery, is necessarily fatal to the purity of a people. That unprotected females, stripped by their degraded condition of woman's self-respect, should be used to minister to other passions in men than the love of gain, is next to inevitable. Accordingly, in such a community the reins are given to youthful licentiousness. Youth, every where in perils, is in these circumstances urged to vice with a terrible power. And the evil cannot stop at youth. Early licentiousness is fruitful of crime in mature life. How far the obligation to conjugal fidelity, the sacredness of domestic ties, will be revered amidst such habits, such temptations, such facilities to vice, as are involved in slavery, needs no exposition.

A slave-country reeks with licentiousness. It is tainted with a deadlier pestilence than the plague.

But the worst is not told. As a consequence of criminal connexions, many a master has children born into slavery.

Our slave-holding brethren, who tell us that the condition of the slave is better than that of the free laborer at the North, talk igno- rantly and rashly. They do not, cannot know, what to us is a matter of daily observation, that from the families of our farmers and me- chanics have sprung our most distinguished men, men who have done most for science, arts, letters, religion, and freedom; and that the noblest spirits among us would have been lost to their country and mankind, had the laboring class here been doomed to slavery.

It is said, however, that the slave, if he not be compared to the free laborer at the North, is in a happier condition than the Irish peasantry. Let this be granted. Let the security of the peasant's do- mestic relations, let his church, and his schoolhouse, and his faint hope of a better lot pass for nothing.

But still we are told the slave is gay. He is not as wretched as our theories teach. After his toil, he sings, he dances, he gives no signs of an exhausted frame or gloomy spirit. The slave happy! Why, then, contend for Rights?

The slave happy! Then happiness is to be found in giving up the distinctive attributes of a man; in darkening intellect and con- science; in quenching generous sentiments; in servility of spirit; in living under a whip; in having neither property nor rights; in hold- ing wife and child at another's pleasure; in toiling without hope; in living without an end!

That there are those among the free, who are more wretched than slaves, is undoubtedly true; just as there is incomparably greater misery among men than among brutes. The brute never knew the agony of a human spirit torn by remorse or wounded in its love.

But the slave, we are told, is taught Religion. This is the most cheering sound which comes to us from the land of bondage. We are rejoiced to learn that any portion of the slaves are instructed in that truth, which gives inward freedom.

Religion, though a great good, can hardly exert its full power on the slave. Will it not be taught to make him obedient to his master rather than to raise him to the dignity of a man? Is slavery, which tends so proverbially to debase the mind, the preparation for spiri- tual truth? Can the slave comprehend the principle of Love, the es- sential principle of Christianity, when he hears it from the lips of those whose relations to him express injustice and selfishness?

Scripture

Attempts are often made to support slavery by the authori[ty of] Revelation. "Slavery," it is said, "is allowed in the Old Testan[ent,] and not condemned in the New. Paul commands slaves to obey. [Paul] commands masters, not to release their slaves, but to treat th[em] justly. Therefore slavery is right, is sanctioned by God's Word."

This reasoning proves too much. If usages sanctioned in the Ol[d] Testament and not forbidden in the New are right, then our mora[l] code will undergo a sad deterioration. Polygamy was allowed to the Israelites, was the practice of the holiest men, and was common and licensed in the age of the Apostles. But the Apostles no where condemn it, nor was the renunciation of it made an essential condition of admission into the Christian church. Why may not Scripture be used to stock our houses with wives as well as with slaves?

What was slavery in the age of Paul? It was the slavery, not so much of black as of white men, not merely of barbarians but of Greeks, not merely of the ignorant and debased, but of the virtuous, educated, and refined. Piracy and conquest were the chief means of supplying the slave-market, and they heeded neither character nor condition. Sometimes the greater part of the population of a captured city was sold into bondage, sometimes the whole, as in the case of Jerusalem. Noble and royal families, the rich and great, the learned and powerful, the philosopher and poet, the wisest and best men, were condemned to the chain. Such was ancient slavery. And this we are told is allowed and confirmed by the Word of God!

Slavery, in the age of the Apostle, had so penetrated society, was so intimately interwoven with it, and the materials of servile war were so abundant, that a religion, preaching freedom to its foundation, would have armed against itself the whole power of the State. Of consequence Paul did not assail it. He satisfied himself with spreading principles, which, however slowly, could not but work its destruction. He commanded Philemon to receive his fugitive slave, Onesimus, "not as a slave, but above a slave, as a brother beloved;" and he commanded masters to give to their slaves that which was "*just* and *equal*;" thus asserting for the slave the rights of a Christian and a Man; and how, in his circumstances, he could have done more for the subversion of slavery, I do not see.

of Scripture to the support of slavery is singu-
in this country. Paul not only commanded slaves
masters. He delivered these precepts: "Let every
ct unto higher powers. For there is no power but of
owers that be are ordained of God. Whosoever, there-
teth the power, resisteth the ordinance of God; and they
st shall receive to themselves damnation." This passage
ritten in the time of Nero. It teaches passive obedience to
otism more strongly than any text teaches the lawfulness of
very.

The very course, which the Gospel takes on this subject, seems
to have been the only one that could have been taken in order to effect the universal abolition of slavery. The gospel was designed, not
for one race or for one time, but for all men and for all times. It
looked not at the abolition of this form of evil for that age alone,
but for its universal abolition . . .

Means of Removing Slavery

In this country no power but that of the slaveholding States can remove the evil, and none of us are anxious to take the office from
their hands. They alone can determine and apply the true and sure
means of emancipation.

What, then, is to be done for the removal of slavery? In the first
place, the slaveholders should solemnly disclaim the right of property in human beings. The great principle, that man cannot belong
to man, should be distinctly, solemnly recognised. The slave should
be acknowledged as a partaker of a common nature, as having the
essential rights of humanity. This great truth lies at the foundation
of every wise plan for his relief.

There is, indeed, a grandeur in the idea of raising more than two
millions of human beings to the enjoyment of human rights, to the
blessings of Christian Civilization, to the means of indefinite improvement.

The slave cannot rightfully and should not be owned by the Individual. But, like every other citizen, he belongs to the Community, he is subject to the community, and the community has a right
and is bound to continue all such restraints, as its own safety and
the well-being of the slave demand. It would be cruelty, not kind-

ness, to the latter to give him a freedom, which he is unprepared to understand or enjoy. It would be cruelty to strike the fetters from a man, whose first steps would infallibly lead him to a precipice. The slave should not have an owner, but he should have a guardian. He needs authority, to supply the lack of that discretion which he has not yet attained; but it should be the authority of a friend; an official authority, conferred by the state, and for which there should be responsibleness to the state, an authority especially designed to prepare its subjects for personal freedom. The slave should not, in the first instance, be allowed to wander at his will beyond the plantation on which he toils; and if he cannot be induced to work by rational and natural motives, he should be obliged to labor; on the same principles on which the vagrant in other communities is confined and compelled to earn his bread.

There is but one weighty argument against immediate emancipation, mainly, that the slave would not support himself and his children by honest industry; that, having always worked on compulsion, he will not work without it; that having always labored from another's will, he will not labor from his own; that there is no spring of exertion in his own mind; that he is unused to forethought, providence in self-denial, and the responsibilities of domestic life; that freedom would produce idleness; idleness, want; want, crime; and that crime, when it should become the habit of numbers, would bring misery, perhaps ruin, not only on the offenders, but the state.

The great step, then, towards the removal of slavery is to prepare the slaves for self support. The colored man is not a savage, to whom toil is torture, who has centred every idea of happiness and dignity in a wild freedom, who must exchange the boundless forests for a narrow plantation, and bend his proud neck for an unknown yoke. Labor was his first lesson, and he has been repeating it all his life. Can it be a hard task to teach him to labor for himself, to work from impulses in his own breast?

One of the great means of elevating the slave, in calling forth his energies is to place his domestic relations on new ground. This is essential. We wish him to labor for his family. Then he must have a family to labor for. Then his wife and children must be truly his own. Then his home must be inviolate. Then the responsibilities of a husband and father must be laid on him. No measure for preparing the slave for liberty can be so effectual as the improvement of the domestic lot. The whole power of religion should be employed to impress him with the sacredness and duties of marriage.

To carry this and all other means of improvement into effect, it is essential that the slave should no longer be bought and sold. As long as he is made an article of merchandise, he cannot be fitted for the offices of a man. While treated as property, he will have little encouragement to accumulate property, for it cannot be secure. While his wife and children may be exposed at auction, and carried, he knows not where, can he be expected to feel and act as a husband and father? It is time, that this Christian and civilized country should no longer be dishonored by one of the worst usages of barbarism. Break up the slave-market, and one of the chief obstructions to emancipation will be removed.

I have said nothing of colonization among the means of removing slavery, because I believe that to rely on it for this object would be equivalent to a resolution to perpetuate the evil without end. Whatever good it may do abroad, and I trust it will do much, it promises little at home. If the slaveholding States, however, should engage in colonization, with a firm faith in its practicableness, with an energy proportionate to its greatness, and with a sincere regard to the welfare of the colored race, I am confident it will not fail from want of sympathy and aid on the part of the other States.

I have said nothing of the inconveniences and sufferings, which, it is urged, will follow emancipation, be it ever so safe; for these, if real, weigh nothing against the claims of justice. The most common objection is, that a mixture of the two races will be the result. Can the slaveholder use the word "amalgamation" without a blush? That emancipation will have its evils we know; but the evils of slavery exceed beyond measure the greatest which attend its removal . . .

Abolitionism

Of the abolitionists I know very few; but I am bound to say of these, that I honor them for their strength of principle, their sympathy with their fellow-creatures and their active goodness. As a party, they are singularly free from political and religious sectarianism, and have been distinguished by the absence of management, calculation, and worldly wisdom.

The abolitionists have done wrong, I believe; nor is their wrong to be winked at, because done fanatically or with good intention; for how much mischief may be wrought with good design! They have fallen into the common error of enthusiasts, that of exaggerating their object, of feeling as if no evil existed but that which they oppose, and as if no guilt could be compared with that of countenancing or upholding it.

Very unhappily they preached their doctrine to the colored people, and collected these into their societies. To this mixed and excitable multitude, minute, heart rending descriptions of slavery were given in the piercing tones of passion; and slaveholders were held up as monsters of cruelty and crime. Now to this procedure I must object as unwise, as unfriendly to the spirit of Christianity, and as increasing, in a degree, the perils of the slaveholding States. Among the unenlightened, whom they so powerfully address, was there not reason to fear that some might feel themselves called to subvert this system of wrong, by whatever means?

I earnestly desire that abolitionism may lay aside the form of public agitation, and seek its end by wiser and milder means. I desire as earnestly, and more earnestly, that it may not be put down by lawless force. There is a worse evil than abolitionism, that is the suppression of it by lawless force . . .

SOURCE NOTE: William Ellery Channing, *Slavery* (Boston, 1835).

Gerrit Smith (1797–1874)

Gerrit Smith was born on March 6, 1797, into a patrician upstate New York family who provided him with good schooling and a college education. He was graduated from Hamilton College in the class of 1818. He was also endowed with a considerable income from his family's investments. Although Smith had studied law, he became immersed in the antislavery movement early in his career, and was active in the Underground Railroad. He was also involved in the intense political life of the midcentury United States, was a frequent contributor to antislavery periodicals and literature, and was fully engaged in the antebellum slavery debates. He served in the United States House of Representatives and once ran for governor of New York.

Smith was not, however, noted for his political skill or his power as a politician. Rather, he exerted influence through his writing and rhetoric, as the example included here, the "Letter of Gerrit Smith to Rev. James Smylie, of the State of Mississippi," makes clear. Smith courted danger in his antislavery abolitionism; he was a supporter of John Brown, providing him with financial aid, and he became an advocate of the use of violence in abolitionist activity. An aggressive "Garrisonian" abolitionist, he was politically a Republican and supported Abraham Lincoln; later, as a delegate to the Republican National Convention of 1872, he supported General Ulysses S. Grant. He died in New York City on December 28, 1874. See *Webster's American Biographies,* ed. Charles Van Doren, Springfield, Mass.: Merriam-Webster, 1975, pp. 960–61.

Smith's antislavery writings may be found in the Thomas and Ruchames collections of abolitionist writings cited in the "Suggestions for Further Reading" that follows the general introduction.

LETTER OF GERRIT SMITH TO
REV. JAMES SMYLIE, OF
THE STATE OF MISSISSIPPI (1837)

. . . There was such a community of interest—so much of mutual confidence—between Abraham and his servants, that they fought his battles. Indeed, the terms of this patriarchal servitude were such, that in the event of the master's dying without issue, one of his servants inherited his property (Gen. 15:3). But, according to the code of Southern Slavery, the slave can no more own property, than he can own himself. "All that a slave possesses belongs to his master"—"Slaves are incapable of inheriting or transmitting property." These, and many similar phrases, are found in that code. Severe as was the system of Roman slavery, yet in this respect, it was far milder than yours; for its subjects could acquire property (their peculium); and frequently did they purchase their liberty with it. So far from Southern slaves being, as Abraham's servants were, a dependence in war, it is historically true, that they are accustomed to improve this occasion to effect their escape, and strengthen the hands of the enemy. As a further proof that Southern slavery begets none of that confidence between master and slave, which characterized the mutual intercourse of Abraham and his servants—the slave is prohibited, under severe penalties, from having any weapons in his possession, even in time of peace; and the nightly patrol, which the terror-stricken whites of Southern towns keep up, in peace, as well as in war, argues anything, rather than the existence of such confidence. "For keeping or carrying a gun, or powder or shot, or a club, or other weapon whatsoever, offensive or defensive, a slave incurs," says a Southern statute book, "for each offense, thirty-nine lashes."

3d. When I read your quotation from the twenty-fourth chapter of Genesis, made for the purpose of showing that God allowed Abraham to have slaves, I could not but wonder at your imprudence, in meddling with this chapter, which is itself, enough to convince any unbiased mind, that Abraham's servants held a relation to their master and to society, totally different from that held by Southern slaves. Have you ever known a great man in your state to send his slave into another to choose a wife for his son?—And, if so, did the lily white damsel he selected call the sable servant "my Lord?"—And did her family spare no pains to manifest respect for their distinguished guest, and promote his comfort? But this chapter, which you call to your aid, informs us, that Abraham's servant was honored with such tokens of confidence and esteem . . .

4th. Did you ever know Southern slaves to contend for their

rights with their masters? When a Southern master reads the thirteenth verse of the thirty-first chapter of Job, he must think that Job
was in the habit of letting down his dignity very low.

5th. So Southern masters accord religious privileges and impart
religious instruction equally to their slaves and their children? Your
laws, which visit with stripes, imprisonment, and death, the attempt
to teach slaves to read the Bible, show but too certainly, that the
Southern master, who should undertake to place "his children and
his household" on the same level, in respect to their religious advantages, as it is probable that Abraham did (Gen. 18:19), would
soon find himself in the midst of enemies, not to his reputation
only, but to his life also.

. . . The Southern slave would obey God in respect to marriage,
and also to the reading and studying of His word. But this, as we
have seen, is forbidden him. He may not marry; nor may he read
the Bible. Again, he would obey God in the duties of secret and social prayer, but he may not attend the prayer-meeting—certainly
not that of his choice; and instances are known, where the master
has intruded upon the slave's secret audience with heaven, to teach
him by the lash, or some other instrument of torture, that he would
allow "no other God before" himself.

. . . After you shall have allowed, as you will allow, that slavery,
as it exists, is at war with God, you will be likely to say, that the
fault is not in the theory of it; but in the practical departure from
that theory; that it is not the system, but the practice under it,
which is at war with God. Our concern, however, is with slavery as
it is, and not with any theory of it. But to indulge you, we will look
at the system of slavery, as it is presented to us, in the laws of the
slave States; and what do we find here? Why, that the system is as
bad as the practice under it. Here we find the most diabolical de-
vices to keep millions of human beings in a state of heathenism—in
the deepest ignorance and most loathsome pollution. But you will
tell me, that I do not look far enough to find the true theory of slavery; and that the cruelties and abominations, which the laws of the
slave States have ingrafted on this theory, are not acknowledged by
the good men in those States to be a part of the theory. Well, you
shall have the benefit of this plea; and I admit, for the sake of argument, that this theory of slavery, which lies far back, and out of

sight of every thing visible and known about slavery, is right. And what does this admission avail you? It is slavery as it is—as it is seen and known, that the abolitionists are contending against. But, say you, to induce our forbearance, "We good men of the South are restoring slavery, as fast as we can, to what it should be; and we will soon make its erring practice quadrate with its perfect and sinless theory." Success to your endeavors! . . .

We must continue to judge slavery by what it is, and not by what you tell us it will, or may be. Until its character be righteous, we shall continue to condemn it; but when you shall have brought it back to you sinless and beautiful theory of it, it will have nothing to fear from the abolitionists. There are two prominent reasons, however, for believing that you will never present Southern slavery to us in this lovely character, the mere imagination of which is so dear to you. The first is, that you are doing nothing to this end. It is an indisputable fact that Southern slavery is continually getting wider and wider from God, and from an innocent theory of servitude; and the "good men at the South," of whom we have spoken, are not only doing nothing to arrest this increasing divergency, but they are actually favoring it . . . The other of these reasons for believing that Southern slavery will never be conformed to your *beau ideal* of slavery, in which it is presupposed there are none but principles of righteousness, is, that on its first contact with these principles, it would "vanish into thin air," leaving "not a wreck behind." In proof of this, and I need not cite any other case, it would be immediate death to Southern slavery to concede to its subjects, God's institution of Marriage; and hence it is, that its code forbids marriage. The rights of the husband in the wife, and of the wife in the husband, and of the parents in their children, would stand directly in the way of that traffic in human flesh, which is the very life-blood of slavery; and the assumptions of the master would, at every turn and corner, be met and nullified by these rights . . .

1st. Is not Southern slavery guilty of a most heaven-daring crime, in substituting concubinage for God's institution of marriage?

2nd. Would not that slavery, and also every theory and modification of slavery, for which you may contend, come speedily to naught, if their subjects were allowed to marry? Slavery, being an abuse, is incapable of reformation. It dies, not only when you aim a fatal blow at its life principle—its foundation doctrine of man's right to property in man[1]—but it dies as surely, when you prune it of its manifold incidents of pollution and irreligion.

1. I mean by this phrase, "right to property in man," a right to hold man as property, and I do not see with what property certain writers construe it to mean, a property in the mere services of a man. [author]

SOURCE NOTE: Gerrit Smith, "Letter to Rev. James Smylie, of the State of Mississippi" (New York, 1837).

Angelina Emily Grimké (1805–1879)
and Sarah Moore Grimké (1792–1873)

Angelina E. Grimké and her sister, Sarah Moore Grimké, were both social reformers who were committed to abolitionism and the emerging women's movement. Born in Charleston, South Carolina, on February 20, 1805, Angelina grew up surrounded by wealth, privilege, and slavery. Both women instinctively disliked the institution on which the family's privilege was based, and they moved to New England, where both became Quakers and joined the abolition movement inspired by William Lloyd Garrison. Both sisters wrote passionately concerning slavery, Sarah authoring "An Epistle to the Clergy of the Southern States" (1836) and Angelina writing the longer treatise excerpted here, *An Appeal to the Christian Women of the South* (1836). Angelina was married to the abolitionist Theodore Dwight Weld, and she also wrote *An Appeal to the Women of the Nominally Free States* (1837), another antislavery treatise. Also excerpted here is Angelina Grimké's exchange of correspondence with Catharine E. Beecher (1800–1874), which is her response to Beecher's 1837 book entitled *An Essay on Slavery and Abolitionism, with Reference to the Duty of American Females*. This dialogue over the roles of women in the antislavery cause marks a division in women's views of the fusion of suffrage and antislavery. Catharine Beecher, who always opposed women's suffrage, regarded abolitionists like Weld and Grimké to be excessive, and she deplored the entry of women into public discourse concerning slavery. As Beecher's publications indicate, she was deeply committed to the domestic roles of women. The exchange between Angelina Grimké and Catharine Beecher constitutes yet another dimension of the antebellum slavery debates, the essential place of women in the rapidly fragmenting Union.

AN APPEAL TO THE CHRISTIAN WOMEN
OF THE SOUTH (1836)

Then Mordecai commanded to answer Esther. Think not within thyself that thou shalt escape in the king's house more than all the Jews. For if thou altogether holdest thy peace at

*this time, then shall there enlargement and deliverance arise to
the Jews from another place: but thou and thy father's house
shall be destroyed: and who knoweth whether thou art come
to the kingdom for such time as this. And Esther bade them
return Mordecai this answer:—and so will I go in unto the
king, which is not according to law, and if I perish, I perish.*"

ESTHER IV. 13–16.

Yes! Sisters in Christ I feel an interest in *you*, and often has the secret prayer arisen on your behalf, Lord "open thou their eyes that
they may see wondrous things out of thy Law"—It is then, because
I *do feel* and *do pray* for you, that I thus address you upon a subject
about which of all others, perhaps you would rather not hear anything.

It is true, I am going to tell you unwelcome truths, but I mean to
speak those *truths in love* . . .

The *women of the South can overthrow* this horrible system of
oppression and cruelty, licentiousness and wrong. Such appeals to
your legislatures would be irresistible, for there is something in the
heart of man which *will bend under moral suasion*. There is a swift
witness for truth in his bosom, which *will respond to truth* when it
is uttered with calmness and dignity. If you could obtain but six
signatures to such a petition in only one state, I would say, send up
that petition, and be not in the least discouraged by the scoffs and
jeers of the heartless, or the resolution of the house to lay it on the
table. It will be a great thing if the subject can be introduced into
your legislatures in any way, even by *women*, and *they* will be most
likely to introduce it there in the best possible manner, as a matter
of *morals* and *religion*, not of expediency or politics. You may petition, too, the different ecclesiastical bodies of the slave states. Slavery must be attacked with the whole power of truth and the sword
of spirit. You must take it up on *Christian* ground, and fight against
it with Christian weapons, whilst your feet are shod with the preparation of the gospel of peace. And *you are now* loudly called upon
by the cries of the widow and the orphan, to arise and gird yourselves for this great moral conflict, with the whole armour of righteousness upon the right hand and on the left.

There is every encouragement for you to labor and pray, my friends, because the abolition of slavery as well as its existence, has been the theme of prophecy. "Ethiopia (says the Psalmist) shall stretch forth her hands unto God." And is she not now doing so? Are not the Christian negroes of the south lifting their hands in prayer for deliverance, just as the Israelites did when their redemption was drawing nigh? Are thy not sighing and crying by reason of the hard bondage? Think you, that He, of whom it was said, "and God heard their groaning, and their cry came up unto him by reason of the hard bondage," think you that his ear is so heavy that he cannot *now* hear the cries of his suffering children? Or that He who raised up a Moses, an Aaron, and a Miriam, to bring them up out of the land of Egypt from the house of bondage, cannot now, with a high hand and a stretched out arm, rid the poor negroes out of the hands of their masters? Surely you believe that his arm is *not* shortened that he cannot save. And would not such work of mercy redound to his glory? But another string of the harp of prophecy vibrates to the song of deliverance: "But they shall sit every man under his vine, and under his fig-tree, and *none shall make them afraid;* for the mouth of the Lord of Hosts hath spoken it." The *slave* never can do this as long as he is a *slave;* whilst he is a "chattel personal" he can own *no* property; but the time *is to come* when *every* man is to sit under *his own* vine and *his own* fig-tree, and no domineering driver, or irresponsible master, or irascible mistress, shall make him afraid of the chain or the whip.

Slavery, then, must be overthrown before the prophecies can be accomplished, but how are they to be fulfilled? Will the wheels of the millennial car be rolled onward by miraculous power? NO! God designs to confer this holy privilege upon *man;* it is through *his* instrumentality that the great and glorious work of reforming the world is to be done. And see you not how the mighty engine of *moral power* is dragging in its rear the Bible and peace societies, anti-slavery and temperance, sabbath schools, moral reform, and missions? Or to adopt another figure, do not these seven philanthropic associations compose the beautiful tints in that bow of promise which spans the arc of our moral heaven? Who does not believe, that if these societies were broken up, their constitutions burnt, and the vast machinery with which they are laboring to regenerate mankind was stopped, that the black clouds of vengeance would soon burst over our world, and every city would witness the fate of the devoted cities of the plain! Each one of these societies is walking abroad through the earth scattering the seeds of truth over the wide field of our world . . .

But I will now say a few words on the subject of Abolitionism. Doubtless you have all heard Anti-Slavery Societies denounced as insurrectionary and mischievous, fanatical and dangerous. It has been said they publish the most abominable untruths, and that they are endeavoring to excite rebellions at the South. Have you believed these reports, my friends? Have *you* also been deceived by these false assertions? Listen to me, then, whilst I endeavor to wipe from the fair character of Abolitionism such unfounded accusations. You know that I am a Southerner; you know that my dearest relatives are now in a slave State. Can you for a moment believe I would prove so recreant to the feelings of a daughter and a sister, as to join a society which was seeking to overthrow slavery by falsehood . . . and it was not until I was fully convinced that their principles were *entirely pacific,* and their efforts *only moral,* that I gave my name as a member to the Female Anti-Slavery Society of Philadelphia. Since that time, I have regularly taken the *Liberator,* and read many Anti-Slavery pamphlets and papers and books, and can never read any account of cruelty which I could not believe. Southerners may deny the truth of these accounts, but why do they not *prove* them to be false? Their violent expressions of horror at such accounts being believed, *may* deceive some, but they cannot deceive *me* for I lived too long in the midst of slavery, not to know what slavery is. When I speak of this system, "I speak that I do know," and I am not at all afraid to assert, that Anti-Slavery publications have *not* overdrawn the monstrous features of slavery at all. And many a Southerner *knows* this as well as I do. A lady in North Carolina remarked to a friend of mine, about eighteen months since, "Northerners know nothing at all about slavery; they think it is perpetual bondage only; but of the *depth of degradation* that word involves, they have no conception; if they had, *they would never cease* their efforts until *so horrible* a system was overthrown." She did not know haw faithfully some Northern men and Northern women had studied this subject; how diligently they had searched out the cause of "him who had none to help him," and how fearlessly they had told the story of the negro's wrongs. Yes, Northerners know *every* thing about slavery now. This monster of iniquity has been unveiled to the world, her frightful features unmasked, and soon, very soon will she be regarded with no more complacency by the American republic than is the idol of Juggernaut, rolling its bloody wheels over the crushed bodies of its prostrate victims.

But you will probably ask, if Anti-Slavery societies are not insurrectionary, why do Northerners tell us they are? Why, I would ask you in return, did Northern senators and Northern representatives give their votes, at the last sitting of congress, to the admission of Arkansas Territory as a state? Take those men, one by one, and ask them in their parlours, do you *approve of slavery?* ask them on *Northern* ground, where they will speak the truth, and I doubt not *every man* of them will tell you, *no!* Why then, I ask, did *they* give their votes to enlarge the mouth of that grave which has already destroyed its tens of thousands? All our enemies tell *us* they are as much anti-slavery as we are. Yes, my friends, thousands who are helping you to bind the fetters of slavery on the negro despise you in their hearts for doing it . . .

But you will say, a great many other Northerners tell us so, who can have no political motives. The interests of the North, you must know my friends, are very closely combined with those of the South. The Northern merchants and manufacturers are making *their* fortunes out of the *produce of slave labor;* the grocer is selling our rice and our sugar; how then can these men bear a testimony against slavery without condemning themselves? But there is another reason, the North is most dreadfully afraid of Amalgamation. She is alarmed at the very idea of a thing so monstrous, as she thinks. And lest this consequence *might* flow from emancipation, she is determined to resist all efforts at emancipation without expatriation. It is not because *she approves of slavery,* or believes it to be "the corner stone of our republic," for she is as much *anti-slavery* as we are; but amalgamation is too horrible to think of. Now I would ask *you,* is it right, is it generous, to refuse the colored people in this country the advantages of education and the privilege, or rather the *right* to follow honest trades and callings merely because they are colored? The same prejudice exists here against our colored brethren that existed against the Gentiles in Judea. Great numbers cannot bear the idea of equality, and fearing lest, if they had the same advantages we enjoy, they would become as intelligent, as moral, as religious, and as respectable and wealthy, they are determined to keep them as low as they possibly can. Is this doing as they would be done by? Is this loving their neighbors *as themselves?* Oh! That *such* opposers of Abolitionism would put their souls in the stead of the free colored man's and obey the apostolic injunction, to "remember them that in bonds *as bound with them.*"

You need not be surprised, then, at all, at what is said *against* Abolitionists by the North, for they are wielding a two-edged sword, which even here, cuts through the *cords of caste,* on one side, and the *bonds of interest* on the other. They are only sharing the fate of other reformers, abused and reviled whilst they are in the minority; but they are neither angry nor discouraged by the invective which has been heaped upon the slaveholders of the South and their apologists at the North.

Abolitionists understand the slaveholding spirit too well to be surprised at anything that has yet happened at the South or the North. They know that the greater the sin is, which is exposed, the more violent will be the efforts to blacken the character and impugn the motives of those who are engaged in bringing to light the hidden things of darkness. They understand the work of Reform too well to be driven back by the furious waves of opposition, which are only foaming out of their own shame.

I can prove the *safety* of immediate Emancipation by history. In St. Domingo in 1793 six hundred thousand slaves were set free in a white population of forty-two thousand. That Island "marched as by enchantment towards its ancient splendor, cultivation prospered, every day produced perceptible proofs of its progress, and the negroes all continued quietly to work on the different plantations, until 1802, France determined to reduce these liberated slaves again to bondage. It was at *this time* that all those dreadful scenes occurred, which we so often *unjustly* hear spoken of, as the effects of Abolition. They were occasioned *not* by Emancipation, but by the base attempt to fasten the chains of slavery on the limbs of liberated slaves.

And why not try it in the Southern States, if it *never* has occasioned rebellion; if *not* a *drop* of *blood* has ever been shed in consequence of it, though it has been so often tried, why should we suppose it would produce such disastrous consequences now? "Be not deceived then, God is not mocked," by such false excuses for not doing justly and loving mercy. There is nothing to fear from immediate Emancipation, but *every thing* from the continuance of slavery.

Sisters in Christ, I have done. As a Southerner, I have felt it was my duty to address you. I have endeavoured to set before you the exceeding sinfulness of slavery, and to point you to the example of those noble women who have been raised up in the church to effect great revolutions, and to suffer for the truth's sake . . .

SOURCE NOTE: Angelina E. Grimké, *An Appeal to the Christian Women of the South* (Boston, 1836).

SARAH M. GRIMKÉ,
AN EPISTLE TO THE CLERGY OF
THE SOUTHERN STATES (1836)

. . . "Let us make man in OUR IMAGE, after our likeness, and let them have dominion over the fish of the sea, and over the fowl of the air, and over the cattle, and over all the earth, and over every creeping thing, that creepeth upon the earth." Here is written in characters of fire continually blazing before the eyes of every man who holds his fellow man in bondage—In the image of God created he man. Here is marked a distinction which can never be effaced between a man and a *thing,* and we are fighting against God's unchangeable decree by depriving this rational and immortal being of those inalienable rights which have been conferred upon him. He was created a little lower than the angels, crowned with glory and honor, and designed to be God's vice-regent upon earth—but slavery has wrested the sceptre of dominion from his hand, slavery has seized with an iron grasp this God-like being, and torn the crown from his head. Slavery has disrobed him of royalty, put on him the collar and the chain, and trampled the image of God in the dust.

. . . Can any crime, tremendous as is the history of human wickedness, compare in turpitude with this?—No, the immutable difference, the *heaven-wide distinction* which God has established between *that* being, whom he has made a little lower than the angels, and all the other works of this wonderful creation, cannot be annihilated without incurring a weight of guilt beyond expression terrible.

. . . Permission ample was given to shed the blood of all inferior creatures, but of this *being, bearing the impress of divinity,* God said, "And surely your blood of your lives will I require, at the hand of every beast will I require it, and at the hand of man, at the hand of every man's brother will I require the life of man. Who so sheddeth man's blood, by man shall his blood be shed, for in the IMAGE OF GOD made he man." Let us pause and examine this passage.—Man may shed the blood of the inferior animals, he may use them as *mere means*—he may convert them into food to sustain existence—but if the top-stone of creation, the *image of God* had his blood shed by a beast, that blood was required even of this irrational brute: as if Deity had said, over *any likeness* I will spread a panoply divine that all creation may instinctively feel that he is precious to his Maker—so precious, that if his life be taken by his fellow man—if man degrades himself to the level of a beast by destroying his brother—"by man shall his blood be shed."

This distinction between *man* and *things* is marked with equal care and solemnity under the Jewish dispensation. "If a man steal an ox, or a sheep, and kill it, or sell it, he shall restore five oxen for an ox, and four sheep for a sheep." But, "he that stealeth a man and selleth him or if he be found in his hand, he shall surely be put to death." If this law were carried into effect now, what must be the inevitable doom of all those who now hold man as property? If Jehovah were to exact the execution of this penalty upon the more enlightened and more spiritually minded men who live under the Christian dispensation, would he not instantly commission his most tremendous thunderbolts to strike from existence those who are thus trampling upon his laws, thus defacing his image?

. . . And here I cannot but advert to a most important distinction which God has made between immortal beings and the beasts that perish.—No one can doubt that by the fall of man the whole creation underwent a change. The apostle says, "We know that the whole creation groaneth and travaileth in pain together." But it was for *man* alone that the Lord Jesus "made himself of no reputation and took upon him the form of a servant." . . .

Mr. Calhoun of Norfolk, in a speech in the House of Delegates of Virginia, on the subject of negro slavery in 1832, speaking of our right to hold our colored brethren in bondage, says:

"As a Virginian, I do not question the master's title to his slave;

but I put it to that gentleman, as a man, as a moral man, as a Christian man, whether he has not some doubts of his claim to his slaves, being as absolute and unqualified as that to other property. Let us in the investigation of this title go back to its origin—Whence came slaves into this country?—From Africa. Were they free men there? At one time they were. How came they to be converted into slaves?—By the stratagem of war and the strong arm of the conqueror; they were vanquished in battle, sold by the victorious party to the slave trader; who brought them to our shores, and disposed of them to the planters of Virginia . . . The truth is, our ancestors had *no title* to this property, and we have acquired it only by legislative enactment."

. . . Another plea by which we endeavor to silence the voice of conscience is, "that the child is invariably born to the condition of the parent." Hence the law of South Carolina, says "ALL THEIR (THE SLAVES) ISSUE AND OFFSPRING, BORN, OR TO BE BORN, SHALL BE, AND THEY ARE HEREBY DECLARED TO BE, AND REMAIN FOREVER HEREAFTER ABSOLUTE SLAVES, AND SHALL FOREVER FOLLOW THE CONDITION OF THE MOTHER." To support this assumption, recourse is had to the page of inspiration. Our colored brethren are said to be the descendants of Ham who was cursed with all his posterity, and their condition only in accordance with the declaration of Jehovah, that he visits the iniquities of the fathers upon the children.—I need only remark that Canaan, not Ham, was the object of Noah's prophecy, and that upon his descendants it has been amply fulfilled.

. . . The present position of my country and of the church is one of deep and solemn interest. The times of our ignorance on the subject of slavery which God may have winked at, *have passed away*. We are no longer standing unconsciously and carelessly on the brink of a burning volcano. The strong arm of Almighty power has rolled back the dense cloud which hung over the terrific crater, and has exposed it to our view, and although no human eye can penetrate the abyss, yet enough is seen to warn us of the consequences of trifling with Omnipotence. Jehovah is calling to us as he did to Job out of the whirlwind, and every blast bears on its wings the sound, Repent! Repent! God, if I may so speak, is waiting to see whether we will hearken unto his voice. He has sent out his light and his truth, and as regards us it may perhaps be said—there is now silence in heaven. The commissioned messengers of grace to this guilty nation are rapidly traversing our country, through the medium of the Anti-Slavery Society, through its agents and its presses, whilst the "ministering spirits" are marking with breathless interest the influence produced by these means of knowledge thus mercifully furnished to our land . . .

What an appalling spectacle do we now present! With one hand we clasp the cross of Christ, and with the other grasp the neck of the down-trodden slave! With one eye we are gazing imploringly on the bleeding sacrifice of Calvary, as if we expected redemption through the blood which was shed there, and with the other we cast the glance of indignation and contempt at the representative of Him who there made his soul an offering for sin! My Christian brethren, if there is any truth in the Bible, and in the God of the Bible, *our hearts bear us witness* that he can no more acknowledge us as his disciples, if we willfully persist in this sin, than he did the Pharisees formerly, who were strict and punctilious in the observance of the ceremonial law, and yet devoured widow's houses. *We have added a deeper shade to their guilt,* we make widows by tearing from the victims of a cruel bondage, the husbands of their bosoms, and then devour the widow herself by robbing her of her freedom, and reducing her to the level of a brute. I solemnly appeal to your consciences . . .

And this is the sin which the Church is fostering in her bosom—This is the leprosy over which she is casting the mantle of charity, to hide, if possible, the "putrefying sores"—This is the monster around which she is twining her maternal arms, and before which she is placing her anointed shield inscribed "holiness to the Lord"—Oh, ye ministers of Him who so loved the slave that he gave his precious blood to redeem him from sin, can ye any longer with your eyes fixed upon the Cross of Christ, plant your feet on his injured representative, and sanction and sanctify this heartbreaking, this soul destroying system?

SOURCE NOTE: Sarah M. Grimké, "An Epistle to the Clergy of the Southern States" (Boston, 1836).

Catharine E. Beecher (1800–1874)

AN ESSAY ON SLAVERY AND
ABOLITIONISM ADDRESSED TO
MISS A. E. GRIMKÉ (1837)

The object I have in view, is to present some reason why it seems unwise and inexpedient for ladies of the non-slave-holding States to unite themselves in Abolition Societies; and thus, at the same time, to exhibit the inexpediency of the course you propose to adopt.

Your remarks seem to assume, that the *principles* held by Abolitionists on the subject of slavery, are peculiar to them, and are not generally adopted by those at the North who oppose their *measures*. In this you are not correctly informed.

I know not where to look for northern Christians, who would deny that every slave-holder is bound to treat his slaves exactly as he would claim that his own children ought to be treated in similar circumstances; that the holding of our fellow men as property, or the withholding of any of the rights of freedom, for mere purposes of gain, is a sin, and ought to be immediately abandoned.

The distinctive peculiarity of the Abolition Society is this: it is a voluntary association in one section of the country, designed to awaken public sentiment against a moral evil existing in another section of the country, and the principal point of effort seems to be, to enlarge the numbers of this association as a means of influencing public sentiment.

Experience has shown, that when certain moral evils exist in a community, efforts to awaken public sentiment against such practices, and combinations for the exercise of personal influence and example, have in various cases tended to rectify these evils. Thus in respect to intemperance;—the collecting of facts, the labours of public lecturers and the distribution of publications, have had much effect in diminishing the evil. So in reference to the slave-trade and slavery in England.

Clarkson, Wilberforce, and their coadjutors, commenced a system of operations to arouse and influence public sentiment, and they succeeded in securing the suppression of the slave trade, and the gradual abolition of slavery in the English colonies.

The second reason I would urge against joining the Abolition Society is, that its character and measures are not either peaceful or Christian in tendency, but they rather are those which tend to generate party spirit, denunciation, recriminations, and angry passions.

I believe, that as a body, Abolitionists are men of pure morals, of great honesty of purpose, of real benevolence and piety, and of great activity in efforts to promote what they consider the best interest of their fellow men. I believe, that, in making efforts to abolish slavery, they have taken measures, which they supposed were best calculated to bring this evil to an end, with the greatest speed, and with the least danger and suffering to the South. I do not believe they ever designed to promote disunion, or insurrection, or to stir up strife.

I regard individuals among them, as having taken a bold and courageous stand, in maintaining the liberty of free discussion, the liberty of speech and of the press.

Although Abolitionists may be lauded for many virtues, still much evidence can be presented, that the character and measures of the Abolition Society are not either peaceful or Christian in tendency, but that they are in their nature calculated to generate party spirit, denunciation, recrimination, and angry passions.

Let us now look at the leaders of the Abolition movement in America. The man who first took the lead was William L. Garrison, who, though he professes a belief in the Christian religion, is an avowed opponent of most of its institutions. The character and spirit of this man have for years been exhibited in *The Liberator,* of which he is the editor. That there is to be found in that paper, or in anything else, any evidence of his possessing the peculiar traits of Wilberforce, not even his warmest admirers will maintain. How many of the opposite traits can be found, those can best judge who have read his paper. Gradually others joined themselves in the effort commenced by Garrison; but for a long time they consisted chiefly of men who would fall into one of these three classes; either good men who were so excited by a knowledge of the enormous evils of slavery, that *anything* was considered better than entire inactivity, or else men accustomed to a contracted field of observation, and more qualified to judge of immediate results than of general tendencies, or else men of ardent and impulsive temperament, whose feelings are likely to take the lead, rather than their judgement.

The editors of the *Emancipation,* the *Friend of Man,* the *New York Evangelist,* and the other abolition periodicals, may therefore be considered as among the chief leaders of the enterprise, and their papers are the mirror from which their spirit and character are reflected.

One of the first measures of Abolitionists was an attack on a benevolent society, originated and sustained by some of the most pious and devoted men of the age. It was imagined by Abolitionists, that the influence and measure of the colonization society tended to retard the abolition of slavery, and to perpetuate injurious prejudices against the coloured race. The peaceful and Christian method of meeting this difficulty would have been, to collect all the evidence of this supposed hurtful tendency, and privately, and in a respectful and conciliating way, to have presented it to the attention of the wise and benevolent men, who were most interested in sustaining this institutions . . .

Instead of this, when the attempt was first made to turn public opinion against the Colonization Society . . .

. . . In public, the enterprise was attacked as a plan for promoting the selfish interests and prejudice of the whites, at the expense of the coloured population . . .

And the style in which the thing was done was at once offensive, inflammatory, and exasperating. Denunciation, sneers, and public rebuke, were bestowed indiscriminately upon the conductors of the enterprise, and of course they fell upon many sincere, upright, and conscientious men, whose feelings were harrowed by a sense of the injustice, the indecorum and the unchristian treatment, they received . . .

. . . Compare this method of carrying a point, with that adopted by Wilberforce and his compeers, and I think you will allow that there was a way that was peaceful and Christian, and that this was not the way which was chosen.

The next measure of Abolitionism was an attempt to remove the prejudices of whites against the blacks, on account of natural peculiarities. Now, prejudice is an *unreasonable* and *groundless* dislike of persons or things . . .

If the friends of the blacks had quietly set themselves to work to increase their intelligence, their usefulness, their respectability, their meekness, gentleness, and benevolence, and then had appealed to the pity, generosity, and Christian feelings of their fellow citizens, a very different result would have appeared. Instead of this, reproaches, rebukes, and sneers, were employed to convince the whites that their prejudices were sinful, and without any just cause. They were accused of pride, of selfish indifference, of un-Christian neglect. This tended to irritate the whites, and to increase their prejudice against the blacks, who thus were made the cause of rebuke and exasperation . . .

. . . Now, the question is not, whether these things, that were urged by Abolitionists, were true. The thing maintained is, that the method taken by them to remove this prejudice was neither peaceful nor Christian in its tendency, but, on the contrary, was calculated to increase the evil, and to generate anger, pride, and recrimination, on one side, and envy, discontent, and revengeful feelings on the other . . .

. . . It was an entire disregard of the prejudices and properties of society, and calculated to stimulate pride, anger, ill-will, contention, and all the bitter feelings that spring from such collisions. Then, instead of adopting measures to soothe and conciliate, rebukes, sneers and denunciation, were employed . . .

. . . The whole system of Abolition measures seems to leave entirely out of view, the obligation of Christians to save their fellow men from all needless temptations. If the thing to be done is only lawful and right, it does not appear to have been a matter of effort to do it in such a way as would not provoke and irritate; but often, if the chief aim had been to do the good in the most injurious and offensive way . . .

. . . It is a fact, that Abolitionists have taken the course most calculated to awaken illegal acts of violence, and that when they have ensued, they have seemed to rejoice in them, as calculated to advance and strengthen their cause. The violence of mobs, the denunciations and unreasonable requirements of the South, the denial of the right of petitions, the restrictions attempted to be laid upon freedom of speech, and freedom of the press, are generally spoken of with exultation by Abolitionists, as what are among the chief means of promoting the cause. It is not so much by exciting feelings of pity and humanity, and Christian love, towards the oppressed, as it is by awakening indignation at the treatment of Abolitionists themselves, that their cause has prospered . . .

. . . The leaders of the Abolition Society disclaim all such wishes or intentions; they only act apparently on the assumption that they are exercising just rights, which they are not bound to give up, because other men will act unreasonably and wickedly.

Another measure of Abolitionists, calculated to awaken evil feelings, has been the treatment of those who objected to their proceedings . . .

. . . The peaceful and Christian method of encountering such opposition, would have been to allow the opponents full credit for purity and integrity of motive, to have avoided all harsh and censorious language, and to have employed facts, arguments and persuasions, in a kind and respectful way with the hope of modifying their views and allaying their fears. Instead of this, the wise and good who opposed Abolition measures, have been treated as though they were the friends and defenders of slavery, or as those who, from a guilty, timid, time-serving policy, refused to take the course which duty demanded . . .

Now there is nothing more irritating, when a man is conscientious and acting according to his own views of right, than to be dealt with in this manner. The more men are treated as if they were honest and sincere—the more they are treated with respect, fairness, and benevolence, the more likely they are to be moved by evidence and arguments. On contrary, harshness, uncharitableness, and rebuke, for opinions and conduct that are in agreement with a man's own views of duty and rectitude, tend to awaken evil feelings, and indispose the mind properly to regard evidence. Abolitionists have not only taken this course, but in many cases, have seemed to act on the principle, that the abolition of Slavery, in the particular mode in which they were aiming to accomplish it, was of such paramount importance, that every thing must be overthrown that stood in the way . . .

. . . Another measure of Abolitionists, which has greatly tended to promote wrath and strife, is their indiscreet and incorrect use of terms . . .

. . . Now if men take words and give them a new and peculiar use, and are consequently misunderstood, they are guilty of deception, and are accountable for all the evils that may ensue as a consequence . . .

. . . Now Abolitionists are before the community, and declare that all slavery is sin, which ought to be immediately forsaken; and that it is their object and intention to promote the *immediate emancipation* of all slaves in this nation . . .

. . . The true and only proper meaning of such language is, that it is the duty of every slaveholder in this nation, to go immediately and make out the legal instruments, that, by the laws of the land, change all his slaves to freemen . . .

. . . The meaning which the Abolitionist attaches to his language is this, that every man is bound to treat his slaves, as nearly as he can, like freemen; and to use all his influence to bring the system of slavery to an end as soon as possible. And they allow that when men do this they are free from guilt, in the matter of slavery, and undeserving of censure . . .

The great mistake of Abolitionists is in using terms which inculcate the immediate annihilation of the relation, when they only intend to urge the Christian duty of treating slaves according to the gospel rules of justice and benevolence, and using all lawful and appropriate means for bringing a most pernicious system to a speedy end . . .

But so long as they persevere in using these terms in a new and peculiar sense, which will always be misunderstood, they are guilty of a species of deception and accountable for the evils that follow.

One other instance of a similar misuse of terms may be mentioned. The word "man-stealer" has one peculiar signification, and it is no more synonymous with "slave-holder" than it is with "sheep-stealer." But Abolitionists show that a slave-holder, in fact does very many of the evils that are perpetrated by a man-stealer, and that the crime is quite as evil in this nature, and very similar in character, and, therefore, he calls a slave-holder a man-stealer . . .

. . . Abolitionism, on the contrary, is a system of *coercion* by public opinion; and in its present operation, its influence is not to convince the erring, but to convince those who are not guilty, of the sins of those who are . . .

Now what is the evil to be cured?

SLAVERY IN THIS NATION.

That this evil is at no distant period to come to an end, is the unanimous opinion of all who either notice the tendencies of the age, or believe in the prophecies of the Bible. All who act on Christian principles in regard to slavery, believe that in a given period (variously estimated) it will end. The only question then, in regard to the benefits to be gained, or the evils to be dreaded in the present agitation of the subject, relates to the *time* and the *manner* of its extinction. The Abolitionists claim that their method will bring it to an end in the shortest time, and in the sagest and best way. Their opponents believe, that it will tend to bring it to an end, if at all, at the most distant period, and in the most dangerous way . . .

The position then I would aim to establish is, that the method taken by the Abolitionists is the one that, according to the laws of mind and past experience, is least likely to bring about the results they aim to accomplish . . .

It is the maxim then of experience, that when men are to be turned from evils, and brought to repent and reform, those only should interfere who have the best right to approach the offender. While on the other hand, rebuke from those who are deemed obtrusive and inimical, or even indifferent, will do more harm than good.

It is another maxim of experience, that such dealings with the erring should be in private, not in public. The moment a man is publicly rebuked, shame, anger, and pride of opinion, all combine to make him defend his practice, and refuse either to own himself wrong, or to cease from his evil ways.

The Abolitionists have violated all these laws of mind and of experience, in dealing with their southern brethren.

Their course has been most calculated to awaken anger, fear, pride, hatred, and all the passions most likely to blind the mind to truth, and make it averse to duty.

They have not approached them with the spirit of love, courtesy, and forbearance . . .

While Abolition Societies did not exist, men could talk and write, at the South, against the evils of slavery, and northern men had free access and liberty of speech, both at the South and at the North. But now all is changed. Every avenue of approach to the South is shut. No paper, pamphlet, or preacher, that touches on that topic, is admitted in their bounds. Their own citizens, that once laboured and remonstrated, are silenced; their own clergy, under the influence of the exasperated feelings of their people, and their own sympathy and sense of wrong, either entirely hold their peace, or become the defenders of a system they once lamented, and attempted to bring to an end. This is the record of experience as to the tendencies of Abolitionism, as thus far developed. This is no picture of fancied dangers, which are not near. The day has come, when already the feelings are so excited on both sides, that I have heard intelligent men, good men, benevolent and pious men, in moments of excitement, declare themselves ready to take up the sword—some for the defense of the master, some for the protection and right of the slave. There will be men from the North and West, standing breast to breast with murderous weapons, in opposing ranks . . .

. . . Is not the South in a state of high exasperation against Abolitionists? Does she not regard them as enemies, as reckless madmen, as impertinent intermeddlers? Will the increase of their numbers tend to allay this exasperation? Will the appearance of a similar body in their own boundaries have any tendency to soothe? Will it not still more alarm and exasperate? . . .

When this point is reached, will the blacks, knowing, as they will know, the sympathies of their Abolition friends, refrain from exerting their physical power? *The Southampton insurrection occurred with far less chance of sympathy and success* . . .

I only say, that if Abolitionists go on as they propose, such results are *more* probable than those they hope to attain.

I have not here alluded to the probabilities of the severing of the Union by the present mode of agitating the question. This may be one of the results, and, if so, what are the probabilities for a Southern republic, that has torn itself off for the purpose of excluding foreign interference, and for the purpose of perpetuating slavery? Can any Abolitionist suppose that, in such a state of things, the great cause of emancipation is as likely to progress favorably, as it was when we were one nation, . . . on those fraternal terms that existed before the Abolition movement began? . . .

Women in Society

It is the grand feature of the Divine economy, that there should be different stations of superiority and subordination, and it is impossible to annihilate this beneficent and immutable law . . .

The master of a family the superior, the domestic a subordinate—the ruler a superior, the subject a subordinate. Nor do these relations at all depend upon superiority either in intellectual or moral worth. However weak the parents, or intelligent the child, there is no reference to this, in the immutable law. However incompetent the teacher, or superior the pupil, no alteration of station can be allowed. However unworthy the master or worthy the servant, while their mutual relations continue, no change in station as to subordination can be allowed. In fulfilling the duties of these relations, true dignity consists in confronting to all those relations that demand subordination, with propriety and cheerfulness . . .

Heaven has appointed to one sex the superior, and to the other the subordinated station, and this without any reference to the character or conduct of either. It is therefore as much for the dignity as it is for the interest of females, in all respects to conform to the duties of this relation. And it is as much a duty as it is for the child to fulfil similar relations to parents, or subjects to rulers. But while woman holds a subordinate relation in society to the other sex, it is not because it was designed that her duties or her influence should be any the less important, or all-pervading. But it was designed that the mode of gaining influence and of exercising power should be altogether different and peculiar.

It is Christianity that has given to woman her true place in society. And it is the peculiar trait of Christianity alone that can sustain her therein . . .

A man may act on society by the collision of intellect, in public debate; he may urge his measure by a sense of shame, by fear and by personal interests; he may coerce by the combination of public sentiment; he may drive by physical force, and he does not out step the boundaries of his sphere. But all the power, and all the conquests that are lawful to woman, are those only which appeal to the kindly, generous, peaceful and benevolent principles.

Woman is to win every thing by peace and love; by making herself so much respected, esteemed and loved, that to yield to her opinions and to gratify her wishes, will be the free-will offering of the heart. But this is to be all accomplished in the domestic and social circle. There let every woman become so cultivated and refined in intellect, that her taste and judgment will be respected; so benevolent in feeling and action, that her motives will be reverenced;—so unassuming and unambitious, that collision and competition will be banished . . .

But the moment woman begins to feel the promptings of ambition, or the thirst for power, her aegis of defence is gone. All the sacred protection of religion, all the generous promptings of chivalry, all the poetry of romantic gallantry, depend upon woman's retaining her place as dependent and defenceless, and making no claims, and maintaining no right but what are the gifts of honour, rectitude and love.

A woman may seek the aid of co-operation and combination among her own sex, to assist her in her appropriate offices of piety, charity, maternal and domestic duty; but whatever, in any measure, throws a woman into the attitude of a combatant, either for herself or others—whatever binds her in a party conflict—whatever obliges her in any way to exert coercive influences, throws her out of her appropriate sphere. If these general principles are correct, they are entirely opposed to the plan of arraying females in any abolition movement; because it enlists them in an effort to coerce the South by the public sentiment of the North; because it brings them forward as partisans in a conflict that has been begun and carried forward by measures that are any thing rather than peaceful in their tendencies; because it draws them forth from their appropriate retirement, to expose themselves to the ungoverned violence of mobs, and to sneers and ridicule in public places; because it leads them into the arena of political collision, not as peaceful mediators to hush the opposing elements, but as combatants to cheer up and carry forward the measure of strife . . .

If petitions from females will operate to exasperate; if they will be deemed obtrusive, indecorous, and unwise, by those to whom they are addressed; if they will increase, rather than diminish the evil which it is wished to remove; if they will be the opening wedge, that will tend eventually to bring females as petitioners and partisans into every political measure that may tend to injure and oppress their sex . . .

Then it is neither appropriate nor wise, nor right, for a woman to petition for the relief of oppressed females.

In this country, petitions to congress, in reference to the official duties of legislators, seem, IN ALL CASES, to fall entirely without the sphere of female duty. Men are the proper persons to make appeals to the rulers whom they appoint, and if their female friends, by arguments and persuasions, can induce them to petition, all the good that can be done by such measures will be secured. But if females cannot influence their nearest friends, to urge forward a public measure in this way, they surely are out of their place, in attempting to do it themselves . . .

We need *ten thousand* teachers at this moment, and an addition of *two thousand every year*. Where is this army of teachers to be found? Is it at all probable that the other sex will afford even a moderate portion of this supply? . . .

Will men turn aside from these high and exciting objects to become the patient labourers in the school-room, and for only the small pittance that rewards such toil? No, they will not do it. Men will be educators in the college, in the high school, in some of the most honourable and lucrative common schools, but the *children,* the *little children* of this nation must, to a wide extent, be taught by females, or remain untaught . . .

And as the value of education rises in the public mind, and the importance of a teacher's office is more highly estimated, women will more and more be furnished with those intellectual advantages which they need to fit them for such duties.

By the concession of all travellers, American females are distinguished above all other for their general intelligence, and yet they are complimented for their retiring modesty, virtue, and domestic faithfulness, while the other sex is as much distinguished for their respectful kindness and attentive gallantry. There is no other country where females have so much public respect and kindness accorded to them as in America, by the concession of all travellers. And it will ever be so, while intellectual culture in the female mind, is combined with the spirit of that religion which so strongly enforces the appropriate duties of a woman's sphere.

But it may be asked, is there nothing to be done to bring this national sin of slavery to an end? . . .

To this it may be replied, that Christian females may, can say and do much to bring these evils to an end . . . and to the present.

It is a sacred and imperious duty, that rests on every human being, to exert all his influence in opposing every thing that he believes is dangerous and wrong, and in sustaining all that he believes is safe and right . . .

If the female advocate chooses to come upon a stage, and expose her person, dress, elocution to public criticism, it is right to express disgust at whatever is offensive and indecorous, as it is to criticise the book of an author, or the dancing of an actress, or any thing else that is presented to public observation. And it is right to make all these things appear as odious and reprehensible to others as they do to ourselves.

In the present aspect of affairs among us, when everything seems to be tending to disunion and distraction, it surely has become the duty of every female instantly to relinquish the attitude of a partisan, in every matter of clashing interests, and to assume the office of a mediator, and an advocate of peace. And to do this, it is not necessary that a woman should in any manner relinquish her opinion as to the evils or the benefits, the right or the wrong, of any principle or practice . . .

There are certain prominent maxims which every woman can adopt as peculiarly belonging to her, as the advocate of charity and peace, and which it should be her especial office to illustrate, enforce, and sustain, by every method in her power . . .

Is a woman surrounded by those who favour the Abolition measures? Can she not with propriety urge such inquiries as these?

Is not slavery to be brought to an end by free discussion, and is it not a war upon the right of free discussion to impeach the motives and depreciate the character of the opposers of Abolition measures? When the opposers of the Abolition movement claim that they honestly and sincerely believe that these measure tend to perpetuate slavery, or to bring it to an end by servile wars, and civil disunion, and the most terrific miseries—when they object to the use of their pulpits, to the embodying of literary students, to the agitation of the community, by Abolition agents—when they object to the circulation of such papers and tracts as Abolitionists prepare, because they believe them most pernicious in their influence and tendencies, is it not as much persecution to use invidious insinuations, depreciating accusation and impeachment of motive, in order to intimidate, as it is for the opposers of Abolitionism to use physical force? Is not the only method by which the South can be brought to relinquish slavery, a conviction that not only her *duty,* but her highest *interest,* requires her to do it? And is not *calm, rational Christian* discussion the only proper method of securing this end? . . .

Is a woman among those who oppose Abolition movements? She can urge such inquiries as these: Ought not Abolitionists to be treated as if they were actuated by the motives of benevolence which they profess? . . .

If Abolitionism prospers by the abuse of its advocates, are not the authors of this abuse accountable for the increase of the very evils they deprecate? . . .

The South, in the moments of angry excitement, have made unreasonable demands upon the non-slave-holding States, and have employed overbearing and provoking language. This has provoked re-action again at the North, and men, who heretofore were unexcited, are beginning to feel indignant, and to say, "Let the Union be sundered." Thus anger begets anger, unreasonable measures provoke equally unreasonable returns.

Abolitionists are men who come before the public in the character of *reprovers.* That the gospel requires Christians sometimes to assume this office, cannot be denied; but it does as unequivocally point out those qualifications which alone can entitle a man to do it. And no man acts wisely or consistently, unless he can satisfy himself that he possesses the qualifications for this duty, before he assumes it.

The first of these qualifications is more than common exemption from the faults that are reproved . . .

For a man is to judge of himself, not by a comparison with other men, but as he stands before God, when compared with a perfect law, and in reference to all his peculiar opportunities and restraints. Who is there that in this comparison, cannot find cause for the deepest humiliation? . . .

. . . A reprover, therefore, if he would avoid a quarrel and do the good he aims to secure, must be possessed of that meekness which can receive evil for good, with patient benevolence. And a man is not fitted for the duties of a reprover, until he can bring his feelings under his control.

The peculiar qualifications, then, which make it suitable for a man to be an Abolitionist are, an exemplary discharge of all the domestic duties; humility, meekness, delicacy, tact, and discretion, and these should especially be the distinctive traits of those who take the place of leaders in devising measures.

And in performing these difficult and self-denying duties, there are no men who need more carefully to study the character and imitate the example of the Redeemer of mankind . . .

SOURCE NOTE: Catharine Beecher, *An Essay on Slavery and Abolitionism with Reference to the Duty of American Females* (Philadelphia, 1837).

ANGELINA GRIMKÉ
*LETTERS TO CATHARINE E. BEECHER,
IN REPLY TO AN ESSAY ON SLAVERY
AND ABOLITIONISM, ADDRESSED TO
A. E. GRIMKÉ* (1838)

*Letter I. Fundamental Principle of
Abolitionists*

*Brookline, Mass.
6 month, 12th, 1837*

My Dear Friend: Thy book has appeared just at a time, when, from the nature of my engagements, it will be impossible for me to give it that attention which so weighty a subject demands. Incessantly occupied in prosecuting a mission, the responsibilities of which task all my powers, I can reply to it only by desultory letters, thrown from my pen as I travel from place to place. I prefer this mode to that of taking as long a time to answer it, as thou didst to determine upon the best method by which to counteract the effect of my testimony at the north—which, as the preface of thy book informs me, was thy main design.

. . . The great fundamental principle of Abolitionists is, that man cannot rightfully hold his fellow man as property. Therefore, we affirm, that *every slaveholder is a man-stealer.* We do so, for the following reasons: to steal a man is to rob him of himself. It matters not whether this be done in Guinea, or Carolina; a man is a *man*, and *as* a man he has *inalienable* rights, among which is the right to personal *liberty*. Now if every man has an *inalienable* right to personal liberty, it follows, that he cannot rightfully be reduced to slavery. But I find in these United States, 2,250,000 men, women and children, robbed of that to which they have an *inalienable* right. How comes this to pass? Where millions are plundered, are there no *plunderers?* If, then, the slaves have been robbed of their liberty, *who* has robbed them? Not the man who stole their forefathers from Africa, but he who now holds them in bondage; no matter *how* they came into his possession, whether he inherited them, or bought them, or seized them at their birth on his own plantation. The only difference I can see between the original manstealer, who caught the African in his native country, and the American slaveholder, is, that the former committed *one* act of robbery, while the other perpetrates the same crime *continually.* Slaveholding is the perpetrating of acts, all of the same kind, in a *series,* the first of which is technically called man-stealing. The *first* act robbed the man of himself; and the same state of mind that prompted *that act, keeps up the series,* having *taken* his all from him: it *keeps* his all from him, not only *refusing to restore,* but still robbing him of all he gets, and as fast as he gets it. Slaveholding, then, is the *constant or habitual perpetration of the act of manstealing.* To *make* a slave is *man-stealing—the ACT itself—*to *hold* him such is man-stealing—the *habit,* the *permanent* state, made up of *individual* acts. In other words—to *begin* to hold a slave is manstealing—to *keep on* holding him is merely a *repetition* of the first act—a doing of the same identical thing *all the time.* A series of the same acts continued for a length of time is a *habit—a permanent state.* And the *first* of this series of the *same* acts that make up this *habit* or state is just like all the rest.

If every slave has a right to freedom, then surely the man who withholds that right from him today is a man-stealer, though he may not be the first person who has robbed him of it. Hence we find that Wesley says, "Men-*buyers* are *exactly on a level with* men-*stealers.*" And again—"Much less is it possible that any child of man should ever be *born a slave.*" Hear also Jonathan Edwards— "To hold a man in a state of slavery, is to be *every day guilty* of robbing him of his liberty, or of *man-stealing.*" And Grotius says—"Those are men-stealers who abduct, *keep,* sell or buy *slaves* or freemen."

If thou meanest merely that *acts* of that *same nature,* but differently located in a series, are designated by different terms, thus pointing out their different *relative positions*, then thy argument concedes what we affirm—the identity in the *nature* of the acts, and thus it dwindles to a mere philological criticism, or rather a mere play upon words.

These are Abolition sentiments on the subject of slaveholding; and although our principles are universally held by our opposers at the North, yet I am told on the 44th page of thy book, that "the word man-stealer has one peculiar signification, and is no more synonymous with slaveholder than it is with sheep-stealer." I must acknowledge, thou hast only confirmed my opinion of the difference which I had believed to exist between Abolitionists and their opponents. As well might Saul have declared, that he held similar views with Stephen, when he stood by and kept the raiment of those who slew him.

. . . But there is another peculiarity in the views of the Abolitionists. We hold that the North is guilty of the crime of slaveholding—we assert that it is a *national* sin: on the contrary, in thy book, I find the following acknowledgment: "*Most* persons in the non-slaveholding States, have considered the matter of southern slavery as one in which they were no more called to interfere, than in the abolition of the press-gang system in England, or the tithe-system in Ireland." Now I cannot see how the same principle can produce such entirely different opinions. "Can a good tree bring forth corrupt fruit?" This I deny, and cannot admit what thou art anxious to prove, viz. that "Public opinion may have been *wrong* on this point, and yet *right* on all those great *principles* of rectitude and justice relating to slavery." If abolition principles are generally adopted at the North, how comes it to pass, that there is no abolition action here, except what is put forth by a few despised fanatics, as they are called? Is there any living faith without works? Can the sap circulate vigorously, and yet neither blossoms put forth nor fruit appear?

Again, I am told on the 7th page, that all Northern Christians believe it is a sin to hold a man in slavery for *"mere purposes of gain"*; as if this was the *whole* abolition principle on this subject. I can assure thee that Abolitionists do not stop here. Our principle is, that *no circumstances can ever justify* a man in holding his fellow man as *property;* it matters not what *motive* he may give for such a monstrous violation of the laws of God. The claim to him as *prop-*

erty is an annihilation of his right to himself, which is the foundation upon which all his other rights are built. It is high-handed robbery of Jehovah; for He has declared, "All souls are *mine*." For myself, I believe there are hundreds of thousands at the South, who do *not* hold their slaves, by any means, as much "for the purpose of gain," as they do from *the lust of power:* this is the passion that reigns triumphant there, and those who do not know this, have much yet to learn. Where, then, is the similarity in our views?

> *I forbear for the present, and subscribe myself,*
> *Thine, but not in the bonds of gospel Abolitionism,*
> *A. E. Grimké*

SOURCE NOTE: Angelina Grimké, *Letters to Catharine E. Beecher, in Reply to an Essay on Slavery and Abolitionism, Addressed to A. E. Grimké* (Boston, 1838).

Theodore Dwight Weld

AMERICAN SLAVERY AS IT IS: TESTIMONY OF A THOUSAND WITNESSES (1839)

See the headnote for Theodore Dwight Weld in the "Biblical Antislavery Arguments" section of this volume.

Advertisement to the Reader

A majority of the facts and testimony contained in this work rests upon the authority of SLAVEHOLDERS, whose names and residences are given to the public, as vouchers for the truths of their statements. That they should utter falsehoods, for the sake of proclaiming their own infamy, is not probable.

Their testimony is taken, mainly, from the recent newspapers, published in the slave states. Most of those papers will be deposited at the office of the American Anti-Slavery Society, 143 Nassau Street, New York City. Those who think the atrocities, which they describe, incredible, are invited to call and read for themselves . . .

from the Introduction

Reader, you are empanelled as a juror to try a plain case and bring in an honest verdict. The question at issue is not one of law, but of fact—"What is the actual condition of the slaves in the United States?" . . . You have a wife, or a husband, a child, a father, a mother, a brother, a sister—make the case your own, make it theirs, and bring in your verdict. The case of Human Rights against Slavery has been adjudicated in the court of conscience times innumerable. The same verdict has always been rendered—"Guilty;" the same sentence has always been pronounced, "Let it be accursed;" and human nature, with her million echoes, has rung it round the world in every language under heaven, "Let it be accursed. Let it be accursed." . . .

It is no marvel that slaveholders are always talking of their *kind treatment* of their slaves. The only marvel is, that men of sense can be gulled by such professions. Despots always insist that they are merciful. The greatest tyrants that ever dripped with blood have assumed the titles of "most gracious," "most clement," "most merciful," &c., and have ordered their crouching vassals to accost them thus. When did not vice lay claim to those virtues which are the opposites of its habitual crimes? The guilty, according to their own showing, are always innocent, and cowards brave, and drunkards sober, and harlots chaste, and pickpockets honest to a fault. Every body understands this. When a man's tongue grows thick, and he begins to hiccough and walk cross-legged, we expect him, as a matter of course, to protest that he is not drunk; . . .

Slaveholders, the world over, have sung the praises of their tender mercies towards their slaves. Even the wretches that plied the African slave trade, tried to rebut Clarkson's proofs of their cruelties, by speeches, affidavits, and published pamphlets, setting forth the accommodations of the "middle passage," and their kind attentions to the comfort of those whom they had stolen from their homes, and kept stowed away under hatches, during a voyage of four thousand miles . . .

As slaveholders and their apologists are volunteer witnesses in their own cause, and are flooding the world with testimony that their slaves are kindly treated; that they are well fed, well clothed, well housed, well lodged, moderately worked, and bountifully provided with all things needful for their comfort, we propose—first, to disprove their assertions by the testimony of a multitude of impartial witnesses, and then to put slaveholders themselves through a course of cross-questioning which shall draw their condemnation out of their own mouths. We will prove that the slaves in the United States are treated with barbarous inhumanity; that they are overworked, underfed, wretchedly clad and lodged, and have insufficient sleep; that they are often made to wear round their necks iron collars armed with prongs, to drag heavy chains and weights at their feet while working in the field, and to wear yokes, and bells, and iron horns; that they are often kept confined in the stocks day and night for weeks together, made to wear gags in their mouths for hours or days, have some of their front teeth torn out or broken off, that they may be easily detected when they run away; that they are frequently flogged with terrible severity, have red pepper rubbed in their lacerated flesh, and hot brine, spirits of turpentine, &c., poured over the gashes to increase the torture; that they are often stripped naked, their backs and limbs cut with knives, bruised and mangled by scores and hundreds of blows with the paddle, and terribly torn by the claws of cats, drawn over them by their tormentors; that they are often hunted with blood hounds and shot down like beasts, or torn in pieces by dogs; that they are often suspended by the arms and whipped and beaten till they faint, and when revived by restoratives, beaten again till they faint, and sometimes till they die; that their ears are often cut off, their eyes knocked out, their bones broken, their flesh branded with red hot irons, that they are maimed, mutilated and burned to death over slow fires. All these things, and more, and worse, we shall *prove*. Reader, we know whereof we affirm, we have weighed it well; *more and worse* **WE WILL PROVE.** Mark these words, and read on; we will establish all these facts by the testimony of *slaveholders* in all parts of the slave states, by slaveholding members of Congress and of state legislatures, by ambassadors to foreign courts, by judges, by doctors of divinity, and clergymen of all denominations, by merchants, mechanics, lawyers and physicians, by presidents and professors in colleges and *professional* seminaries, by planters, overseers and drivers. We shall show, not merely that such deeds are committed, but that they are frequent; not done in corners, but before the sun; not in one of the slave states, but in all of them; not perpetrated by brutal overseers and drivers merely, but by magistrates, by legislators, by professors of religion, by preachers of the gospel, by governors of states, by "gentlemen of property and standing," and by delicate females moving in the "highest circle of society." We know, full well, the outcry that will be made by multitudes, at these declarations; the multiform cavils, the flat denials, the charges of "exaggeration" and "falsehood" so often bandied, the sneers of affected contempt at the credulity that can believe such things, and the rage and imprecations against those who give them currency. We know, too, the threadbare sophistries by which slaveholders and their apologists seek to evade such testimony. If they admit that such deeds are committed, they tell us that they are exceedingly rare, and therefore furnish no grounds for judging of the general treatment of slaves; that occasionally a brutal wretch in the *free* states barbarously butchers his wife, but that no one thinks of inferring from that, the general treatment of wives at the North and West.

. . . The foregoing declarations touching the inflictions upon slaves, are not haphazard assertions, nor the exaggerations of fiction conjured up to carry a point; nor are they the rhapsodies of enthusiasm, nor crude conclusions, jumped at by hasty and imperfect investigation, nor the aimless outpourings either of sympathy or poetry; but they are proclamations of deliberate, well weighed convictions, produced by accumulations of proof, by affirmations and affidavits, by written testimonies and statements . . .

We will first present the reader with a few Personal Narratives furnished by individuals, natives of slave states and others, embodying, in the main, the results of their own observation in the midst of slavery—facts and scenes of which they were eyewitnesses.

In the next place, to give the reader as clear and definite a view of the actual condition of slaves as possible, we propose to make specific points, to pass in review the various particulars in the slave's condition, simply presenting sufficient testimony under each head to settle the question in every candid mind. The examination will be conducted by stating distinct propositions, and in the following order of topics.

1. THE FOOD OF THE SLAVES, THE KIND, QUALITY AND QUANTITY, ALSO, THE NUMBER AND TIME OF MEALS EACH DAY, &C.
2. THEIR HOURS OF LABOR AND REST.
3. THEIR CLOTHING.
4. THEIR DWELLINGS.
5. THEIR PRIVATIONS AND INFLICTIONS.
6. *In conclusion,* a variety of OBJECTIONS and ARGUMENTS will be considered which are used by the advocates of slavery to set aside the force of testimony, and to show that the slaves are kindly treated.

SOURCE NOTE: Theodore Dwight Weld, *American Slavery As It Is: Testimony of a Thousand Witnesses* (New York: The American Antislavery Society, 1839), reprint edition, 1968, Ayer Company for Arno Press (New York, 1991).

AN ANTISLAVERY MANUAL,
CONTAINING A COLLECTION OF
FACTS AND ARGUMENTS ON AMERICAN
SLAVERY BY REV. ROY SUNDERLAND
(NEW YORK: PIERCY AND REED, 1837)

—This information for the benefit of anyone who
believes cats are benevolent, precious pets!!!

CAT-HAWLING

A whole gang of slaves had been flogged to make one of them confess that he had stolen a hog. Finally, one was fixed upon as the culprit, and the following method taken for his punishment:—

"A boy was then ordered to get up, run to the house, and bring a cat, which was soon produced. The cat, which was a large gray tomcat, was then taken by the well-dressed gentleman, and placed upon the bare back of the prostrate black man, near the shoulders and forcibly dragged by the tail down the back, and along the bare thighs of the sufferer. The cat sunk his nails into the flesh, and tore off pieces of the skin with his teeth. The man roared with pain of this punishment, and would have rolled along the ground had he not have been held in his place by the force of four other slaves, each of whom confined a hand or a foot. As soon as the cat was drawn from him, the man said he would tell who stole the hog, and confessed that he and several others, three of whom were holding, had stolen the hog—killed, dressed, and eaten it. In return for this confession, the overseer said he should have another touch of the cat, was again drawn along his back, not as before, from the head downwards, but from below the heels to the head. The man was then permitted to rise, and each of those who had been named by him as a participator in stealing the hog, was compelled to lie down, and have the cat twice drawn along his back—first downwards, and then upwards. After the termination of this punishment, each of the sufferers was washed with salt water by a black woman, and they were then dismissed.

This was the most excruciating punishment that I ever saw inflicted on black people—and, in my opinion, it is very dangerous, for the claws of the cat are poisonous, and wounds made by them are very subject to inflammation."

Horace Bushnell (1802–1876)

A leading nineteenth-century theologian and Congregational minister, Horace Bushnell was a man of exceptional talents, and following his education at Yale College, he studied law and then theology at the Yale Divinity School, where he became a tutor. Bushnell was intellectually keen, and approached both social and theological problems as a scholar, as the sermon excerpted here clearly shows. He was pastor of the North Church in Hartford, but regularly received invitations from educational institutions to become president. He declined both Middlebury College and the college that was to become the University of California at Berkeley, but he con-tinued to write often controversial books on theology and religious history, including *Christian Nurture* (1847), *Nature and the Supernatural* (1861), and *God in Christ* (1849). These works showed his allegiance to a new European theology, a mystical romanticism, espoused by Friedrich Schleiermacher in Germany and Samuel Taylor Coleridge in England, whose *Aids to Reflection* was a work that influenced not only Bushnell, but also Ralph Waldo Emerson. Bushnell's 1839 "A Discourse on the Slavery Question" is represented here not because Bushnell was a leading abolitionist, for he was not. Although he opposed the Fugitive Slave Act and the Compromise of 1850, he did not participate in the reform movements of his time. His opposition to women's suffrage is found in his book *Women's Suffrage: The Reform Against Nature* (1869), and his primary radicalism is found in his new theology, based on a rejection of Edwardsean Calvinism and a belief in the essential, natural goodness of human beings, including children, who were free from innate depravity. These theological views no doubt contributed to his opposition to slavery in the United States.

SUGGESTIONS FOR FURTHER READING

Bushnell, Horace. *Christ in Theology.* 1851.
———. *Christian Nurture.* 1847.
———. *God in Christ.* 1849.

————. *Nature and the Supernatural.* Reprt., 1903.
————. *Women's Suffrage: The Reform Against Nature.* 1869.
Smith, James Ward, and A. Leland Jamison, eds. *Religion in American Life,
    vol. I: The Shaping of American Religion.* Princeton, N.J.: Princeton
    University Press, 1961.

A DISCOURSE ON
THE SLAVERY QUESTION (1839)

As regards the matter of abolishing slavery in the Southern portions
of our country, there are two great questions, which arise for discussion and settlement.

I. Whether such abolition is possible, or a duty obligatory on the
Southern Legislatures.
And
II. What is our duty in reference to the subject; what measures, If
any, ought we to adopt with a view to hasten the result . . .

There are some three of our features in American slavery, which
no Christian, no man who has the common feelings of humanity,
can think of without pity, disgust, and shame . . .
The obnoxious features in American slavery of which I speak are
these . . .
First and chief of all is the non-permission of the family state, by
the denial of marriage rites; by tearing asunder those parents whom
God, more merciful than the laws, has doubtless accepted in the
rites of nature; by stripping their children from their arms; by disal-
lowing, if I should not rather say, extinguishing every affection
which makes life human . . .
Another feature of American slavery is the absence of any real
protection to the body of the slave, in respect to limb, life, or
chastity. It is philosophically true, that there are no such statutes, and they are not to be named in making out the legal view of
slavery . . .
A third feature of American slavery, as a legal institution is that it
nowhere recognizes, in the slave, a moral or intellectual nature. He
exists for another;—in himself he is no man. He is a muscular being

only, in the laws, or, rather I should say, he is a muscular tool, a thing composed of arms and legs and various integuments convenient to do work with. A frightful system of legalized selfishness has robbed him of himself. Light is denied him, the windows of his soul are shut up by express statute. As a creature of conscience, a creature of immortal wants, a creature in God's image, he has no legal existence . . .

Now observe—when I fix upon these features of slavery and take my stand for abolition before them, I do by no means regard the view they present, as a picture of slavery in the life. The condition of the slave, thus deserted, is seldom as desperate as the law suffers it to be. In this matter, he depends entirely upon the mercy, or the caprice of his master. Sometimes, of course, he finds a parent in his master. For myself, I cannot think of slavery, in this view, knowing as I do, the selfishness, the ferocity, the demoralized passions of men, without such a sense of its woes and cruelties as I cannot restrain. It compels me to say—I will not reason the matter farther. No facts, no arguments, no apprehension of mischief in a change, shall put me at peace with these things. They ought to be, will be, must be put away. And this to me is the abolition of slavery . . .

I say to the South, this institution is your own, not ours. Take your own way of proceeding. Modify your system as you please. But let me declare to you that, until you have established the family state and made it sacred, till you have given security to the body, till you have acknowledged the immortal mind and manhood of your slave, you do an offence to God and humanity, in the continuance of this institution, which we must condemn. In this sense, I am ready to go for the abolition of slavery, and I cannot think that any man in New England, is so lost to the spirit of liberty and humanity as to feel otherwise . . .

I turn here, on the one hand, to our Southern brethren, and say, here is a force in motion which you cannot long resist. The law of human society is against you, and you can as easily drive back the sun. The moral position of the world begins to reflect a peculiar disgrace on your institutions. You feel it now; you will feel it more; you will be compelled to yield to the feeling. I make no doubt that you are now firmly resolved to face out the odium of the human race; but cannot hold that resolve. Man's will is stout enough for a short time, but it can no more hold out in a long strain, than the muscles of his arms or his leg . . .

I turn on the other hand, to our Anti-Slavery brethren, and say, do not regard yourselves in the organization you have raised up. Neither conclude, too hastily, at the beginning of a movement for liberty, or assume too much consequence to yourselves in the organization you have raised up. Neither conclude, too hastily, that what you are doing is a real advantage. The destruction of slavery will be accomplished, either with you, or without you; or, if you make it necessary, in spite of you . . .

I am obliged to say that I do not anticipate any such bright destiny opening on the African race in their country, as seems to occupy the vision of our Anti-Slavery brethren. They cherish egregious expectations, in this matter, I am confident, and the zeal which actuates them is, so far, out of proportion. Their action would be more healthful, if they had a more moderate estimate of the good, which is probably to be accomplished, in behalf of the colored race . . .

There is no example in history, where an uncultivated and barbarous stock has been elevated in the midst of a cultivated and civilized stock; and I have no expectation that there ever will be . . .

My expectation is that the African races, in this country, would soon begin to dwindle towards extinction, in the same way, if emancipated. Some few persons would, of course, be much elevated by their new privileges; as we see in the case of individuals among our Indian tribes. I am far from thinking that the African is incapable of elevation. We have facts enough to prove the contrary. The difficulty is to elevate the race, *as a race,* among us . . .

In attempting to elevate the African race among us, there is too great a disadvantage against them in the beginning, to allow any hope of success. They need five hundred or a thousand years of cultivation to give them a fair chance. They cannot maintain the competition, they will be preyed upon and over-reached, they will, many of them, betake themselves to idleness, vice, and crime; by all these conjoint influences they will be kept down and gradually diminished in numbers. At present they are kept from a decline in population, only by the interest their masters have in them . . .

If we suppose that Christian benevolence will undertake for the race and will rescue them from the doom, otherwise sure to over-take them, doubtless much will be attempted and much done in that way. But the work is so great, the amount of Christian instruction and patronage requisite, so far beyond the possible supply, as effec-tually to cut off all hope of success . . .

Furthermore, I have facts to show the probable decline of our colored population in a state of freedom, which leave us no need of speculation. Take the case of the Irish. It is not true, as many sup-pose, that they become an integral part of our nation to any consid-erable extent: They become extinct. It is very seldom that their children born in this country live to mature age. Intemperance and poor living sweep them away, both old and young together. If you will glance over the catalogues of our colleges and legislatures, the advertisements of merchants and mechanics, you will almost never find an Irish name among them, which shows you at least that they do not rise to any rank among us. At the same time, if you will search the catalogues of alms-houses, and prisons, and potter's fields, there you will find their names in thick order . . .

If then slavery ought thus to be given up, or abolished by the South, let us inquire—

II. What is our duty, at the North, in reference to this subject; what measures, if any, ought we to adopt . . .

Many, who are offended by the Anti-Slavery movements, do not stay to settle their own minds, as they ought, but declare at once, that we have nothing to do with the subject, and have even no right to touch it. But that is a doctrine which cannot be yielded to for a moment . . .

Again we are linked with slavery, by duties of mutual aid and de-fence. Thus if an insurrection arises, we may be called, according to the Constitution, to march down our troops and aid in restoring the laws . . .

We have also a common character with the South, we are one na-tion, and have as dear a property in their good name, as they have in their own . . .

A man's right hand cannot be a thief's and his left an honest man's. No more can a nation have its honor or its dishonor in single limbs and fragments . . .

Then again our holy religion is a spirit of universal humanity and benevolence. By it we are constituted brothers of mankind . . .

The first movement here at the North was a rank onset and explosion . . .

The first sin of this organization was a sin of ill manners. They went to work much as if they were going to drive the masters—as they do their negroes. The great convention, which met at Philadelphia, drew up a declaration of their sentiments, in which they visibly affected the style and tone of the Declaration of Independence . . .

The Union is undervalued, and its preservation is often spoken of with lightness!

The movements of our societies have not touched the consciences of the Southern people, as many would be glad to believe, when they see the heat that is excited . . .

We have been greatly mistaken, as to the moral power of associations generally, but here they are specially impotent. If you wish to put a man of real weight quite out of the way, to *hide* him, or make his name a cipher, as regards this question, you need only put him into an Anti-Slavery association. He *will lie there sweltering* under the heated mass of numbers, like the giant under Aetna, and by men as little felt or regarded . . .

The three great features of American slavery, which I have named, must be an offence to every principle of goodness in your hearts. I charge you, then, in every sphere of life, as citizens and as Christians, to justify your own consciences, and be true to your post, as friends of God and humanity . . .

You cannot be indifferent to these weighty interests. You are the sons of New England; you are friends, too, of humanity, and lovers of your country. I invoke you also in the higher name of GOD and duty.—May He whose distinction it is, that he bringeth out of the land of Egypt and out of the house of bondage; the wheels of whose chariot were filled, of old, with the eyes of an all-inspecting and equal justice; who sent forth His Son, in the later ages, proclaiming liberty to the captives . . .

SOURCE NOTE: Horace Bushnell, *A Discourse on the Slavery Question* (1839).

James McCune Smith (1813–1865)

James McCune Smith was one of the most prominent of the black abolitionists of the nineteenth century. Born in New York City in 1813, he was,
like Frederick Douglass, his contemporary, a mulatto of mixed white and
black parentage. He received an excellent education, but not all of it in the
United States. First he attended the African Free School in Manhattan that
was then located near Hester Street, which was to become the site of Jewish
immigration settlement later in the nineteenth century. For his university
education, he was compelled to emigrate to Great Britain, as most American universities were closed to African American students. Therefore, he
studied at the University of Glasgow, from which he received the B.A. degree in 1835, the M.A. in 1836, and the M.D. in 1837. His medical residency
was pursued in Paris, and then he practiced medicine in New York City for
a quarter century, simultaneously remaining active in the black abolitionist
movement of antebellum America.

Because he was the first African American to hold a medical degree, his
medical practice in New York prospered; however, he is best remembered
for his activism and writings as an abolitionist. "Smith's intellect, integrity,
and lifelong commitment to abolitionism brought him state and national
recognition. From the early 1840s, he provided leadership for the campaign
to expand black voting rights in New York, although he initially refused to
ally with any political party. In the 1850s, Smith continued his suffrage activity through the black state conventions. He eventually gravitated to the
political antislavery views of the Radical Abolition party, and received the
party's nomination for New York Secretary of State in 1857" (*Encyclopedia
of Black Americans* [New York, 1994], pp. 2493–95).

James McCune Smith was primarily a pamphlet writer; however, he authored several important books, including *A Lecture on the Haytien Revolutions: with a Sketch of the Character of Toussaint L'Ouverture* (1841) and
the book which is excerpted here, *The Destiny of a People of Color* (1843).
He also authored the introductions to Frederick Douglass, *My Bondage
and My Freedom* (1855), the second of the Douglass autobiographies, and
Henry Highland Garnet's *Memorial Discourse* (1865). Smith was offered a
teaching position at Wilberforce University, but his poor health (he suffered from heart disease) made it impossible for him to accept the position,

and he moved his family to Williamsburg, Long Island, New York, where he died on November 17, 1865.

SUGGESTIONS FOR FURTHER READING

Blight, David. "In Search of Learning, Liberty, and Self-Definition: James McCune Smith and the Ordeal of the Antebellum Black Intellectual." *African-Americans in New York Life and History* 9 (1985), pp. 7–25.

Quarles, Benjamin. *The Black Abolitionists.* New York: Oxford University Press, 1969.

Ripley, C. Peter, et al., eds. *The Black Abolitionist Papers.* Vol. 3, *The United States, 1830–1846.* Chapel Hill: University of North Carolina Press, 1991.

———. *The Black Abolitionist Papers.* Vol. 4, *The United States, 1847–1858.* Chapel Hill: University of North Carolina Press, 1991.

Smith, James McCune. *Autographs for Freedom.* 1853, 1854.

———, ed. *The Colored American* (after May issue, 1839).

THE DESTINY OF
A PEOPLE OF COLOR (1843)

But how shall we enquire into the future? With what line and rule shall we step beyond the bounds of the present and read with an intelligent eye the fate of men and empires? . . . The rule is announced in the simple proposition: What hath been will be or like causes under like circumstances will produce like effects. This proposition is the very basis of all our belief, all our hope—it is the very essence of that Faith in the stability of things without which life would be made up of dismal, because uncertain, anticipation. Reposing on the belief that because our planet, for thousands of years, hath described its orbit round the sun, and that because day and night, seed-time and harvest, summer and winter, have run their successive course, therefore they will continue in the same, we live on free from apprehensions which would turn life into a curse . . .

May we not, then, guided by a proposition so universal in its application, the basis at once of our faith and of our knowledge,—may we not venture upon the investigation of the probable destiny of those with whom we are more immediately linked? . . .

It has been asserted, by intelligent men, that the day will come when the colored population of these United States shall have entirely disappeared, and when the various nations of men that now make up our "chequered Union," shall, in the words of our national motto, "of many nations make one." The statistical reports seem to announce the slow but certain approach of such a time; for, the census of the United States, from 1790 to 1840 show, that whilst the white population has maintained the same ratio of increase, the increase of the colored population has been by a gradually diminishing ratio. In other words, the whites are increasing more rapidly, relatively, than the colored people.

But, notwithstanding a time may come, when the descendants of our people shall no longer be distinguished by any physical peculiarity, yet it is clear, that a destiny awaits them which they must fulfil, and which will greatly affect whoever may live during and after its fulfilment. In order to investigate that destiny, it is necessary, first, to examine into our present position, by which our fate must necessarily be governed.

First: We are a minority held in servitude by a majority.

Secondly: That majority simulate a Republican form of Government.

Thirdly: We, the minority, held in servitude, are distinguished by a different complexion from the majority who hold us in thrall.

Such is our position. Men have been held in servitude in other times and places, under one or two of the above conditions, and the destiny of such men has been recorded; but until now, and in our case, there has not happened a concurrence of all these conditions in the position of any people upon the earth . . .

Let us now take up the propositions which describe our condition. And first, let us enquire into the probable destiny of men enslaved, and who differ in complexion from their masters.

The white slaves on the coast of Barbary, have as yet wrought out no general fact in history; as if slavery was natural to them, they have tamely remained in bondage, occasionally escaping by flight or ransom. But the Jews, held in slavery by the Egyptians, after suffering dreadful oppression, at length gathered themselves under a leader raised up by God, and migrated from the house of Bondage. A remarkable characteristic of this slavery was that there was no amalgamation between the masters and their slaves. Escape from slavery, by migration, was in this instance the law obeyed by the minority (the Jews) who differed in complexion from their masters. Can this law be applied to our destiny? To a certain extent, we do escape from slavery in this manner. But thirty thousand, which is, in full, the number of people who have migrated to Canada, Liberia, and the West Indies, is too small a number from which to draw a general inference, it is only one eighty-third portion of our population. No! we are not a migrating people. The soil of our birth is dear to our hearts, and we cling to it with a tenacity which no force can unhinge, no contumely sever . . .

Alike in servitude, and in being distinguished by complexion from our task-masters, we act differently from the Israelites? Why? It must be for the accomplishment of some end different from what they effected. They emigrated from the scene of their slavery, and in the search for Liberty. *"Ubi libertas, ibi patria,"* is an expression of their rule of conduct; and from the time of their escape from the House of Bondage, until now, the persecuted, or oppressed few have for the most part fled from their homes in search of Liberty. By remaining upon the scene of our oppressions we are acting out the converse of their rule of conduct. We proclaim to the oppressed few, *"Ubi patria, ibi libertas,"* "Where our country is, there shall Liberty dwell!" . . .

By remaining in this country, the scene of our enslavement, we shall overcome slavery, and consequently confute, by the resistless evidence of facts, the doctrines upon which slavery rests. This will do more for human Liberty than could be accomplished by emigration. By the latter course we might escape from, but would leave untouched an evil institution, which, by our present course, we are destined to overthrow.

But in overcoming the Institution of Slavery, we must by our conduct confute the doctrines on which it is based. One of these doctrines is, that "Might makes Right." Because men have the power, therefore they have the right to keep other men enslaved. This doctrine has also been the basis of several modern revolutions. For when the dogma of the Divine Right of Kings, and the reign of superstition lost their influence upon the minds of the masses, these masses arose in their might, and relying upon their physical might, endeavored to obtain those rights which had been so long withheld from them. Their success has been only partial, because, perchance, their efforts were based upon an unstable foundation—mere might.

We are not in possession of physical superiority: yet we must overturn the doctrine "might makes right," and we can only do so by demonstrating that "right makes right." This very doctrine is contained in the American Declaration of Independence, which declares that "all men have certain inalienable rights." But the Constitution of these United States, professedly constructed on the above principles, holds that there are some "other persons"—besides all men—who are not entitled to these rights! It is our destiny to prove that even this exception is wrong, and therefore contrary to the highest interests of the whole people, and to eradicate from the Constitution this exception, so contrary to its general principles.

There is another doctrine which we are destined, nay, that we are daily illustrating by our conduct. It has been the History of nearly all great Revolutions, that Reformers have followed out the doctrine of returning evil for evil. So soon as the oppressed have found the opportunity and the power, they have retaliated upon the oppressor with a similarity of oppression. They have returned evil for evil. **We are destined to show the infinite superiority of returning Good for Evil.** Even at this hour, bound with bands of iron at the South, and the fetters of prejudice at the North, scorned, jeered at, tortured with the fangs of ferocious and malignant slanders, and with the merciless lash of the slave whip, we have refrained from deluging our country in blood. The beautiful edifices of our oppressors spring up on every side, gathering into villages, towns, and cities, and the broad rivers run by them, swollen with the tears of the oppressed, but untinged with the blood of the oppressors. They drive us from the magnificent temples which they erect for the worship of the Most High, as if He were a "respecter of persons." In our humble way, we raise humble tenements in which we approach the footstool of our common Father, and we pray, not for vengeance, but for mercy on our oppressors, and we throw open the doors that all, even those who exclude us, all who thirst may come in and drink, that all who are heavily laden may unburthen themselves before altars erected to the Living Lord; in a word, in our every act, and all our relations we are already rendering Good for Evil, and what can be more glorious in the destiny of any people!

We are an oppressed minority, then, and are men of kindred power with those who oppress us. What has been the fate of oppressed minorities who have resisted oppression? History is full of evidence on this subject. The Jews, for example, in comparatively modern times have been persecuted and oppressed very much in almost every European kingdom. The Inquisition of Spain was specially instituted against them. They were expelled from country after country by a series of laws which are the prototypes or precedents of the Ohio-code. Even at this hour they are excluded from the privileges of citizenship in free, enlightened and philanthropic Great Britain. And yet we find that the Jews, the so pitilessly oppressed minority, now hold in their hands the rule, the very fate of some of the kingdoms which were formerly foremost in persecuting them. The very persecutions which they suffered drove them to amass that influence—MONEY—which enables them to rule their former oppressors.

SOURCE NOTE: James McCune Smith, *The Destiny of a People of Color* (Boston, 1843). The allusion above to the "Ohio-code" specifically refers first, to the manly resistance of the people of color to mob violence in Cincinnati, and second, to the fact that in spite of the odious Black Code of Ohio, the colored people of Ohio had advanced more rapidly and energetically than the same population in any other state, according to McCune's calculations. The nonviolent and Christian doctrine of returning "good for evil" is of course an early expression of the doctrine that Martin Luther King, Jr., would adopt for the civil rights movement of the 1950s and 1960s.

Wendell Phillips (1811–1884)

Like his contemporary, William Lloyd Garrison, Wendell Phillips was a pioneering reformer who championed a number of unpopular causes, including abolitionism, women's suffrage, prison reform, prohibition, and an improvement in the federal policy toward the displaced Native Americans. Unlike Garrison, Phillips advocated occasional violence in the cause of abolitionism. Both men called for unconditional emancipation and were critics of the U.S. Constitution as a proslavery document, and both men called for secession of the North from the slaveholding South and a rejection of the Compromise of 1850, which included the Fugitive Slave Law, which most abolitionists viewed as a compact with Satan. Unlike Garrison, Phillips was superbly educated, having attended the Boston Latin School and Harvard College (class of 1831). He was also a graduate of the Harvard Law School (1834). As closely as they worked and as many issues as they agreed upon, Garrison and Phillips disagreed on several prominent questions and were eventually disunited in 1865 when the American Anti-Slavery Society elected Phillips as president to succeed Garrison. Phillips's achievement was in his writing and his oratory, not in his political acumen or elected positions. He is represented in this volume by his treatise *The Constitution, a Pro-Slavery Compact* (1845), which engages the legalisms of Lysander Spooner's *The Unconstitutionality of Slavery* (1845), also antislavery but different in its approach to the issues. Phillips also wrote *The Philosophy of the Abolitionist Movement* (1854), which is a defense of abolitionism at a time when its principles were under assault not only in the South, but also by conservative abolitionists in the North. Phillips was a powerful speaker—perhaps, with Frederick Douglass, one of the two most effective orators in antebellum America. He died in Boston on February 2, 1884.

THE CONSTITUTION, A PRO-SLAVERY
COMPACT: SELECTIONS FROM THE
MADISON PAPERS, &C. (1845)

from the Introduction

... These extracts develop most clearly all the details of that "compromise," which was made between freedom and slavery, in 1787; granting to the slaveholder distinct privileges and protection for his slave property, in return for certain commercial concessions on his part toward the North. They prove also that the Nation at large were fully aware of this bargain at the time, and entered into it willingly and with open eyes.

... The clauses of the Constitution to which we refer as of a pro-slavery character are the following:

Art. 1, Sect. 2.—Representatives and direct taxes shall be apportioned among the several States, which may be included within this Union, according to their respective numbers, which shall be determined by adding to the whole number of free person, including those bound to service for a term of years, and excluding Indians not taxed, *three-fifths of all other persons.*

Art. 1, Sect. 8.—Congress shall have power ... to suppress insurrections.

Art. 1, Sect. 9.—The migration or importation of such persons as any of the States now existing, shall think proper to admit, shall not be prohibited by the Congress, prior to the year one thousand eight hundred and eight: but a tax or duty may be imposed on such importation, not exceeding ten dollars for each person.

Art. 4, Sect. 2.—No person, held to service or labor in one State, under the laws thereof, escaping into another, shall, in consequence of any law or regulation therein, be discharged from such service or labor; but shall be delivered up on claim of the party to whom such service or labor may be due.

Art. 4, Sect. 4.—The United States shall guarantee to every State in this Union a republican form of government; and shall protect each of them against invasion; and, on application of the legislature, or of the executive (when the legislature cannot be convened) *against domestic violence.*

The first of these clauses, relating to representation, confers on a slaveholding community additional political power for every slave held among them, and thus tempts them to continue to uphold the system: the second and the last, relating to insurrection and domestic violence, perfectly innocent in themselves—yet being made with the fact directly in view that slavery exists among us, do deliberately pledge the whole national force against the unhappy slave if he imitate our fathers and resist oppression—thus making us partners in the guilt of sustaining slavery: the third, relating to the slave-trade, disgraces the nation by a pledge not to abolish that traffic till after twenty years, *without obliging Congress to do so even then,* and thus the slave-trade may be legalized tomorrow if Congress choose: the fourth is a promise on the part of the whole Nation to return fugitive slaves to their masters, a deed which God's law expressly condemns and which every noble feeling of our nature repudiates with loathing and contempt.

... A few persons, to be sure, of late years, to serve the purposes of a party, have tried to prove that the Constitution makes no compromise with slavery. Notwithstanding the clear light of history; the unanimous decision of all the courts in the land, both State and Federal; the action of Congress and the State Legislatures; the constant practice of the Executive in all its branches; and the deliberate acquiescence of the whole people for half a century, still they contend that the Nation does not know its own meaning, and that the Constitution does not tolerate slavery! Every candid mind, however, must acknowledge that the language of the Constitution is clear and explicit.

Its terms are so broad, it is said, that they include many others beside slaves, and hence it is wisely (!) inferred that they cannot include the slaves themselves! Many persons besides slaves in this country doubtless are "held to service and labor under the laws of the States," but that does not at all show that slaves are not "held to service;" many persons beside the slaves may take part "in insurrections," but that does not prove that when the slaves rise, the National Government is not bound to put them down by force. Such a thing has been heard of before as one description, including a great variety of persons—and this is the case in the present instance.

But granting that the terms of the Constitution are ambiguous—

that they are susceptible of two meanings, if the unanimous, concurrent, unbroken practice of every department of the Government, judicial, legislative, and executive, and the acquiescence of the whole people for fifty years do not prove which is the true construction, then how and where can such a question ever be settled? If the people and the Courts of the land do not know what they themselves mean, who has authority to settle their meaning for them?

If then the people and the Courts of a country are to be allowed to determine what their own laws mean, it follows that at this time and for the last half century, the Constitution of the United States has been, and still is, a pro-slavery instrument, and that any one who swears to support it, swears to do pro-slavery acts, and violates his duty both as a man and as an abolitionist. What the Constitution may become a century hence, we know not; we speak of it *as it is,* and repudiate it *as it is.*

But the purpose, for which we have thrown these pages before the community, is this. Some men, finding the nation unanimously deciding that the Constitution tolerates slavery, have tried to prove that this false construction, as they think it, has been foisted into the instrument by the corrupting influence of slavery itself, tainting all it touches. They assert that the known anti-slavery spirit of revolutionary times never *could* have consented to so infamous a bargain as the Constitution is represented to be, and has in its present hands become. Now these pages prove the melancholy fact, that willingly, with deliberate purpose, our fathers bartered honesty for gain, and became partners with tyrants, that they might share in the profits of their tyranny.

And in view of this fact, will it not require a very strong argument to make any candid man believe, that the bargain which the fathers tell us they meant to incorporate into the Constitution, and which the sons have always thought they found there incorporated, does not exist there, after all? Forty of the shrewdest men and lawyers in the land assemble to make a bargain, among other things, about slaves, after months of anxious deliberations they put it into writing and sign their names to the instrument, fifty years roll away, twenty millions, at least, of their children pass over the stage of life, courts sit and pass judgment, parties arise and struggle fiercely; still all concur in finding in the instrument just that meaning which the fathers tell us they intended to express: must not he be a desperate man, who, after all this, sets out to prove that the fathers were bunglers and the sons fools, and that slavery is not referred to at all?

Besides, the advocates of this new theory of the Anti-slavery character of the Constitution, quote some portions of the Madison Papers in support of their views; and this makes it proper that the community should hear *all* that these Debates have to say on the subject. The further we explore them, the clearer becomes the fact, that the Constitution was meant to be, what it has always been esteemed, a compromise between slavery and freedom.

If then the Constitution be, what these Debates show that our fathers intended to make it, and what, too, their descendants, this nation, say they did make it and agree to uphold, then we affirm that it is a "covenant with death and an agreement with hell," and ought to be immediately annulled. No abolitionist can consistently take office under it, or swear to support it.

But if, on the contrary, our fathers failed in their purpose, and the Constitution is all pure and untouched by slavery, then, Union itself is impossible, without guilt. For it is undeniable that the fifty years passed under this (anti-slavery) Constitution, show us the slaves trebling in numbers; slaveholders monopolizing the offices and dictating the policy of the Government; prostituting the strength and influence of the Nation to the support of slavery here and elsewhere; trampling on the rights of the free States, and making the courts of the country their tools. To continue this disastrous alliance longer is madness. The trial of fifty years with the best of men and the best of Constitutions, on this supposition, only proves that it is impossible for free and slave States to unite on any terms, without all becoming partners in the guilt and responsibility for the sin of slavery. We dare not prolong the experiment, and with double earnestness we repeat our demand upon every honest man to join in the outcry of the American Anti-Slavery Society,—

NO UNION WITH SLAVEHOLDERS!

SOURCE NOTE: Wendell Phillips, *The Constitution, a Pro-Slavery Compact* (Boston, 1845), in the collections of the Widener Library, Harvard University, and the Boston Public Library.

PHILOSOPHY OF THE ABOLITION
MOVEMENT (1854)

... I wish, Mr. Chairman, to notice some objections that have been made to our course ever since Mr. Garrison began his career, and which have been lately urged again, with considerable force and emphasis, in the columns of *The London Leader,* the able organ of a very respectable and influential class in England ...

The charges to which I refer are these: that, in dealing with slave-holders and their apologists, we indulge in fierce denunciations, in-stead of appealing to their reason and common sense by plain statements and fair argument—that we might have won the sympa-thies and support of the nation, if we would have submitted to ar-gue this question with a manly patience; but, instead of this, we have outraged the feelings of the community by attacks, unjust and unnecessarily severe, on its most valued institutions, and gratified our spleen by indiscriminate abuse of leading men, who were often honest in their intentions, however mistaken in their views—that we have utterly neglected the ample means that lay around us to convert the nation, submitted to no discipline, formed no plan, been guided by no foresight, but hurried on in childish, reckless, blind, and hotheaded zeal—bigots in the narrowness of our views, and fa-natics in our blind fury of invective and malignant judgment of other men's motives ...

What is the denunciation with which we are charged? It is en-deavoring, in our faltering human speech, to declare the enormity of the sin of making merchandise of men—of separating husband and wife—taking the infant from its mother, and selling the daugh-ter to prostitution—of a professedly Christian nation denying, by statute, the Bible to every sixth man and woman of its population, and making it illegal for "two or three" to meet together, except a white man be present! What is the harsh criticism of motives with which we are charged? It is simply holding the intelligent and delib-erate actor responsible for the character and consequences of his acts. Is there anything inherently wrong in such denunciation or such criticism? This we may claim—we have never judged a man but out of his own mouth. We have seldom, if ever, held him to account, except for acts of which he and his own friends were proud. All that we ask the world and thoughtful men to note are the principles and deeds on which the American pulpit and American public men plume themselves. We always allow our opponents to paint their own pictures. Our humble duty is to stand by and assure the spectators that what they would take for a knave or a hypocrite is really, in American estimation, a Doctor of Divinity or Secretary of State.

So far, however you distrust my philosophy, you will not doubt my statements. That we have denounced and rebuked with unsparing fidelity will not be denied. Have we not also addressed ourselves to that other duty, of arguing our question thoroughly?—of using due discretion and fair sagacity in endeavoring to promote our cause? Yes, we have. Every statement we have made has been doubted. Every principle we have laid down has been denied by overwhelming majorities against us. No one step has ever been gained but by the most laborious research and the most exhausting argument. And no question has ever, since Revolutionary days, been so thoroughly investigated or argued here, as that of slavery. Of that research and that argument, of the whole of it, the old-fashioned, fanatical, crazy Garrisonian antislavery movement has been the author. From this band of men has proceeded every important argument or idea which has been broached on the antislavery question from 1830 to the present time . . . How shall a feeble minority, without weight or influence in the country, with no jury of millions to appeal to—denounced, vilified, and contemned—how shall we make way against the overwhelming weight of some colossal reputation, if we do not turn from the idolatrous present, and appeal to the human race? saying to your idols of today, "Here we are defeated; but we will write our judgment with the iron pen of a century to come, and it shall never be forgotten, if we can help it, that you were false in your generation to the claims of the slave!"

At present, our leading men, strong in the support of large majorities, and counting safely on the prejudices of the community, can afford to despise us. They know they can overawe or cajole the Present; their only fear is the judgment of the Future. Strange fear, perhaps, considering how short and local their fame! But however little, it is their all. Our only hold upon them is the thought of that bar of posterity, before which we are all to stand . . . We are weak here—out-talked, out-voted. You load our names with infamy, and shout us down. But our words bide their time. We warn the living that we have terrible memories, and that their sins are never to be forgotten. We will gibbet the name of every apostate so black and high that his children's children shall blush to bear it. Yet we bear no malice—cherish no resentment . . .

So far from the antislavery cause having lacked a manly and able discussion, I think it will be acknowledged hereafter that this discussion has been one of the noblest contributions to a literature really American. Heretofore, not only has our tone been but an echo of foreign culture, but the very topics discussed and the views maintained have been too often pale reflections of European politics and European philosophy. No matter what dress we assumed, the voice was ever "the voice of Jacob." At last we have stirred a question thoroughly American; the subject has been looked at from a point of view entirely American; and it is of such deep interest, that it has called out all the intellectual strength of the nation. For once, the nation speaks its own thoughts in its own language, and the tone also is all its own . . .

Sir, when a nation sets itself to do evil, and all its leading forces, wealth, party, and piety, join in the career, it is impossible but that those who offer a constant opposition should be hated and maligned, no matter how wise, cautious, and well planned their course may be. We are peculiar sufferers in this way. The community has come to hate its reproving Nathan so bitterly, that even those whom the relenting part is beginning to regard as standard-bearers of the antislavery host think it unwise to avow any connection or sympathy with him. I refer to some of the leaders of the political movement against slavery. They feel it to be their mission to marshal and use as effectively as possible the present convictions of the people. They cannot afford to encumber themselves with the odium which twenty years of angry agitation have engendered in great sects sore from unsparing rebuke, parties galled by constant defeat, and leading men provoked by unexpected exposure. They are willing to confess, privately, that our movement produced theirs, and that its continued existence is the very breath of their life. But, at the same time, they would fain walk on the road without being soiled by too close contact with the rough pioneers who threw it up. They are wise and honorable, and their silence is very expressive.

When I speak of their eminent position and acknowledged ability, another thought strikes me. Who converted these men and their distinguished associates? It is said we have shown neither sagacity in plans, nor candor in discussion, nor ability. Who, then, or what, converted Burlingame and Wilson, Sumner and Adams, Palfrey and Mann, Chase and Hale, and Phillips and Giddings? Who taught the *Christian Register,* the *Daily Advertiser,* and that class of prints, that there were such things as a slave and a slaveholder in the land, and so gave them some more intelligent basis than their mere instincts to hate William Lloyd Garrison? What magic wand was it whose touch made the toadying servility of the land start up the real demon that it was, and at the same time gathered into the slave's service the professional ability, ripe culture, and personal integrity that grace the Free Soil ranks? We never argue! These men, then, were converted by simple denunciation! They were all converted by the "hot," "reckless," "ranting," "bigoted," "fanatic" Garrison, who never troubled himself about facts, nor stopped to argue with an opponent, but straightway knocked him down! . . . Do not criticise too much the agency by which such men were converted. That blade has a double edge. Our reckless course, our empty rant, our fanaticism, has made Abolitionists of some of the best and ablest men in the land. We are inclined to go on, and see if even with such poor tools we cannot make some more . . .

Caution is not always good policy in a cause like ours. It is said that, when Napoleon saw the day going against him, he used to throw away all the rules of war, and trust himself to the hot impetuosity of his soldiers. The masses are governed more by impulse than conviction; and even were it not so, the convictions of most men are on our side, and this will surely appear, if we can only pierce the crust of their prejudice or indifference. I observe that our Free Soil friends never stir their audience so deeply as when some individual leaps beyond the platform, and strikes upon the very heart of the people. Men listen to discussions of laws and tactics with ominous patience . . .

It would be superfluous to say that we grant the entire sincerity and true-heartedness of these men. But in critical times, when a wrong step entails most disastrous consequences, to "mean well" is not enough. Sincerity is no shield for any man from the criticism of his fellow-laborers. I do not fear that such men as these will take offense at our discussion of their views and conduct. Long years of hard labor, in which we have borne at least our share, have resulted in a golden opportunity. How to use it, friends differ. Shall we stand courteously silent, and let these men play out the play, when, to our thinking, their plan will slacken the zeal, balk the hopes, and waste the efforts of the slave's friends?

Every thoughtful and unprejudiced mind must see that such an evil as slavery will yield only to the most radical treatment. If you consider the work we have to do, you will not think us needlessly aggressive, or that we dig down unnecessarily deep in laying the foundations of our enterprise. A money power of two thousand millions of dollars, as the prices of slaves now range, held by a small body of able and desperate men; that body raised into a political aristocracy by special constitutional provisions; cotton, the product of slave labor, forming the basis of our whole foreign commerce, and the commercial class thus subsidized; the press bought up, the pulpit reduced to vassalage, the heart of the common people chilled by a bitter prejudice against the black race; our leading men bribed, by ambition, either to silence or open hostility—in such a land, on what shall an Abolitionist rely? On a few cold prayers, mere lip-service, and never from the heart? On a church resolution, hidden often in its records, and meant only as a decent cover for servility in daily practice? On political parties, with their superficial influence at best, and seeking ordinarily only to use existing prejudices to the best advantage? Slavery has deeper root here than any aristocratic institution has in Europe; and politics is but the common pulse-beat, of which revolution is the fever-spasm. Yet we have seen European aristocracy survive storms which seemed to reach down to the primal strata of European life. Shall we, then, trust to mere politics, where even revolution has failed? How shall the stream rise above its fountain? Where shall our church organizations or parties get strength to attack their great parent and moulder, the Slave Power? Shall the thing formed say to him that formed it, Why hast thou made me thus? The old jest of one who tried to lift himself in his own basket, is but a tame picture of the man who imagines that, by working solely through existing sects and parties, he can destroy slavery.

SOURCE NOTE: Wendell Phillips, *Philosophy of the Abolition Movement* (Boston, 1854), in the collections of Widener Library, Harvard University.

Lysander Spooner (1808–1891)

Lysander Spooner was a Massachusetts constitutional theorist who argued, in print, the viability of slavery under the charter agreement of the new nation. He vigorously opposed slavery and used legal reasoning to convince his readers that the Declaration of Independence, the constitutions of the various founding states, and the Articles of Confederation (which preceded the Constitution as a charter document of the new nation) were all documents that did not allow slavery as part of founding agreements. He did not agree with the Garrisonians, particularly Wendell Phillips, who saw in the Constitution an "agreement with Hell" and a "Proslavery Compact." Spooner debated in print with Wendell Phillips and with Henry Bowditch, whose *Slavery and the Constitution* (1849) was a response to Spooner's *Unconstitutionality of Slavery.* According to John Thomas, "As a trained lawyer, Bowditch was not impressed by Spooner's cranky and seemingly factitious argument. His own *Slavery and the Constitution* (1849) was intended as a rebuttal to Spooner's book based on an examination of the Constitution 'according to the common meaning of its terms' and establishing the 'uncontrovertible conclusion' that it legalized and upheld slavery" (John Thomas, *Slavery Attacked: The Abolitionist Crusade* [Englewood Cliffs, N.J.: Prentice-Hall, 1969]). Spooner's arguments may have been significant for constitutional theorists, but they did not have the widespread public appeal of Wendell Phillips's oratory. Phillips's *The Constitution, a Pro-Slavery Compact* (1845), also an engagement with the Spooner argument, is excerpted in this volume.

SUGGESTIONS FOR FURTHER READING

Bowditch, Henry Ingersoll. *Slavery and the Constitution.* 1849.
Spooner, Lysander. *The Unconstitutionality of Slavery.* 1845.
Thomas, John L., ed. *Slavery Attacked: The Abolitionist Crusade.* Englewood Cliffs, N.J.: Prentice-Hall, 1969.

THE UNCONSTITUTIONALITY OF
SLAVERY (1845)

from Chapter 8,
"The Constitution of the United States"

. . . Let us now look at the *positive* provisions of the constitution, *in favor of liberty,* and see whether they are not only inconsistent with any legal sanction of slavery, but also whether they must not, of themselves, have necessarily extinguished slavery, if it had had any constitutional existence to be extinguished.

And, first, the constitution made all "the people of the United States" *citizens* under the government to be established by it; for all of those, by whose authority the constitution declares itself to be established, must of course be presumed to have been made citizens by it . . .

Who, then, established the constitution?

The preamble to the constitution has told us in the plainest possible terms, to wit, that "We, *the people* of the United States" "do ordain and establish this constitution," &c.

By "the people of the United States," here mentioned, the constitution intends *all* "the people" then permanently inhabiting the United States. If it does not intend all, who were intended by "the people of the United States"?—The constitution itself gives no answer to such a question.—It does not declare that "we, the *white* people," or "we, the *free* people," or "we, a *part* of the people"—but that "we, *the* people"—that is, we the *whole* people—of the United States, "do ordain and establish this constitution."

If the *whole* people of the United States were not recognized as citizens by the constitution, then the constitution gives no information as to what portion of the people were to be citizens under it. And the consequence would then follow that the constitution established a government that could not know its own citizens.

. . . That the designation, "We the people of the United States," included the whole people that properly belonged to the United States, is also proved by the fact that no exception is made in any other part of the instrument.

If the constitution had intended that any portion of "the people of the United States" should be excepted from its benefits, disfranchised, outlawed, enslaved, it would of course have designated these exceptions with such particularity as to make it sure that none but the true persons intended would be liable to be subjected to such wrongs. Yet, instead of such particular designation of the exceptions, we find no designation whatever of the kind. But on the contrary, we *do* find, in the preamble itself, a sweeping declaration to the effect that there are no such exceptions; that the whole people of the United States are citizens, and entitled to liberty, protection, and the dispensation of justice under the constitution.

. . . Again. If the constitution was established by authority of all "the people of the United States," they are all legally parties to it, and citizens under it. And if they were parties to it, and citizens under it, it follows that neither they, *nor their posterity,* nor any nor either of them, can ever be legally enslaved within the territory of the United States; for the constitution declares its object to be, among other things, "to secure the blessings of liberty to *ourselves, and our posterity.*" This purpose of the national constitution is a law paramount to all state constitutions; for it is declared that "this constitution, and the laws of the United States that shall be made in pursuance thereof, and all treaties made, or which shall be made under the authority of the United States, shall be the supreme law of the land; and the judges *in every state* shall be bound thereby, any thing in the constitution or laws of any state to the contrary notwithstanding."

. . . But however clear it may be, that the constitution, in reality, made citizens of all "the people of the United States," yet it is not necessary to maintain that point, in order to prove that the constitution gave no guaranty or sanction to slavery—or if it had not already given citizenship to all, it nevertheless gave to the government of the United States unlimited power of offering citizenship to all. The power given to the government of passing naturalization laws, is entirely unrestricted, except that the laws must be uniform throughout the country. And the government has undoubted power to offer naturalization and citizenship to every person in the country, whether foreigner or native, who is not already a citizen. To suppose that we have in the country three millions of native born inhabitants, not citizens, and whom the national government has no power to make citizens, when its power of naturalization is entirely unrestricted, is a palpable contradiction.

from Chapter 13,
"The Children of Slaves Are Born Free"

... This law of nature, that all men are born free, was recognized by this country in the Declaration of Independence.—But it was no new principle then. Justinian says, "Captivity and servitude are both contrary to the law of nature; for by that law all men are born free." But the principle was not new with Justinian; it exists in the nature of man, and is as old as man—and the race of man generally has acknowledged it. The exceptions have been special; the rule general.

The constitution of the United States recognizes the principle that all men are born free; for it recognizes the principle that natural birth in the country gives citizenship—which of course implies freedom. And no exception is made to the rule. Of course all born in the country since the adoption of the constitution of the United States, have been born free, whether there were, or were not any legal slaves in the country before that time.

Even the provisions, in the several state constitutions, that the legislatures shall not *emancipate* slaves, would, if allowed their full effect, unrestrained by the constitution of the United States, hold in slavery only those who were then slaves; it would do nothing towards enslaving their children, and would give the legislatures no authority to enslave them.

It is clear, therefore, that on this principle alone, slavery would now be extinct in this country, unless there should be an exception of a few aged persons.

SOURCE NOTE: Lysander Spooner, *The Unconstitutionality of Slavery* (Boston, 1845).

James Russell Lowell (1819–1891)

James Russell Lowell was born in Cambridge, Massachusetts, on February 22, 1819, and was educated at Harvard College (1838) and the Harvard Law School. But it was his career as a writer and poet that occupied him, and he soon published *A Year's Life* (1844) and *Poems* (1845). He edited a literary journal, *The Pioneer,* in which he published the writings of his contemporaries Nathaniel Hawthorne, Edgar Allan Poe, and John Greenleaf Whittier, the Quaker poet and abolitionist. Both Lowell and his wife were deeply committed to the abolitionist cause, and in his *Biglow Papers,* which have the satirical character of Washington Irving's *Salmagundi Papers,* Lowell used a persona-narrator to attack the war with Mexico over the annexation of Texas, and the extension of slavery into the new territories. He wrote regularly for *The Atlantic,* and published new *Biglow Papers* during the Civil War that were serialized there and then released in book form. In this volume Lowell is represented by a wide variety of selections, indicating his wide-ranging interests in the issues of his day. As an abolitionist, he focused much energy on the hypocrisy of the institutional church for its support of slavery, and wrote "Politics and the Pulpit" in 1849, "The Church and the Clergy" in 1845, and one month later, "The Church and the Clergy Again." He also contributed to the debates concerning the essential nature of the African, and in 1849 wrote "Ethnology." Lowell wrote extremely well, as these selections clearly show, and his regular contributions to the *Atlantic* and to antislavery papers gave him a leading voice in the abolitionist cause.

SUGGESTIONS FOR FURTHER READING

Duberman, Martin. *James Russell Lowell: A Biography.* 1966.

Howard, Leon. *Victorian Knight Errant: The Early Literary Career of James Russell Lowell.* 1952.

Lowell, James Russell. *The Biglow Papers. First Series.* Edited by Thomas Wortham. 1977.

See also the James Russell Lowell entries in *American Literary Scholarship,* published annually by *American Literature* and the Duke University Press.

MR. CALHOUN'S REPORT (1849)

. . . As a general rule, the race has been distinguished for its steady habits, but individuals have been known to fall into habits of dissipation, scattering their pocketfuls of rocks in the most spendthrift manner, and some have displayed a dangerous predilection for playing with fire, which has rendered them very uncomfortable neighbors . . .

Mr. Calhoun's document is not so much a report as a Jeremiad. It consists mainly of a catalogue of the wrongs and grievances which the Southern Israel has sustained at the hands of the Heathen round about. In one respect it is meritoriously distinguished from the doleful palaver of Northern pro-slavery. Its tone is gentlemanly, and there is no snuffle, no piety in it from beginning to end. Ham is not alluded to, and there is no hypocritical twaddle about the mysterious designs of an inscrutable Providence. Let us be thankful that we have at least a pro-slavery appeal in which the slaveholder and not slavery is defended, in which the guilt of wrong and inhumanity is not laid to the charge of the benign Father of us all . . .

Mr. Calhoun and other pleaders for the peculiar institution seem to think that the claim to buy and sell human beings gathers validity by the distance of time at which it was recognized as a portion of our political system, and that its respectability is proportionate to its antiquity. But, however true this may be of just and rightful things, it is certain that age only attracts a deeper damnation toward what is wrong and unjust. The force of the antagonism to it is cumulative, like the poison of arsenic. Every year adds to its horror and its odium, lengthening out the loathsome vista with new objects for indignation, and new claims for retribution and redress. The age of slavery, like the gray hairs of Scenic, only heightens the sense of its atrocity. Shall it claim a privilege for cruelty because it has been cruel long? Shall it sanctify tyranny by the plea of invariable usage?

After showing what divinity doth constitutionally hedge Slavery in the Southern States, Mr. Calhoun proceeds to draw a charming picture of the precautions taken to prevent the escape of runaways, and of the assistance which the pursuing masters received from citizens of free states in those earlier and simpler days of the Republic. But, like other pictures of a bygone Arcadia, it unfortunately is not founded on truth. There was never so much or so sincere anti-slavery feeling in the Northern States as at the period immediately following the Revolution. This is made evident by the emancipation, or the movements toward it, which took place at that time . . .

THE ABOLITIONISTS AND
EMANCIPATION (1849)

Next to the charge of being possessed of only a single idea, the accusation most often brought against Abolitionists has been that they have retarded the progress of emancipation and made more galling the fetters of the slave. If emancipation at all hazards be the one idea of the Abolitionists, this is the one idea of their opponents . . .

In the first place has there really been a change of public opinion for the worse, either at the North or the South, since *The Liberator* came into existence eighteen years ago? We select this period as the point of departure, and not because we have forgotten Woolman, Benezet, and Lundy, but because these stand in the same relation to the Anti-slavery movement in America that Dante, the Lollards and Huss hold in respect to Luther.

. . . Moreover, at the time when the movement began, Slavery was regarded as a distant and detached object. The immense spread of its roots, and how they had forced themselves into every crevice in the foundations of Church and State, was not even suspected . . .

Any one who has read Clarkson's *History of the Abolition of the Slave Trade* cannot fail to be struck with the similarity of the objections brought against the advocate of that measure in England and those which are constantly thrown in the way of American Anti-slavery . . .

. . . The simple fact undoubtedly is that were the Abolitionists now to go back to the position from which they started, they would find themselves less fanatical than a very respectable minority of the people . . . The Garrison of 1831 might be a popular man and a member of Congress now. But it is part of the order of Providence that there should be always Garrisons as well as popular men and members of Congress.

. . . So much for the retarding effect of the Anti-slavery agitation at the North. At the South, if violent opposition has been excited, it has been a mere offset to equal violence on the other side. It has arisen from the fact that the defenders of slavery instinctively felt that their weakness was in their own camp. How could what is in its own nature the most unreasonable of institutions, be reasonably defended? How could that which is founded on force and fraud be gently and honestly supported? ... The efforts of the Abolitionists have drawn so much attention toward slavery, and their sentiments have found so much sympathy even in some of the Slave States themselves, that every evil, cruelty and misery belonging to the system had become painfully conspicuous. The slaveholder in the remotest rice swamp of Florida feels that the walls have eyes and ears.

The fanaticism of the Abolitionists has retarded emancipation, just in the same way that Luther retarded the Reformation. Considering the immense odds against which they have had to struggle, they have brought about a revolution in a wonderfully short space of time. It does not matter that the advocates of emancipation in the Slave states shrink from accepting the abolition doctrine in all its length and breadth ... Along the slender wire of Northern Anti-slavery the Southern Abolitionist receives the inspiring influx of the religious sentiment, the love of freedom, and the humanity of entire Christendom. Slavery has nothing behind it but the sheer precipice, nothing before it but the inevitable retributive Doom.

POLITICS AND THE PULPIT (1849)

... There can be no fallacy greater or more dangerous than is contained in the popular axiom that politics and religion should be kept carefully disjoined. It is an axiom which had its origin in the unprincipled self-interest of politicians. It is of a piece with the system which would shut God out from the secular part of the week and imprison Him in a particular day and in certain buildings. With equal propriety the merchant might banish religion from business, and the tradesman keep it carefully away from his shop. Indeed it is too often true that, as the clergyman leaves his robes hanging in the vestry, the congregation doff their religion to be locked up in the church where it will be kept safely till they need it to put on again when the seventh day, appropriate to that ceremony, shall have come round again.

Next to having no religion at all, this kind, which can be put on and off at will, is certainly the most convenient . . .

The great hardship of the Christian revelation lies in the exact closeness with which it will fit you and me. Embodying a universal truth, it possesses within itself a principle of development which renders it a test for the church, the state and the individual in every possible phase of society. It is a standard which cannot warp or shrink, and which indicates with impartial indifference every deviation from the immutable line of right and duty. It cannot well be a very comfortable instrument in the hands of a faithful minister.

. . . Abolitionists have no quarrel with the Church as a Church, but only with the Church as it is. This is the reason why they are odious to sect-wrights and divinity-mongers. They do not deny the great services which the Church and the Clergy have rendered to truth and progress as the instruments of order and organization. But they affirm that a Church, to be of any benefit, must be in advance of the social ideas of the age, and demand of the Clergy that they no longer organize sects, but society. It is not politics which they ask them to preach, but Christianity itself.

To state the matter more strictly, it is not the Abolitionist who makes the demands. They are the requisitions of our present social condition. Nor is the Church so much called upon to be a Reformer, as to be truly a Church. The clergy, at least in America, are no longer a privileged order. They do not and cannot any longer occupy the position which they held when the mouth and the pen were the only vehicles and disseminators of truth. They are no longer the only priests, and there are other pulpits than those on churches . . .

Nevertheless a certain amount of prestige still attaches itself to the clergy. They are still looked upon as guardians specially set apart to watch over religion and spiritual things. A seventh part of the year is reserved for them, and their obligations to truth are larger in proportion to the opportunity afforded them to disseminate and enforce it . . .

THE CHURCH AND THE CLERGY (1845)

. . . There is no such short and easy way to popularity among the thoughtless and uneducated portion of the people as that of assuming to be the defender of their religious prejudices, however absurd and monstrous they may be. When a system has become corrupt, an indifferent skepticism gradually pervades the more refined and intellectual classes of society, while the zeal of the brutal and unintelligent in its defence becomes proportioned always to the nearness of its approach to their sympathies and tastes, and the indulgences it allows to their appetites . . .

Every true abolitionist is thoroughly persuaded that the most terrible weapon which they can bring to bear, not only against slavery, but against all other social vices, is the religious sentiment of the country. But it is the *true* religious sentiment, and not that of which the churches and clergy of the land are the present exponents, which they are striving to reach; and the religious system of the country, as now existing, is the greatest obstacle in their way . . . The political and religious principles of a nation must, in order to have any useful vitality, be in advance of that nation's civilization. When they have brought the civilization of that nation up to their own higher level, they must move forward another step. In this country the civilization of the people has not yet come nearly up to the political principles set forth in the Declaration of Independence, but it has already gone beyond the religious principle as now represented by the church. It is time, then, for the church to re-form itself so as to be the emblem of something higher and purer—of something which shall satisfy the demand of the foremost spirits of the age—and no longer be content, by remaining fixed in a traditionary and retrospective excellence, to be the time-serving cloak and excuse for the indolent or interested who lag behind . . .

THE CHURCH AND
THE CLERGY AGAIN (1845)

. . . If the church carry this divine authority with it, it should be always in advance of public opinion. It should not wait till the Washingtonians, by acting the part which, in virtue of the station it arrogates to itself, should have been its own, had driven it to sign the pledge and hold fellowship with the degraded and fallen. It should not wait until the abolitionists, by working a change in the public sentiment of the people, have convinced it that it is more politic to sympathize with the slave than with the slave-owner, before it ventures to lisp the alphabet of anti-slavery. The glorious privilege of leading the forlorn hope of truth, of facing the desperate waves of prejudice, of making itself vile in the eyes of men by choosing the humblest means of serving the despised cause of the Master it professes to worship, all these belong to it in right of the position it has assumed.

Instead of timidly yielding to, and in many instances encouraging, the prejudices or the ignorant rage of the mob, it is the clergy themselves who should have been the victims (if any there must be) of the first wrath of assaulted sin. It is they who should have been mobbed, who should have endured insult and contumely . . .

The church is, in its true sense, merely the outward symbol of the religious sentiment as that sentiment ought to be. When it becomes merely the symbol of that sentiment as it is, there is no longer any use or fitness in it, and it degrades the moral sense of the nation which it was its duty to elevate. Then it is time for all those who have some innate principle of religion, and who are therefore competent to reform it, to begin an attack upon it which shall compel it to move forward in reality to that lofty stand which it has duped men into believing that it occupies already . . .

DANIEL WEBSTER (1846)

"Mr. Edward Webster has arrived in town for the purposes of recruiting a company of volunteers for the Mexican War. He has taken this step, we understand, with the full approval of his distinguished father."

—(BOSTON PAPERS.)

. . . Among the thousand and one so-called great men of this so-called democracy, Daniel Webster always excites in us the most painful feeling of regret. A man who might have done so much, and who will die without having disburthened the weary heart of Humanity of one of its devouring griefs! What has freedom to thank Daniel Webster for? What has Peace? What has Civilization? What has that true Conservatism, which consists in bringing the earth forward and upward to the idea of its benign Maker? In one word, how is God the better served, how are heaven and earth more at one for His having bestowed upon this man that large utterance, that divine faculty of eloquent speech? How was man made in the image of God, save that the capacity was given him of being an adequate representative on earth of some one of the attributes of the Great Father, and His loyal ambassador to man?

Who that has ever witnessed the wonderful magnetism which Webster exerts over masses of men can doubt that his great powers have been staked against the chances of the presidential chair and lost, gambled, thrown away by the fortune of the dice? The influence of his physical presence is prodigious. He owes half his fame to it . . .

It is said that great occasions summon forth great minds to be their servants and to do their work. Rather, we should say, the world is full of great occasions, but only great minds can see them, and surrender themselves unreservedly to their dictation. Such men as Washington are called providential men. And so they are; yet there were men of far greater intellectual capacity than Washington in the day of the Revolution. Washington had a great *character,* and it is in proportion as they possess this mysterious faculty (we may call it) that men make their mark upon their age, and are valued by posterity. Herein consists the great strength of such men as Garrison, and it is precisely here that Webster is wanting . . .

Will God decide that the occasion has been wanting to Daniel Webster? How far might not that trumpet voice have reached, in behalf of the oppressed, from the commanding position conceded to his powerful intellect! How far might it not have aroused who now sleep, forgetful of their duty to their fellow-man! God has given him eminent faculties, and what is the harvest? Will they who from among the crowding tares of the world glean the sparse wheat ears for God's hungry poor, be forced to pull down their barns and build greater because Daniel Webster has lived? . . . He has won the title "Defender of the Constitution" by his zeal in fostering the corrupt public sentiment which sets the political shifts of men above the law of nature and of God . . . And finally, he has sent his youngest son, (a youth who has just about brains enough to be conveniently come at by a cannon ball) to Boston to recruit company for the Mexican War, as if his subserviency to the slave power had not already amply atoned for his federalism in the last war, and richly earned for him the title of *patriot* as it is understood in America.

. . . Verily, we say again, there is no sadder sentence than *"might have been."*

THE MORAL MOVEMENT AGAINST
SLAVERY (1849)

. . . The American Anti-Slavery Society advocates disunion . . .

Whatever opinion the editor of an anti-slavery paper may entertain as to the evils or benefits which would result from a dissolution of the union, he should never himself (nor let his readers) lose sight of the fact that those who urge that measure do so from an intense appreciation of the horrors of slavery. They are men and women who keep the popular mind alive to an example of self-devotion in behalf of a purely moral object and charge it with a portion of the magnetism of their self-sacrifice, who attack fearlessly and without question of odds every institution, however venerable with time or hallowed with associations, which affords shelter or vantage ground to the forces of the evil principle they are at war with . . .

Meanwhile, a pure Ethical Idea can never be defeated. It cannot, indeed, be brought into conflict with material organizations, but only applied to them as an impartial test. It cannot attract to itself the rancorous animosity, nor the imputation of motives of personal aggrandizement, to which a political association, however pure, is liable. It does not present to the gross and indiscriminating popular eye a divided object. Its activity is not sensible of any seasons of peculiar intensity or depression. It is not restricted to time and place—the year long caucuses are held in the family and the workshop. It knows no distinction of age or sex, but draws to itself the yet undissipated sympathies of youth and contracts indissoluble alliance with the finer instinct and more persistent enthusiasm of woman.

Two things especially absorb the admiration and sympathy of men—practical success and that weariless devotion which does not need the stimulus of success. The former is the key to the popularity of Taylor, the latter to the power of Garrison. People without ideas laugh at the man of one. But these men are not so common as is generally imagined. That mind is of no ordinary strain which, through long years of obloquy and decision, can still keep its single object as fresh and attractive as at first. It is the man of one idea who attains his end. Narrowness does not always imply bigotry, but sometimes concentration.

. . . But the necessity of renewed and continuous exertion on the part of non-political abolitionists is enforced by all the signs of the times. It is they who keep alive the scattered sparks which are fanned into flame during the gusty days of electioneering excitement. Nay, at what altar was the firebrand lighted which the Fox of Kinderhook carried into the standing corn of the Philistines?

SOURCE NOTE: All of the Lowell essays excerpted here originally appeared in *The National Antislavery Standard.* They were collected in *The Antislavery Papers of James Russell Lowell* (New York: Houghton-Mifflin, 1902), reprinted in 1969 by the Negro Universities Press, a division of Greenwood Publishing, New York.

Horace Mann (1796–1859)

The name "Horace Mann" is rightly associated with education, and numerous schools in the United States are named after him. In his sixty-three years, he succeeded in becoming a graduate of Brown University and the Litchfield School of Law, a practicing attorney, a Massachusetts state senator, and the president of Antioch College in Ohio. He is remembered for his fierce dedication to the improvement of the school systems of Massachusetts, which were disorganized and less effective in antebellum America than they had been in colonial times. Mann was an effective speaker, as his "Speech to the United States House of Representatives on the Institution of Slavery, February 15, 1852," makes clear. He is also associated with the founding of the common-school movement in the United States, arguing for universal, free, public education for precollege young people. Although he eventually succeeded to the presidency of an institution of higher learning, his reputation was built on his lifelong support for public secondary education and his opposition to slavery. He was born in Franklin, Massachusetts, on May 4, 1796, and died in Yellow Springs, Ohio, on August 2, 1859.

SUGGESTIONS FOR FURTHER READING

Auer, J. Jeffrey, ed. *Antislavery and Disunion, 1858–1861: Studies in the Rhetoric of Compromise and Conflict.* New York: Harper and Row, 1963.

Dumond, Dwight L. *A Bibliography of Antislavery in America.* Ann Arbor: University of Michigan Press, 1961.

SPEECH ON THE INSTITUTION OF
SLAVERY (1852)

If the word "Abolitionist" is to be used in a reproachful and contumelious sense, does it not more properly belong to those who would extend a system which in its very nature abolishes freedom, justice, equity, and a sense of human brotherhood? Does it not belong to those who would abolish not only social and political, but all natural rights; who would abolish "liberty and the pursuit of happiness;" who would close up all the avenues to knowledge; who would render freedom of thought and liberty of conscience impossible, by crushing out the faculties by which alone we can think and decide; who would rob a fellow-man of his parental rights, and innocent children of the tenderness and joys of a filial love; who would introduce a foul concubinage in place of the institution of marriage, and who would remorselessly trample upon all the tenderest and holiest affections which the human soul is capable of feeling? After Mr. Jefferson, in the Declaration of Independence, had enumerated a few oppressive deeds of the British king towards his American colonists, he denominated him "a prince whose character was marked by every act that could define a tyrant." There are now as many slaves in this country as there were colonists in 1776. Compare the condition of these three million slaves with the condition of the three million colonists. The conduct of that sovereign who was denounced before earth and heaven as having committed all the atrocities that could "define a tyrant" was mercy and loving-kindness compared with the wrongs and privations of three millions of our fellow beings, now existing among us. If the word "Abolitionist," then is to be used in a reproachful sense, let it be applied to those who, in the middle of the nineteenth century, and in defiance of all the lights of the age, would extend the horrors of an institution which by one all-comprehending crime towards a helpless race, makes it impossible to commit any new crime against them,—unless it be to enlarge the area of their bondage, and to multiply the number of the victims . . .

If we are abolitionists, then we are abolitionists of human bondage; while those who oppose us are abolitionists of human liberty. We would prevent the extension of one of the greatest wrongs that man ever suffered upon earth; they would carry bodily chains and mental chains,—chains in a literal and chains in a figurative sense,—into realms where even half-civilized descendants of the Spaniard and the Indians have silenced their clanking . . .

I know it said that the *fact* of slavery always precedes the *law* of slavery; that *law* does not go before the institution and create it, but comes afterwards to sanction and regulate it. But this is no more true of slavery than of every other institution or practice among mankind whether right or wrong. Homicide existed before law; the law came in subsequently and declared that he who took an innocent man's life without law, should lose his own by law. The law came in to regulate homicide; to authorize the taking of human life for crime just as we authorize involuntary servitude for crime; and it may just as well be argued that murder is a natural right because it existed before law, as that slavery is a natural right because it existed before the law. *This argument appeals to the crime which the law was enacted to prevent, in order to establish the supremacy of the crime over the law that forbids it* . . .

Having, as I trust, refuted the argument of the slaveholder, that the prohibition of slavery in the territories is an act of injustice to his rights, I will consider his next assertion, that it is an insult to his feelings. We are told that the exclusion of slavery from the territories is an affront to the honorable sensibilities of the south; and that acquiescence in the exclusion would involve their dishonor and degradation . . .

There are two answers to this complaint. The first is, that among gentlemen, no insult is ever offered where none is intended . . .

But there is another consideration,—one which appertains to the party supposed to be insulted, rather than the party charged with the insult. In his "Theory of Moral Sentiments," Adam Smith maintains that it is the judgment of men,—the opinion of the bystanders,—that gives us the pleasure of being approved, or the pain of being disapproved, on account of our conduct. Now, in this contest between the north and the south, on the subject of extending slavery, who are the bystanders? They are the civilized nations of the earth. We, the north and south, are contending in an arena. All civilized men stand around us. They are a ring of lookers-on. It is an august spectacle. It is a larger assemblage than ever witnessed any other struggle in the history of mankind; and their shouts of approbation or hisses of scorn are worthy of our heed. And what do these spectators say, in the alternations of the combat? Do they urge on the south to mightier efforts, to the wider spread of slavery, and the multiplication of its victims? Do they shout when she triumphs? When new chains are forged and riveted, when new realms are subdued by haughty taskmasters, and overrun by imbruted slaves, do their plaudits greet your ears and rouse you to more vehement efforts? All the reverse; totally the reverse. They are now looking on with disgust and abhorrence. They groan, they mock, they hiss. The brightest pages of their literature portray you, as covered with badges of dishonor; their orators hold up your purposes as objects for the execration of mankind; their wits hurl the lightnings of satire at your leaders . . .

And do those gentlemen who make these threats soberly consider how deeply they are pledging themselves and their constituents by them? Threats of dissolution, if executed, become rebellion or treason. The machinery of this government is now moving onward in its majestic course . . .

I cannot contemplate this spectacle without a thrill of horror. If the two sections of this country ever marshal themselves against each other, and squadrons rush to the conflict, it will be a war carried on by such powers of intellect, animated by such vehemence of resources, as the world has never before witnessed. "Ten foreign wars," it has been well said, "are a luxury compared with one civil war." But I turn from this scene with a shudder. If, in the retributive providence of God, the volcano of civil war should ever burst upon us, it will be amid thunderings above, and earthquakes below, and darkness around; and when that darkness is lifted up, we shall see this once glorious union,—this oneness of government, under which we have been prospered and blessed as Heaven never prospered and blessed any other people,—rifted in twain from east to west, with a gulf between us wide and profound, save that this gulf will be filled and heaped high with the slaughtered bodies of our countrymen; and when we reawaken to consciousness, we shall behold garments and the hands of the survivors red with fratricidal blood . . .

And what is the object for which we are willing to make this awful sacrifice? Is it to redeem a realm to freedom? No! But to subjugate a realm to slavery. Is it to defend the rights of man? No! But to abolish the rights of man!

I know it is said that some of the Northern States are averse to the reception of blacks. Let us analyze this idea. There are now by estimation three million of slaves. Say one half of these are either too old or too young to have the strength or the intelligence to escape. A million and a half are left; five hundred thousand of these will have attachments to their own parents or children, or to their masters, too strong to be broken; or they may be so degraded as to be contented with bondage; for their contentment is always one of the measures of their degradation. This would leave a million for fugitives, consisting wholly of the most able bodied and intelligent. The Northern States comprise a territory of five hundred thousand square miles. A million of escaped slaves would give but two to a square mile, and this surely would not be a formidable number, even, where colorphobia is strongest . . .

Southern gentlemen, when they threaten disunion cannot surely be so much at fault as to forget that slavery exists here as it never existed before in the world. In Greece there were slaves;—in some cases highly intelligent and accomplished slaves. They could have escaped if they would; but where should they escape to? All conterminous nations,—the whole circle round,—were barbarians. These slaves, therefore, had no place to flee to, where better institutions and juster laws prevailed . . .

But it is said that if dissolution occurs, the "United States South" can form an alliance with Great Britain. And are there no instigators and abolitionists in England? Yes, sir, ten in England where there is one at the north. Frederick Douglass has just returned from England, where he has enjoyed the honors of an oration. William Wells Brown, another fugitive slave, is now traveling England. His journeys from place to place are like the "progresses" of one of the magnates of that land . . .

Sir, every man who has traveled in England knows that there are large, wealthy, and refined circles there, no member of which would allow a slaveholder to sit at his table or enter his doors. Not only churches, but moral and religious men, the world over, have begun to read slaveholders out of their communion and companionship. If the south expects to rid itself of agitation and abolitionism by rupturing its bonds with the north and substituting an alliance with Great Britain for our present constitution they may envy the wisdom of the geese who invited the fox to stand sentinel over them while they slept . . .

I said that the slave does not know much of geography; but he understands enough of it to know where lies the free frontier. The slave does not know much astronomy; but there is one star in the firmament, which is dearer to him than all the heavenly host were to the Chaldeans . . .

Is the case of the *Amistad* forgotten, where a few ignorant, degraded wretches, fresh from the jungles of benighted Africa herself, seized upon the vessel in which they were transported, and compelled the master, under peril of his life, to steer for the north star,—that light which God kindled in the heavens, and which he will as soon extinguish as he will extinguish the love of liberty which he has kindled in every human breast?

And will they find a model of their manifesto in that glorious Declaration of American Independence which their own immortal Jefferson prepared, and to which many of the greatest of all their historic names are subscribed? Alas, they will have to read that Declaration, as the devil reads Scripture, backwards! I know not what may be the rhetorical terms and phrases of the new Declaration but I do know that its *historic* form and substance cannot be widely different from this:—

"We hold these truths to be self-evident, that men are not created equal; that they are not endowed by their Creator with inalienable rights; that white men, of the Anglo-Saxon race, were born to rob, and tyrannize, and enjoy, and black men, of the African race, to labor, and suffer, and obey; that a man, with a drop of African blood in his veins, has no political rights, and therefore shall never vote; that he has no pecuniary rights, and therefore whatever he may earn or receive, belongs to his master; that he has no judicial rights, and therefore he shall never be heard as a witness to redress wrong, or violence, or robbery, committed by white men upon him; that he has no parental rights, and therefore his children may be torn from his bosom, at the pleasure or caprice of his owner; that he has no marital rights, and therefore his wife may be lawfully sold away into distant bondage, or violated before his eyes; that he has no religious rights, and therefore he shall never read the Bible; that he has no heaven-descended, God-given rights of freedom, and therefore he and his posterity shall be slaves forever. We hold that governments were instituted among men to secure and fortify this ascendency of one race over another; that this ascendency has its foundation in force ratified by law and in ignorance and debasement inflicted by intelligence and superiority; and when any people, with whom we are politically associated, would debar us from propagating our doctrines or extending our domination into new realms and over free territories, it becomes our duty to separate from them, and to hold them, as we hold the rest of mankind,—friends when they make slaves, enemies when they make freemen."

I say, sir, of whatever words and phrases the southern "Magna Carta" may consist, this, or something like this, must be its substance and reality.

So preamble to their constitution must run in the wise: "We, the people of the 'United States South,' in order to form a more perfect conspiracy against the rights of the African race, establish injustice, insure domestic slavery, provide for holding three millions of our fellow-beings, with all the countless millions of their posterity, in bondage, and to secure to ourselves and our posterity the enjoyment of power, and luxury, and sloth, do ordain and establish this constitution for the 'United States South.' "

Sir, should a civil war ensue between the north and the south, (which may God in his mercy avert,) in consequence of an attempt to dissolve this Union, and the certain resistance which would be made to such an attempt, it would be difficult to exaggerate the immediate evils which would befall the interests of New England and some other parts of the north. Our manufacturers and our commerce would suffer at least a temporary derangement . . .

SOURCE NOTE: Horace Mann, *A Speech Delivered in the United States House of Representatives, February 15, 1852, on the Subject of Slavery in the Territories, and the Consequences of a Dissolution of the Union* (Washington, D.C., 1852).

Theodore Parker (1810–1860)

EDITED BY DEAN GRODZINS

In September 1850, Congress passed a new Fugitive Slave Law. According to its terms, any African American accused of being a fugitive slave could be arrested, given a summary hearing before a federal court commissioner, and sent into slavery in a matter of hours. At the hearing, there was no jury. The accused was not required to have counsel. The accused could not even testify on his or her own behalf (only self-incriminatory testimony could be admitted as evidence). Moreover, the new law imposed heavy fines and a jail term on anyone who helped a fugitive escape. Supporters of the law, many of them in the North, argued it was needed to protect the constitutional rights of slave owners and to appease the South in order to keep it from rebelling against the Union.

Not everyone was convinced by these arguments to obey the law. Some saw it as fundamentally inhumane. Some believed its terms grossly violated the most basic legal rights of the accused. Some resented that the terms of the law obliged them to lend active support to a slave system they hated. For all these reasons, in the fall of 1850, blacks and whites across the North began organizing what turned out to be one of the most extensive and long-lasting campaigns of civil disobedience in American history. While the law was in effect (it was not repealed until 1862), its opponents provided fugitives with money, hiding places, and legal counsel; they helped fugitives escape to Canada; they harassed slave owners, or their representatives, who came North to claim fugitives; they even, in a few cases, broke into the jails where fugitives were being held and rescued them.

Boston, Massachusetts, was a hotbed of resistance to the law, and near the epicenter of Boston resistance stood the Reverend Theodore Parker. The Sunday after the law went into effect, he announced to his congregation that "I will shelter, and I will help, and I will defend the fugitive with all my humble means and power." Within weeks, Parker had been named by a large public meeting to be minister-at-large to all fugitive slaves in the city. He also became chair of the executive committee of the "Boston Vigilance Committee," which soon had hundreds of members, all pledged to help fugitives. Parker himself began breaking the law as early as October 1850, when he harbored a fugitive slave woman in his home. He had worked out the rationale for his actions in his sermon on "The Function and Place of Conscience," preached on September 22, and later published. An excerpt appears below.

Parker was the leader of the New England transcendentalist movement, along with Ralph Waldo Emerson. The transcendentalists held that truth, including moral truth, could be known intuitively. Because they believed our innate ability to know right from wrong was given by God, and that the law of God was "higher" than human law, they held that the dictates of conscience had priority over any statute. Another transcendentalist, Henry David Thoreau, famously developed this argument in his essay on "Civil Disobedience" (published 1849), as a rationale for "resistance to civil government." According to Thoreau, if the law requires you to do something you think is evil, you should decline to obey the law. He seems less interested in affecting political change than in teaching people how to keep their personal integrity intact in a compromised world. He therefore shows no interest in political institutions or organized political activity.

Parker, by contrast, shows much interest in both. For example, he advocates what is today called "jury nullification": that is, he tells jurors never to vote to convict someone who has rescued a fugitive, even when the law and the facts would seem to require it. Parker makes this case in terms as strong as possible. Although a juror has taken an oath to decide according to the law and the facts alone, Parker argues, that oath should be ignored or reinterpreted. Moreover, he urges opponents of the Fugitive Slave Law to become jurors in such cases, even when they know beforehand that they will have to take an oath they do not intend to keep.

Also, Thoreau, in "Civil Disobedience," does not advocate violence. Parker, in this sermon, does advocate it, under certain circumstances at least. He clearly states that someone who tries to enslave another has by that act lost the right to live and may be rightfully killed. In asserting this point, Parker is taking issue with the pacifism of some of his fellow abolitionists, notably William Lloyd Garrison. Yet while sounding emphatic here, Parker in fact struggled with the issue of when murder was justified and tried to limit the circumstances as much as possible. In October 1850, he told a fugitive slave, William Craft, that killing should be used only "in the last extremity," and that if you cannot kill "without hating the man you strike, then your action will not be without sin." [*The Papers of Daniel Webster: Correspondence* (Dartmouth, 1986), 7:190]

Another major theme of Parker's sermon is "manliness," which he equates with being strong and protecting the weak. Among the weak he numbers fugitives—and women. Parker was in fact an advocate of women's rights (he was one of the only ministers in the country during the 1850s to support the women's suffrage movement, and he championed women's education), but he also had a somewhat conservative conception of gender roles, according to which men were obliged to protect their women dependants. He therefore approves, in his note on "The Function of the Jury" below, of juries that acquitted men who murdered rapists; that he declares such approval, while elsewhere in the sermon rejecting the death penalty, shows that his ideas about manhood were more important to him than his ideas about capital punishment. Again, in October 1850, he told William Craft that while Craft might choose not to kill a man trying to enslave him, he was obliged to kill one trying to enslave his wife, if killing him was the only way to save her.

Parker's sermon is worth reading partly as the eloquent testimony of someone on the front lines of the fugitive slave controversy. As he says, he had to act to save fugitives who belonged to his congregation. Also, the sermon reveals how stark, and sometimes disturbing, were the choices facing those who decided to defy the Fugitive Slave Law.

SUGGESTIONS FOR FURTHER READING

Campbell, Stanley W. *The Slave Catchers: Enforcement of the Fugitive Slave Law, 1850–1860.* Chapel Hill: University of North Carolina Press, 1970.

Collison, Gary. *Shadrach Minkins: From Slave to Citizen.* Cambridge, Mass.: Harvard University Press, 1998.

Von Frank, Albert. *The Trials of Anthony Burns: Freedom and Slavery in Emerson's Boston.* Cambridge, Mass.: Harvard University Press, 1998.

FROM *THE FUNCTION AND PLACE OF CONSCIENCE IN RELATION TO THE LAWS OF MEN* (1850)

Last winter a bill for the capture of fugitive slaves was introduced into the Senate of the United States of America . . . that bill, with various alterations, some for the better, others for the worse, has become a law . . . The statute allows the slaveholder, or his agent, to come here, and by summary process seize a fugitive slave, and without the formality of a trial by jury, to carry him back to eternal bondage. The statute makes it the official business of certain magistrates to aid in enslaving a man; it empowers them to call out force enough to overcome any resistance which may be offered, to summon the bystanders to aid in that work. It provides a punishment for anyone who shall aid and abet, directly or indirectly, and harbor or conceal the man who is seeking to maintain his natural and unalienable right to life, liberty and the pursuit of happiness. He may be fined a thousand dollars, imprisoned six months, and be liable to a civil action for a thousand dollars more!

. . . This is now the law of the land. It is the official business of judges, commissioners and marshals, as magistrates, to execute the statute and deliver a fugitive up to slavery; it is your official business and mine, as citizens, when legally summoned, to aid in capturing the man. Does the command make it any man's duty? The natural duty to keep the law of God overrides the obligation to observe any human statute, and continually commands us to love a man and not hate him, to do him justice, and not injustice, to allow him his natural rights not alienated by himself; yes, to defend him in them, not only by all means legal, but by all means moral.

Let us look a little at our duty under this statute. If a man falls into the water and is in danger of drowning, it is the natural duty of the bystanders to aid in pulling him out, even at the risk of wetting their garments. We should think a man a coward who could swim, and would not save a drowning girl for fear of spoiling his coat. He would be indictable at common law. If a troop of wolves or tigers were about to seize a man, and devour him, and you and I could help him, it would be our duty to do so, even to peril our own limbs and life for that purpose. If a man undertakes to murder or steal a man, it is the duty of the bystanders to help their brother, who is in peril, against wrong from the two-legged man, as much as against the four-legged beast. But suppose the invader who seizes the man is an officer of the United States, has a commission in his pocket, a warrant for his deed in his hand, and seizes as a slave a man who has done nothing to alienate his natural rights—does that give him any more natural right to enslave a man than he had before? Can any piece of parchment make right wrong, and wrong right?

The fugitive has been a slave before: does the wrong you committed yesterday, give you a natural right to commit wrong afresh and continually? Because you enslaved this man's father, have you a natural right to enslave his child? The same right you would have to murder a man because you butchered his father first. The right to murder is as much transmissible by inheritance as the right to enslave! It is plain to me that it is the natural duty of citizens to rescue every fugitive slave from the hands of the marshal who essays to return him to bondage; to do it peaceably if they can, forcibly if they must, but by all means to do it. Will you stand by and see your countrymen, your fellow-citizens of Boston, sent off to slavery by some commissioner? Shall I see my own parishioners taken from under my eyes and carried back to bondage, by a man whose constitutional business it is to work wickedness by statute? Shall I never lift an arm to protect him? When I consent to that, you may call me a hireling shepherd, an infidel, a wolf in sheep's clothing, even a defender of slave-catching if you will; and I will confess I was a poor dumb dog, barking always at the moon, but silent as the moon when the murderer comes near.

I am not a man who loves violence. I respect the sacredness of human life. But this I say, solemnly, that I will do all in my power to rescue any fugitive slave from the hands of any officer who attempts to return him to bondage. I will resist him as gently as I know how, but with such strength as I can command; I will ring the bells, and alarm the town; I will serve as the head, as foot, or as hand to any body of serious and earnest men, who will go with me, with no weapons but their hands, in this work. I will do it as readily as I would lift a man out of the water, or pluck him from the teeth of a wolf, or snatch him from the hands of a murderer. What is a fine of a thousand dollars, and jailing for six months, to the liberty of a man? My money perish with me, if it stand between me and the eternal law of God. I trust there are manly men enough in this house to secure the freedom of every fugitive slave in Boston, without breaking a limb or rending a garment.

One thing more I think is very plain, that the fugitive has the same natural right to defend himself against the slave-catcher, or his constitutional tool, that he has against a murderer or a wolf. The man who attacks me to reduce me to slavery, in that moment of attack alienates his right to life, and if I were a fugitive, and could escape in no other way, I would kill him with as little compunction as I would drive a mosquito from my face. It is high time this was said. What grasshoppers we are before the statute of men! What Goliaths against the law of God! What capitalist heeds your statute of usury when he can get illegal interest? How many banks are content with six *per cent.* when money is scarce? Did you ever hear of a merchant evading the duties of the custom-house? When a man's liberty is concerned, we must keep the law, must we? Betray the wanderer, and expose the outcast?

In the same manner the natural duty of a man over-rides all the special obligations which a man takes on himself as a magistrate by his official oath. Our theory of office is this: The man is sunk in the magistrate; he is *un homme couvert;* his individual manhood is covered up and extinguished by his official cap; he is no longer a man, but a mere president, general, governor, representative, sheriff, juror, or constable; he is absolved from all allegiance to God's law of the universe when it conflicts with man's law of the land; his official business as a magistrate supersedes his natural duty as a man. In virtue of this theory, President Polk, and his coadjutors in Congress and out of it, with malice aforethought and intent to rob and to kill, did officially invade Mexico, and therein "slay, kill and murder" some thousands of men, as well Americans as Mexicans. This is thought right because he did it officially. But the fact that he and they were magistrates, doing official business, did not make the killing any the less a wrong than if he and they had been private men, with General Lopez and not General Taylor to head or back them. The official killing of a man who has not alienated his right to life, is just as much a violation of the law of God, and the natural duty of a man, as the unofficial killing of such a person. Because you and I and some other foolish people put a man in a high office, and get him to take an oath, does that, all at once, invest him with a natural right to kill any body he sees fit; to kill an innocent Mexican? All his natural rights he had before, and it would be difficult to ascertain where the people could find the right to authorize him to do a wrong. A man does not escape from the jurisdiction of natural law and the dominion of God by enlisting in the army, or by taking the oath of the President; for justice, the law paramount of the universe, extends over armies and nations.

A little while ago a murderer was hanged in Boston, by the sheriff of Suffolk county, at the command of certain persons called grand and petit jurors, all of them acting in their official capacity, and doing the official business they had sworn to do. If it be a wrong thing to hang a man, or to take his life except in self-defence, and while in imminent peril, then it is not any less a wrong because men do it in their official character, in compliance with their oath. I am speaking of absolute wrong, not merely what is wrong relatively to the man's own judgment, for I doubt not that all those officers were entirely conscientious in what they did, and therefore no blame rests on them. But if a man believes it wrong to take human life deliberately, except in the cases named, then I do not see how, with a good conscience, he can be partaker in the death of any man, notwithstanding his official oath.

Let me suppose a case which may happen here and before long. A woman flies from South Carolina to Massachusetts to escape from bondage. Mr. Greatheart aids her in her escape, harbors and conceals her, and is brought to trial for it. The punishment is a fine of one thousand dollars and imprisonment for six months. I am drawn to serve as a juror, and pass upon this offence. I may refuse to serve and be punished for that, leaving men with no scruples to take my place, or may take the juror's oath to give a verdict according to the law and the testimony. The law is plain, let us suppose, and the testimony conclusive. Greatheart himself confesses he did the deed alleged, saving one ready to perish. The judge charges, that if the jurors are satisfied of that fact, then they must return that he is guilty. This is a nice matter. Here are two questions. The one, put to me in my official capacity as juror, is this: "Did Greatheart aid the woman?" The other, put to me in my natural character as man, is this: "Will you help punish Greatheart with fine and imprisonment for helping a woman obtain her unalienable rights?" I am to answer both. If I have extinguished my manhood by my juror's oath, then I shall do my official business and find Greatheart guilty, and I shall seem to be a true man; but if I value my manhood, I shall answer after my natural duty to love a man and not hate him, to do him justice, not injustice, to allow him the natural rights he has not alienated, and shall say "not guilty." Then foolish men, blinded by the dust of courts, may call me forsworn and a liar; but I think human nature will justify the verdict.*

In cases of this kind, when justice is on one side and the court on the other, it seems to me a conscientious man must either refuse to serve as a juror, or else return a verdict at variance with the facts and what courts declare to be his official business as juror; but the eyes

---

*   THE FUNCTION OF THE JURY.

There are two theories of the function of the jury in criminal trials. One I will call the theory of the Government; the other the theory of the People. The first has of late been insisted on in certain courts, and laid down by some judges in their charges to the jury. The second lies, perhaps dimly, in the consciousness of the people, and may be gathered from the conduct of juries in trials where the judges' law would do obvious injustice to the prisoner.

I. According to the theory of the Government. The judge is to settle the law for the jury. This involves two things:

1. He is to declare the law denouncing punishment on the alleged crime.

2. To declare what constitutes the crime. Then the jury are only to determine whether the prisoner did the deed which the judge says constitutes the crime. He, exclusively, is to decide what is the law, and what deed constitutes the crime; they only to decide if the prisoner did the deed. For example, to take a case which has not happened yet, to my knowledge: John Doe is accused of having eaten a Medford cracker; and thereupon, by direction of the Government, has been indicted by a grand jury for the capital offense of treason, and is brought before a traverse jury for trial. The judge tells the jury, 1. That eating a Medford cracker constitutes the crime of treason. 2. That there is a law denouncing death on that crime. Then the jury are to hearken to the evidence, and if it is proved to their satisfaction that John Doe ate the Medford cracker, they are to return a verdict of guilty. They are only to judge of the matter of fact, and take the law on the judge's authority.

II. According to the theory of the People, in order to render their verdict, the jury are to determine three things:

1. Did the man do the deed alleged?

2. If so, Is there a legal and constitutional statute denouncing punishment upon the crime? Here the question is twofold: (a) as to the deed which constitutes the crime, and (b) as to the statute which denounces the crime.

3. If all this is settled affirmatively, then, Shall this man suffer the punishment thus legally and constitutionally denounced?

For example: John Doe is accused of having eaten a Medford cracker, is indicted for treason, and brought to trial; the judge charges as above. Then the jury are to determine:

1. Did John Doe eat the Medford cracker in the manner alleged?

2. If so: (a) Does that deed constitute the crime of treason? and (b) Is there a legal and constitutional statute denouncing the punishment of death on that crime?

3. If so likewise, Shall John Doe suffer the punishment of death?

of some men have been so long blinded by what the court declares
is the law, and by its notion of the juror's function, that they will
help inflict such a punishment on their brother, and the judge decree the sentence, in a case where the arrest, the verdict and the sentence are the only wrong in which the prisoner is concerned. It
seems to me it is time this matter should be understood, and that it
should be known that no official oath can take a man out of the jurisdiction of God's natural law of the universe.

A case may be brought before a commissioner or judge of the
United States, to determine whether Daniel is a slave, and therefore to be surrendered up. His official business, sanctioned by his
oath, enforced by the law of the land, demands the surrender; his
natural duty, sanctioned by his conscience, enforced by absolute
justice, forbids the surrender. What shall he do? There is no serving

---

The first question, as to the fact, they are to settle by the evidence presented in
open court, according to the usual forms, and before the face of the prisoner; the
testimony of each witness forms one element of that evidence. The jury alone are to
determine whether the testimony of the witnesses proves the fact.

The second question, (a) as to the deed which constitutes the crime, and (b) as to
the law which denounces the crime, they are to settle by evidence; the testimony of
the Judge, of the State's Attorney, of the Prisoner's counsel, each forms an element
of that evidence. The jury alone are to determine whether that testimony proves
that the deed constitutes the crime, and that there is a law denouncing death against
it; and the jury are to remember that the judge and the attorney who are the
creatures of the Government, and often paid to serve its passions, may be, and often
have been, quite as partial, quite as unjust, as the prisoner's counsel.

The third question, as to punishing the prisoner, after the other questions are
decided against him, is to be settled solely by the mind and conscience of the jury.
If they know that John Doe did eat the Medford cracker; that that deed legally
constitutes the crime of treason, and that there is a legal and constitutional statute
denouncing death on that crime, they are still to determine, on their oath as jurors,
on their manhood as men, Whether John Doe shall suffer the punishment of death.
They are jurors to do justice, not injustice; what they think is justice, not what they
think injustice.

The Government theory, though often laid down in the charge, is seldom if ever
practically carried out by a judge in its full extent. For he does not declare on his
own authority what is the law and what constitutes the crime, but gives the statutes,
precedents, decisions and the like; clearly implying by this very course that the jury
are not to take his authority barely, but his reasons as reasonable.

In the majority of cases, the statute and the ruling of the court come as near to
real justice as the opinion of the jury does; then if they are satisfied that the
prisoner did the deed alleged, they return a verdict of guilty with a clear conscience,

of God and Mammon both. He may abandon his commission and refuse to remain thus halting between two opposites. But if he keeps his office, I see not how he can renounce his nature and send back a fugitive slave, and do as great a wrong as to make a free man a slave!

Suppose the Constitution had been altered, and Congress had made a law, making it the business of the United States' commissioners to enslave and sell at public outcry all the red-haired men in the nation, and forbid us to aid and abet their escape, to harbor and conceal them under the same penalties just now mentioned; do you think any commissioner would be justified before God by his oath in kidnapping the red-haired men, or any person in punishing such

---

and subject the man to what they deem a just punishment for an unjust act. Their conduct then seems to confirm the Government theory of the juror's function. Lawyers and others sometimes reason exclusively from such cases, and conclude such is the true and actual theory thereof. But when a case occurs, wherein the ruling of the judge appears wrong to the jury; when he declares legal and constitutional what they think is not so; when he declares that a trifling offence constitutes a great crime; when the statute is manifestly unjust, forbidding what is not wrong, or when the punishment denounced for a real wrong is excessive, or any punishment is provided for a deed not wrong, though there is no doubt of the facts, the jury will not convict. Sometimes they acquit the prisoner; sometimes they fail to agree. The history of criminal trials in England and America proves this. In such cases the jury are not false to their function and juror's oath, but faithful to both, for the jurors are the "country"—the justice and humanity of men.

Suppose someone should invent a machine to be used in criminal trials for determining the testimony given in court. Let me call it a Martyrion. This instrument receives the evidence and determines and reports the fact that the prisoner did, or did not, do the deed alleged. According to the government theory, the Martyrion would perfectly perform all the functions of the jury in a criminal case; but would any community substitute the machine for the jury of "twelve good men and true"? If the jury is to be merely the judge's machine, it had better be made of iron and gutta-percha than of human beings.

In Philadelphia, some years ago, a man went deliberately and shot a person who had seduced his sister under circumstances of great atrocity. He was indicted for wilful murder. There was no doubt as to the fact, none as to the law, none as to the deed which constituted that crime. The jury returned, "Not guilty"—and were justified in their verdict. In 1850, in New Jersey, a man seduced the wife of another, under circumstances even more atrocious. The husband, in open day, cooly and deliberately shot the seducer; was tried for wilful murder. But the jury, perfectly in accordance with their official function, returned "Not guilty." . . .

as harbored or concealed them, such as forcibly took the victims out of the hand of officials who would work mischief by statute? Will the color of a hair make right wrong, and wrong right?

Suppose a man has sworn to keep the Constitution of the United States, and the Constitution is found to be wrong in certain particulars: then his oath is not morally binding, for before his oath, by his very existence, he is morally bound to keep the law of God as fast as he learns it. No oath can absolve him from his natural allegiance to God. Yet I see not how a man can knowingly, and with a good conscience, swear to keep what he deems wrong to keep, and will not keep, and does not intend to keep . . .

I will tell you a portion of the story of a fugitive slave whom I have known. I will call his name Joseph, though he was in worse than Egyptian bondage. He was "owned" by a notorious gambler, and once ran away, but was retaken. His master proceeded to punish him for that crime, took him to a chamber, locked the door and lighted a fire; he then beat the slave severely. After that he put the branding-iron in the fire, took a knife,—I am not telling what took place in Algiers, but in Alabama,—and proceeded to cut off the ears of his victim! The owner's wife, alarmed by the shrieks of the sufferer, beat down the door with sledge-hammer, and prevented that catastrophe. Afterwards, two slaves of this gambler, for stealing their master's sheep, were beaten so that they died of the stripes. The "Minister" came to the funeral, told the others that those were wicked slaves, who deserved their fate; that they would never "rise" in the general resurrection, and were not fit to be buried! Accordingly their bodies were thrown into a hole and left there. Joseph ran away again; he came to Boston; was sheltered by a man whose charity never fails; he has been in my house, and often has worshipped here with us. Shall I take that man and deliver him up?—do it "with alacrity"? Shall I suffer that gambler to carry his prey from this city? Will you allow it—though all the laws and constitutions of men give the commandment? God do so unto us if we suffer it.

This we need continually to remember: that nothing in the world without is sacred as the Eternal Law of God; of the world within nothing is more venerable than our own conscience, the permanent, everlasting oracle of God. The Urim and Thummim were but Jewish or Egyptian toys on the breastplate of the Hebrew priest; the

Delphic oracle was only a subtle cheat, but this is the true Shekinah and presence of God in your heart: as this

> —*"pronounces lastly on each deed,*
> *Of so much fame in heaven expect your meed."*

If I am consciously and continually false to this, it is of no avail that I seem loyal to all besides; I make the light that is in me darkness, and how great is that darkness! The centre of my manhood is gone, and I am rotten at my heart. Men may respect me, honor me, but I am not respectable; I am a base, dishonorable man, and like a tree, broad-branched, and leafed with green, but all its heart gnawed out by secret worms, at some slight touch one day, my rotten trunk will fall with a horrid squelch, bringing my leafy honors to dishonored dust, and men will wonder that bark could hide such rottenness and ruin.

But if I am true to this Legate of God, holding his court with my soul, then my power to discover the just and right will enlarge continually; the axis of my little life will coincide with the life of the infinite God, His Conscience and my own will be one. Then my character and my work will lie in the plane of his Almighty action; no other will in me, His infinite wisdom, justice, holiness and love will flow into me, a ceaseless tide, filling with life divine and new the little creeklets of my humble soul. I shall be one with God, feel His delight in me and mine in Him, and all my mortal life run o'er with life divine and bless mankind. Let men abhor me, yea, scourge and crucify, angels are at hand; yes, the Father is with me!

SOURCE NOTE: Theodore Parker, "The Function and Place of Conscience in Relation to the Laws of Men," a sermon Parker preached on September 22, 1850, in Theodore Parker, *Speeches, Addresses, and Occasional Sermons* (Boston, 1852), vol. 2, pp. 255–273.

Theodore Parker had a special position in the faction-ridden abolitionist movement as a mediator between different hostile groups. He worked hardest to bridge the bitter divide in the antislavery ranks between the political opponents of slavery, who recognized the legitimacy of the U.S. Constitution and tried to work within its constraints, and the Garrisonians, who rejected the Constitution as a proslavery "covenant with hell," and so repudiated most routine political action, such as voting.

Both camps respected Parker as a religious reformer (he was pastor of the most famous "free church" in America, the Twenty-eighth Congregational Society in Boston). He used this prestige to mediate personal disputes between antislavery leaders of the two sides. More importantly, he worked hard to explain each side to the other. He expounded a comprehensive vision of how historical change occurs in which both political and antipolitical abolitionists played necessary roles (although he held the antipolitical one to be more important). In the address excerpted below, delivered to a convention of Garrisonians in New York, Parker tried to convince them to be more tolerant of political antislavery leaders, whom they often attacked as trimmers and compromisers.

SUGGESTIONS FOR FURTHER READING

Kraditor, Aileen. *Means and Ends in American Abolitionism: Garrison and His Critics on Strategy and Tactics, 1834–1850.* 1967; Chicago, 1989.

FROM PRESENT ASPECT OF
THE ANTI-SLAVERY ENTERPRISE (1856)
(SPEECH TO THE AMERICAN
ANTI-SLAVERY SOCIETY)[1]

In all great movements of mankind, there are three special works to be done, so many periods of work, and the same number of classes of persons therein engaged.

First is the period of sentiment. The business is the produced right feeling,—a sense of lack, and a fore-feeling of desire for the special thing required. The aim is to produce a sense of need, and also a feeling of want. That is the first thing.

The next period is that of ideas, where the work is to furnish the thought of what is wanted,—a distinct, precise, adequate idea. The sentiment must precede the thought: for the primitive element in all human conduct is a feeling; everything begins in a spontaneous emotion.

The third is the period of action, when the business is to make the thought a thing, to organize it into institutions. The idea must precede the action, else man begins to build and is not able to finish; he runs before he is sent, and knows not where he is going, or the way thither.

Now these three special works go on in the anti-slavery movement; there are these three periods observable, and three classes of persons engaged in the various works. The first is to excite the anti-slavery feeling; the next, to furnish the anti-slavery idea; and the third is to make the thought a thing,—to organize the idea into institutions which shall be as wide as the idea, and fully adequate to express the feeling itself . . .

Now look at the special forces which are engaged in this [anti-slavery] enterprise. I divide them into two great parties.

The first party consists of the political reformers, men who wish to act by political machinery, and are in government offices, legislative, judicial, or executive.

The second party is the non-political reformers, who are not, and do not wish to be, in government offices, legislative, judicial, or executive . . .

The business of the political man, legislative, judicial, and executive, is confined to the third part of the anti-slavery work; namely, to organizing the idea, and making the anti-slavery thought a thing. The political reformer, as such, is not expected to kindle the sentiment or create the idea, only to take what he finds ready and put it into form . . .

If the politician is to keep in office, he must accommodate himself to the ideas of the people; for the people are sovereign, and reign, while the politicians only govern with delegated power, but do not reign: they are agents, trustees, holding by a special power of attorney, which authorizes them to do certain things, for doing which they are responsible to the people. In order to carry his point, the politician must have a majority on his side: he cannot wait for it to grow, but must have it now, else he loses his post. He takes the wolf by the ears; and if he lets go, the wolf eats him up: he must therefore lay hold where he can clinch fast and continue. If Mr. Sumner,[2] in his place in the Senate, says what Massachusetts does not indorse, out goes Mr. Sumner. It is the same with all the rest. All the politicians are well aware of that fact. I have sometimes thought they forgot a great many other things; they very seldom forget that.

See the proof of what I say. If you will go into any political meeting of Whigs or Democrats, you will find the ablest men of the party on the platform,—the great Whigs, the great Democrats; "the rest of mankind" will be on the floor. Now, watch the speeches. They do not propose an idea, or appeal to a sentiment that is in advance of the people. But, when you go into an anti-slavery meeting, you find that the platform is a great ways higher than the pews, uniformly so. Accordingly, when an African speaks (who is commonly supposed to be lower than the rest of mankind) and says a very generous thing, there is a storm of hisses all round this hall.[3] What does it show? That the anti-slavery platform which the African stands on is somewhat higher than the general level of the floor . . . The politician on his platform often speaks to the bottom of the floor, and not to the top of the ceiling.

So much for the political reformers: I am not speaking of political hunkers.[4] Now a word of the non-political reformers. Their business is, first, to produce the sentiment; next, the idea; and thirdly, to suggest a mode of action. The anti-slavery non-political reformer is to raise the cotton, to spin it into thread, to weave it into web, to prescribe the pattern after which the dress is to be made; and then he is to pass over the cloth and pattern to the political reformer, and say "Now, sir, take your shears, and cut it out, and make it up." You see how very inferior the business of the political reformer is, after all. The non-political reformer is not restricted by any law, any constitution, any man, nor by the people, because he is not to deal with institutions; he is to make the institutions better . . .

The political reformer must have a majority with him, else he cannot do anything; he has not carried his point or accomplished his end. But the non-political reformer has accomplished part of his end, if he has convinced one man out of a million; for that one man will work to convince another, and by and by the whole will be convinced. A political reformer must get a majority; a non-political reformer has done something if he has the very smallest minority, even if it is a minority of one . . .

. . . [As] the anti-slavery idea and sentiment are not very widespread, the ablest ... [political anti-slavery reformers] are forced to leave their special business as politicians, and go into the elementary work of the non-political reformers. Accordingly, Mr. Wilson[5] stumped all Massachusetts last year,—yes, all the North; not working for a purpose purely political, but for a purpose purely anti-slavery,—to excite the anti-slavery sentiment, to produce an anti-slavery idea. And Mr. Sumner has had to do that work, even in our city of Boston. Yet New England is further advanced in anti-slavery work than any other part of America ... But, notwithstanding New England is the most anti-slavery portion of the whole land, these political men, whose business ought to be only to organize the anti-slavery ideas, and give expression to anti-slavery sentiments in the Senate, or House of Representatives, are forced to abandon that work from time to time, to go about amongst the people, and produce the anti-slavery sentiment itself. Let us not be very harsh in criticising these men, remembering that they are not so well supported behind as we could all wish they were ...

... This has been charged against [the non-political anti-slavery reformers]: that they quarrel among themselves; two against three, and three against two; Douglass against Garrison, and Garrison against Douglass;[6] the liberty-party men against the old anti-slavery men;[7] and all that. That is perfectly true. But remember why it is so. You can bring together a Democratic body, draw your line, and they all touch the mark; it is so with the Whigs. They have long been drilled into it. But whenever a body of men with new ideas comes to organize, there are as many opinions as persons. Pilate and Herod, bitter enemies of each other, were made friends by a common hostility to Jesus; but when the twelve disciples came together, they fell out: Paul resisted Peter; James differed from John; and so on. It is always so on every platform of new ideas, and will always be so—at least for a long time. We must bear one another the best we can.

I think that the [non-political] anti-slavery party has not always quite done justice to the political men. See why. It is easy for Mr. Garrison[8] and Mr. Phillips[9] or me to say all of our thought. I am responsible to nobody, and nobody to me. But it is not easy for Mr. Sumner, Mr. Seward,[10] and Mr. Chase[11] to say all of their thought; because they have a position to maintain, and they must keep that position ...

The anti-slavery non-political reformer is to excite the sentiment, and give the idea; he may tell his whole scheme at once, if he will. But the political reformer, who, for immediate action, is to organize the sentiment and idea he finds ready for him, cannot do or propose all things at once: he must do one thing at a time, tell one thing at a time . . .

Still, this non-political, anti-slavery party—averse to fighting,[12] hostile to voters under present, if not all possible circumstances[13]— has been of immense value to mankind. It has been a perpetual critic on the politicians; and now it has become so powerful that every political man in the North is afraid of it; and, when he makes a speech, he asks not only, What will the Whigs and the Democrats think of it? but, What will the anti-slavery men say; what will the *Liberator*[14] and the *Standard*[15] say of it? And, when a candidate is to be presented for the office of President, the men who make the nomination go to the Quakers of Pennsylvania, and say, "Whom do you want?" They go to the non-resistants of Massachusetts—men that never vote or take office—and ask if it will do to nominate this, that, or the other man. A true Church is to criticize the world by a higher standard. The non-political anti-slavery party is the Church of America to criticize the politics of America. It has been of immense service; it is now a great force.

ENDNOTES

1. The text is taken from Parker's *Works,* vol. 12 (*The Rights of Man in America* [Boston, Centennial Edition, 1911]), 397–429.

2. Charles Sumner was an antislavery senator from Massachusetts.

3. Parker may be referring to an incident which had happened minutes earlier; he had been preceded on the platform by a black speaker.

4. "Hunker" was an insulting political term, originally used to derogate a faction of New York Democrats who did not support the Free Soil Party in 1848: they were accused of loving political patronage more than political principles or the good of the country. Parker used "hunker" to refer to any Northern politician who was not antislavery.

5. Henry Wilson was an antislavery senator from Massachusetts and later vice president of the United States.

6. The abolitionists William Lloyd Garrison and Frederick Douglass had a famous and bitter dispute—partly political, partly personal—in the early 1850s.

7. In 1840 the American Antislavery Society split between those who demanded the society endorse political action, in the form of the Liberty Party, the first antislavery political party, and those who argued that the society should endorse no particular means of furthering the antislavery cause. Many who made the latter argument were nonpolitical abolitionists.

8. William Lloyd Garrison, the most famous nonpolitical abolitionist, edited the famous antislavery newspaper *The Liberator*.

9. Wendell Phillips, a close ally of Garrison, was the most well known abolitionist orator.

10. William Henry Seward was the antislavery senator from New York and later secretary of state.

11. Salmon P. Chase was the antislavery governor of Ohio and later secretary of the treasury and chief justice of the United States Supreme Court.

12. Parker is referring to the "nonresistant" abolitionists, who were pacifists.

13. Some abolitionists refused to vote because they believed the United States Constitution was a proslavery document, but in theory were willing to vote if the Constitution were changed. Other abolitionists refused to vote because they believed all governments, except only the government of God, were sinful.

14. *The Liberator*, the famous abolitionist newspaper out of Boston, was edited by William Lloyd Garrison.

15. The *American Anti-Slavery Standard* was the principal antislavery newspaper in New York.

Harriet Beecher Stowe (1811–1896);
Mary Eastman (1818–1880)

Harriet Beecher Stowe was possibly the most influential of the antebellum abolitionists, if only because her book *Uncle Tom's Cabin* (1852) reached so many readers. Few people today realize that Stephen Foster's "My Old Kentucky Home," now a classic in the repertoire of American folk music, was originally composed to accompany stage versions of *Uncle Tom's Cabin*. The song, a lamentation, was originally scored for Tom's character, as he longs for his wife, Chloe, and his children who are still in Kentucky after he has been sold to the slave trader, Haley. Stowe's early writing was unspectacular; she taught at a girls' academy and wrote temperance tales and advice tracts for women. But her masterpiece was an astonishing media event for its time.

She was the daughter of Lyman Beecher, a prominent evangelist and president of Lane Theological Seminary in Cincinnati, Ohio. She was born in Litchfield, Connecticut, and had five brothers who became ministers, so the religious influences on her thinking and writing were Protestant evangelical Christianity and orthodox Calvinism. In 1836, she married a professor of theology from Lane Seminary, Calvin Stowe, and returned to New England when he accepted a position at Bowdoin College in Maine. The Stowes had seven children; one drowned in 1857, one became a drunkard, and one daughter became a morphine addict. In the 1850s, the Stowes left Bowdoin and moved to Hartford, Connecticut, where her home was next door to Mark Twain's. (Both the Twain and Stowe houses are now museums and are open to the public.)

In Cincinnati, Harriet Beecher was provided with a firsthand look at American slavery; the seminary was a depot on the Underground Railroad, and she interviewed slaves who had recently escaped across the Ohio River, which that separates Ohio from Kentucky. In 1853, following the success of her antislavery novel, Stowe published *A Key to Uncle Tom's Cabin*, which is a compilation of sources she used in writing her novel. The *Key* was produced to establish the credibility of her work in the face of loud attacks on the novel's veracity, since Stowe had not traveled widely in the antebellum South. When the Congress of the United States passed the

Fugitive Slave Act in 1850 as part of the Compromise of 1850, Stowe responded with a moral energy unmatched in American literary history. While taking communion in 1851, she experienced a vision of an elderly male slave being whipped to death, and this epiphany became the ending for her powerful novel. *Uncle Tom's Cabin* was first serialized in *The National Era* (1851–52). It appeared bound in hardcover in the spring of 1852.

In the first week the book sold ten thousand copies, and by the end of six months it had sold three hundred thousand copies. The printers were unable to keep up with the demand, and in 1861, on the eve of the Civil War, the novel was being read in sixteen languages and had sold over four and one-half million copies. This is a remarkable statistic even today; in 1861, however, the population of the United States was only thirty-two million, and some five million of that number were semiliterate slaves living in the South. Moreover, the book was banned by most Southern legislatures. Thus, the population remaining among whom the book circulated was only twenty-two million, of whom only sixteen million were sufficiently literate or old enough to read the book through. There was therefore one copy of *Uncle Tom's Cabin* for every four or five readers in America in 1862.

The impact of the work was enormous. Abraham Lincoln met Mrs. Stowe in the White House in 1862, and reportedly greeted her by saying, "So this is the little lady who started this great war." He was not far off the mark. Together with Hinton Rowan Helper's 1857 publication *The Impending Crisis of the South: How to Meet It*, Stowe's book stirred up anti-Southern sentiment in the North and highlighted the moral arguments concerning American slavery. The book's popularity aroused deep resentment in the South, where feeling ran strong that Stowe had misrepresented Southern slavery by emphasizing the cruelty of owners like Simon Legree and barbarous practices like the separation of families at slave auctions. Proslavery novels appeared immediately to counter the arguments and impressions left by *Uncle Tom's Cabin.* Prominent among these was Mary Eastman's *Aunt Phillis's Cabin* (1852), which is represented in this volume by its preface.

Slave narratives like Frederick Douglass's *Narrative of the Life of Frederick Douglass, an American Slave* (1845) and Harriet Jacobs's *Linda: Incidents in the Life of a Slave Girl* (1861) corroborated Stowe's fictional version with detailed accounts of cruelty, and one of Stowe's sources, Theodore Dwight Weld's *American Slavery As It Is: The Testimony of a Thousand Witnesses* (1839), provided journalistic accounts of mistreatment and cruelty gathered from newspapers published both "at the South" and in the North. Still, Southern writers responded immediately to Stowe, not only by openly condemning her inexperience with slavery, but also by attacking her fictional account in the political arena. Southern congressmen railed against Stowe's popular depiction of the degrading effects slavery had on everyone, from Legree's alcoholism to Tom's untimely sacrifice and Cassy's concubinage to Legree's lust. Viewing Southern slavery as a paternalistic institution that provided opportunities for "Christianizing" and "civilizing" the heathen and barbarous African slaves, Southern writers like Mary Eastman portrayed slavery as a beneficial institution that made salvation available to pagans and family life in the monogamous, Western mode available to the polygamous tribal members fortunate enough to be sold into American slavery.

Aunt Phillis's Cabin is a romantic fantasy of life on the plantation, showing how paternalistic slavery is a necessary institution for the African children, who are essentially unable to govern or care for themselves, an insipid image of slavery Eastman and her proslavery contemporaries sought to portray. Here, happy slaves dance and frolic around a well-tended slave cabin, which has curtains in the windows and flower boxes decorating the exterior of the house. All of this joy is viewed, from a distance, by the Lord of the Manor, the plantation owner, who sits in the "big house" or "Great House" high on the hill, supervising the play of his dependent children. Similar to Eastman's paternalistic account was that of John Pendleton Kennedy, who wrote *Swallow Barn* (1832), a romantic novel of plantation life that eulogizes the Virginia planter and his treatment of his slaves.

These conflicting representations of slavery continued for several decades, well into the era of Reconstruction, and while Stowe's version had an enormous impact on antebellum America, Eastman's romanticized description of plantation life reappeared in 1936 in Margaret Mitchell's *Gone with the Wind*, an antebellum (and postbellum) romance that sanitized slavery and provided the reading and moviegoing world with characters such as Big Sam and Mammy, portrayed in the 1939 film version by Hattie McDaniel, who won the first Oscar ever by an African American for her role. This benign view of the "peculiar institution" corroborated early-twentieth-century views of antebellum America as a pastoral world in which Southern planters presided over large extended families at "Tara" and "Twelve Oaks" while the Africans, whose total dependence on the slave master was demonstrated by these proslavery novels, would never evolve beyond the status of children that they had enjoyed in the antebellum world. Eastman's *Aunt Phillis's Cabin* never achieved the status of Stowe's novel in the decade before the Civil War, but the antebellum world it depicted held fast in the popular imagination until the mid–twentieth century, when college courses in Reconstruction, African American history, and race relations began to provide less romantic and more realistic accounts of slavery. Stowe's *Uncle Tom's Cabin* has also enjoyed a resurrection since the civil rights movement of the 1960s, and in 1994, Joan Hedrick's masterful biography *Harriet Beecher Stowe: A Life* (New York: Oxford University Press, 1994) won the Pulitzer Prize for biography. See also the collection of essays edited by Mason Lowance, et al., *The Stowe Debate: Rhetorical Strategies in* Uncle Tom's Cabin (Amherst: University of Massachusetts Press, 1994).

"CONCLUDING REMARKS," FROM *UNCLE TOM'S CABIN* (1852)

To fill up Liberia with an ignorant, inexperienced, half-barbarized race, just escaped from the chains of slavery, would be only to prolong, for ages, the period of struggle and conflict which attends the inception of new enterprises. Let the church of the north receive these poor sufferers in the spirit of Christ; receive them to the educating advantages of Christian republican society and schools, until they have attained to somewhat of a moral and intellectual maturity, and then assist them in their passage to those shores, where they may put in practice the lessons they have learned in America.

There is a body of men at the north, comparatively small, who have been doing this; and, as the result, this country has already seen examples of men, formerly slaves, who have rapidly acquired property, reputation, and education. Talent has been developed, which, considering the circumstances, is remarkable; and, for moral traits of honesty, kindness, tenderness of feeling—for heroic efforts and self-denials, endured for the ransom of brethren and friends yet in slavery—they have been remarkable to a degree that, considering the influence under which they were born, is surprising.

The writer has lived, for many years, on the frontier-line of slave states, and has had great opportunities of observation among those who formerly were slaves. They have been in her family as servants; and, in default of any other school to receive them, she has, in many cases, had them instructed in a family school, with her own children. She has also the testimony of missionaries, among the fugitives in Canada, in coincidence with her own experience; and her deductions, with regard to the capabilities of the race, are encouraging in the highest degree.

The first desire of the emancipated slave, generally, is for *education*. There is nothing that they are not willing to give or do to have their children instructed; and, so far as the writer has observed herself, or taken the testimony of teachers among them, they are remarkably intelligent and quick to learn. The results of schools, founded for them by benevolent individuals in Cincinnati, fully establish this . . .

This is an age of the world when nations are trembling and convulsed. A mighty influence is abroad, surging and heaving the world, as with an earthquake. And is America safe? Every nation that carries in its bosom great and unredressed injustice has in it the elements of this last convulsion.

For what is this mighty influence thus rousing in all nations and languages those groanings that cannot be uttered, for man's freedom and equality?

O, Church of Christ, read the signs of the times! Is not this power the spirit of HIM whose kingdom is yet to come, and whose will to be done on earth as it is in heaven?

But who may abide the day of his appearing? "For that day shall burn as an oven: and he shall appear as a swift witness against those that oppress the hirelings in his wages, the widow and the fatherless, and that *turn aside the stranger in his right:* and he shall break in pieces the oppressor."

Are not these dread words for a nation bearing in her bosom so mighty an injustice? Christians! every time that you pray that the kingdom of Christ may come, can you forget that prophecy associates, in the dread fellowship, the *day of vengeance* with the year of his redeemed?

A day of grace is yet held out to us. Both North and South have been guilty before God; and the *Christian church* has a heavy account to answer. Not by combining together, to protect injustice and cruelty, and making a common capital of sin, is this Union to be saved—but by repentance, justice and mercy; for, not surer is the eternal law by which the millstone sinks in the ocean, than that stronger law, by which injustice and cruelty shall bring on nations the wrath of Almighty God!

———

SOURCE NOTE: Harriet Beecher Stowe, *Uncle Tom's Cabin,* ed. Ann Douglas (New York: Penguin Classics, 1981).

FROM *AUNT PHILLIS'S CABIN; OR, SOUTHERN LIFE AS IT IS* (1852)

A writer on Slavery has no difficulty in tracing back its origin. There is also the advantage of finding it, with its continued history, and the laws given by God to govern his own institution, in the Holy Bible. Neither profane history, tradition, nor philosophical research are required to prove its origin or existence; though they, as all things must, come forward to substantiate the truth of the Scriptures. God, who created the human race, willed they should be holy like himself. Sin was committed, and the curse of sin, death, was induced: other punishments were denounced for the perpetration of particular crimes—the shedding of man's blood for murder, and the curse of slavery. The mysterious reasons that here influenced the mind of the Creator it is not ours to declare. Yet may we learn enough from his revealed word on this and every other subject to confirm his power, truth and justice. There is no Christian duty more insisted upon in Scripture than reverence and obedience to parents. "Honor thy father and thy mother, that thy days may be long in the land which the Lord thy God giveth thee." The relation of child to parent resembles closely that of man to his Creator. He who loves and honors his God will assuredly love and honor his parents. Though it is evidently the duty of every parent so to live as to secure the respect and affection of his child, yet there is nothing in the Scriptures to authorize a child treating with disrespect a parent, though he be unworthy in the greatest degree.

We are told in Gen. ix. 22, "And Ham, the father of Canaan, saw the nakedness of his father, and told his two brethren without"; and in the 24th, 25th, 26th, and 27th verses we read, "And Noah awoke from his wine, and knew what his younger son had done unto him; and he said, Cursed be Canaan; a servant of servants shall he be unto his brethren. And he said, Blessed be the Lord God of Shem, and Canaan shall be his servant. God shall enlarge Japeth, and he shall dwell in the tents of Shem, and Canaan shall be his servant." Is it not preposterous that any man, any Christian, should read these verses and say slavery was not instituted by God as a curse on Ham and Canaan and their posterity?

And who can read the history of the world and say this curse has not existed ever since it was uttered?

"The whole continent of Africa," says Bishop Newton, "was peopled principally by the descendants of Ham; and for how many ages have the better parts of that country lain under the dominion of the Romans, then of the Saracens, and now of the Turks! In what wickedness, ignorance, barbarity, slavery, misery, live most of the inhabitants! And of the poor negroes, how many hundreds every year are sold and bought like beasts in the market, and conveyed from one quarter of the world to do the work of beasts in another!"

But does this curse authorize the slave-trade? God forbid. He commanded the Jews to enslave the heathen around them, saying, "they should be their bondmen forever"; but he has given no such command to other nations. The threatenings and reproofs uttered against Israel, throughout the Old Testament, on the subject of slavery, refer to their oppressing and keeping in slavery their own countrymen. Never is there slightest imputation of sin, as far as I can see, conveyed against them for holding in bondage the children of heathen nations.

Yet do the Scriptures evidently permit slavery, even to the present time. The curse on the serpent, ("And the Lord God said unto the serpent, Because thou hast done this, thou art cursed above all cattle and above every beast of the field,") uttered more than sixteen hundred years before the curse of Noah upon Ham and his race, has lost nothing of its force and true meaning. "Cursed is the ground for thy sake: in sorrow shalt thou eat of it, all the days of thy life," said the Supreme Being. Has this curse failed or been removed?

Remember the threatened curses of God upon the whole Jewish tribe if they forsook his worship. Have not they been fulfilled?

But it has been contended that the people of God sinned in holding their fellow-creatures in bondage! Open your Bible, Christian, and read the commands of God as regards slavery—the laws that he made to govern the conduct of the master and the slave!

But again—*we* live under the glorious and new dispensation of Christ; and He came to establish God's will, and to confirm such laws as were to continue in existence, to destroy such rules as were not to govern our lives!

When there was but one family upon the earth, a portion of the family was devoted to be slaves to others. God made a covenant with Abraham: he included in it his slaves. "He that is born in thy house, and he that is bought with thy money," are words of Scripture. A servant of Abraham says, "And the Lord has blessed my master greatly, and he is become great, and he hath given him flocks and herds, and silver and gold, and men-servants and maid-servants, and camels and asses."

The Lord has called himself the God of Abraham and Isaac and Jacob. These holy men were slaveholders!

The existence of slavery then, and the sanction of God on his own institution, is palpable from the time of the pronouncing of the curse, until the glorious advent of the Son of God. When he came, slavery existed in every part of the world.

Jesus Christ, the Son of God, came from the heaven and dwelt upon the earth: his mission to proclaim the will of God to a world sunk in the lowest depths in iniquity.

Look at his miracles—the cleansing of the leper, the healing of the sick, the casting out of unclean spirits, the raising of the dead, the rebuking of the winds and seas, the control of those possessed with devils—and say, was he not the Son of God—yea, was he not God?

He came on an errand of mercy to the world, and he was all powerful to accomplish the Divine intent; but, did he emancipate the slave? The happiness of the human race was the object of his coming; and is it possible that the large portion of them then slaves could have escaped his all-seeing eye! Did he condemn the institution which he had made? Did he establish universal freedom? Oh! No; he came to redeem the world from the power of sin; his was no earthly mission; he did not interfere with the organization of society.

The application made by the Abolitionists of the golden rule is absurd: it might then apply to the child, who *would have* his father no longer control him; to the apprentice, who *would* no longer that the man to whom he is bound should have a right to direct him.

Thus the foundations of society would be shaken, nay, destroyed. Christ would have us deal with others, not as they desire, but as the law of God demands: in the condition of life in which we have been placed, we must do what we conscientiously believe to be our duty to our fellow-men.

Christ alludes to slavery, but does not forbid it. "And the servant abideth not in the house forever, but the son abideth ever. If the Son therefore shall make you free, you are free indeed."

Show me in the history of the Old Testament, or in the life of Christ, authority to proclaim *as a sin* the holding of the race of Ham and Canaan in bondage.

In the times of the apostles, what do we see? Slaves are still in bondage, the children of Ham are menials as they were before. Christ had come, had died, had ascended to heaven, and slavery still existed. Had the apostles authority to do it away? Had Christ left it to them to carry out, in this instance, his revealed will?

It is well known and often quoted that the holy apostle did all he could to restore a slave to his master—one whom he had been the means of making free in a spiritual sense. Yet he knew that God had made Onesimus a slave, and, when he had fled from his master, Paul persuaded him to return and to do his duty toward him. Open your Bible, Christian, and carefully read the letter of Paul to Philemon, and contrast its spirit with the incendiary publications of the Abolitionists of the present day. St. Paul was not a fanatic, and therefore *could not be* an Abolitionist. The Christian age advanced and slavery continued, and we approach the time when our fathers fled from persecution to the soil we now call our own, when they fought for the liberty to which they felt they had a right. Our fathers fought for it, and our mothers did, more when they urged forth their husbands and sons, not knowing whether the life-blood that was glowing with religion and patriotism would not soon be dyeing the land that had been their refuge, and where they fondly hoped they should find a happy home. Oh, glorious parentage! Children of America, trace no farther back—say not the crest of nobility once adorned thy father's breast, the gemmed coronet thy mother's brow—stop here! It is enough that they earned for thee a home—a free, a happy home. And what did they say to the slavery that existed then and had been entailed upon them by the English government?

In the North, slavery was useless; nay, more, it was a drawback to the prosperity of that section of the union—it was dispensed with. In other sections, gradually, our people have seen their condition would be more prosperous without slaves—they have emancipated them. In the South, they are necessary: though an evil, it is one that cannot be dispensed with; and here they have been retained, and will be retained, unless God should manifest his will to the contrary.

The whole nation sanctioned slavery by adopting the Constitution which provides for them, and for their restoration (when figure) to their owners. Our country was then like one family—their souls had been tried and made pure by a united struggle.

The subject of slavery was agitated among them; many difficulties occurred, but they were all settled—and, they thought, effectually. They agreed then, on the propriety of giving up runaway slaves, unanimously.

As long as England needed sons and daughters of Africa to do her bidding, she trafficked in the flesh and blood of her fellow-creatures; but our immortal fathers put an end to the disgraceful trade. They saw its heinous sin, for they had no command to emancipate the slave; therefore they wisely forbore farther to interfere. They drew the nice line of distinction between an unavoidable evil and a sin.

Slavery was acknowledged, and slaves considered as property all over our country, at the North as well as the South—in Pennsylvania, New York, and New Jersey. Now, has there been any law reversing this, except in the States that have become free? Out of the limits of these States, slaves are property, according to the Constitution.

Let the people of the North take care of their own poor.

Let the people of the South take care of theirs.

Let each remember the great and awful day when they must render a final account to their Creator, their Redeemer, and their Judge.

SOURCE NOTE: Mary Eastman, *Aunt Phillis's Cabin; or, Southern Life As It Is* (Philadelphia, 1852).

Ralph Waldo Emerson (1803–1882)

EDITED BY WILLIAM PANNAPACKER

Ralph Waldo Emerson was always a deeply committed social reformer, but he was often ambivalent about the means to achieve his ends. Born in Boston, Emerson studied theology at Harvard and was ordained a Unitarian minister in 1829. Plagued by spiritual doubts, he resigned his ministry in 1832, traveled abroad, and settled in Concord, Massachusetts, in 1834. After the publication of his short treatise *Nature* (1836), Emerson became the central figure of the transcendentalist movement in the United States and a guiding intellect for numerous American writers including Henry David Thoreau and Walt Whitman.

Although Emerson resided near the geographic and social center of abolitionism, he initially resisted an open alliance with the more militant leaders of the movement whom he regarded, at first, as lawless, unkempt, and self-righteous. Emerson was suspicious of organizations and a reluctant leader, viewing himself as a scholar and poet rather than as a political agitator. Much as he hoped for the abolition of slavery, he thought this could best be achieved by reforming the nature of the individual rather than through collective action. Emerson resisted the notion that society could be improved by single-issue reform movements aimed at the passage of legislation; morality had to come from the consonance of individual hearts, each independently perceiving the same ideal truths. In "Self-Reliance," Emerson actually chides abolitionists for being overly concerned with the sins of faraway neighbors while neglecting their own shortcomings.

Nevertheless, Emerson's journals show that he was concerned with the evil of slavery from his youth forward, and he even dreamed that he might somehow deliver slaves from bondage. As a minister, Emerson frequently used slavery as an example of a human injustice. But it was not until 1837 that Emerson was provoked by the murder of an abolitionist publisher, Elijah P. Lovejoy, in Alton, Illinois, into delivering a moderate antislavery address. At this point, Emerson still maintained that reform was best achieved by the moral suasion of individuals rather than by the militant action of groups. Over the next seven years Emerson read more deeply into the horrors of slavery, his fears concerning its expansion grew, and he acquired a deep admiration for the abolitionist movement, which he expressed in a moving speech in Concord on August 1, 1844. He stated, "we are indebted mainly to this movement, and to the continuers of it, for the popular discussion of every point of practical ethics." Thereafter, he was welcomed by the abolitionists with enthusiasm.

Emerson shared the outrage of abolitionists at the Compromise of 1850 and the Fugitive Slave Law, which required states to return escaped slaves to their owners. Denouncing what he believed to be an unjust law, Emerson finally became willing to advocate open resistance to civil government. Conventional political means were incapable of redressing an immoral law; the "higher law" of the individual conscience was of more importance than a corrupted Constitution. Emerson's outrage escalated in 1854 when Massachusetts chief justice Lemuel Shaw returned the fugitive slave Anthony Burns to bondage and Congress passed the Kansas-Nebraska Act, effectively nullifying the Compromise of 1820 by permitting the expansion of slavery into the territories. It was shortly after these events that Emerson wrote the "Lecture on Slavery" which is reprinted here. He first delivered the lecture in Boston on January 25, 1855, before the Massachusetts Anti-Slavery Society, and he delivered it four more times over the next month. It was received warmly by abolitionists, but it earned Emerson a great deal of criticism from those who supported the paternalistic doctrines of George Fitzhugh.

Rather than emphasizing individual reflection, Emerson's "Lecture on Slavery" assumes a more activist posture: "I do not cripple but exalt the social action," he writes. He asserts unequivocally that slavery is a moral evil, a violation of America's sacred mission, and a threat to the integrity of the entire nation. The Fugitive Slave Law is unjust, he argues, and honest men are not obliged to uphold it. Most specifically, Emerson proposes that a negotiated settlement should be reached with the slaveholders, offering them compensation for emancipating their slaves without acknowledging their right to ownership. Although Emerson continued to resist the inflexibility of the Garrisonians, the crisis of the mid-1850s provoked him out of his intellectual malaise into a specific—if moderate—plan to end the "peculiar institution."

SUGGESTIONS FOR FURTHER READING

The Complete Works of Ralph Waldo Emerson, edited in twelve volumes by Edward Waldo Emerson (1903–1904), has long been the standard edition. It will be superseded by the *Collected Works of Ralph Waldo Emerson*, edited by Alfred R. Ferguson et al., which remains under production by Harvard University Press; five volumes have appeared as of 2000. Other useful primary sources are *The Journals and Miscellaneous Notebooks of Ralph Waldo Emerson*, edited by William H. Gilman et al. (1960–1982); *The Letters of Ralph Waldo Emerson*, 6 vols., edited by Ralph L. Rusk (1939); volumes 7–8, ed. Eleanor Tilton (1990–1991); *The Correspondence of Emerson and Carlyle*, ed. Joseph Slater (1964); *The Complete Sermons of Ralph Waldo Emerson*, 4 vols., ed. Albert J. Von Frank et al. (1989–1992); and *The Early Lectures of Ralph Waldo Emerson*, ed. Robert E. Spiller et al. (1966–1972). Widely available anthologies of Emerson's writings are published by the Library of America: *Essays and Lectures*, ed. Joel Porte (1983), and *Collected Poems and Translations*, eds. Harold Bloom and Paul Kane (1994). Joel Myerson has edited the authoritative *Ralph Waldo Emerson: A Descriptive Bibliography* (1982).

The most comprehensive general biography is Ralph Leslie Rusk's *The Life of Ralph Waldo Emerson* (1949). It is well complemented by the intellectual biographies of Stephen Whicher, *Freedom and Fate: An Inner Life of Ralph Waldo Emerson* (1953), and Robert Richardson, *Emerson: The Mind on Fire* (1995). Particularly useful essay collections are *Ralph Waldo Emerson: A Collection of Critical Essays*, ed. Lawrence Buell (1993), and *On Emerson: The Best from* American Literature, ed. Edwin H. Cady and Louis J. Budd (1988). The reception of Emerson's works may be traced in *Emerson and Thoreau: The Contemporary Reviews*, ed. Joel Myerson (1992). Examinations of Emerson's relationship with abolitionism may be found in *Virtue's Hero: Emerson, Antislavery, and Reform*, by Len Gougeon (1990); *Emerson's Antislavery Writings*, eds. Len Gougeon and Joel Myerson (1995); and *The Trials of Anthony Burns: Freedom and Slavery in Emerson's Boston*, by Albert J. Von Frank (1998).

FROM LECTURE ON SLAVERY (1855)

Gentlemen,

I approach the grave and bitter subject of American slavery with diffidence and pain . . .

The subject seems exhausted. An honest man is soon weary of crying "Thief!" Who can long continue to feel an interest in condemning homicide, or counterfeiting, or wife-beating? Tis said, endless negation is a flat affair . . .

We have to consider that, however strongly the tides of public sentiment have set or are setting towards freedom, the code of slavery in this country is at this hour more malignant than ever before. The recent action of Congress has brought it home to New England, and made it impossible to avoid complicity.

The crying facts are these, that, in a Republic professing to base its laws on liberty, and on the doctrines of Christianity, slavery is suffered to subsist: and, when the poor people who are the victims of this crime, disliking the stripping and peeling process, run away into states where this practice is not permitted,—a law has been passed requiring us who sit here to seize these poor people, tell them they have not been plundered enough, and must go back to be stripped and peeled again, and as long as they live.

But this was not yet the present grief. It was shocking to hear of the sufferings of these men: But the district was three hundred, five hundred, and a thousand miles off, and, however leagued with ours, was yet independent. And, for the national law which enacted this complicity, and threw us into conspiracy with the thief, it was an old dead law, which had been made in an hour of weakness and fear, and which we guarded ourselves from executing,—now revived and made stringent. But there was no fear that it would be valid.

But the destruction was here. We found well-born, well-bred, well-grown men among ourselves, not outcasts, not foreigners, not beggars, not convicts, but baptised, vaccinated, schooled, high-placed, official men, who abetted this law. "O by all means, catch the slave, and drag him back." And when we went to the courts, the interpreters of God's right between man and man said, "catch the slave, and force him back."

Now this was disheartening. Slavery is an evil, as cholera or typhus is, that will be purged out by the health of the system. Being unnatural and violent, I know that it will yield at last, and go with cannibalism, tattooing, inquisition, dueling, burking; and as we cannot refuse to ride in the same planet with the New Zealander, so we must be content to go with the southern planter, and say, you are you, and I am I, and God send you an early conversion. But to find it here in our sunlight, here in the heart of Puritan traditions in an intellectual country, in the land of schools, of sabbaths and sermons, under the shadow of the White Hills, of Katahdin, and under the eye of the most ingenious, industrious, and self-helping men in the world,—staggers our faith in progress . . . [The White Mountains are in New Hampshire; Mount Katahdin is in Maine.]

Look at our politics. The great parties coeval with the origin of the government,—do they inspire us with any exalted hope? Does the Democracy stand really for the good of the many? of the poor? for the elevation of entire humanity? Have they ever addressed themselves to the enterprise of relieving this country of the pest of slavery?

The Party of Property, of education, has resisted every progressive step. Did Free Trade come from them? Have they urged the abolition of Capital Punishment? Have they urged any of the prophetic action of the time? No. They would nail the stars to the sky. With their eyes over their shoulders, they adore their ancestors, the framers of the Constitution. *Nolumus mutari* ["We are unwilling to be changed"]. We do not wish to touch the Constitution. They wish their age should be absolutely like the last. There is no confession of destitution like this fierce conservatism. Can any thing proclaim so loudly the absence of all aim or principle? What means this desperate grasp on the past, if not that they find no principle, no hope, no future in their own mind? Some foundation we must have, and, if we can see nothing, we cling desperately to those whom we believe can see.

Our politics have run very low, and men of character will not willingly touch them. This is fast becoming, if it has not already become, discreditable work. Those who have gone to Congress were honest well-meaning men. I heard congratulations from good men, their friends, in relation to certain recent members, that "these were honest and thoroughly trustworthy, obstinately honest." Yet they voted on the late criminal measures with the basest of the populace. They ate dirt, and saw not the sneer of the bullies who duped them with an alleged state-necessity: and all because they had no burning splendor of law in their own minds. Well, what refuge for them? They had honor enough left to feel degraded: they could have a place in which they could not preserve appearances. They become apathized and indifferentists. We leave them in their retreats. They represented the property of their constituency. Our merchants do not believe in anything but their trade. They loll in republican chairs, they eat and drink in republican Astor, Tremont, and Girard Houses [elite hotels in New York, Boston, and Philadelphia, respectively]. They roll in easy and swift trains, telegraphing their wishes before them. And the power of money is so obtrusive as to exclude the view of the larger powers that control it.

I am sorry to say, that, even our political reforms show the same desperation. What shall we think of the new movement? We are clear that the old parties could not lead us. They were plainly bankrupt, their machineries and politicians discredited. We will have none of them. Yes, but shall we therefore abdicate our common sense? I employed false guides and they misled me; shall I therefore put my head in a bag?

The late revolution in Massachusetts no man will wonder at who sees how far our politics had departed from the path of simple right. The reigning parties had forfeited the awe and reverence which always attaches to a wise and honest government. And as they inspired no respect, they were turned out by an immense frolic. But to persist in a joke;—I don't like joking with edge-tools, and there is no knife so sharp as legislation . . .

There are periods of occulation when the light of mind seems to be partially withdrawn from nations as well as from individuals. This devastation reached its crisis in the acquiescence in slavery in this country,—in the political servitude of Europe, during the same age. And there are moments of greatest darkness, and of total eclipse. In the French Revolution, there was a day when the Parisians took a strumpet from the street, seated her in a chariot, and led her in procession, saying, "This is the Goddess of Reason." And, in 1850, the American Congress passed a statute which ordained that justice and mercy should be subject to fine and imprisonment, and that there existed no higher law in the universe than the Constitution and this paper statute which uprooted the foundations of rectitude and denied the existence of God.

Thus in society, in education, in political parties, in trade, and in labor, in expenditure, or the direction of surplus capital, you may see the credence of men; how deeply they live, how much water the ship draws. In all these, it is the thought of men, what they think, which is the helm that turns them all about. When thus explored, instead of rich belief, of minds great and wise sounding the secrets of nature, announcing the laws of science, and glowing with zeal to act and serve, and life too short to read the revelations inscribed on earth and heaven, I fear you will find non-credence, which produces nothing, but leaves sterility and littleness.

This skepticism assails a vital part when it climbs into the Courts, which are the brain of the state. The idea of abstract right exists in the human mind, and lays itself out in the equilibrium of nature, in the equalities and periods of our system, in the level of seas, in the action and reaction of forces, that nothing is allowed to exceed or absorb the rest; if it do, it is disease, and is quickly destroyed.

Among men, this limitation of my liberty by yours,—allowing the largest liberty to each compatible with the liberty of all,—protection in seeking my benefit, as long as it does not interfere with your benefit,—is justice,—which satisfies everybody . . .

The fathers, in July 1787, consented to adopt population as the basis of representation, and to count only three-fifths of the slaves, and to concede the reclamation of fugitive slaves;—for the consideration, that there should be no slavery in the Northwest Territory. They agreed to this false basis of representation and to this criminal complicity of restoring fugitives: and the splendor of the bribe, namely, the magnificent prosperity of America from 1787, is their excuse for the crime. It was a fatal blunder. They should have refused it at the risk of making no Union. Many ways could have been taken. If the southern section had made a separate alliance with England, or gone back into colonies, the slaves would have been emancipated with the West Indians, and then the colonies could have been annexed to us. The bribe, if they foresaw the prosperity we have seen, was one to dazzle common men, and I do not wonder that common men excuse and applaud it. But always so much crime brings so much ruin. A little crime, a minor penalty; a great crime, a great disaster.

If the south country thinks itself enriched by slavery, read the census, read the valuation tables, or weigh the men. I think it impoverished. Young men are born in that country, I suppose, of as much ability as elsewhere, and yet some blight is on their education: in the present generation is there one living son to make good the

reputation of the Past? If the north think it a benefit, I find the
north saddled with a load which has all the effect of a partnership in
a crime, on a virtuous and prosperous youth. It stops his mouth,
ties his hands, forces him to submit to every sort of humiliation,
and now it is a fountain of poison which is felt in every transaction
and every conversation in this country.

Well, certain men were glad perceivers of this Right, with more
clearness and steadiness than others, and labored to establish the application of it to human affairs. They were Lawgivers or Judges.
And all men hailed the Laws of Menu, the Laws of Lycurgus, laws
of Moses, laws of Confucius, laws of Jesus, the laws of Alfred, and
of men of less fame, who in their place, believing in an ideal right,
strove to make it practical,—the Code of Justinian, the famous jurists, Grotius, Vattel, Daguesseau, Blackstone, and Mansfield.[1]
These were original judges, perceivers that this is no child's play, no
egotistic opinion, but stands on the original law of the world. And
the reputation of all the judges on earth stands on the real perception of these few natural or God-anointed judges. All these men
held that law was not an opinion, not an egotism of any king or the
will of any mob, but a transcript of natural right. The judge was
there as its organ and expounder, and his first duty was to read the
law in accordance with equity. And, if it jarred with equity, to dis-
own the law. All the great lawgivers and jurists of the world have
agreed in this, that an immoral law is void. So held Cicero, Selden,
Hooker; and Coke, Hobart, Holt, and Mansfield, chief justices of
England.[2] Even the Canon law says, "Neither allegiance nor oath
can bind to obey that which is unlawful." Grotius, Vattel, Dagues-

---

1. The Laws of Menu (or Manu) are commentaries on Indian law compiled
between 200 B.C. and A.D. 200. Lycurgus was a Spartan statesperson; Alfred "the
Great" (840–899), an English king who drew up a legal code; Justinian I (483–565),
known as "the Great," a Byzantine emperor who codified Roman law; Hugo
Grotius (1583–1645), a Dutch scholar who wrote the first treatise on international
law; Daguesseau is Henri-François d'Aguesseau (1668–1751), a French magistrate
and legal scholar; William Blackstone (1723–1780), a famous British jurist whose
four-volume *Commentaries* (1765–1769) was the standard treatment of English law;
and William Murray, Lord Mansfield (1704–1793), an English jurist.
2. John Selden (1584–1654) was an English jurist; Richard Hooker (1554–1600), an
English theologian. Edward Coke (1552–1634), Henry Hobart, John Holt
(1642–1710), and William Murray, Lord Mansfield (1704–1793), were all eminent
English magistrates.

seau, and Blackstone teach the same. Of course they do. What else could they? You cannot enact a falsehood to be true, nor a wrong act to be right.

And I name their names, not of course to add authority to a self-evident proposition, but only to show that black-letter lawyers supposed to be more than others tied to precedent and statute, saw the exquisite absurdity of enacting a crime.

And yet in America justice was poisoned at its fountain. In our northern states, no judge appeared of sufficient character and intellect to ask not whether it was constitutional, but whether it was right.

This outrage of giving back a stolen and plundered man to his thieves was ordained and under circumstances the most painful. There was enough law of the State of Massachusetts to resist the dishonor and the crime, but no judge had the heart to invoke, no governor was found to execute it. The judges feared collision of the State and Federal Courts. The Governor was a most estimable man—we all knew his sterling virtues, but he fell in an era when governors do not govern, when judges do not judge, when Presidents do not preside, and when representatives do not represent.[3]

The judges were skeptics too and shared the sickness of the time. The open secret of the world was hid from their eyes, the art of subliming a private soul with inspirations from the great and public and divine soul from which we live. A man is a little thing whilst he works by and for himself. A judge who gives voice as a judge should, to the rules of love and justice, is godlike; his word is current in all countries. But a man sitting on the Bench servile to precedent, or a windy politician, or a dangler trying to give authority to the notions of his superiors or of his set, pipes and squeaks and cheeps ridiculously . . .

Now what is the effect of this evil government? To discredit government. When the public fails in its duty, private men take its place. When the British ministry is weak, the *Times'* editor governs the realm. When the American government and courts are false to

---

3. Emerson is probably referring to one of four governors of Massachusetts during this period: George N. Briggs (1796–1861), governor 1844–1851; George S. Boutell (1818–1905), governor 1851–1853; John H. Clifford (1809–1876), governor 1853–1854; and Emory Washburn (1800–1877), governor 1854–1855.

their trust, men disobey the government, put it in the wrong; the government is forced into all manner of false and ridiculous attitudes. Men hear reason and truth from private men who have brave hearts and great minds. This is the compensation of bad governments,—the field it affords for illustrious men. And we have a great debt to the brave and faithful men who in the very hour and place of the evil act, made their protest for themselves and their countrymen by word and deed. They are justified and the law is condemned.

It is not to societies that the secrets of nature are revealed, but to private persons, to each man in his organization, in his thoughts. A serious man who has used his opportunities will early discover that he only works and thinks securely when he is acting on his own experience. All forcible men will agree that books and learned societies could not supply what their own good sense taught them . . .

But whilst I insist on the doctrine of the independence and the inspiration of the individual, I do not cripple but exalt the social action. Patriotism, public opinion, have a real meaning, though there is so much counterfeit rag money abroad under it, that the name is apt to disgust . . .

And as the state is a reality, so it is certain that societies of men, a race, a people have a public function, a part to play in the history of humanity. Thus, the theory of our government is Liberty. The thought and experience of Europe had got thus far, a century ago, to believe that, as soon as favorable circumstances permitted, the experiment of self-government should be made. America afforded the circumstances, and the new order began. All the mind in America was possessed by that idea. The Declaration of Independence, the Constitution of the States, the Parties; the newspapers, the songs, star-spangled banner, land of the brave and home of the free, the very manners of the Americans, all showed them as the receivers and propagandists of this lesson to the world. Liberty; to each man the largest liberty compatible with the liberty of every other man. It was not a sect, it was not a private opinion, but a gradual and irresistible growth of the human mind. That is the meaning of our national pride. It is a noble office. For liberty is a very serious thing. It is the severest test by which a government can be tried. All history goes to show, that it is the measure of all national success. Religion, arts, science, material production are as is the degree of liberty.

Montesquieu said, "Countries are not cultivated in proportion to their population, but in proportion to their freedom."

Most unhappily, this universally accepted duty and feeling has been antagonized by the calamity of southern slavery. And that institution in its perpetual encroachment has had through the stronger personality, shall I say, of the southern people, and through their systematic devotion to politics, the art so to league itself with the government, as to check and pervert the natural sentiment of the people by their respect for law and statute.

And this country exhibits an abject regard to the forms, whilst we are swindled out of the liberty . . .

Men inspire each other. The affections are the Muses. Hope is a muse, Love is, Despair is not, and selfishness drives away the angels. It is so delicious to act with great masses to great aims. For instance the summary or gradual abolition of slavery. Why in the name of common sense and the peace of mankind is not this made the subject of instant negotiation and settlement? Why do not the men of administrative ability in whose brain the prosperity of Philadelphia is rooted;—the multitude of able men who lead each enterprise in the City of New York; in Boston, in Baltimore; why not the strong courageous leaders of the south; join their heads and hearts to form some basis of negotiation to settle this dangerous dispute on some ground of fair compensation, on one side, and of satisfaction, on the other, to the conscience of the Free States. Is it impossible to speak of it with reason and good nature? Why? Because it is property? Why, then it has a price. Because it is political? Well then, it ultimately concerns us, threatens us, and there will never be a better time than the present time. It is really the great task fit for this country to accomplish, to buy that property of the planters, as the British nation bought the West Indian slaves. I say *buy,*—never conceding the right of the planter to own, but that we may acknowledge the calamity of his position, and bear a countryman's share in relieving him, and because it is the only practicable course, and is innocent.

Well, here is right social or public function which one man cannot do, which all men must do. We shall one day bring the states shoulder to shoulder, and the citizens man to man, to exterminate slavery. It is said, it will cost two thousand millions of dollars. Was there ever any contribution levied that was so enthusiastically paid as this will be? The United States shall give every inch of the public lands. The states shall give their surplus revenues, their unsold lands. The citizen his private contribution. We will have a chimney-tax. We will give up our coaches, and wine, and watches. The churches will melt their plate. The Father of his country shall wait well-pleased a little longer for his monument: Franklin for his; the Pilgrim Fathers for theirs.[4] We will call on those rich benefactors who found Asylums, Hospitals, Athenaeums, Lowell Institutes, Peabody Institutions, Bates and Astor City Libraries.[5] On wealthy bachelors and wealthy maidens to make the State their heir as they were wont in Rome. The merchant will give his best voyage. The mechanic will give his fabric. The needlewoman will give. Children will have cent societies. If really the matter could come to negotiation and a price were named, I do not think any price founded on an estimate that figures could tell would be quite unmanageable. Every man in the land would give a week's work to dig away this accursed mountain of sorrow once and forever out of the world.

---

4. The Washington Monument was started in 1848 but not completed until 1885.
5. John Lowell, Jr. (1799–1836) established the Lowell Institute in Boston; George Peabody (1795–1869) established the Peabody Institute in Baltimore; Joshua Bates (1788–1864) funded the Boston Public Library; and John Jacob Astor (1763–1848) helped to form the New York Public Library.

SOURCE NOTE: Emerson first delivered this lecture before the Massachusetts Anti-Slavery Society in Boston on January 25, 1855. Emerson repeated the lecture in New York on February 6, in Philadelphia on February 8, in Rochester on February 21, and in Syracuse on February 25. This reprinting is derived from *Emerson's Antislavery Writings*, edited by Len Gougeon and Joel Myerson (New Haven and London: Yale University Press, 1995), pp. 91–106.

Charles Sumner (1811–1874)

Born in Boston on January 6, 1811, Charles Sumner graduated from Harvard College and the Harvard Law School. (Most Bostonians today remember him as namesake of the Sumner Tunnel, under Boston Harbor, leading to Logan Airport.) In antebellum America, Sumner was a strong abolitionist and powerful speaker whose oratorical authority led to his repeated election to the U.S. Senate from Massachusetts. His views were often controversial, and after the Civil War he supported Reconstruction measures that would have granted full Negro suffrage throughout the South as a requirement for the readmission of those states that had seceded from the Union at the outbreak of the war. He openly opposed the Compromise of 1850 and its inclusion of the Fugitive Slave Law. "His oratory typically was of the nature of tirade; in vituperation he was peerless, and his uncompromising stand on slavery made him a favorite and most powerful abolitionist. He bitterly opposed the Kansas-Nebraska Bill in 1854 and in May 1856, in a [Senate] debate on the admission of Kansas, made his most famous address, 'The Crime Against Kansas.' He scorned the Kansas-Nebraska Act as a swindle and he heaped invective upon its authors, Senators Andrew Butler and Stephen A. Douglas, in the most vindictive terms. Two days later, while at his desk in the Senate chamber, he was set upon and severely beaten by Preston S. Brooks, a congressman from South Carolina who was a nephew of Butler. For three years, Sumner was unable to resume his official duties, but the outraged Massachusetts legislature reelected him in 1857 despite his incapacitation." (*Webster's American Biographies*, p. 1008) On March 11, 1874, Sumner died in Washington, D.C. His career had been filled with reform causes, and he vigorously opposed slavery and was, consequently, favored among abolitionists.

SUGGESTIONS FOR FURTHER READING

Dumond, Dwight Lowell. *Antislavery Origins of the Civil War in the United States.* Ann Arbor: University of Michigan Press, 1961.
———. *Antislavery: The Crusade for Freedom in America.* Ann Arbor, University of Michigan Press, 1961.

————, ed. *A Bibliography of Antislavery in America.* Ann Arbor: University of Michigan Press, 1961.

McKitrick, Eric L., ed. *Slavery Defended: The Views of the Old South.* Englewood Cliffs, N.J.: Prentice-Hall, 1963.

THE BARBARISM OF SLAVERY (1860)

from the Dedication

To the young men of the United States, I dedicate this new edition of a speech on the barbarism of Slavery, in token of heartfelt gratitude to them for brave and patriotic service rendered in the present war for civilization.

. . . The election of Mr. Lincoln was a judgment against Slavery, and its representatives were aroused.

. . . It was under the shadow of this constitutional assumption that the assumption for Slavery grew into virulent vigor, so that, at last, when Mr. Lincoln was elected, it broke forth in open war; but the war was declared in the name of State Rights.

Therefore, there are two *apparent* rudiments to this war. One is Slavery and the other is State Rights. But the latter is only a cover for the former. If Slavery were out of the way there would be no trouble from State Rights.

The war, then, is for Slavery, and nothing else. It is an insane attempt to vindicate by arms the lordship which had been already asserted in debate. With mad-cap audacity it seeks to install this Barbarism as the truest civilization. Slavery is declared to be the "corner-stone" of the new edifice. This is enough.

The question is thus presented between Barbarism and Civilization; not merely between two different forms of Civilization, but between Barbarism on the one side and Civilization on the other side. If you are for Barbarism, join the Rebellion, or, if you can not join it, give it your sympathies. If you are for Civilization, stand by the Government of your country with mind, soul, heart, and might!

Such is the issue simply stated. On the one side are women and children on the auction-block; families rudely separated; human flesh lacerated and seamed by the bloody scourge; labor extorted without wages; and all this frightful, many-sided wrong is the declared foundation of a mock commonwealth. On the other side is the Union of our Fathers, with the image of "Liberty" on its coin and the sentiment of Liberty in its Constitution, now arrayed under a patriotic government, which insists that no such mock Commonwealth, having such a declared foundation, shall be permitted on our territory, purchased with money and blood, to impair the unity of our jurisdiction and to insult the moral sense of mankind.

Therefore, the battle which is now waged by the Union is for Civilization itself, and it must have aid and God-speed from all who are not openly for Barbarism. There is no word of peace, no tone of gentleness, no whisper of humanity, which does not become trumpet-tongued against the Rebellion. War itself seems to "smooth its wrinkled front" as it undertakes the championship of such a cause. The armed soldier becomes a minister of mercy.

from the Speech

. . . By various voices, is the claim made for Slavery, which is put forward defiantly as a form of civilization—as if its existence were not plainly inconsistent with the first principles of anything that can be called Civilization—except by that figure of speech in classical literature, where a thing takes its name from something which it has not, as the dreadful Fates were called merciful because they were without mercy . . .

Such are the two assumptions, the *first* an assumption of fact, and the *second* an assumption of constitutional law, which are now made without apology or hesitation. I meet them both. To the first I oppose the essential Barbarism of Slavery, in all its influences, whether high or low, as Satan is Satan still, whether towering in the sky or squatting in the toad. To the second I oppose the unanswerable, irresistible truth, that the Constitution of the United States nowhere recognizes property in man. These two assumptions naturally go together. They are "twins" suckled by the same wolf. They are the "couple" in the present slave-hunt. And the latter can not be answered without exposing the former. It is only when Slavery is exhibited in its truly hateful character, that we can fully appreciate the absurdity of the assumption, which, in defiance of the express letter of the Constitution, and without a single sentence, phrase, or word, upholding human bondage, yet it foists into this blameless text the barbarous idea that man can hold property in man.

. . . The Barbarism of Slavery appears; *first* in the *character of Slavery*, and *secondly* in the *character of Slave-masters*. Under the first head we shall naturally consider (1) the Law of Slavery and its Origin, and (2) the practical results of Slavery as shown in a comparison between the Free States and the Slave States. Under the *second* head we shall naturally consider (1) Slave-masters as shown in the Law of Slavery; (2) Slave-masters in their relations with slaves, here glancing at their three brutal instruments; (3) Slave-masters in their relations with each other, with society, and with Government; and (4) Slave-masters in their unconsciousness.

. . . (1.) I begin with the *Law of Slavery and its Origin*, and here this Barbarism paints itself in its own chosen definition. It is simply this: Man, created in the image of God, is divested of his human character, and declared to be a "chattel"—that is, a beast, a thing or article of property. That this statement may not seem to be put forward without precise authority, I quote the statutes of three different States, beginning with South Carolina, whose voice for Slavery always has an unerring distinctiveness. Here is the definition supplied by this State:

"Slaves shall be deemed, held, taken, reputed, and adjudged in law, to be *chattel personal* in the hands of their owners and possessors and their executors, administrators, and assigns, to all intents, constructions, and purposes whatsoever." —*2 Brev. Dig., 229.*

And here is the definition supplied by the Civil Code of Louisiana:

"A slave is one who is in the power of a master to whom he belongs. The master may sell him, depose of his person, his industry, and his labor. He can do nothing, possess nothing, nor acquire anything, but what must belong to his master." —*Civil Code, Art. 35.*

In similar spirit, the law of Maryland thus indirectly defines a slave as an *article:*

"In case the personal property of a ward shall consist of specific *articles, such as slaves*, working beasts, animals of any kind, the court, if it deem it advantageous for the ward, may at any time pass an order for the sale thereof." —*Statutes of Maryland.*

Not to occupy time unnecessarily, I present a summary of the pretended law defining Slavery in all the Slave States, as made by a careful writer, Judge Stroud, in a work of juridical as well as philanthropic merit:

"The careful principle of Slavery—that the slave is not to be ranked among *sentient* beings, but among *things*—is an article of property—a chattel personal—obtains as undoubted law in all of these (Slave) States." —*Stroud's Law of Slavery.*

. . . The slave is held simply *for the use of his master*, to whose behest, his life, liberty, and happiness are devoted, and by whom he may be bartered, leased, mortgaged, bequeathed, invoiced, shipped as cargo, stored as goods, sold on execution, knocked off at public auction, and even staked at the gaming-table on the hazard of a card or a die; all according to law. Nor is there anything, within the limit of life, inflicted on a beast which may not be inflicted on the slave. He may be marked like a hog, branded like a mule, yoked like an ox, hobbled like a horse, driven like an ass, sheared like a sheep, maimed like a cur, and constantly beaten like a brute; all according to law. And should life itself be taken, what is the remedy?

. . . *Secondly.* Slavery paints itself again in its complete *abrogation of marriage,* recognized as a sacrament by the church, and recognized as a contract wherever civilization prevails. Under the law of Slavery, no such sacrament is respected, and no such contract can exist. The ties that may be formed between slaves are all subject to the selfish interests or more selfish lust of the master, whose license knows no check. Natural affections, which have come together, are rudely torn asunder; nor is this all. Stripped of every defense, the chastity of a whole race is exposed to violence, while the result is recorded in the tell-tale faces of children, glowing with their master's blood, but doomed for their mother's skin to Slavery, through all descending generations . . .

Thirdly. Slavery paints itself again in its complete *abrogation of the parental relation,* which God in his benevolence has provided for the nurture and education of the human family, and which constitutes an essential part of Civilization itself. And yet, by the law of Slavery—happily beginning to be modified in some places—this relation is set at naught, and in its place is substituted the arbitrary control of the master, at whose mere command little children, such as the Savior called unto him, though clasped by a mother's arms, may be swept under the hammer of the auctioneer. I do not dwell on this exhibition. Sir, is not Slavery barbarous?

Fourthly. Slavery paints itself again *in closing the gates of knowledge,* which are also the shining gates of civilization. Under its plain unequivocal law, the bondman may, at the unrestrained will of his master, be shut out from all instruction; while in many places, incredible to relate! the law itself, by cumulative provisions, positively forbids that he shall be taught to read. Of course, the slave can not be allowed to read, for his soul would then expand in larger air, while he saw the glory of the North Star, and also the helping truth, that God, who made iron, never made a slave; for he would then become familiar with the Scriptures, with the Decalogue still speaking in the thunders of Sinai; with that ancient text, "He that stealeth a man and selleth him, or if he be found in his hands, he shall surely be put to death"; with that other text, "Masters, give unto your servants that which is just and equal"; with that great story of redemption, when the Lord raised the slave-born Moses to deliver his chosen people from the house of bondage; and with that sublimer story, where the Savior died a cruel death, that all men, without distinction of race, might be saved—leaving to mankind commandments, which, even without his example, make Slavery impossible.

. . . This same testimony also found expression from the fiery soul of Jefferson. Here are some of his words:

"There must be an unhappy influence on the manners of our people, produced by the existence of Slavery among us. The whole commerce between master and slave is a perpetual exercise of the most boisterous passions, THE MOST UNREMITTING DESPOTISM on the one part, and degrading submission on the other; our children see this, and learn to imitate it . . . *The man must be a prodigy who can retain his manners and morals undepraved by such circumstances.* And with what execration should the statesman be loaded, who, permitting one half the citizens thus to trample on the rights of the other, *transforms those into despots,* and these into enemies, destroys the morals of the one part, and the *amor patriae* of the other! . . . With the morals of the people, their industry also is destroyed."

. . . In the recent work of Mr. [Frederick Law] Olmsted, a close observer and traveler in the Slave States, which abounds in pictures of Slavery, expressed with caution and evident regard to truth, will be found still another, where a Slave-master thus frankly confesses his experience:

" 'I can tell you how you can break a nigger of running away, certain,' says the Slave-master. 'There was an old fellow I used to know in Georgia, that always cured his so. If a nigger ran away, when he caught him, he would bind his knee over a log, and fasten him so he couldn't stir; and then he'd take a pair of pincers, and pull one of his toe-nails out by the roots; and tell him, that if he ever run away again, he would pull out two of them; and if he run away again after that, he told him he'd pull out four of them, and so on, doubling each time. He never had to do it more than twice; it always cured them.' " —*Olmsted's Texas Journey, 105.*

Like this story, which is from the lips of a Slave-master, is another, where the master, angry because his slave had sought to regain his God-given liberty, deliberately cut the tendons of his heel, thus horribly maiming him for life.

. . . The enormity of the pretensions that Slavery is sanctioned by the Constitution becomes still more apparent, when we read the Constitution in the light of great national acts and of contemporaneous declarations. First comes the Declaration of Independence, the illuminated initial letter of our history, which in familiar words announces that "all men are created equal; that they are endowed by their Creator with certain unalienable rights; that among these are Life, *Liberty,* and the Pursuit of Happiness; that to secure these rights governments are instituted among men, deriving their just powers from the consent of the governed." . . . "Let it be remembered, that it has ever been the pride and the boast of America, *that the rights for which she has contended were the rights of human nature.* By the blessing of the Author of *these rights,* they have prevailed over all opposition, and form THE BASIS of thirteen independent States." Now, whatever may be the privileges of States in their individual capacities, with their several local jurisdictions, no power can ever be attributed to the nation, in the absence of positive unequivocal grant, inconsistent with these two national declarations. Here is the national heart, the national soul, the national will, the national voice, which must inspire our interpretation of the

Constitution, and enter into and diffuse itself through all the national legislation. Such are the commanding authorities which constitute "Life, Liberty, and the Pursuit of Happiness," and in more general words, "the Rights of Human Nature," without distinction of race, or recognition of the curse of Ham, as the basis of our national institutions. They need no additional support.

SOURCE NOTE: Charles Sumner, *The Barbarism of Slavery: Speech by Hon. Charles Sumner on the Bill for the Admission of Kansas as a Free State*, United States Senate, June 4, 1860 (Boston, 1860). Copy owned by the editor, the gift of his daughter, Susan Lowance.

ACTS OF CONGRESS

RELATING TO

SLAVERY

EMBRACING THE FUGITIVE SLAVE LAW OF 1793,
THE MISSOURI COMPROMISE ACT OF 1820,
THE FUGITIVE SLAVE LAW OF 1850,
THE ORDINANCE OF 1787,
AND THE WILMOT PROVISO OF 1847

❖

Fugitive Slave Law of 1793

SECOND CONGRESS—Sess. 2, Chap. 7, 1793

Statute 2, February 12, 1793

CHAP. VII.—AN ACT respecting fugitives from justice, and persons escaping from the service of their masters.

SEC. 1. Be it enacted by the Senate and House of Representatives of the United States of America in Congress assembled, That whenever the executive authority of any state in the Union, or of either of the territories, northwest or south of the river Ohio, shall demand any person, as a fugitive from justice, of the executive authority of any such state or territory to which such person shall have fled, and shall, moreover, produce the copy of an indictment found, or an affidavit made before a magistrate of any state or territory as aforesaid, charging the person so demanded with having committed treason, felony, or other crime, certified as authentic by the governor or chief magistrate of the state or territory from whence the person so charged fled, it shall be the duty of the executive authority of the state or territory to which such person shall have fled, to cause him or her to be arrested and secured, and notice of the arrest to be given to the executive authority making such demand, or to the agent of such authority appointed to receive the fugitive, and to cause the fugitive to be delivered to such agent when he shall appear.—But if no such agent shall appear within six months from the time of the arrest, the prisoner may be discharged. And all costs or expenses incurred in the apprehending, securing, and transmitting such fugitive to the state or territory making such demand, shall be paid by such state or territory.

SEC. 2. And be it further enacted, That any agent appointed as aforesaid, who shall receive the fugitive into his custody, shall be empowered to transport him or her to the state or territory from which he or she shall have fled. And, if any person or persons shall by force set at liberty, or rescue the fugitive from such agent while transporting as aforesaid, the person or persons so offending, shall, on conviction, be fined not exceeding five hundred dollars, and be imprisoned not exceeding one year.

SEC. 3. And be it also enacted, That when a person held to labor in any of the United States, or in either of the territories on the northwest or south of the river Ohio, under the laws thereof, shall escape into any other of the said states or territory, the person to whom such labor or service may be due, his agent or attorney is hereby empowered to seize or arrest such fugitive from labor, and to take him or her before any judge of the Circuit or District Courts of the United States, residing or being within the state, or before any magistrate of a county, city or town corporate, wherein such seizure or arrest shall be made, and upon proof to the satisfaction of such judge or magistrate, either by oral testimony or affidavit taken before, and certified by, a magistrate of any such state or territory, that the person so seized or arrested, doth, under the laws of the state or territory from which he or she fled, owe services or labor to the person claiming him or her, it shall be the duty of such judge or magistrate to give a certificate thereof to such claimant, his agent or attorney which shall be sufficient warrant for removing the said fugitive from labor, to the state or territory from which he or she fled.

SEC. 4. And be it further enacted, That any person who shall knowingly and willingly obstruct or hinder such claimant, his agent or attorney, in so seizing or arresting such fugitive from labor, or shall rescue such fugitive from such claimant, his agent or attorney, when so arrested pursuant to the authority herein given or declared; or shall harbor or conceal such person after notice that he or she was a fugitive from labor as aforesaid, shall, for either of the said offences, forfeit and pay the sum of five hundred dollars. Which penalty may be recovered by and for the benefit of such claimant, by action of debt, in any court proper to try the same; saving, moreover, to the person claiming such labor or service, his right of action for or on account of the said injuries, or either of them.

Approved February 12, 1793.

Missouri Compromise

SIXTEENTH CONGRESS—Sess. 1,
Chap. 22, 1820

Statute 1, March 6, 1820

CHAP. XXII.—An Act to authorize the people of the Missouri territory to form a Constitution and State Government, and for the admission of such State into the Union on an equal footing with the original States, and to prohibit slavery in certain territories.

(All the previous sections of this Act relate entirely to the formation of the Missouri Territory in the usual form of territorial bills—the 8th section only relating to the slavery question.)

Sec. VIII. And be it further enacted, That in all that territory ceded by France to the United States, under the name of Louisiana, which lies north of thirty-six degrees, and thirty minutes north latitude, not included within the limits of the state contemplated by their act, slavery and involuntary servitude, otherwise than in the punishment of crimes, whereof the parties shall have been duly convicted, shall be, and is hereby, forever prohibited. Provided always that any person escaping into the same, from whom labor or service is lawfully claimed, in any state or territory of the United States, such fugitive may be lawfully reclaimed and conveyed to the person claiming his or her labor or service as aforesaid.

Approved March 6, 1820.

Fugitive Slave Law of 1850

THIRTY-FIRST CONGRESS—Sess. 1,
Chap. 60, 1850

September 18, 1850

CHAP. LX.—An Act to amend, and supplementary to, the Act entitled, "An Act respecting Fugitives from Justice, and Persons escaping from, the Service of their Masters," approved February twelfth, one thousand seven hundred and ninety-three.

Be it enacted by the Senate and House of Representatives of the United States of America in congress assembled, That the persons who have been, or may hereafter be, appointed Commissioners, in Virtue of any Act of Congress, by the Circuit Courts of the United States, and who, in consequence of such appointment, are authorized to exercise the powers that any justice of the peace, or other magistrate of any of the United States, may exercise in respect to offenders for any crime or offence against the United States, by arresting, imprisoning, or bailing the same under and by virtue of the thirty-third section of the act of the twenty-fourth of September, seventeen hundred and eighty-nine, entitled "An Act to establish the judicial courts of the United States," shall be, and are hereby, authorized and required to exercise and discharge all the powers and duties conferred by this act.

SEC. 2. And be it further enacted, That the Superior Court of each organized Territory of the United States shall have the same power to appoint commissioners to take acknowledgments of bail and affidavits, and to take depositions of witnesses in civil causes, which is now possessed by the Circuit Court of the United States; and all commissioners who shall hereafter be appointed for such purposes by the Superior Court of any organized Territory of the United States, shall possess all the powers, and exercise all the duties, conferred by law upon the commissioners appointed by the Circuit Courts of the United States for similar purposes, and shall moreover exercise and discharge all the powers and duties conferred by this act.

SEC. 3. And be it further enacted, That the Circuit Courts of the

United States, and the Superior Courts of each organized Territory of the United States, shall from time to time enlarge the number of Commissioners with a view to afford reasonable facilities to reclaim fugitives from labor, and to the prompt discharge of the duties imposed by this Act.

SEC. 4. And be it further enacted, That the Commissioners above named shall have concurrent jurisdiction with the judges of the Circuit and District Courts of the United States, in their respective circuits and districts within the several States, and the judges of the Superior Courts of the Territories severally and collectively, in term-time and vacation; and shall grant certificates to such claimants upon satisfactory proof being made, with authority to take and remove such fugitives from service or labor, under the restrictions herein contained, to the State or Territory from which such persons may have escaped or fled.

SEC. 5. And be it further enacted, That it shall be the duty of all marshals and deputy marshals to obey and execute all warrants and precepts issued under the provisions of this act, when to them directed; and should any marshal or deputy marshal refuse to receive such warrant, or other process, when tendered, or to use all proper means diligently to execute the same, he shall, on conviction thereof, be fined in the sum of one thousand dollars, to the use of such claimant, on the motion of such claimant, by the Circuit or District Court for the district of such marshal; and after arrest of such fugitive, by such marshal or his deputy, or whilst at any time in his custody, under the provisions of this act, should such fugitive escape, whether with or without the assent of such marshal or his deputy, such marshal shall be liable, on his official bond, to be prosecuted for the benefit of such claimant, for the full value of the service or labor of said fugitive in the State, Territory, or District whence he escaped; and the better to enable said commissioners, when thus appointed, to execute their duties faithfully and efficiently, in conformity with the requirements of the Constitution of the United States, and of this act, they are hereby authorized and empowered, within their counties respectively, to appoint, in writing under their hands, any one or more suitable persons, from time to time, to execute all such warrants and other process as may be issued by them in the lawful performance of their respective duties; with authority to such commissioners, or the persons to be appointed by them, to execute process as aforesaid, to summon and call to their aid the bystanders, or *posse comitatus* of the proper county, when necessary to insure a faithful observance of the clause of the Constitution referred to, in conformity with the provisions of this act; and all good citizens are hereby commanded to aid and assist in the prompt and efficient execution of this law, whenever their services may be required, as aforesaid, for that purpose; and said warrants shall run, and be executed by said officers, anywhere in the State within which they are issued.

SEC. 6. And be it further enacted, That when a person held to service or labor in any State or Territory of the United States, has heretofore or shall hereafter escape into another State or Territory of the United States, the person or persons to whom such service or labor may be due, or his, her, or their agent or attorney, duly authorized by power of attorney, in writing acknowledged and certified under the seal of some legal officer or Court of the State or Territory in which the same may be executed, may pursue and reclaim such fugitive person, either by procuring a warrant from some one of the Courts, judges, or commissioners aforesaid, of the proper circuit, district, or county, for the apprehension of such fugitive from service or labor, or by seizing and arresting such fugitive where the same can be done without process, and by taking, or causing such person to be taken forthwith before such Court, Judge or Commissioner, whose duty it shall be, to hear and determine the case of such claimant in a summary manner; and upon satisfactory proof being made, by deposition or affidavit, in writing, to be taken, and certified by such Court, Judge, or Commissioner, or by other satisfactory testimony, duly taken and certified by some Court, Magistrate, Justice of the Peace, or other legal officer authorized to administer an oath and take depositions under the laws of the State or Territory from which such person owing service or labor may have escaped, with a certificate of such magistracy, or other authority as aforesaid, with the seal of the proper Court or officer thereto attached, which seal shall be sufficient to establish the competency of the proof, and with proof, also by affidavit, of the identity of the person whose service or labor is claimed to be due as aforesaid, that the person so arrested does in fact owe service or labor to the person or persons claiming him or her, in the State or Territory from which such fugitive may have escaped as aforesaid, and that said person escaped, to make out and deliver to such claimant, his or her agent or attorney, a certificate setting forth the substantial facts as to the service or labor due from such fugitive to the claimant, and of his or her escape from the State or Territory in which such service or labor was due to the State or Territory in which he or she was arrested, with authority to such claimant, or his, or her agent, or attorney, to use such reasonable force and restraint as may be necessary, under the circumstances of the case, to take and remove such fugitive person back to the State or Territory whence he or she may have escaped as aforesaid. In no trial or hearing under this Act shall the testimony of such alleged fugitive be admitted in evidence; and the certificates in this and the first (fourth) section mentioned, shall be conclusive of the right of the person or persons in whose favor granted, to remove such fugitive to the State or Territory from which he escaped, and shall prevent all molestation of such person or persons by any process issued by any Court, Judge, Magistrate or other person whomsoever.

SEC. 7. And be it further enacted, That any person who shall knowingly and willingly obstruct, hinder, or prevent such claimant, his agent or attorney, or any person or persons lawfully assisting him, her or them, from arresting such a fugitive from service or labor, either with or without process as aforesaid, or shall rescue or attempt to rescue such fugitive from service or labor from the custody of such claimant, his, or her agent, or attorney, or other person or persons lawfully assisting as aforesaid, when so arrested pursuant to the authority herein given, and declared, or shall aid, abet, or assist such person so owing service or labor as aforesaid, directly or indirectly, to escape from such claimant, his agent or attorney, or other person or persons legally authorized as aforesaid; or shall harbor or conceal such fugitive so as to prevent the discovery and arrest of such person, after notice or knowledge of the fact that such person was a fugitive from service or labor as aforesaid, shall, for either of said offences, be subject to a fine not exceeding one thousand dollars, and imprisonment not exceeding six months, by indictment and conviction before the District Court of the United States, for the district in which such offence may have been committed, or before the proper Court of Criminal jurisdiction, if committed within any one of the organized territories of the United States, and shall moreover forfeit and pay, by way of civil damages to the party injured by such illegal conduct, the sum of One thousand dollars, for each fugitive so lost as aforesaid, to be recovered by action of debt in any of the District or Territorial Courts aforesaid, within whose jurisdiction the said offence may have been committed.

SEC. 8. And be it further enacted, That the Marshals, their deputies, and the clerks of the said District and Territorial Courts, shall be paid for their services the like fees as may be allowed to them for similar services in other cases; and where such services are rendered exclusively in the arrest, custody, and delivery of the fugitive to the claimant, his or her agent or attorney, or where such supposed fugitive may be discharged out of custody for the want of sufficient proof as aforesaid, then such fees are to be paid in the whole by such claimant, his agent or attorney; and in all cases where the proceedings are before a Commissioner, he shall be entitled to a fee of Ten dollars in full for his services in each case, upon the delivery of the said certificate to the claimant, his or her agent or attorney; or a fee of five dollars in cases where the proof shall not, in the opinion of such Commissioner, warrant such certificate and delivery, inclusive of all services incident to such arrest and examination to be paid in either case, by the claimant, his or her agent, or attorney. The person or persons authorized to execute the process to be issued by such Commissioner for the arrest and detention of fugitives from service or labor as aforesaid, shall also be entitled to a fee of five dollars each, for each person he or they may arrest and take before any such Commissioner, as aforesaid, at the instance and request of such claimant, with such other fees as may be deemed reasonable by such Commissioners for such other additional services as may be necessarily performed by him or them; such as attending at the examination, keeping the fugitive in custody, and providing him with food and lodging during his detention and until the final determination of such Commissioner; and, in general, for performing such other duties as may be required by such claimant, his or her attorney, or agent, or Commissioner in the premises. Such fees to be made up in conformity with the fees usually charged by the officers of the courts of justice within the proper district or county, as near as may be practicable, and paid by such claimants, their agents or attorneys, whether such supposed fugitives from service or labor be ordered to be delivered to such claimants by the final determination of such Commissioner or not.

SEC. 9. And be it further enacted, That, upon affidavit made by the claimant of such fugitive, his agent or attorney, after such certificate has been issued that he has reason to apprehend that such fugitive will be rescued by force from his or her possession before he can be taken beyond the limits of the State in which the arrest is made, it shall be the duty of the officer making the arrest to retain such fugitive in his custody, and to remove him to the State whence he fled, and there to deliver him to said claimant, his agent or attorney. And to this end, the officer aforesaid is hereby authorized and required to employ so many persons as he may deem necessary to overcome such force, and to retain them in his service so long as circumstances may require. The said officer and his assistants while so employed to receive the same compensation, and to be allowed the same expenses as are now allowed by law for transportation of criminals, to be certified by the judge of the district within which the arrest is made, and paid out of the treasury of the United States.

SEC. 10. And be it further enacted, That when any person held to service or labor in any State or Territory, or in the District of Columbia, shall escape therefrom, the party to whom such service or labor may be due, his, her, or their agent or attorney, may apply to any court of record therein, or judge thereof in vacation, and make satisfactory proof to such court, or judge in vacation, of the escape aforesaid, and that the person escaping owed service or labor to such party. Whereupon the court shall cause a record to be made of the matters so proved, and also a general description of the person so escaping with such convenient certainty as may be; and a transcript of such record authenticated by the attestation of the clerk and of the seal of the said court, being produced in any other State, Territory or district in which the person so escaping may be found, and being exhibited to any judge, commissioner, or other officer authorized by the law of the United States to cause persons escaping from service or labor to be delivered up, shall be held and taken to be full and conclusive evidence of the fact of the escape, and that the service or labor of the person escaping is due to the party in such record mentioned. And upon the production by the said party of other and further evidence if necessary, either oral or by affidavit, in addition to what is contained in the said record of the identity of the person escaping, he or she shall be delivered up to the claimant. And the said court, commissioner, judge, or other person authorized by this act to grant certificates to claimants of fugitives, shall, upon the production of the record and other evidences aforesaid, grant to such claimant a certificate of his right to take any such person identified and proved to be owing service or labor as aforesaid, which shall authorize such claimant to seize or arrest and transport such person to the State or Territory from which he escaped: Provided, That nothing herein contained shall be construed as requiring the production of a transcript of such record as evidence as aforesaid. But in its absence the claim shall be heard and determined upon other satisfactory proofs, competent in law.

Approved September 18, 1850.

The Ordinance of 1787

PASSED BY CONGRESS PREVIOUS TO THE ADOPTION OF THE NEW CONSTITUTION, AND SUBSEQUENTLY ADOPTED BY CONGRESS, AUGUST 7, 1789

ENTITLED—An ordinance for the Government of the Territory of the United States North West of the River Ohio

(All the Articles of this Ordinance previous to Article VI, relate to the organization and powers of the government of the territory. The following section being all that relates to slavery.)

Article VI.

There shall be neither slavery nor involuntary servitude in the said Territory, otherwise than in punishment of crimes, whereof the party shall have been duly convicted: Provided always, that any person escaping into the same from whom labor or service is lawfully claimed in any one of the original States, such fugitive may be lawfully reclaimed and conveyed to the person claiming his or her labor or service as aforesaid.

Done by the United States in Congress assembled the thirteenth day of July, in the year of our Lord, 1787, and of the sovereignty and Independence the twelfth.

WILLIAM GRAYSON, CHAIRMAN.

CHARLES THOMPSON, SEC'Y.

The Wilmot Proviso

HOUSE OF REPRESENTATIVES,
FEBRUARY 1, 1847

The Chair allowed the Hon. Preston King to read as a part of his argument (upon the appropriation of $3,000,000 to enable the President to conclude a treaty of peace with Mexico,) the amendment which was prepared by Mr. Wilmot and which is commonly called the Wilmot Proviso, viz:

SECTION—And be it further enacted, that there shall be neither slavery nor involuntary servitude in any Territory on the Continent of America, which shall hereafter be acquired by, or annexed to, the United States, except for crimes whereof the party shall have been duly convicted: Provided always, that any person escaping into such Territory, from whom labor or service is lawfully claimed, in any one of the United States, such fugitive may be lawfully reclaimed and conveyed out of said territory to the persons claiming his or her labor or service.

FOR THE BEST IN PAPERBACKS, LOOK FOR THE 🐧

In every corner of the world, on every subject under the sun, Penguin represents quality and variety—the very best in publishing today.

For complete information about books available from Penguin—including Puffins, Penguin Classics, and Arkana—and how to order them, write to us at the appropriate address below. Please note that for copyright reasons the selection of books varies from country to country.

In the United Kingdom: Please write to *Dept. EP, Penguin Books Ltd, Bath Road, Harmondsworth, West Drayton, Middlesex UB7 0DA.*

In the United States: Please write to *Penguin Putnam Inc., P.O. Box 12289 Dept. B, Newark, New Jersey 07101-5289* or call 1-800-788-6262.

In Canada: Please write to *Penguin Books Canada Ltd, 10 Alcorn Avenue, Suite 300, Toronto, Ontario M4V 3B2.*

In Australia: Please write to *Penguin Books Australia Ltd, P.O. Box 257, Ringwood, Victoria 3134.*

In New Zealand: Please write to *Penguin Books (NZ) Ltd, Private Bag 102902, North Shore Mail Centre, Auckland 10.*

In India: Please write to *Penguin Books India Pvt Ltd, 11 Panchsheel Shopping Centre, Panchsheel Park, New Delhi 110 017.*

In the Netherlands: Please write to *Penguin Books Netherlands bv, Postbus 3507, NL-1001 AH Amsterdam.*

In Germany: Please write to *Penguin Books Deutschland GmbH, Metzlerstrasse 26, 60594 Frankfurt am Main.*

In Spain: Please write to *Penguin Books S. A., Bravo Murillo 19, 1° B, 28015 Madrid.*

In Italy: Please write to *Penguin Italia s.r.l., Via Benedetto Croce 2, 20094 Corsico, Milano.*

In France: Please write to *Penguin France, Le Carré Wilson, 62 rue Benjamin Baillaud, 31500 Toulouse.*

In Japan: Please write to *Penguin Books Japan Ltd, Kaneko Building, 2-3-25 Koraku, Bunkyo-Ku, Tokyo 112.*

In South Africa: Please write to *Penguin Books South Africa (Pty) Ltd, Private Bag X14, Parkview, 2122 Johannesburg.*